Prosperous Descent

Samuel Alexander

PROSPEROUS DESCENT: CRISIS AS OPPORTUNITY IN
AN AGE OF LIMITS

Published by the Simplicity Institute, Melbourne, 2015
www.simplicityinstitute.org

WHAT OTHERS ARE SAYING ABOUT *PROSPEROUS DESCENT*:

'*Prosperous Descent* is a creative and important contribution to a movement with surprising momentum, one that challenges the very notions of progress and wellbeing on which our societies are constructed. It is a radical challenge in the best sense of the term. We can all learn a great deal from Samuel Alexander, both about our societies and about how to live our lives.'

– Clive Hamilton, author of *Affluenza: When Too Much is Never Enough* and *Growth Fetish*

'In this treatise, Samuel Alexander strives with great persuasiveness and using all the right arguments to convince us to switch from the misery of the present into the utopia of frugal abundance, to escape the Apocalypse looming.'

– Serge Latouche, author of *Farewell to Growth*

'This timely book reminds us that the good life is the simple life; a life within limits. It is a truly interdisciplinary volume, covering topics from the macroeconomics of a planned degrowth, to the ecology of planetary limits, to the sociology of voluntary simplifiers. A must read.'

– Giorgos Kallis, co-editor of *Degrowth: A Vocabulary for a New Era*

'Consumer capitalist society is characterised by a deep feeling of anxiety and isolation. It persists by inculcating a deep sense of disempowerment and diluting our radical imagination. The strength of this book lies in its ability to delicately weave together not only the theory but also the practice of simplicity. It carries with it the moral weight of generations of people who have demonstrated a different way of living and the shallowness of consumer society.'

– Peter D. Burdon, author of *Earth Jurisprudence* and co-editor of *Wild Law: In Practice*

CONTENTS

Acknowledgements   *vii*

INTRODUCTION   *ix*

1. A Critique of Techno-Optimism
Efficiency without sufficiency is lost   1

2. Post-Growth Economics
A paradigm shift in progress   29

3. Planned Economic Contraction
The emerging case for degrowth   63

4. Degrowth Implies Voluntary Simplicity
Overcoming barriers to sustainable consumption   89

5. Reimagining the Good Life Beyond Consumer Culture
A revolution in consciousness   113

6. Ted Trainer and The Simpler Way
A sympathetic critique   135

7. The New Economics of Oil
Energy, economics, and the twilight of growth   159

8. The Paradox of Oil
The cheaper it is, the more it costs   175

9. Voluntary Simplification as an Alternative to Collapse
Prosperous descent in the Anthropocene   199

10. Radical Simplicity and the Middle Class
Exploring the lifestyle implications of a 'Great Disruption'   229

11. Voluntary Simplicity as an Aesthetics of Existence
The art of ethics in a consumer age   253

12. The Hour is Darkest Just Before Dawn
Crisis as opportunity   293

Appendix – Contents of SUFFICIENCY ECONOMY   299

About the Author   301

Acknowledgements

These collected essays are an outgrowth of work initiated in 2006, when I began working on my doctoral thesis, 'Property Beyond Growth: Toward a Politics of Voluntary Simplicity'. Since then the ideas and perspectives they express have developed in the process of establishing and teaching a course called 'Consumerism and the Growth Economy: Interdisciplinary Perspectives', which forms part of the Masters of Environment at the University of Melbourne, Australia. Over this time, most of the essays have been published in peer-reviewed journals or other academic publications, as detailed below:

A version of Ch. 1 was published as a *Post Carbon Pathways* report, with the Melbourne Sustainable Society Institute (January, 2014); a version of Ch. 2 was published in *Arena* (2014) 41/42: 93-122; a version of Ch. 3 was published in *Environmental Politics* (2012) 21(3): 349-368; versions of chapters 4, 8, and 10 were published as *Simplicity Institute Reports* 12b, 15a, and 12p, respectively; a version of Ch. 5 was published in the *International Journal of Environmental, Cultural, Economic, and Social Sustainability* (2011) 7(3): 133-150; a version of Ch. 6 was published in *Capitalism Nature Socialism* (2014) 25(2): 95-111; a version of Ch. 7 was published as an *Issues Paper* with the Melbourne Sustainable Society Institute (March, 2014); a version of Ch. 9 was published in *Foresight* (2014) 16(6): 550-566 ('Descent Pathways' Special Issue). I am grateful for the opportunity to reprint. Chapters 11 and 12 have not previously been published.

In writing these essays I was encouraged, challenged, and inspired by my colleagues and fellow authors at the Simplicity Institute, especially Ted Trainer, Mark Burch, Simon Ussher, David Holmgren, Serge Latouche, Esther Alloun, and Johnny Rutherford. I owe special thanks to Antoinette Wilson and Johnny Rutherford for helping proof and prepare this manuscript. I would also like to thank Professor John Wiseman and the Melbourne Sustainable Society Institute for the support offered as I prepared this manuscript for publication. Debts of gratitude and Guinness are also owed to my very good friend Andrew Doodson for designing the cover for this book. Your time and creativity are always greatly appreciated.

Finally, to Helen and Laurie – whose love, support, and tolerance make all my efforts possible. Thank you, as always, for everything.

There is one way forward: the creation of flesh and blood examples of low-consumption, high-quality alternatives to the mainstream pattern of life. This we can see happening already on the counter-cultural fringes. And nothing – no amount of argument or research – will take the place of such living proof. What people must see is that ecologically sane, socially responsible living is *good* living; that simplicity, thrift, and reciprocity make for an existence that is free.

– Theodore Roszak, *Where the Wasteland Ends*

INTRODUCTION

I sometimes tell my students that I am an 'apocaloptimist'. While, in truth, I am neither apocalyptic nor optimistic, this neologism serves as a fruitful conversation starter. It allows me to begin stating the case for why we, the human species, are facing overlapping crises of unprecedented magnitude – crises that are threatening the very persistence of our civilisation. At the same time, I explain why all of these problems are of our own making and, indeed, that their solutions already exist and are within our grasp, if only we decide that solving them is seriously what we want. I also maintain that the process of solving or at least responding appropriately to these problems can be both meaningful and fulfilling, if only we are prepared to let go of dominant conceptions of the good life. This means embracing very different ways of living, while also re-structuring our societies to support a very different set of values – especially the values of frugality, moderation, and sufficiency. In short, I argue that the problems we face today are as grave as the solutions are available and attractive, and this tension is reflected in the title of this book – *PROSPEROUS DESCENT* – which I use provocatively to signify a paradox whose meaning will be unpacked in the following pages and chapters.

Before outlining the content of the following chapters, let me introduce some of the basic themes which shape all the essays collected in this book (and its companion volume, *SUFFICIENCY ECONOMY*). To begin with, I take a global perspective, even if my focus is generally on the cultures and economies prevalent in what are called the 'developed' nations. One of the normative assumptions underlying the essays is that we, human beings, are not citizens of any particular nation-state, the borders of which are artificial constructs of limited moral relevance. Rather, I contend that we are, as Diogenes claimed long ago, 'citizens of the cosmos', members of a global community of life, today more so than ever before. Our moral obligations, therefore – our commitments to justice and sustainability, in particular – cannot and should not stop at the borders of our own communities or our own nations. Justice and sustainability are global, seemingly abstract challenges demanding a global perspective, even if our actions and inter-ventions must inevitably be local and concrete.

In globalising one's perspective, however, one is inevitability radicalised. As soon as we start asking questions about what a just distribution of the world's resources would look like, or what material standard of living could be *universalised* on our already overburdened planet, it immediately becomes clear that justice and sustainability, if these fuzzy notions are to mean anything, require nothing short of a revolution of the existing order of things. As this book will argue, we cannot merely tinker with the systems and cultures of global capitalism and hope that things will magically improve; those systems and cultures are not the symptoms but the causes of our overlapping social, economic, and ecological crises, so ultimately those systems and cultures must be replaced with fundamentally different forms of human interaction and organisation, driven and animated by different values, hopes, and myths. Uncivilising ourselves from our destructive civilisation and building something new is the great, undefined, creative challenge we face in coming decades – which is a challenge both of opposition and renewal. Together we must write a new future, a task that has already begun as individuals and communities begin to build the new world within the shell of the old. But this new future must look radically different from the past if the crises we face are to be tolerably resolved. There are no prizes, of course, for being the most 'radical' theorist or movement, yet if evidence, ethical reflection, and logic all demand a radical position, then as a matter of intellectual integrity, radical we must be – even if it is unclear why a position should be called 'radical' if the forces of reason and evidence are on our side. Such is the state of things.

Today there are unfathomable amounts of wealth and power concentrated in the hands of a tiny minority of super-rich elites, while great multitudes of our fellow human beings live lives of humiliating destitution. Early in 2014, for example, it was reported that the richest 85 people today have as much accumulated wealth as the poorest half of humanity.[1] This is not 'civilisation' as I understand the term. Nothing – no amount of fancy theorising – can justify such a skewed distribution of wealth and power, nor can this distribution be passed off as a 'natural' outcome of free individuals operating within free markets. It would be more accurate to say it is the natural outcome of unfree individuals operating within unfree markets. The current distribution of wealth and power, both within nations and between them, is a function of decisions human beings have made about how to structure our economies and political systems, and one does not need a fancy

---

[1] See R. Fuentes-Nieva and N. Galasso. 2014. 'Working for the few: Political capture and economic inequality', Oxfam Briefing Paper, 20 January 2014.

moral or political theory to conclude that the existing distribution, shaped by the existing, globalised economy, is shamefully unjust. It is self-evidently, painfully, and hideously unjust, even if usually we divert our eyes from this distasteful reality, it being too difficult to dwell on for long. Nevertheless, the point is that if human beings made these oppressive and destructive systems, so too can we unmake them and remake them into different systems, better systems, more humane systems – if we commit ourselves to that enormous task.

Our challenges, however, go well beyond distributional questions and call on us to rethink contemporary understandings of 'progress', 'development', 'sustainability', and even the meaning of 'civilisation' itself. What does it mean to be 'civilised' today? What is it that we want sustained? How will we sustain those things? At what cost? And for whom? Sustainability must not be conceived of as the project of sustaining anything resembling the status quo, although that is a common assumption and, indeed, it currently defines the international development agenda. The high consumption way of life which is enjoyed by the richest one or two billion people on Earth, and which is widely celebrated as the peak of civilisation, simply cannot, due to ecological limits, be universalised to the world's seven billion people, let alone the eight, or nine, or ten billion people that are expected to inhabit the planet in coming decades. What are the implications of this ecological impossibility? When we ask ourselves what way of life would be consistent with a 'fair share' of the world's finite resources, it quickly becomes evident that a just and sustainable civilisation must not seek to universalise the high impact consumer way of life. That would be ecologically catastrophic – a catastrophe that is, however, in the process of unfolding as conventional modes of 'sustainable development' are pursued tragically into the future.

If the global population is to live safely within the sustainable carrying capacity of the planet, we must be prepared – especially those of us in the developed regions of the world – to reimagine the good life by embracing 'simpler ways' of living based on notions of moderation, frugality, appropriate technology, and sufficiency. These notions are rarely discussed in mainstream environmental literature, and they are unspeakable by our politicians, yet I hope to show that they are indispensable to the proper understanding of our predicament and signify our only way out of it. If once it was thought that technology would 'save the day', producing efficiencies that would allow a growing global population to live high consumption lifestyles while remaining within the sustainable carrying capacity of the planet, today it is increasingly clear that such techno-optimism lacks all evidential credibility. Universal affluence is nice in theory, perhaps, or perhaps not even nice in theory. But empirically, the promise of technological salvation has failed us. Despite decades of extraordinary technological advance, the ecological burdens humanity places on nature continue to increase. The face of Gaia is vanishing. Efficiency without sufficiency is lost.

Although there is a demonstrable ecological imperative to embrace simpler lifestyles of moderate consumption, there are, fortunately, many reasons to think that such lifestyles would actually be in our immediate self-interest. As will be seen, evidence indicates that even those who have attained the consumerist ideal so often find that it does not satisfy them, suggesting that human beings just do not find consumption a source of much fulfillment – despite what the advertisements insist. Most people living in consumer cultures today are materially richer than at any other time in history, yet too many of us also tend to be poor in time, poor in community engagement, and lack an intimate connection with nature. Our wealth is dubious. It has come at too high a price.

Human beings all have basic biophysical needs, of course, that must be met in order for us to flourish, but not far beyond those basic needs it seems that consumption has fast diminishing marginal returns. The never-ending pursuit of affluence is like a treadmill on which we keep running without advancing, eventually becoming a zero-sum game of 'status competition' which degrades the planet while distracting us from more worthy pursuits. And so the logic of sufficiency is clear: we *must* step off that consumerist treadmill for ecological reasons, and we *should* step off it for social justice reasons, but we should *want* to step off it because if we transcend consumer culture we will discover that there are simply more fulfilling ways to live. Consumerism is a tragic failure of the human imagination. Certainly, we can do much better.

This book holds up 'simple living' or 'voluntary simplicity' as the most coherent alternative to consumerism. I use these terms not to imply crudely regressing to old ways of living but instead to imply *post-consumerist* ways of living. These ways of living would weave together the best human innovations and traditions but use these knowledges and practices to create low-impact lifestyles of moderate consumption, which are nevertheless rich in their non-material dimensions. Although this way of life defies simplistic definition, practically it can mean growing organic food in backyards or urban farms, or supporting local farmers' markets; it can mean wearing second-hand clothes or mending existing items, and creating or making necessary goods out of recycled materials rather than always acquiring them new; it can mean purchasing solar panels or supporting renewable energy initiatives, while also radically reducing household energy consumption by riding a bike, taking public transport, co-housing, or simply using a washing line instead of a dryer. A process not a destination, the practical implications of voluntary simplicity are endless, which presents us with an immensely creative challenge, especially in consumer cultures. It implies the general attempt to minimise wasteful and superfluous consumption, sharing what we have, and knowing how much is 'enough', all the while redirecting life's vital energies toward non-materialist sources of meaning and fulfillment, such as friends and family, social engagement, creative activity, home production, meeting our civic duties, or exploring whatever one's private passions might be. The fundamental premise of this book – of all my work – is that a simple life can be a good life.

Nevertheless, although I argue that true sustainability certainly implies living more simply in a material sense, the following essays also maintain that we must simultaneously build structures and institutions that reflect, embody, and foster the same ethics of sufficiency. This means moving away from macroeconomic systems that have an inbuilt imperative to 'grow or die', toward post-growth systems that provide for the material needs of all but which do not seek to provide people with ever-higher levels of affluence. These would be highly localised, zero-growth economies based on permaculture principles, which use mostly local resources to meet mostly local needs. (I tried to describe such an economy – a sufficiency economy – in my last book, *Entropia: Life Beyond Industrial Civilisation*, which was inspired by the likes of Henry David Thoreau, William Morris, Serge Latouche, David Holmgren, and Ted Trainer.)

For social and ecological reasons, the problem of population growth must also be confronted (somehow) with dedication and equity, since population is obviously a multiplier of everything, including ecological impact. Nevertheless, the population problem must not be used as a scapegoat to deflect attention away from the more fundamental problems: consumerist aspirations shaping the dominant myth of progress and structures of growth locking us into that myth.

If our civilisation does not embrace an ethics of sufficiency – and if we persist in the fantasy of globalising affluence and hoping technology and 'free markets' will solve our social and ecological problems – we will meet the same fate as the snake that eats its own tail. Before this century is out, our civilisation will have collapsed; will have consumed itself to death.

◆ ◆ ◆

At this stage the paradox of PROSPEROUS DESCENT – the paradox that less can be more – should appear somewhat less paradoxical. The phrase is intended to signify the 'upside of down', a positive response to the impending limits to growth which necessitate post-consumerist ways of living. One way or another, for better or for worse, the descent of industrial civilisation is approaching us – in fact, it would seem that the descent is already underway. But currently, the unfolding descent is unplanned and far from prosperous, because most efforts are directed, consciously or unconsciously, toward *sustaining the existing civilisation* rather than *creating something new*. Resource limits – especially oil constraints – are beginning to squeeze the life-force out of economies that are dependent on cheap energy inputs to grow, and the reckless burning of fossil energy has begun to destabilise our climate. This is industrial civilisation. It is grossly unsustainable. It is not serving the vast majority of humankind. It has no future.

In order to make the best of the overlapping crises we face – in order to turn those crises into opportunities – the following essays argue that we need to develop cultures that reject consumerism and create far less energy and resource intensive ways of living. To support this cultural revolution in consciousness, we must also build economic and political structures that support and promote the practice of sufficiency. In the most developed regions of the world, this means radically downshifting away from high consumption ways of living and embracing far simpler ways of reduced and restrained consumption. This is the 'descent' – the descent away from growth and consumerism – that I argue can be 'prosperous', if we negotiate the transition wisely and take to the task with vigour, creativity, and urgency. This book and its companion volume, SUFFICIENCY ECONOMY, attempt to unpack and defend this bold vision, as well as explore the thorny question of how to realise it.

Before proceeding I should briefly anticipate an objection that will no doubt arise even from this preliminary overview. Let me be clear: the notion of 'prosperous descent' is not a prediction. I am not arguing that human beings are *going* to create a global village of thriving, sufficiency economies, nor do I even suggest that this is *likely*. And I am certainly not arguing that an unplanned, chaotic civilisational collapse into poverty is going to be 'prosperous' (so please do not accuse me of that). My argument is simply that economies of sufficiency, in which the entire community of life can flourish, are the *only* way to respond effectively to the overlapping crises of industrial civilisation. To oppose Margaret Thatcher with her own words: 'there is no alternative'.

If this can be established, as I believe it can, it would follow that we should try to create sufficiency economies, here and now, even if our chances of success do not look good. We may never realise the ideal of a sufficiency economy, but having a coherent ideal functions as a compass to guide action. Without a compass, our energies and efforts would lack direction and thus could easily be misdirected with the best of intentions. Indeed, I worry that dominant strains of the environmental movement today can be understood primarily as misdirected good intentions, efforts which tend to be mistaken in attempting to 'green' a growth-orientated mode of production that can never be green. Others oppose the existing order without having any conception of what should replace it. Even those who reject the growth economy sometimes fail to understand the radical implications of such a proposal; fail to understand that we cannot give up growth while other aspects of life more or less go on as usual. Sufficiency, I contend, is a revolutionary project.

While I believe the practical question of 'strategy' – the question of how to realise a sufficiency economy – should remain open and dependent on context, the 'theory of change' that informs these essays is one grounded in grassroots, community-based action and initiatives. That is to say, I contend that until we have a *culture* or *social consciousness* that embraces sufficiency, our politicians are not going to be driven to create the necessary *structures* of sufficiency, nor, in the absence of such a culture, are we going to build new structures ourselves. In fact, even if such a culture of sufficiency emerged, our politicians are likely to be sluggish and non-responsive in supporting it. This means that the primary (although not necessarily the exclusive) forces of societal change must come 'from below', from people like you and me, working in our local communities, at the grassroots level. Before all else, we need to create the social conditions for deep transformation. There is a huge amount our governments *could do*, of course, to create just and sustainable economies of sufficiency, and in certain chapters I explore some available policy options. This can help us imagine alternative forms of human society and organisation. But we must not wait for governments to act, or we will still be waiting while the ship of civilisation sails over the cliff and crashes into the dark abyss below.

In any case, we should not want our governments to *impose* justice and sustainability upon us, and perhaps that would not be possible even if they wanted to. Instead, we must become politically mature enough to govern ourselves toward a better world and shape our own fates. To the extent that governments can assist us, I argue that they should be aiming to *deconstruct the barriers* to a sufficiency economy, and provide us with the freedom to choose it.

Currently that freedom is disastrously constrained, which sadly seems to be part of the design of Empire.

◆ ◆ ◆

I will close this introduction by providing a brief outline of the chapters that follow. These essays have been ordered to reflect steps in an argument, however they all stand alone well enough, so there is no need, necessarily, to read them in order. Certain lines of argument, in places, are repeated or summarised, but I hope this serves primarily to emphasise key points and weave the essays together into a coherent whole.

Chapter 1 lays the foundation for the book by presenting an evidenced-based critique of techno-optimism. Most people today, including many environmentalists, assume that technological advancement will eventually 'decouple' our economic growth from environmental impact, thereby allowing us to grow our economies without limit while at the same time reducing ecological impact. This position – which I am calling techno-optimism – is the foundation of dominant conceptions of 'sustainable development' and the primary reason so many people assume there are no 'limits to growth'. If this techno-optimism is justifiable, sustained economic growth may eventually solve global poverty and raise the living standards of all, without destroying the necessary ecosystems that sustain life as we know it. But it is not justifiable. The opening chapter presents a critique of techno-optimism, showing it to be without evidential foundation and dangerously flawed. There are limits to growth – limits which in fact seem to be upon us – and we ignore them at our own peril. The implication is that any adequate response to today's overlapping crises requires a global shift away from growth economics toward a macroeconomics 'beyond growth'.

Chapter 2 reviews the key thinkers and movements in the emerging paradigm of 'post-growth' economics. It begins by presenting a brief overview of the conventional growth paradigm, in order to later highlight, by way of contrast, some of the most prominent features of the alternative paradigm. A substantial literature review of post-growth economics is then provided, after which some of the outstanding issues in this emerging paradigm are outlined. This chapter raises questions about what prospects this alternative paradigm has for the economics of growth; what significance it may have if it were ever to succeed; and what the implications could be if it were to remain marginalised. The chapter concludes by outlining a research agenda of critical issues.

Chapter 3 outlines the sociological, ecological, and economic foundations of a macroeconomics 'beyond growth', focusing on the idea of degrowth. Degrowth opposes conventional growth economics on the grounds that growth in the highly developed nations has become socially counter-productive, ecologically unsustainable, and uneconomic. Stagnating energy supplies and rising prices also suggest an imminent 'end of growth'. In response to growth economics, degrowth scholars call for a politico-economic policy of *planned economic contraction*, an approach which has been broadly defined as 'an equitable downscaling of production and consumption that increases human wellbeing and enhances ecological conditions'. After defining growth economics and outlining the emerging case for degrowth, this chapter considers the feasibility of a macroeconomics beyond growth and sketches an outline of what such a macroeconomics might look like as a politico-economic programme.

Chapter 4 is based on the idea that a degrowth process of planned economic contraction depends on, and must be driven by, a culture of 'simple living' – or, as the title of this chapter puts it, 'degrowth implies voluntary simplicity'. Be that as it may, this chapter shows that things are not that simple. Our lifestyle decisions, especially our consumption practices, are not made in a vacuum. They are made within social, economic, and political *structures of constraint*, and those structures make some lifestyle decisions easy or necessary and other lifestyle decisions difficult or impossible. These structures can even 'lock' people into high consumption lifestyles. Change the social, economic, and political structures, however, and different consumption practices would or could emerge. This chapter seeks to deepen the understanding of the relationship between consumer behaviour and the structures which shape that behaviour, in the hope that the existing barriers to sustainable consumption can be overcome or avoided.

Chapter 5 outlines in more detail the theory and practice of 'voluntary simplicity'. This term defies easy definition but can be preliminarily understood as a way of life in which people choose to restrain or reduce their material consumption, while at the same time seeking a higher quality of life. For reasons discussed in previous chapters, there is a desperate need for alternative practices and narratives of consumption beyond those prevalent in the most developed regions of the world today, and increasingly people see voluntary simplicity or 'simple living' as a coherent and attractive alternative to the 'work-and-spend' cycle of consumer culture. After addressing issues of definition, justification, and practice, this chapter concludes by considering some objections that can be levelled against voluntary simplicity, both as a living strategy and as a nascent social movement.

Chapter 6 presents a sympathetic critique of Ted Trainer's vision of 'The Simpler Way', which he has been developing and refining for several decades. Trainer's essential premise is that overconsumption in the most developed regions of the world is the root cause of our global predicament, and upon this premise he argues that a necessary part of any transition to a sustainable and just world involves the consumer class adopting far 'simpler' lifestyles in terms of material and energy consumption. That is the radical implication of our global predicament which most people seem unwilling to acknowledge or accept, but which Trainer does not shy away from, and, indeed, which he follows through to its logical conclusion. Trainer's complex position can be understood to merge and build upon various strains of socialist, anarchist, and environmentalist thinking. Of particular importance is his critical analysis of the literature on renewable energy, which he argues does not support the assumption that renewable energy can sustain consumer societies. If Trainer is correct, sustainability implies moving toward societies with far lower energy demands than the developed economies, with all that this implies about reduced consumption and production. Needless to say, this directly contradicts the techno-optimism of most sustainability discourse, which assumes that existing and projected energy demands can easily and affordably be met with renewable energy.

Chapter 7 provides a review of the peak oil situation and offers a response to recent claims that 'peak oil is dead'. The analysis shows that oil issues remain at the centre of global challenges facing humanity, despite recent claims of oil abundance, and that the challenges are only going to intensify in coming years as competition increases over the world's most important source of fossil energy. The main issue, however, is not whether we will have enough oil, but whether we can afford to produce and burn the oil we have.

Chapter 8 provides an outline and analysis of various explanations for why the price of oil has fallen so dramatically between June 2014 and February 2015 (the time of writing). The main conclusion defended is that so-called 'cheap oil' (at ~$50 per barrel) is just as problematic as expensive oil (at $100+ per barrel), but for very different social, economic, political, and environmental reasons. Just as expensive oil suffocates industrial economies that are dependent on cheap energy inputs to function, cheap oil merely propagates and further entrenches the existing order of global capitalism that is in the process of growing itself to death.

Chapter 9 presents the most important theoretical contribution of the book, but it is a contribution that I suggest has hugely significant practical implications. The analysis revisits

Joseph Tainter's theory of complexity and collapse and responds to his argument that 'voluntary simplification' (which is essentially Tainter's term for degrowth or the simpler way) is not a viable path to a stable civilisation. Tainter argues forcefully, I admit, that in order to solve the problems facing our species we will need increased energy supplies, and on that basis he rejects the strategy of voluntarily reducing consumption. While I accept many aspects of Tainter's profound theoretical framework, this chapter ultimately rejects his conclusion, arguing that we are at a stage in our civilisational development where increasing energy consumption is now causing some of the primary problems that energy consumption is supposed to allow us to solve. In order to 'solve' some of the central crises of our times – in particular, in order to solve the problem of diminishing marginal returns on complexity which Tainter argues has led to the collapse of civilisations throughout history – I maintain that we must embrace a process of voluntary simplification. The primary contribution of this chapter lies in showing why Tainter's dismissal of this strategy is misguided and that, in fact, voluntary simplification is the only alternative to collapse.

Chapter 10 is a thought experiment based on a 'collapse scenario', which attempts to explore the lifestyle implications of what Paul Gilding has called a 'Great Disruption'. The question the chapter poses is this: how would an ordinary member of the consumer class deal with a lifestyle of radical simplicity? By radical simplicity I do not mean poverty. Rather, I mean a very low but biophysically sufficient material standard of living. This chapter argues that radical simplicity, in this sense, would not be as bad as it might first seem, provided we were ready for it and wisely negotiated its arrival, both as individuals and communities. The aim of this chapter is to provoke readers to reflect deeply on the question of what material standard of living is really necessary to live a full, human life. If it turns out that much less might be needed than is commonly thought, then in our age of ecological overshoot, this should provide us with further grounds for attempting to minimise our consumption and move toward lifestyles of sufficiency. If we do not choose this path, then my concern is that lifestyles of radically reduced consumption will be soon enough imposed upon us, but in ways that are unlikely to be experienced positively. As Thoreau once said, 'when a dog runs at you, whistle for him' – which I interpret as suggesting that we should embrace those things that necessarily await us whether we want those things or not. Nietzsche expressed a similar point: *amor fati* ('love thy fate').

Chapter 11 is the most philosophical of these collected essays, and is also the longest. It is placed toward the end because it may also be the least accessible, but I include it because I am convinced that the issues it raises are of the utmost importance. The chapter summarises then applies the ethical writings of Michel Foucault to the theory and practice of voluntary simplicity, drawing in particular on his notion of an 'aesthetics of existence'. Foucault argued that 'the self' is socially constructed. So far as that is true, inhabitants of consumer societies have probably internalised the social and institutional celebration of consumer lifestyles to varying degrees, and this will have shaped our identities and worldviews, often in subtle, even insidious, ways. But Foucault also argued that 'the self', as well as being shaped by society, can act on itself and change itself through a process of 'self-fashioning'. This raises the ethical question: what type of person should one create? Given that overconsumption is driving many of the world's most pressing problems, it may be that ethical activity today requires that we critically reflect on our own subjectivities in order to *refuse who we are* – so far as we are uncritical consumers. This Great Refusal would open up space to create new, post-consumerist forms of subjectivity, which is surely part of the revolution in consciousness needed in order to produce a society based on a 'simpler way'. After outlining Foucault's ethics and situating them in the context of consumption practices, the chapter concludes by describing several 'techniques of the self' that could be employed by those who wish to practise the idea of voluntary simplicity as an aesthetics of existence.

Chapter 12, the final chapter, is a short essay which was delivered at the Festival of Ideas, at the University of Melbourne, Australia in October 2013. It looks back from the year 2033 to consider how a transition to a low-carbon society might transpire, based on the notion that a crisis is also an opportunity.

It is worth acknowledging that the essays in this book do not answer all questions and, in fact, may raise as many questions as they answer. A second book of essays is also being published, which I hope will fill some of the gaps. A provisional contents page of that volume, called SUFFICIENCY ECONOMY: ENOUGH, FOR EVERYONE, FOREVER, is included as an appendix to this book.

1

A CRITIQUE OF TECHNO-OPTIMISM
Efficiency without sufficiency is lost

The solution to the unintended consequences of modernity is, and has always been, more modernity – just as the solution to the unintended consequences of our technologies has always been more technology.
— Ted Nordhaus and Michael Shellenberger

1. Introduction

As the human species evolved, one of our most significant evolutionary advantages proved to be our opposable thumbs, which made it easier for us to make fire and other basic tools, like knives and spears. These early 'technological' advances, primitive though they seem to us today, nevertheless shaped the course of human history. They helped solve some of our problems, such as staying warm and gaining advantage over other species, as well as securing a more reliable source of food, especially protein, which contributed to the development of our brains. With larger brains, we came to understand the world better and were able to manipulate it to our apparent advantage. Thus the conscious development of technology is arguably what defines us as humans and separates us from all other forms of life.

Science and technology have continued to play a central role in the development of civilisation. Through their advancement human beings have been able to produce electricity, cure diseases, split the atom, travel into space, invent computers and the internet, and map the human genome, among an unending list of things that often seem like miracles. Notably, these scientific and technological advancements have also assisted in the unprecedented expansion of our productive capacities, primarily through harnessing the energy

1

in fossil fuels and developing machines to augment human labour. This has allowed many people, primarily in the developed nations, to achieve lifestyles of material comfort that would have been unimaginable even a few generations ago. Increasingly all seven billion people on the planet seem set on achieving these high consumption lifestyles for themselves, and at first consideration the universalisation of affluence indeed seems a coherent and plausible path of progress.

But, however awesome the advancement of science and technology has been as a means of raising material living standards, there are also well known social and environmental dark sides that flow from this mode of development. Economic activity depends on nature for resources, and as economies and populations have expanded, especially since the industrial revolution, more pressure has been placed on those natural resources, ecosystems, and waste sinks. Today, we face a series of overlapping crises owing to the heavy burden our economies are placing on the planet (Meadows *et al.*, 2004; Ehrlich and Ehrlich, 2013). According to the best available evidence, the global economy now exceeds the sustainable carrying capacity of the planet by 50% (Global Footprint Network, 2013), with deforestation, ocean depletion, soil erosion, biodiversity loss, pollution, water shortages, and climate change being just a sample of these acute, unfolding problems (Rockstrom, *et al.*, 2009; Brown, 2011). The latest publication from the IPCC (2013) reiterates the immense challenge of climate change in particular, with the necessity of rapid emissions reductions becoming ever more pressing as carbon budgets continue to shrink through lack of committed action. At the same time, great multitudes of people around the planet still live in material destitution, and global population continues to grow (UNDSEA, 2012), suggesting the environmental burden is only going to be exacerbated as the global development agenda – the goal of promoting growth in global economic output – is pursued into the future (Turner, 2012).

Technological optimists believe, however, that just as the application of technology has been a primary cause of environmental problems, so too does it provide the primary solution (Lovins, 1998; Lovins, 2011; Lomborg, 2001). From this view, humanity will be able to solve environmental problems primarily through technological advancement, while continuing to focus attention on economic growth (see, e.g., Grantham Institute, 2013). By implementing this approach it is widely believed we will be able to eliminate global poverty and raise living standards for all, without destroying the necessary ecosystem services that sustain life as we know it. There can be no doubt that this promise of technology is seductive – material abundance for all, while solving environmental problems. But is this promise credible? If not, what are the implications?

This chapter presents an evidence-based critique of such techno-optimism, arguing that the vision of progress it promotes is unrealisable due to the limits of technology and the inherent structure of growth economics. The focus of this critique, however, is not on the techno-wizardry that holds up desalination plants as the solution to water shortages, genetically modified foods as the solution to global hunger, or geo-engineering as the solution to climate change, etc., important though those critiques are (see Huesemann and Huesemann, 2011; Hamilton, 2013). Rather, the present focus is on the subtler faith that many people place in 'efficiency' as the environmental saviour. Techno-optimism, in this sense, can be broadly defined as the belief that science and technology will be able to solve the major social and environmental problems of our times, without fundamentally rethinking the structure or goals of our growth-based economies or the nature of Western-style, affluent lifestyles. In other words, techno-optimism is the belief that the problems caused by economic growth can be solved by more economic growth (as measured by GDP), provided we learn how to produce and consume more efficiently through the application of science and technology. Proponents of this view argue that advancements in knowledge and design, in conjunction with market mechanisms, will mean that we will be able to decouple our economic activity from environmental impact, thus avoiding the implication that economic growth has biophysical limits. Should any resource become scarce, it is assumed that 'free markets' and high prices will incentivise more exploration or the development of substitute resources (see, e.g., Simon and Kahn, 1984; Beckerman, 2002). Rather than questioning growth economics, then, this dominant school of thought advocates 'green growth' or 'sustainable development' (see Purdey, 2010). This general perspective defines the present era more than any other, but the evidence reviewed below shows that the vision is profoundly flawed.

The critical analysis begins in Section 2 by placing techno-optimism in theoretical context. It is important to understand the structure of techno-optimism and see why it forms a central part of the ideology of growth. In Section 3, the notion of an Environmental Kuznets's Curve (EKC) is outlined and considered. This hypothesis holds that environmental harm tends to increase in early stages of industrialisation, but as economies get richer and their technologies develop, environmental impact tends to decrease. The evidence for this position is reviewed and analysed, and it is shown that the EKC hypothesis is generally without substance. At least, the EKC has to be qualified so heavily that it essentially disappears. In sections 4 and 5 the notion of 'decoupling' is examined, and this analysis is used to explain why efficiency improvements have not produced sustainable economies despite extraordinary technological advancements in recent decades. It turns out efficiency improvements have not often been able to keep up with continued economic and population growth – largely due to 'rebound effects' – meaning that overall environmental impact continues to grow, despite efficiency improvements. Section 6 unpacks the arithmetic of growth to expose how unrealistic techno-optimism really is. In the concluding sections the implications of the analysis are discussed. The central conclusion of this critique is that technology cannot and will not solve environmental problems so long as it is applied within a growth-based economic model. In order to take advantage of efficiency gains, which are without doubt an essential part of the transition to a just and sustainable world (von Weizsacker *et al.*, 2009), it is argued that a value-shift is required to move cultures and structures away from growth-orientated consumerism toward a 'post-growth' or 'steady state' economy based on material sufficiency. The nature of this alternative is briefly outlined, although the purpose of this chapter is primarily diagnostic rather than prescriptive.

2. Techno-Optimism and the Ideology of Growth

In 1971, Paul Ehrlich and John Holdren published an article that greatly advanced the understanding and communication of environmental problems and their potential solutions (Ehrlich and Holdren, 1971). In this article they developed what has become known as the IPAT equation. This equation holds that environmental impact (I) equals, or is a function of, Population (P), Affluence (A), and Technology (T). While this equation is not without its limitations and drawbacks – some of which will be discussed below – it nevertheless made it easy for environmentalists to talk about the nature of the unfolding environmental crisis (Meadows *et al.*, 1972). With the IPAT equation, it could be shown in clear terms that environmental impact could be mitigated by the various means of reducing population, reducing per capita income, and increasing productive or energy efficiencies through technological development. Put otherwise, the equation showed that continuous population and consumption growth would exacerbate environmental problems, unless technological advancement could outweigh those impacts through efficiency gains.

One of the attractions of the IPAT equation was the way in which it highlighted the fact that individuals and policy-makers had various options for tackling environmental problems. People who cared about the environment could try to lessen impact either by trying to reduce population, by trying to consume as little as possible, or by trying to produce and consume as efficiently as possible. However, the fact that there were options turned out to be a mixed blessing. It suggested that if people or nations were unable or unwilling to tackle certain parts of the IPAT equation, they could still reduce impacts by addressing one or more of the other variables. As it turned out, the IPAT equation ended up marginalising population and consumption as sites of environmental action, and privileging technological fixes (see Huesemann and Huesemann, 2011).

In one sense, this was quite understandable. Population control is obviously a thorny issue, in that procreation seems like a very intimate issue that governments should not try to regulate. With some justification, how many children people have is widely considered a private matter. For this reason, population has been, and to a large part remains, one of the great taboo subjects of the environmental debate. We know that population is a multiplier of everything (Alcott, 2010), but so challenging and controversial is it to reduce or regulate population that governments have generally looked elsewhere to respond to environmental problems (Ehrlich and Ehrlich, 1990).

A similar dynamic could explain the marginalisation of consumption (Simms *et al.*, 2009). Since a higher income is almost universally considered better than a lower income, governments and individuals have looked for other ways to lessen environmental impact. Voluntarily reducing consumption was, and is, a hard sell, and it certainly does not suggest itself as a vote-winning basis of a political campaign in consumer-orientated societies (or anywhere). To borrow a phrase from George Monbiot (2006), people do not 'riot for austerity'.

The IPAT equation, however, had within it the win/win solution that people seemed to be seeking: efficiency improvements. Even if a nation was unable to reduce population, and even if it was unwilling to reduce its income, the equation provided a theoretical framework that showed that it was nevertheless possible to reduce environmental impact through technological advancement (Simon and Kahn, 1984). This 'techno-fix' approach was a much more politically, economically, and socially palatable way to address environmental problems – leaving to one side, for the moment, the issue of whether the strategy was likely to succeed. It provided governments and individuals with a means of responding to environmental problems (or being seen to respond to environmental problems), without rethinking population growth or questioning affluent lifestyles. In theory, at least, it seemed like a coherent and politically appropriate strategy, and for this reason it came to define, and remains, the mainstream position on environmental matters. At the Rio+20 conference in 2012, for example, the international declaration repeatedly called for 'sustained economic growth' (UN, 2012; Monbiot, 2012) as an essential ingredient in 'sustainable development'.

In much the same way, and according to the same logic, the IPAT equation also opened up a strategy for the corporate world to try to respond to environmental problems, in ways that would not interfere with the interests of capital expansion (Lovins, 2011). Increases in population means there are more consumers and more labourers, so businesses have an economic incentive to consider population growth as a good thing. Similarly, and even more obviously, businesses are in favour of increased consumption, not decreased consumption. As a means of responding to environmental problems, therefore, the corporate world has a clear incentive to privilege techno-fixes. Not only does this strategy avoid having to confront the non-profitable terrains of population or consumption reduction, but it also opens up a huge market for 'green products' which could be sold to a growing demographic of environmentally aware consumers and governments (Pearse, 2012).

As noted, this 'green growth' approach, based on a profound faith in technological solutions, has come to define our times. Reducing overall population and consumption are notoriously difficult and unpopular policies, so the world shies away from them no matter how necessary they may be. But technology is there to save the day, at least in theory (Trainer, 2012a). While lip service is occasionally paid to the challenge of population, and while occasional comments are made regarding the importance of not over-consuming, the reality is that mainstream environmental discourse, especially in the political realm, has placed its faith, explicitly or implicitly, almost entirely in techno-fixes. That is, it is widely assumed that reducing environmental impact – reducing emissions, in particular – will be achieved not by reducing population or consumption, but by producing and consuming goods more efficiently. In this way, economies can still grow in terms of GDP, and affluence can be universalised, while environmental impact reduces. This, in essence, is the vision encapsulated within notions of 'sustainable development', 'green growth', and 'ecological modernisation'. It is so convenient that governments and businesses tend to believe in it, irrespective of whether it has much empirical support. As the next sections show, that empirical support is lacking, which is a most inconvenient truth for those consciously or unconsciously committed to the ideology of growth (Hamilton, 2003).

3. Is There an Environmental Kuznets Curve?

In 1955, the economist Simon Kuznets published a paper arguing that the relationship between GDP and income inequality showed an inverted U-shape when graphed (Kuznets, 1955). That is, he argued that income inequality first increases as a nation develops, but eventually, as a nation's economy continues to grow, inequality levels off and begins to decline, leading to a broader distribution of wealth. Leaving to one side the validity of that socio-economic thesis, a similar idea was later proposed with respect to environmental degradation instead of income inequality (Grossman and Kruger, 1991). This became known as the Environmental Kuznets curve (EKC).

The EKC hypothesis holds that an economy's environmental impact tends to increase during the early phases of industrialisation, but as a nation becomes richer its environmental impact levels off and eventually begins to decline. The essential reasoning beneath this hypothesis can be summarised as follows: (1) as GDP grows, nations can dedicate more of their attention and resources toward environmental protection (a so-called 'post-materialist' need), whereas the poorest nations must focus solely on meeting their basic material needs, irrespective of environmental impact (Carson *et al.*, 1997; McConnell, K., 1997; cf., Martinez-Alier, 1995); (2) richer nations will be able to develop and afford better technologies, which will make production cleaner and less resource-intensive (Lovins, 1998; Grossman and Kruger, 1995); and (3) as nations get richer their economies tend to shift from 'industrial' economies to 'post-industrial' or 'information' or 'service' economies, which it is claimed rely on lower material and energy flows (Janicke *et al.*, 1997; Lomborg, 2001).

Based on these somewhat overlapping lines of reasoning, the EKC hypothesis is used to argue that there are no environmental limits to growth (c.f. Meadows *et al.*, 2004; Trainer, 2010; Heinberg, 2011) – that growth is ultimately good for the environment, even if at first it seems bad. As Wilfred Beckerman (1992: 482) puts it, 'although economic growth usually leads to environmental degradation in the early stages of the process, in the end the best – and probably the only – way to attain a decent environment in most countries is to become rich'. It should come as little surprise that the EKC hypothesis – at least, its essential message – was enthusiastically embraced by mainstream politicians and businesses (Purdey, 2010). After all, it suggested that economies should remain focused on growth in GDP, not in contradiction of environmental concerns but in support of them. This approach was the path of least resistance, as the win/win message it entailed was that there was no inconsistency with promoting limitless economic growth *and* caring for the environment. In terms of responding to environmental problems, therefore, the EKC propped up the status quo and gave apparent legitimacy to 'business as usual'. The logic, such that it is, becomes: 'Grow now, clean up later' (Van Alstine and Neumayer, 2010). We can have the cake and eat it too – or so the argument goes.

The EKC hypothesis might have some initial theoretical plausibility based on the three lines of argument listed above, but the hypothesis should only shape policy, of course, if it can be empirically substantiated. The empirical foundations of the hypothesis, however, are dubious, at best. A comprehensive review of the literature on EKC hypothesis is beyond the scope of this chapter (see Stern, 2004; Bradshaw, Giam, and Sodhi, 2010), but in broad terms the empirical status of the EKC can be expressed as follows. Some studies have shown that where certain types of environmental damage are generated and suffered locally (or within adjacent cooperating nations) an EKC can indeed be seen (Dinda, 2004; Bo, 2011). These limited circumstances include wastewater discharge, sulphur dioxide emissions, and carbon monoxide emissions. On the other hand, when the environmental problems cross national boundaries or have longer-term impacts, studies conclude that the EKC does not hold (Stern, 2010). Most importantly, an EKC exists neither for carbon dioxide (Luzzati and Orsini, 2009) nor biodiversity loss (Mills and Waite, 2009; Asafu-Adjaye, 2003), two of the most significant environmental crises. It is hard to defend a growth model of progress based on the limited cases of environmental improvement, if sustained growth in GDP fails to address (and indeed exacerbates) problems such as climate change or biodiversity loss. As Brian Czech (2013: 200) puts it, the EKC represents 'a grain of truth embedded in a fallacy'. The environmental costs of growth also tend to impact most on the poorest parts of the world (Woodward and Simms, 2006), at least at first, providing further grounds for questioning whether growth is really the path of progress.

Furthermore, a study by Holm and Englund (2009) has done much to debunk the widely held belief that a movement toward a 'service', 'information', or 'post-industrial' economy leads to reduced environmental impacts. In a review of the evidence on this matter, they show that despite growth of the service sector during the last decades in the world's wealthier countries, overall resource consumption has increased (see also, Fourcroy *et al.*, 2012; Henriques and Kander, 2010). Moreover, to the limited extent that some 'service' economies do seem to be decoupling growth from impact per capita (an issue considered in more detail below), it is arguably due to the outsourcing of manufacturing to developing nations, especially China. Accordingly, any apparent decoupling can often be attributed to dubious or at least incomplete accounting. For example, it is no good claiming a reduction in national deforestation, say, if a nation is simply importing more wood from abroad rather than cutting down its own trees (Asici, 2013); and it is no good claiming a reduced carbon footprint per capita if it simply means China or other industrialising nations are serving as a 'pollution haven' (Cole, 2004) for carbon-intensive manufacturing (see Wiedmann *et al.*, 2013). That would be not so much 'decoupling' as 'recoupling'.

This accounting issue is slowly being recognised even by mainstream institutions like the United Nations, which recently noted, albeit in an understated way, that 'a certain amount of material burden and the associated environmental impacts are being "externalized" from importing countries... Countries may improve their decoupling performance most easily by outsourcing material-intensive extraction and processing to other countries and by importing concentrated products instead' (UNEP, 2011: 60-61). While it may be possible to 'externalise' impacts from any particular nation, the planet as a whole, of course, is a closed system. Accordingly, when 'externalised' manufacturing is 'internalised' from an accounting perspective, much of the perceived dematerialisation of rich nations disappears (Wiedmann *et al.*, 2013).

In one of the most comprehensive reviews of the data and methodologies used to estimate the EKC hypothesis, David Stern (2004: 1435) concludes that 'the statistical analysis on which the EKC is based is not robust. There is little evidence for a common inverted U-shaped pathway that countries follow as their income rises.' This general conclusion finds much evidential support (see Wang *et al.*, 2013; Wiedmann *et al.*, 2013).

Even in those limited cases where the EKC can be shown to exist, it is far too simplistic to suggest that this is solely or primarily because a nation has become rich. Often it can be shown that environmental improvements are associated with new laws, policies, or institutions (see Magnani, 2001). This raises the question of whether such improvements were due to increases in GDP, as the EKC hypothesis holds, or simply due to better regulations. It could not credibly be argued that getting rich is the only relevant variable. Reductions in harm do not happen automatically when nations become rich. Policies are usually needed – such as regulations about factory pollution, land use, the fuel efficiency of cars, or the treatment of rivers – and it is at least arguable that the regulations could have been produced at much lower levels of income and achieved the same or even more positive environmental outcomes.

Perhaps the most damning criticism of the EKC hypothesis, however, comes from the ecological footprint analysis (White, 2007; Caviglia-Harris *et al.*, 2009; Wang *et al.*, 2013; Global Footprint Network, 2013). The EKC, if valid, would suggest that nations should seek growth in GDP if they want to reduce their environmental impact. But when this extraordinary claim is considered in the context of ecological footprint analysis, the hypothesis is simply and obviously wrong. The US is the richest nation on the planet, but if the US way of life were globalised we would need more than four times the biocapacity of Earth (Global Footprint Network, 2013). On that basis, who could possibly argue that environmental degradation decreases as wealth grows? For a further example, take Australia – another of the richest nations – which has the highest per capita carbon footprint in the OECD and one of the highest in the world (Garnaut, 2008: Ch. 7). This strongly suggests that the EKC hypothesis is embraced for political reasons, not scientific foundation.

Even the somewhat less resource-intensive Western European nations – the so-called 'green' economies like Germany, Norway, Denmark, and Sweden – are grossly exceeding their 'fair share' of the planet's biocapacity (Vale and Vale, 2013). We would need approximately three planets if the Western European way of life were globalised, and that is assuming no population growth (Global Footprint Network, 2013). So even if there were an EKC, the turning point in the curve would be occurring much too late in the process of development to validate anything like the conventional development path. Accordingly, the argument that sustainability will arrive when the entire world gets rich or 'developed' is patently wrong, and it is intellectually irresponsible to pretend otherwise (White, 2007). It is a view that simply lacks any evidential foundation.

In sum, one must not get caught up in the smoke and mirrors of isolated studies that show certain aspects of environmental damage or pollution have declined as a nation has gotten richer. Such analyses totally miss the bigger picture, which is that it would be ecologically catastrophic if the entire world tried to become affluent as a means of environmental protection (Turner, 2012; Smith and Positano, 2010). If the EKC hypothesis sounds too good to be true, that is because, on the whole, it is false.

4. Are Economies Decoupling Growth from Impact?

Given that the richest nations demonstrably have the largest ecological footprints, it is surprising, or at least disappointing, that mainstream environmental discourse still tends to assume that sustained growth in GDP, across the globe, will solve the ecological predicament; or at least, that sustained growth is not incompatible with sustainability (UN, 2012). There seems to be an implicit acceptance of the EKC hypothesis, driven by techno-optimism, even though it lacks empirical foundation. This can be explained primarily in terms of political convenience. Politicians seem very reluctant to accept any incompatibility between growth and environmental protection, because that would involve choosing between those goals. Instead of making tough choices, politicians just pretend that there is no incompatibility, which is what people and businesses seem to want to hear. All the while, the biocapacity of the planet continues to decline (Lawn and Clarke, 2010).

There is, however, the *theoretical possibility* that in the future our economies will be able to achieve sustainability by decoupling their economic activity from environmental impact, through efficiency gains (UNEP, 2011). It is this seductive line of reasoning that now deserves deeper consideration. After all, the fact that technology and growth have not been able to produce a sustainable economy does not mean that it is not possible to do so in the future. As Nordhaus and Shellenberger (2011) argue: 'The solution to the unintended consequences of modernity is, and has always been, more modernity – just as the solution to the unintended consequences of our technologies has always been more technology.' While this can be accepted as a theoretical possibility, there are dynamics at play – including the laws of physics – that suggest that decoupling through efficiency gains will not reduce the overall ecological impacts of economic activity if global growth remains the primary economic goal.

In assessing the prospects of efficiency gains as a means of reducing environmental impact, it is imperative to distinguish between 'relative' and 'absolute' decoupling (Jackson, 2009). Relative decoupling refers to a decline in the ecological impact *per unit* of economic output. Absolute decoupling refers to a decline in the *overall* ecological impact of total economic output. While relative decoupling may occur, making each commodity less materially intensive, if the total consumption of commodities increases then there may be no absolute decoupling; indeed, the absolute ecological impact of total economic activity may increase.

Given that the global economy already exceeds the planet's sustainable carrying capacity (Global Footprint Network, 2013), it is clear that absolute decoupling is what is needed. As shown below, however, it is just as clear that absolute decoupling is not occurring. Overall (or absolute) energy use and resource extraction continues to rise, even if in places the energy or resource intensity per capita is in decline (Wiedmann *et al.*, 2013).

Consider, for example, the energy intensity per unit of global economic output, where the evidence of relative decoupling is quite clear. Tim Jackson (2009: 69) reports that the amount of energy needed to produce each unit of the world's economic output has fallen more or less continuously in recent decades, with the global energy intensity per unit now 33 per cent lower on average than it was in 1970. Unsurprisingly, this improved energy efficiency is also leading to relative decoupling in terms of carbon emission intensities. The global carbon intensity per unit of economic output declined by almost one quarter from just over 1 kilogramme of CO_2 per US dollar in 1980 to 770 grams of CO_2 per US dollar in 2006.

However, despite declining energy and carbon intensities, Jackson shows that total CO_2 emissions have increased 80% since 1970. 'Emissions today,' he adds, 'are almost 40% higher than they were in 1990 – the Kyoto base year – and since the year 2000 they have been growing at 3% per year' (Jackson, 2009: 71). This shows that despite significant relative decoupling of energy intensities, absolute levels of carbon emissions are rising significantly. Efficiency gains are not fulfilling their promise to reduce overall impact.

Peter Victor (2008) arrived at essentially the same conclusion when he reviewed studies of decoupling with respect to the total material resource requirements of Germany, the Netherlands, US, and Japan – some of the most technologically advanced nations on the planet. He reports that although a degree of relative decoupling has occurred in recent decades, the decoupling was insufficient to prevent the total use of resources increasing. He explains that '[t]his is because the rate of increase in GDP in each of the four countries was greater than the rate of decrease in material intensity' (Victor, 2008: 55). This suggests that even if these technologically advanced nations were able to fully decarbonise their economies in response to climate change, the material intensity of their economies (in terms of resource consumption) would remain unsustainably high. This points to the important but often forgotten fact that acute environmental crises would remain (e.g., deforestation, ocean depletion, biodiversity loss, soil erosion, etc.) even if the issue of climate change were somehow resolved. Globally the message is essentially the same:

Comparing 2002 with 1980 about 25 per cent less natural resources (measured in physical units) were used to produce one dollar of GDP. This relative decoupling of economic growth and resource use was insufficient to prevent the total quantity of resource extraction increasing, which it did by 36 per cent (Victor, 2008: 55-6).

The message of this analysis is not that decoupling through techno-efficiency improvements is unnecessary – far from it. Decoupling has an absolutely vital role to play in the attainment of a sustainable society (von Weizsacker *et al.*, 2009). But the evidence shows that despite many examples of relative decoupling, growth in overall economic output has meant that absolute impacts on the environment are still increasing. Every year more carbon emissions are sent into the atmosphere and more renewable and non-renewable resources are extracted from our finite Earth. In short, decades of extraordinary technological development have resulted in increased, not reduced, environmental impacts. It is not clear, therefore, whether the 'optimism' in 'techno-optimism' has any rational basis at all.

5. Efficiency, Rebound Effects, and Jevons' Paradox

The evidence reviewed clearly indicates that there has been significant relative decoupling in recent decades, but little or no absolute decoupling – certainly not at the global level. This is somewhat counter-intuitive, perhaps, because one might ordinarily think that efficiency gains (which produce relative decoupling) would lead to absolute decoupling. In other words, it is plausible to think that as the world gets better at producing commodities more efficiently, the absolute impacts of our economic activity would naturally decline. But this assumption has not played out in reality. As will now be explained, one of critical reasons it has not played out is because of what are known as 'rebound effects', or the Jevons paradox (Alcott, 2005; Polimeni *et al.*, 2009; Owen, 2012).

The Jevons paradox acquires its name from the classical economist William Stanley Jevons, who was the first to formalise the idea that efficiency gains would not necessarily lead to a reduction in resource consumption, and could even lead to increased consumption. Writing at a time when there was increasing concern over England's diminishing coal reserves, Jevons (1865) noted that the more efficient steam engines were not reducing but actually increasing the consumption of coal. This was because the new technologies being developed made the engines more accessible and affordable to more people, thus increasing the demand on coal resources even as engines became more efficient. He formalised his view by stating: 'It is a confusion of ideas to suppose that the economical use of fuel is equivalent to diminished consumption. The very contrary is the truth' (Jevons, 1865: 103). What are the dynamics of this paradox and to what extent does it exist?

The Jevons paradox is generally discussed in the scholarly literature with reference to the notion of 'rebound effects' (Herring and Sorrell, 2009; Alcott and Madlener, 2009). A rebound effect is said to have occurred when the benefits of efficiency improvements are partially or wholly negated by consumption growth that was made possible by the efficiency improvements. For example, a 5% increase in energy efficiency may only reduce energy consumption by 2% if the efficiency improvements incentivise people to act in more energy-intensive ways (meaning 60% of anticipated savings are lost or 'taken back'). In other words, efficiency improvements can provoke behavioural or economic responses ('rebounds') that end up reducing some of the anticipated benefits of the efficiency improvements. When those rebounds are significant enough they can even lead to *increased* resource or energy consumption, which is sometimes called 'back-fire' – or the Jevons paradox. As will now be explained, there are three main categories of rebound effects – direct rebounds, indirect rebounds, and a macroeconomic or economy-wide rebound.

A direct rebound occurs when an efficiency gain in production results in increased consumption of the same resource (Khazzoom, 1980; Frondel *et al.*, 2012). For example, a more fuel-efficient car can lead people to drive more often, or further, since the costs of fuel per kilometre have gone down; a more efficient heater can lead people to warm their houses for longer periods or to hotter temperatures, since the relative costs of heating have gone down; energy efficient lighting can lead people to leave the lights on for longer, etc. (Sorrell, 2009). Because efficiency generally reduces the price of a commodity (since it makes production less resource-intensive or time-intensive), this incentivises increased consumption, meaning that some or all of the ecological benefits that flow from efficiency gains are often lost to increased consumption.

An indirect rebound occurs when efficiency gains lead to increased consumption of some other resource. For example, insulating one's home might reduce the annual consumption of energy for electricity, but the money saved from reduced energy costs is often spent on other commodities that require energy (e.g., a plane flight or a new television). This can mean that some or all of the energy saved from insulating one's house is actually consumed elsewhere, meaning overall energy dependence can stay the same or even increase.

A macroeconomic or economy-wide rebound is the aggregate of direct and indirect rebounds. New technologies can create new production possibilities, or make existing production possibilities accessible to more people, thus stimulating economic growth. The result is that efficiency-promoting technologies often facilitate the consumption of more energy and resources even as energy and resource intensities reduce, as Jevons observed long ago.

While the basic mechanism of rebound effects is widely acknowledged, and, indeed, beyond dispute, there is an ongoing debate over the magnitude of the various rebound phenomena. Some argue that the macroeconomic rebound actually exceeds the energy or resource savings (Polimeni *et al.*, 2009; Hanley *et al.*, 2009; Owen, 2012), suggesting that efficiency improvements, designed to reduce overall consumption, sometimes actually back-fire and lead to increased consumption. This would cast into grave doubt the presumed value of efficiency improvements, at least in some circumstances. Other theorists are more circumspect (Herring and Sorrell, 2009), suggesting at the very least that the case for back-fire is unclear. It is also the case that rebounds generally differ according to context and type of rebound, and assessing the degree of rebound also depends on the methodological assumptions used when studying them.

Direct rebounds are estimated to range generally in the vicinity of 10-30% (Sorrell, 2009: 33), meaning that typically 10-30% of the expected environmental benefits of efficiency gains are lost to increased consumption of the same resource. In some circum-stances, direct rebounds can be 75% or higher (Chakravarty *et al.*, 2013). Indirect rebounds are somewhat harder to measure, but are generally thought to be higher than direct rebounds, and estimates of macroeconomic rebound range from 15%-350% (Dimitropoulos, 2007). The huge range here again points to differences in methodo-logical assumptions. Without entering into the intricacies of the complex empirical and theoretical debates, it is fair to say that despite the uncertainties, there is broad agreement that rebound effects exist and that they are significant. The benefits of technology are almost always less than presumed, and, in fact, at times efficiency improvements can lead to more, not fewer, resources being consumed overall.

What seems to be far less widely appreciated, however, is that when efficiency gains occur within a paradigm of growth economics, there is little to no chance of absolute decoupling occurring (Herring, 2009; Huesemann and Huesemann, 2011; Trainer, 2012). This is partly due to rebound effects, and partly due to the inherent structure of growth economics. It will now be shown that in order to achieve the absolute decoupling required for sustainability, efficiency gains must be governed, not by an imperative to grow, but by an economics of sufficiency.

6. The 'Growth Model' Has No Techno-Fix

Perhaps the limits of technology can be most easily understood when clarifying exactly what is expected of technology in terms of achieving sustainability. The global development agenda, as expressed in the Rio+20 declaration, is that all nations should seek 'sustained growth' (UN, 2012) in GDP as a path to sustainable development. But what degree of efficiency improvements would be required to make sustained global growth 'sustainable'? When one does the math on this question, it becomes perfectly clear that technology can never make the growth model 'green'. Consider the following basic arithmetic:

Throughout much of the 20th century, developed economies achieved around 3% growth in GDP per annum, meaning that they doubled in size roughly every 23 years (Purdey, 2010). This has become something of a reference point for signifying politico-economic 'success' (Hamilton, 2003), so let us assume that when the United Nations talks of 'growth' it means continuing levels of growth that have been experienced in recent decades. Furthermore, for social justice reasons, let us assume that the aim of 'development' is ultimately to bring the poorest parts of the world up to the living standards enjoyed by the developed world. After all, from a moral perspective, it is difficult to argue that one section of the global population is entitled to a certain income per capita while denying a similar level to others. If, however, this global development agenda were to be achieved over the next 70 years, how big would the global economy be relative to the existing economy?

The figures are confronting, to say the least. Over 70 years, at 3% growth, the economies of the developed world (populated by roughly 1 billion people) would have doubled in size three times, meaning they would be eight times larger, in terms of GDP, than they are now. If we also assume that by 2080 the world population is going to be around 10 billion (UNDSEA, 2012), and that this population has caught up to the living standards of the developed world by this stage, then the global economy would be around 80 times larger, in terms of GDP, than the size of the developed world's aggregate economy today.

Needless to say, ecosystems are trembling under the pressure of one 'developed world' at the existing size. Who, then, could seriously think our planet could withstand the equivalent of an 80-fold increase? The very suggestion is absurd, and yet this very absurdity defines the vision of the global development agenda. It is the elephant in the room. If we make the rough estimation that the developed world, on its own, currently consumes the earth's entire sustainable biocapacity (Vale and Vale, 2013), then an 80-fold increase would imply that in 70 years we would need 80 planets in order to sustain the global economy. We only have one planet, of course, and its biocapacity is already in decline.

At this stage the techno-optimist may wish to interject and insist that in this scenario, which forecasts GDP growth into the future, we can expect that there would be efficiency improvements, such that the impact of global growth would be less than projected above. There would be efficiency improvements, indeed, meaning that the impact could be significantly less than projected above. For example, a recent study (Wiedmann et al., 2013) shows that with every 10% increase in GDP, the material footprint of economies 'only' increase by 6%. But based on that estimate of decoupling, we would still need 48 planets' worth of biocapacity. Accordingly, even if these figures are overstated by an order of magnitude, the point would remain that efficiency gains could not possibly be expected to make the projected amount of GDP growth sustainable. The levels of decoupling required would simply be too much (Huesemann and Huesemann, 2011; Trainer, 2012). To think otherwise is not being optimistic but delusional.

Even based on more conservative numbers, the decoupling required would be unattainable. For example, Tim Jackson (2009) has done the arithmetic with respect to carbon emissions, envisioning a scenario in which current Western European incomes grow at 2% and by 2050 nine billion people share that same income level. In this more moderate scenario, the global economy still grows 15 times. Jackson shows that in order to meet the IPCC's carbon goal of 450ppm, the carbon intensity of each dollar of GDP must be 130 times lower than the average carbon intensity today. This means carbon intensities must fall 11% every year between now and 2050. By way of context, carbon intensities have declined merely 0.7% per year since 1990 (Jackson, 2009: 79). When these numbers are understood, one can only conclude that techno-optimism is not a scientifically credible position but is instead a 'faith' without foundation.

According to the latest IPCC report (2013), if the world is to have a 50% chance of keeping warming to less than two degrees (the so-called 'safe' level), no more than 820-1445 billion tones of carbon dioxide and other greenhouse gases can be emitted during the rest of this century. Based on existing yearly emissions, and aiming for a 66% chance of success, this carbon budget is going to be used up by

2045. If existing trends of growth in emissions continue or accelerate, or if we demand a higher chance of success than 66%, that budget will be used up even sooner (see also, Moriarty and Honnery, 2011).

The question, therefore, must not be: 'How can we make the growth model sustainable?' The question should be: 'What economic model is sustainable?' And the answer, it seems, must be: 'Something other than the growth model.'

7. Efficiency Without Sufficiency is Lost

The central message of the analysis so far is that efficiency gains that take place within a growth-orientated economy tend to be negated by further growth, resulting in an overall increase in resource and energy consumption, or at least no reduction. Technologies that increase labour productivity, for example, are rarely converted into less labour input; instead of allowing for less work, productivity gains tend to 'rebound' as more overall production (Norgard, 2009). Similarly, developments in the design of commodities that allow for less material or energy inputs end up reducing the cost of production, but cheaper production reduces the price of the commodity, generally resulting in increased con-sumption. Furthermore, capital investments in technology (R&D) are generally driven by the need for a 'return on investment', meaning that the technologies that are developed are generally the ones that maximise profits (Huesemann and Huesemann, 2011). These are the types of dynamics by which the potential ecological benefits of efficiency gains are lost.

In order to take advantage of efficiency gains – that is, in order for efficiency gains to actually *reduce* resource and energy consumption to sustainable levels – what is needed is an economics of sufficiency; an economics that directs efficiency gains into reducing ecological impacts rather than increasing material growth. Sufficiency is a concept that is entirely absent from the paradigm of conventional growth economics, but once the limits of technology (and thus the limits to growth) are recognised, it becomes clear that embracing an economics of sufficiency is absolutely necessary if we are to create an economic model that is ecologically sustainable (Alexander, 2012a; Goodman, 2010; Herring, 2009).

Space does not permit a detailed outline of what an economics of sufficiency would look like, but some general comments are in order. In the poorest parts of the world, of course, economic development *of some form* is still required in order for basic material needs to be sufficiently met. In such contexts, an economics of sufficiency might still imply a phase of economic growth, for using efficiency gains to help eliminate poverty is certainly a part of what 'development' should mean (for a discussion of 'appropriate development', see Trainer, 2010: Ch. 5). But in the most highly developed regions of the world – where the main focus of this analysis is directed – an economics of sufficiency would involve moving away from a focus on continuous economic growth toward a 'post-growth' or 'steady state' economy that operated within the sustainable carrying capacity of the planet (Daly, 1996; Norgard, 2009). Given that those highly developed nations currently all have unsustainably high ecological footprints, any transition to a steady state economy presumably means not simply moving away from continuous economic expansion (in terms of resource and energy use), but actually entering a phase of planned contraction of resource and energy use – a process known as degrowth (Alexander, 2012b). Technology provides no escape from this logic, which is the main point of this chapter.[2]

The broad vision implied by an economics of sufficiency involves the richest nations initiating a degrowth process while the poorest nations grow in order to meet basic needs. If sustainability is to be achieved over coming decades the rich and poor economies will need to converge to produce a global economy that meets the basic needs for all while operating within the sustainable carrying capacity of the planet (Lawn and Clarke, 2010). This may not seem very likely at all – and the necessary policies or mechanisms of change cannot be explored presently – but the vision is presented here as a far more coherent conception of sustainability than the dominant notions of 'sustainable development' based on continuous global growth. Note that this alternative vision does not entail globalising Western-style affluence but rather globalising less-consumption orientated lifestyles of material sufficiency (Princen,

---

[2] The term 'degrowth' obviously has huge public relations challenges and for that reason it is highly unlikely to ever become the basis of a popular campaign. Nevertheless, in an era where growth is widely considered the solution to most societal problems (Hamilton, 2003), the value of the degrowth literature lies in its provocative suggestion that contraction, not growth, of material and energy consumption may be required in overdeveloped areas of the world in order to transition to a just and sustainable world. That is the provocation entirely absent from notions of 'sustainable development' within mainstream environmental discourse (see Goodman, 2010). Whether 'degrowth' is the best way of framing the necessity of contraction is an important issue, but one that must be left for consideration on another occasion.

2005; Trainer, 2010). In short, sustainability in the developed nations does not just meaning producing and consuming more *efficiently*; it also means producing and consuming *less*. This follows from the critique of techno-optimism detailed above.

In order for this admittedly radical vision to be realised – or, at least, to begin moving toward it – what is needed, at a minimum, is for rich nations to stop redirecting efficiency gains into production and consumption growth. Instead, efficiency gains must be used to reduce overall energy and resource consumption. For example, technologies that increase labour productivity should generally lead to decreased working hours, not increased production; technologies that increase energy efficiency must not be used to 'do more with the same inputs' but to 'do enough with fewer inputs'.

Reducing the ecological impacts of developed nations, however, cannot be achieved simply through the application of technology. As well as using technologies to reduce the impact of economic activity, what is also required is that typical levels of consumption and production in developed nations go down. This can be achieved partly by cultural change, through which people practice 'voluntary simplicity' by exchanging superfluous consumption for more free time (Burch, 2012; Alexander, 2012c). But such cultural change needs to be supported and facilitated by structural changes that support an economics of sufficiency (see, e.g., Alcott, 2008; Trainer, 2010; Alexander, 2011; van den Bergh, 2011).

Exactly what form those cultural and structural changes should take, and how they may be achieved, are large and complex questions that cannot be addressed presently. This includes the question of to what extent the required structural changes can arise within a 'market-based' economy (see Trainer, 2011), and whether the necessary change will need to be driven from the 'top down' or 'from below' (Trainer, 2010). There is also the critically important question of what *types* of consumption and production need to 'degrow', and whether some types may still need to 'grow'. For example, it can be fairly presumed, even within a degrowth model of progress, that any transition to a sustainable society is going to depend on a considerable expansion of the production of solar panels and wind turbines. This suggests that the dualism of growth vs. degrowth is somewhat simplistic and needs to be negotiated with some subtlety. But this chapter will have served its purpose if the need for a paradigm-shift in economics is now more clearly evident. Accurate prescription is not possible until there has been an accurate diagnosis, and the evidence-based diagnosis delivered above is that the conventional growth model of progress is cancerous and cannot be saved by technology. Any transition to a just and sustainable economy, therefore, depends on a value-shift in the direction of sufficiency. Until that occurs, sustainability will remain a will-o'-the-wisp.

8. Conclusion

This chapter has reviewed the evidence in support of techno-optimism and found it to be wanting. This is significant because it debunks a widely held view, even amongst many environmentalists, that 'green growth' is a coherent path to sustainability. Perhaps it would be nice if affluence could be globalised without damaging the planet. It would certainly be less confronting than rethinking cultural and economic fundamentals. But there are no credible grounds for thinking that technology is going to be able to protect the environment if economic growth is sustained and high consumption lifestyles continue to be globalised. The levels of decoupling required are simply too great. More efficient growth in GDP, therefore, is not so much 'green' as slightly 'less brown' (Czech, 2013: Ch. 8), which is a wholly inadequate response to the crises facing humanity.

We have seen that as nations get richer, their overall ecological footprints and carbon emissions tend to rise, from which it follows that the argument that higher GDP will produce sustainable economies entirely lacks evidential foundation. The central problem is that in a growth-orientated economy, efficiency gains are almost always reinvested into increasing production and consumption, not reducing them. These rebound effects have meant that the overall impact of economies tends to increase, even though technology has produced many efficiency gains in production. In other words, technological advancement has produced relative decoupling, but little or no absolute decoupling. The latter is obviously what is needed, however, given that the global economy is in gross ecological overshoot (Turner, 2012).

Since there are no reasons to think that more efficient growth is going to reduce humanity's ecological footprint within sustainable bounds, it follows that we must consider alternative models of economy – alternative models of progress – even if these challenge conventional economic wisdom. To draw on the Einsteinian dictum: we cannot solve our problems using the same kinds of thinking that caused them. Among other things, this implies taking population stabilisation and reduction policies much more seriously (Alcott, 2012). But even if population were to be stabilised today, the global economy would remain in gross ecological overshoot. All appropriate technologies must also be exploited – this chapter does not argue otherwise! – it only maintains that technology is not going to be able to solve environmental problems when the application of technology is governed by a growth imperative. Accordingly, this chapter has argued that what is needed for true sustainability (as opposed to 'greenwash') is a transition to a fundamentally different kind of economy – an economy that seeks sufficiency rather than limitless growth. This may not be a popular message, and it may already be too late for there to be a smooth transition beyond the growth model (Gilding, 2011). But on a finite planet, there is no alternative. The sooner the world realises this, the better it will be for both people and planet.

We must embrace life beyond growth before it embraces us.

References

Alcott, B. 2005. Jevons' paradox. *Ecological Economics* 54: 9-21.

Alcott, B. 2008. 'The sufficiency strategy: Would rich-world frugality lower environmental impact?'. *Ecological Economics* 64: 770-86.

Alcott, B. 2012. 'Population matters in ecological economics'. *Ecological Economics* 80: 109-120.

Alcott, B. and Madlener, R. 2009. 'Energy rebound and economic growth: A review of the main issues and research needs'. *Energy* 34: 370-376.

Alexander, S. 2011. 'Property beyond growth: Toward a politics of voluntary simplicity'. Doctoral thesis, Melbourne Law School. Available at: http://papers.ssrn.com/sol3/papers.cfm?abstract_id=1941069 (accessed 10 September 2013).

Alexander, S. 2012a. 'The optimal material threshold: Toward an economics of sufficiency'. *Real-World Economics Review* 61: 2-21.

Alexander, S. 2012b. 'Planned economic contraction: The emerging case for degrowth'. *Environmental Politics* 21 (3): 349-368.

Alexander, S. 2012c. 'The sufficiency economy: Envisioning a prosperous way down'. *Simplicity Institute Report* 12s: 1-31.

Asafu-Adjaye, J. 2003. 'Biodiversity loss and economic growth: A cross-country analysis'. *Contemporary Economic Policy* 21(2): 173: 185.

Asici, A.A. 2013. 'Economic growth and its impact on environment: A panel data analysis'. *Ecolgical Economics* 24: 324-333.

Beckerman, W. 1992. 'Economic growth and the environment: Whose growth? Whose environment?'. *World Development* 20(4): 481-496.

Beckerman, W. 2002. *A poverty of reason: Sustainable*

development and economic growth. Oakland: Independent Institute.

Bo, S. 2011. 'A literature review on environmental Kuznets curve'. *Energy Procedia* 5: 1322-1325.

Bradshaw, C., Giam, X., and Sodhi, N. 2010. 'Evaluating the relative environmental impact of countries'. *PLoS One* 5(5): e10440.

Brown, L. 2011. *World on the edge: How to prevent environmental and economic collapse*. New York: W.W. Norton and Company.

Burch, M. 2012. 'Twenty questions: Technology and simple living'. *Simplicity Institute Report* 12f: 1-31.

Carson, R., Jeon, Y., and McCubbin, D. 1997. 'The relationship between air pollution emissions and income: US data'. *Environment and Development Economics* 2(4): 433-450.

Caviglia-Harris, J., Chambers, D., and Kahn, J. 2009. 'Taking the "U" out of Kuznets: A comprehensive analysis of the EKC and environmental degradation'. *Ecological Economics* 68: 1149-1159.

Chakravarty, D., Dasgupta, S., Roy, J. 2013. 'Rebound effect: How much to worry?'. *Current Opinion in Environmental Sustainability* 5: 216-228.

Cole. M. 2004. 'Trade, the pollution haven hypothesis and the environmental Kuznets curve: Examining the linkages'. *Ecological Economics* 48(1): 71-81.

Czech, B. 2013. *Supply shock: Economic growth at the crossroads and the steady state solution*. Gabriola Island: New Society Publishers.

Daly, H. 1996. *Beyond growth: The economics of sustainable development*. Boston: Beacon Press.

Dimitropoulos, J. 2007. 'Energy productivity improvement and the rebound effect: An overview of the state of knowledge'. *Energy Policy* 35: 6354-6363.

Dinda, S. 2004. 'Environmental Kuznets curve hypothesis: A Survey'. *Ecological Economics* 49(4): 431.

Ehrlich, P. and Ehrlich, A. 1990. *The population explosion*. London: Frederick Muller.

Ehrlich, P. and Ehrlich A. 2013. 'Can a collapse of civilization be avoided?'. *Simplicity Institute Report* 13a: 1-19.

Ehrlich, P. and Holdren, J. 1971. 'Impact of population growth'. *Science* 171: 1212-1217.

Fourcroy, C., Gallouj, F., and Decellas, F. 2012. 'Energy consumption in service industries: Challenging the myth of non-materiality'. *Ecological Economics* 81: 155-164.

Frondel, M., Ritter, N., and Vance, C. 2012. 'Heterogeneity in the rebound effect: Further evidence from Germany'. *Energy Economics* 34: 461-467.

Garnaut, R. 2008. 'The Garnet climate change review'. Available at: http://www.garnautreview.org.au/index.htm (accessed 10 September 2013).

Gilding, P. 2011. *The great disruption: How the climate crisis will transform the global economy*. London: Bloomsbury.

Global Footprint Network. 2013. Reports available at: http://www.footprintnetwork.org/en/index.php/GFN/ (accessed 3 September 2013).

Goodman, J. 2010. 'Responding to the climate crisis: Modernisation, limits, socialism'. *Journal of Australia Political Economy* 66: 144-65.

Grantham Institute for Climate Change. 2013. 'Halving global CO2 by 2050: Technologies and costs'. Available at: http://www3.imperial.ac.uk/climatechange/publications/collaborative/halving-global-co2-by-2050 (accessed 10 October 2013).

Grossman, G. and Kruger, A.B. 1991. 'Environmental impacts of a NAFTA agreement'. (National Bureau of Economic Research Working Paper, 3914.)

Grossman, G. and Kruger, A.B. 1995. Economic growth and the environment. *Quarterly Journal of Economics* 110(2): 353-377.

Hamilton, C. 2003. *Growth fetish*. Crows Nest, NSW: Allen & Unwin.

Hamilton, C. 2013. *Earthmasters: Playing God with the climate*. Crows Nest, NSW: Allen & Unwin.

Hanley, N., McGregor, P.G., Swales, J.K., and Turner, K. 2009. 'Do increases in energy efficiency improve environmental quality and sustainability?'. *Ecological Economics* 68(3): 692-709.

Heinberg, R. 2011. *The end of growth: Adapting to our new economic reality*. Gabriola Island: New Society Publishers.

Henriques, S. and Kander, A. 2010. 'The modest environmental relief resulting from the transition to a service economy'. *Ecological Economics* 70: 271-282.

Herring, H. 2009. 'Sufficiency and the rebound effect', in H. Herring and S. Sorrell (eds). *Energy efficiency and sustainable consumption: The rebound effect*. London: Palgrave Macmillan.

Herring, H. and Sorrell, S. 2009. *Energy efficiency and sustainable consumption: The rebound effect*. London: Palgrave Macmillan.

Holm, S.-O. and G. Englund. 2009. 'Increased ecoefficiency and gross rebound effect: Evidence from USA and six European countries 1960-2002'. *Ecological Economics* 68: 879-887.

Huesemann, M. and Huesemann, J. 2011. *Techno-fix: Why technology won't save us or the environment*. Gabriola Island: New Society Publishers.

Intergovernmental Panel on Climate Change (IPCC), 2013. 'Climate Change 2013: The Physical Science Basis (Fifth Assessment Report)'. Available at: http://www.ipcc.ch/report/ar5/wg1/#. Uk6k-CjqMRw (accessed 4 October 2013).

Jackson, T. 2009. *Prosperity without growth: Economics for a finite planet*. London: Earthscan.

Janicke, M., Binder, M., and Monch, H. 1997. 'Dirty industries: Patterns of change in industrial countries'. *Environmental and Resource Economics* 9: 467; 491.

Jevons, W.S. 1865. *The coal question: An inquiry concerning the progress of the nation and the probable exhaustion of our coal-mines*. MacMillan: London.

Khazzoom, J.D. 1980. 'Economic implications of mandated efficiency in standards for household appliances'. *Energy Journal* 1(4): 21-40.

Kuznets, S. 1955. 'Economic growth and income inequality'. *American Economic Review* 45: 1-28.

Lawn, P. and Clarke, M. 2010. 'The end of economic growth? A contracting threshold hypothesis'. *Ecological Economics* 69: 2213-2223.

Lomborg, B. 2001. *The sceptical environmentalist: Measuring the real state of the world*. Cambridge: Cambridge University Press.

Lovins, A. 1998. *Factor four: Doubling wealth – halving resource use*. London: Earthscan.

Lovins, A. 2011. *Reinventing fire: Bold business solutions for new energy era*. White River Junction, Vt: Chelsea Green Publishing.

Luzzati, T. and Orsini, M. 2009. 'Investigating the energy-environmental Kuznets curve'. *Energy* 34: 291-300.

Magnani, E. 2001. 'The environmental Kuznets curve: Development path or policy result?'. *Environmental Modelling & Software* 16: 157-165.

Martinez-Alier, J. 1995. 'The environment as a luxury good or "too poor to be green"?'. *Ecological Economics* 13(1): 1-10.

McConnell, K. 1997. 'Income and the demand for environmental quality'. *Environment and Development Economics* 2(4): 383-399.

Meadows, D., Randers, J., and Meadows, D., 2004. *Limits to growth: The 30-year update*. White River Junction, Vt: Chelsea Green Publishing.

Mills, J. and Waite, T. 2009. 'Economic prosperity, biodiversity conservation, and the environmental Kuznets curve'. *Ecological Economics* 68: 2087-2095.

Monbiot, G. 2006. *Heat: How we can stop burning the planet.* Penguin: London.

Monbiot, G. 2012. 'After Rio, we know. Governments have given up on the planet'. *Guardian*, 26 June 2013. Available at: http://www.theguardian.com/commentisfree/2012/jun/25/rio-governments-will-not-save-planet (accessed 10 September 2013).

Moriarty, P. and Honnery, D. 2011. *Rise and fall of the carbon civilisation: Resolving global environmental and resource problems.* London: Springer-Verlag.

Nordaus, T. and Schellenberger, M. 2011. 'Evolve: A case for modernization as the road to salvation'. *Orion Magazine* (September/October 2011). Available at: http://www.orion magazine.org/index.php/articles/article/6402/ (accessed 10 September 2013).

Norgard, J. 2009. 'Avoiding rebound through a steady-state economy', in H. Herring and S. Sorrell (eds). *Energy efficiency and sustainable consumption: The rebound effect.* London: Palgrave Macmillan, 204-223.

Owen, D. 2012. *The conundrum: How scientific innovation, increased efficiency, and good intentions can make our energy and climate problems worse.* New York: Riverhead.

Pearse, G. 2012. *Greenwash: Big brands and carbon scams.* Melbourne: Black, Inc.

Polimeni, J. et al. 2009. *The myth of resource efficiency: The Jevons paradox.* London: Earthscan.

Princen, T. 2005. *The logic of sufficiency.* Cambridge, MA: MIT Press.

Purdey, S. 2010. *Economic growth, the environment, and international relations: The growth paradigm.* New York: Routledge.

Rockstrom, J. et al. 2009. Planetary boundaries: Exploring the safe operating space for humanity. *Ecology and Society* 14(2) Article 32.

Simms, A., Johnson, V., Smith, J., Mitchell, S. 2009. 'The consumption explosion: The third UK independence report'. *New Economics Foundation.* Available at: http://www.neweconomics.org/publications/entry/the-consumption-explosion (accessed 3 September 2013).

Simon, J. and Kahn, H. 1984. *The resourceful earth: A response to Global 2000.* London: Blackwell Publishing.

Smith, J. and Positano, S. 2010. *The self-destructive affluence of the first world: The coming crises of global poverty and ecological collapse.* New York: Edwin Mellen.

Sorrell, S. 2009. 'The evidence for direct rebounds', in H. Herring and S. Sorrell (eds). *Energy efficiency and sustainable consumption: The rebound effect*. London: Palgrave Macmillan, 23-46.

Stern, D. 2004. 'The rise and fall of the environmental Kuznets curve'. *World Development* 32(8): 1419-1439.

Stern, D. 2010. 'Between estimates of the emissions-income elasticity'. *Ecological Economics* 69(11): 2173-2182.

Trainer. T. 2010. *The transition to a sustainable and just world*. Sydney: Envirobook.

Trainer, T. 2011. 'The Radical Implications of Zero Growth Economy'. *Real-World Economics Review* 57: 71-82.

Trainer, T. 2012. 'But can't technological advance solve the problems?'. *Simplicity Institute Report* 12g: 1-7.

Turner, G. 2012. 'Are we on the cusp of collapse? Updated comparison of *The Limits to Growth* with historical data'. *Gaia* 21(2): 116-124.

United Nations Environmental Programme (UNEP). 2011. 'Decoupling natural resource use and environmental impacts from economic growth'. Available at: http://www.unep.org/resourcepanel/decoupling/files/pdf/decoupling_report_english.pdf (accessed 10 September 2013).

United Nations Department of Social and Economic Affairs (UNDSEA). 2012. 'World Population Prospects: The 2012 Revision'. Available at: http://esa.un.org/wpp/ (accessed 10 September 2013).

United Nations. 2012. 'The future we want'. A/Res/66/88. Available at: http://daccess-dds-ny.un.org/doc/UNDOC/GEN/N11/476/10/PDF/N1147610.pdf?OpenElement (accessed 10 September 2013).

Vale, R. and Vale, B. 2013. *Living within a fair share ecological footprint*. London: Earthscan.

Van Alstine, J. and Neumayer, E. 2010. 'The environmental Kuznets curve', in K. Gallagher (ed.). *Handbook on trade and the environment*. Cheltenham: Edward Elgar, 49-59.

Van den Bergh, J. 2011. 'Energy conservation more effective with rebound policy'. *Environmental Resource Economics* 48(1): 43-58.

Victor, P. 2008. *Managing without growth: Slower by design, not disaster*. Cheltenham: Edward Elgar Publishing.

Von Weizsacker, E.U., Hargroves, C., Smith, M.H., Desha, C., and Stasinopoulous, P. 2009. *Factor five: Transforming the global economy through 80% improvements in resource productivity*. London: Routledge.

Wang, Y., Kang, L., Wu, X., and Xiao, Y. 2013. 'Estimating the environmental Kuznets curve for ecological footprint at the global level: A spatial econometric approach'. *Ecological Indicators* 43: 15-21.

Weidmann, T., Schandl, H., Lenzen, M., Moran, D., Suh, S., West, J., and Kanemoto, K. 2013. 'The material footprint of nations'. *Proceedings of the National Academy of Sciences (Early Edition)*. Published ahead of print, 3 September 2013: doi:10.1073/pnas.1220362110

White, T. 2007. 'Sharing resources: The global distribution of the ecological footprint'. *Ecological Economics* 64(2): 402-410.

Woodward, D. and Simms, A., 2006. 'Growth isn't working: The uneven distribution of benefits and costs from economic growth'. *New Economics Foundation*. Available at: http://www.neweconomics.org/publications/entry/growth-isnt-working (accessed 10 September 2013).

2

POST-GROWTH ECONOMICS
A paradigm shift in progress

If the earth must lose that great portion of its pleasantness which it owes to things that the unlimited increase of wealth and population would extirpate from it, for the mere purpose of enabling it to support a larger, but not a better or happier population, I sincerely hope, for the sake of posterity, that they will be content to be stationary, long before necessity compels them to it.
— John Stuart Mill

1. Introduction

'Going for growth is the government's number one priority', declared Gordon Brown in 2010, then Prime Minister of the United Kingdom, neatly capturing the spirit of our times (Settle, 2010). It is a worldview that shapes the global economy more so today than ever before (Purdey, 2010), at least as a reflection of economic *desire*, if not as a description of recent or anticipated economic *reality*. As the global economy slowly emerges, at least superficially, from the global financial crisis — a crisis in which many economies around the world suffered recession — the imperative of all governments around the world to maximise growth in Gross Domestic Product (GDP) has never seemed stronger. The underlying economic assumption is that growth in GDP is the most direct path to national prosperity, and this vision of progress is widely embraced across the political spectrum, where growth is used as the touchstone of policy and institutional success (Hamilton, 2003).

Despite the dominance of this growth model of progress around the world, it has never been without its critics, and as this chapter will outline, there are reasons to think that grounds for opposition are growing in number, strength, and sophistication. It was the philosopher of science Thomas Kuhn (1962) who argued that paradigm shifts in the natural sciences occur when the existing paradigm finds itself increasingly unable to solve the critical problems it sets for itself. As anomalies increase in number and severity, the need for an alternative paradigm becomes clearer, and eventually a new paradigm is developed that can solve more problems than the old one. At that stage a paradigm shift is set in motion, and over time the new paradigm becomes accepted and the old one loses its influence, sometimes quite abruptly. In much the same way, this chapter proposes that a paradigm shift in macroeconomics is underway, with a post-growth economic framework threatening to resolve critical anomalies that seem irresolvable from within the existing growth paradigm. We will see that a growing array of theorists, from various disciplinary backgrounds, are questioning the feasibility and even the desirability of continuous growth, especially with respect to the most highly developed regions of the world. Increasingly there is a call to look 'beyond growth' (see, e.g., Costanza *et al.*, 2014; Kubiszewski *et al.*, 2013; Stiglitz, Sen, and Fitoussi, 2010), on the grounds that growth may now be causing the problems it was traditionally hoped to solve. Not only can it be argued that a post-growth paradigm shift is *in progress*, it seems the fundamental importance of this shift lies in the fact that it is *in relation to progress*. That is, it is changing the very nature of what 'progress' means.

In this chapter the key thinkers and movements in this emerging paradigm of 'post-growth' economics will be reviewed. By way of introduction, a brief overview of the growth paradigm is presented, in order to later highlight, by way of contrast, some of the most prominent features of the alternative paradigm. A substantial literature review of post-growth economics is then provided, after which some of the outstanding issues in this emerging movement are outlined. This chapter intends to raise questions about what prosects this movement has for dislodging the growth paradigm from the dominant position it currently holds in popular consciousness; what significance it may have if it were ever to succeed; and what the implications could be if it were to remain marginalised. The chapter concludes by outlining a research agenda of critical issues.

2. The Growth Model of Progress

Economic growth is conventionally defined as a rise in GDP, and that is how the term will be used in this chapter, unless stated otherwise. The result of elaborate national accounting systems, GDP can be broadly understood as 'the market value of all final goods and services [i.e., commodities] produced within a country during a given period of time' (Mankiw, 2008: 510). It can be calculated in three different, but formally equivalent ways, as Tim Jackson (2002: 99) explains:

> [GDP] may be seen, first, as the total of all *incomes* (wages and profits) earned from the production of domestically owned goods and services. Next, it may be regarded as the total of all *expenditures* made in consuming the finished goods and services. Finally, it can be viewed as the sum of the *value added* by all the activities which produce economic goods and services.

GDP accounting first emerged in the early 1930s with the onset of the Great Depression, which highlighted the need for more detailed economic data. Responding to this deficiency, the US' Department of Commerce commissioned Simon Kuznets (who would later receive the Nobel Prize in Economics) to develop a set of national accounts. These were the prototype for what later became the GDP accounts. GDP accounting developed significantly during World War II to assist with planning, but it was really in the post-war era that GDP came to prominence, not just in the US but also increasingly around the world (Collins, 2000). Almost immediately international comparisons of GDP per capita were made as a way of assessing the relative 'progress' of nations (Purdey, 2010).

According to this dominant macroeconomic paradigm, growth in GDP provides governments, by way of taxation, with more resources to pay for the nation's most important social services. It provides the necessary funds needed for national security and a police force, democratic elections, sophisticated heath care, sanitation systems and other infrastructure, public education, unemployment benefits, and so on, as well as funding for such things as environmental protection programmes, foreign aid, and the arts. These are all good things, one might accept, but they cost money, and funds are always limited. Therefore, by maximising growth of the economy a government can secure more funding for those services, thereby contributing directly, so the paradigm implies, to social, economic, and ecological wellbeing. There is a certain coherency to this way of looking at the world, no doubt, and in many ways it even seems commonsensical.

Furthermore, this paradigm also implies that as an economy grows, so too do personal incomes, meaning that individuals, not just governments, have more money and thus more freedom to purchase those things which they desire or need most. From this perspective growth seems unquestionably good – both individually and nationally – from which it would seem to follow that a bigger economy is always better. By essentially conflating economic and social wellbeing, growth in GDP per capita becomes a measure not just of economic success but of a nation's social progress more generally, a view that is being referred to herein as the 'growth model of progress'.

Conventional growth economists accept that there is an optimal scale at the *micro*economic level (Mankiw, 2008) – which is to say, they accept there will eventually come a point where growth in an individual firm's production will cost more than it is worth, and therefore be judged 'uneconomic' growth; at some stage, that is, hiring more employees or buying more industrial plant will not maximise profits. However, there is no place in the growth paradigm for an optimal scale at the *macro*economic level, no optimal scale of the economy as a whole. In particular, growth economists argue that there are no biophysical limits to growth. This is because technological and allocative efficiency improvements are thought to allow for an infinitely expanding economy, despite the fact that the raw materials needed for production are finite. Technological efficiency, it is assumed, will continually allow human beings to consume a finite set of resources more efficiently or, better yet, to consume a set of resources hitherto inaccessible (e.g., Lovins, 1998; Lomborg, 2001). Alternatively, human ingenuity in conjunction with pricing mechanisms will lead to scarce resources being substituted for less scarce resources when the benefits of doing so outweigh the costs (Simon and Kahn, 1984). Allocative efficiency, it is assumed, will ensure that market mechanisms continually move resources into the hands of those who will 'exploit' them best (Posner, 1986). All this is expected to 'decouple' growth from environmental impact, a process through which it is believed GDP can grow while each unit of GDP becomes less resource and energy intensive. When one looks at the world through this neoclassical lens, what matters most is that commodities are available for exchange in the market, for then the 'invisible hand' is said to maximise social wellbeing while protecting the environment better than any other system of structuring society. Prices will ensure that natural resources are consumed to an 'optimal' degree. Since each market transaction under non-coercive conditions is assumed to increase the wealth of both seller and buyer – otherwise why would the parties transact? – the growth paradigm implies that 'free markets' are in everyone's interests and that market activity should be maximised (Friedman, 2002).[3]

---

[3] For a critical examination of free market theory, see Samuel Alexander,

Upon these neoclassical assumptions, advocates of growth purport to show that an economy as a whole can and should continue growing indefinitely. The great social problem according to this influential narrative is that even the richest nations do not have 'enough' and therefore must pursue 'more'. Economic growth is thus heralded across the globe, and across the political spectrum, as the goal toward which all nations should direct their collective energy. Not only are growth and environmental health seen as compatible goals, growth in the rich world is seen as the best means of lifting the poorest individuals and nations out of poverty. Within the growth model, that is, the solution to poverty involves growing a bigger economic pie ('a rising tide lifts all boats'), not slicing the economic pie differently (redistribution).

This growth model strikes many people as basically correct, and, as noted, one can accept that parts of it, at least, have some intuitive plausibility. Nevertheless, according to the latest reports from the Global Footprint Network (2013), the global economy now exceeds the sustainable carrying capacity of the planet by 50%, causing a perfect storm of chronic ecological problems including climate change, biodiversity loss, resource depletion, topsoil erosion, deforestation, water shortages, and pollution (Rockstrom *et al.*, 2009; Brown, 2011; Ehrlich and Ehrlich, 2013). To make the environmental burden heavier still, the human population is set to reach nine or ten billion in coming decades. But despite this fact of gross ecological overshoot, essentially all nations on the planet seek to grow their economies further, and without apparent limit. This is the growth paradigm, and it is in the process of colliding with biophysical reality (Turner, 2012).

Consider the basic arithmetic of growth: if the GDP of developed nations were to grow by 3% per year in coming decades – which seems to be the benchmark for success – and by 2080 a global population of 10 billion has achieved a similarly high material standard of living – which seems to be the goal of the global development agenda – then the global economy could be 40-60 times larger than it is today. Pause for a moment to dwell on those figures. Even allowing for significant uncertainty in these types of forecasts, and even assuming many efficiency improvements are implemented to reduce the resource intensity of each dollar of GDP, it is simply not credible to think that the planet's ecosystems could tolerate the global economy multiplying in size even two or three or

---

'Property Beyond Growth: Toward a Politics of Voluntary Simplicity' (doctoral thesis, Melbourne Law School), Ch. 2. Available here: http://papers. ssrn.com/sol3/papers.cfm?abstract_id=1941069 [accessed 10 November 2013].

four times, let alone 40 or 60 times. And yet this is essentially the global development agenda (UN, 2012).

The point about efficiency deserves some brief elaboration, because it is both the theoretical keystone of growth economics and the point at which that model of progress loses its plausibility. Advocates of green growth or sustainable development insist that nations across the globe can and should pursue continuous growth, but that growth should be progressively decoupled from environmental impact through more efficient production and consumption. This approach is coherent in theory, at best, but demonstrably it does not reflect empirical reality (see Alexander, 2014; Jackson, 2009). Although most economies across the globe have experienced considerable efficiency gains in recent decades, the overall biophysical impact of the global economy continues to increase. This is because those efficiency gains, rather than reducing the absolute impact of economic activity, have been redirected into increased production and consumption – that is, more growth. Within growth-based economies, therefore, efficiency gains are generally functioning to exacerbate rather than solve the ecological crises we face, a point touched on again later in the analysis. This is but one of the critical problems with the 'more is always better' growth model – problems which a growing chorus of theorists argue cannot be dismissed as minor anomalies in an otherwise functional paradigm.

3. A Literature Review of Post-Growth Economics

The following literature review will have a predominately macroeconomic focus, with the macroeconomic tradition beginning, as we will see, with economists such as Thomas Malthus and John Stuart Mill. It is worth noting, however, that many of the post-growth perspectives that eventually found macroeconomic expression can be understood to have had their roots in much earlier thinkers and cultures, whose focus was more on personal and social perspectives than macroeconomics. One of the defining features of post-growth macroeconomics is a questioning of materialistic values – a questioning of the very pursuit of material wealth as a path to wellbeing – and clearly that critical positioning finds its roots in ancient times (Vanenbroeck, 1991). While this body of ideas is vast and deep, representative examples come from thinkers as diverse as the Buddha, Lao-Tzu, Confucius, Diogenes, Socrates, Aristotle, Epictetus, Jesus, Marcus Aurelius, Seneca, and St Francis, while in more modern times one could cite thinkers such as William Morris, John Ruskin, Henry Thoreau, Mahatma Gandhi, and Helen Nearing, as well as cultures such as the Amish or the Quakers (Alexander and McCleod, 2014). All these thinkers and cultures, and a great many more, have expressly denied that 'the good life' depends on an abundance of material things, and instead emphasised the importance of virtues such as moderation, frugality, simplicity, and sufficiency. Accordingly, this diverse wisdom tradition, with deep historical roots, can be understood to provide some of the philosophical and ethical underpinnings of post-growth macroeconomics. Although these perspectives focused mainly on the *individual* benefits of living a life based on material sufficiency, perhaps the closest thing to an expression of a post-growth *macroeconomics* in ancient times can be found in Plato's *Republic*, where a distinction is made between a 'healthy city' based on moderation and a 'fevered city' driven relentlessly on by insatiable desires for luxury and extravagance (Plato, 2004). If one seeks a more developed expression of post-growth economics, however, one must look to the late 18th century and beyond, beginning with Thomas Malthus.

Malthus is most famous for his *Essay on the Principle of Population*, first published in 1798, wherein he made his case for what became known as the 'Malthusian catastrophe'. In essence, Malthus claimed that population growth would outpace the ability of agricultural production to feed people, a dynamic that he proposed would end in a 'gigantic inevitable famine' (Malthus, 2007 [1798]: 54). Although he never used the phrase, Malthus was arguing that there were 'limits to growth'. The critical flaw in his theory, however, was that he failed to take into account the impacts of technology, for what happened was that technological development led to huge productivity gains in agricultural output, making it possible to feed growing populations, thereby averting, or at least delaying, his predicted catastrophe. Today the term 'Malthusian' or 'neo-Malthusian' is generally used as a slanderous epithet to describe those who predict catastrophe based on false premises. Nevertheless, as the global population moves toward eight billion people, the challenges raised by population growth may yet justify Malthus' grim perspective. Paul Ehrlich (1970) has perhaps done more than any other to keep the question of population at the forefront of environmental and social concerns, showing clearly that, all other things being equal, population growth tends to increase environmental impact, especially as the high-impact consumer class expands (Ehrlich and Holdren, 1971; Alcott, 2010). Malthus deserves his place in the history of post-growth economics on the basis that he was first to raise the possibility that unlimited population growth, coupled with the economic growth that such a growing population would depend on, could eventually lead to human suffering and environmental degradation on a tragic scale. Despite the theoretical errors in Malthus' original work, a case can be made that a 'Malthusian catastrophe' of some form remains a worryingly real prospect, with the UN predicting that global population will reach 9.6 billion by 2050, perhaps as high as 10.9 billion (UNDSEA, 2012). Whereas conventional economics sees population growth as a good thing – providing a larger pool of labourers and consumers to stimulate economic activity – there is a very real question over whether planetary ecosystems can sustain such a large population, and what the consequences may be if they cannot.

While Malthus prophesised about population growth inevitably leading to mass starvation, other classical economists, such as David Ricardo, developed similarly gloomy theories – such as the so-called 'Iron Law of Wages' – which held that economic laws would result in wages inevitably moving toward bare subsistence levels (see generally, Hollander, 1992). Owing to such theories, the details of which we need not presently unpack, economics became known as the 'dismal science'. But while other classical economists were theorising pessimistically about how economic laws would constrain the ability of economies to grow and meet human needs, in 1848 John Stuart Mill first published his *Principles of Political Economy*, in which there is a short, neglected chapter arguing that perhaps a non-growing economy may not be such a bad thing. It is this chapter, entitled 'Of the Stationary State', where we find the first explicit defence of a post-growth economy, and on that basis it is Mill, rather than Malthus or Ricardo, who deserves acknowledgement as the true founder of post-growth economics.

Mill posed the question: 'Toward what ultimate end is society tending by its industrial progress?' (Mill, 2004 [1848]: 188). Unremarkable on the surface, perhaps, this question subtly challenges the growth model of progress in three important ways: first, because it acknowledges, implicitly, that industrial progress (or what we today would call economic growth) is only of instrumental value and not of any intrinsic value; second, because it raises the possibility that there might come a time when economic growth no longer serves any worthwhile purposes; and third, and perhaps most importantly, because it prompts us to consider not only how much economic growth is *enough*, but also what we want growth *for*. Mill proposed that if there came a time when economic growth stopped contributing to wellbeing (or began undermining those things upon which wellbeing depends), the most suitable economic system would be what he called 'the stationary state'. By this he meant a society with a stable population and zero growth in physical capital stock, but which continued improvements in technology and what he called the 'Art of Living'. Mill argued that technology in a stationary state would serve not to increase material wealth, but to abridge labour, an approach that is receiving increased attention in the 21st century as a means of promoting quality of life while reducing ecological impact (see, e.g., Coote and Franklin, 2013). As for the Art of Living, Mill was of the view that cultural, moral, and social progress would be much more likely 'when minds ceased to be engrossed by the art of getting on,' later adding that 'it is scarcely necessary to remark that a stationary condition of capital and population implies no stationary state of human improvement' (Mill, 2004 [1848]: 191). Despite its coherency and attractiveness as a vision of a future society, Mill's conception of a stationary state proved to be too far ahead of its time and was essentially ignored by his contemporaries. For generations to come, the growth scepticism it entailed lay dormant and forgotten.

It was not until the 1950s and 60s that growth scepticism re-emerged. More than a century of relatively sustained economic growth had occurred since Mill's work – driven by the fossil-fuelled, industrial revolution – meaning that by this stage most Westerners maintained a material standard of living that Mill may never have dared think possible. Books were being published with titles such as *The Affluent Society* (Galbraith, 1958) and *The Challenge of Abundance* (Theobald, 1961), suggesting that a stationary state with sufficient material resources for all was not the utopian pipedream it may once have seemed to be. Western economies had indeed grown significantly, providing the vast majority of their citizens with unprecedented material comforts, but not everyone took this as an unmitigated social advancement, and some were beginning to doubt both the desirability and feasibility of continued economic growth. Kenneth Boulding (1997 [1966]) was one of the first to argue at any length that economic growth, being dependant on natural resources, could not continue indefinitely on a finite planet. He famously quipped that anyone who thought it could 'was either a madman or an economist' (as quoted in Collins, 2000: 141). In the cultural domain, Herbert Marcuse (2000 [1964]) presented a scathing indictment of how Western nations fixated on growth and consumption were creating 'one-dimension societies'. He argued that the emergence of consumer-orientated cultures was homogenising human experience and providing people with little more than a 'comfortable unfreedom' (Marcuse, 2002 [1964]: 3; see also, Adorno, 2002).

Growth scepticism received its first comprehensive statement, however, in 1967, with the publication of Ezra Mishan's *The Costs of Economic Growth*. In this path-breaking text, directed at affluent Western nations, Mishan expressed deep reservations about whether limitless economic expansion – a policy that he called 'growthmania' (Mishan, 1967: 3) – was in the interests of human welfare. After acknowledging that growth had historically brought significant benefits to the West, lifting many people out of poverty, Mishan set about highlighting the unpleasant *costs* of economic growth that he felt were too often overlooked when governments shaped their pro-growth policies. Casting doubt on the dominant economic paradigm, he provocatively suggested that perhaps the costs of growth – which he argued included psychological ill-health, long working hours, loss of community, ugly cityscapes, traffic congestion, pollution, environmental degradation, etc. – were beginning to outweigh the benefits. Just for a moment, he proposed, we should put our minds to the question of whether it is all really worth it, whether there might not be a better path to follow. In the context of this literature review, what is particularly significant about Mishan's argument is the fact that it exposed how the single-minded pursuit of growth placed severe limits on government action, presumptively excluding any policy or institutional reform that would retard growth in any way. Mishan recognised that if growth were ever to lose its privileged position as the touchstone of policy and institutional success, new avenues would open up for progressive political, legal, and economic reform. In the following decades, however, the desire for growth not only persisted but intensified and the politics of growth became more deeply entrenched (Purdey, 2010; Collins, 2000).

A few years after the publication of Mishan's manifesto, several other texts emerged which made significant contributions to the tradition of growth scepticism. In 1972 a group of systems analysts, known as the Club of Rome, caused much controversy with their publication *Limits to Growth* (Meadows *et al.*, 1972), which has come to be the most widely read environmental text of all time. In this book the authors explored, with the help of computer modelling techniques, the potential consequences of exponential growth in human population and resource consumption in a world of finite resources. Their alarming but arguably commonsensical diagnosis was that if growth trends in world population, industrialisation, and resource depletion were to continue or accelerate, the planet would eventually come up against 'limits to growth', with potentially catastrophic consequences. Widely but erroneously dismissed at the time for ignoring pricing mechanisms, understating the potential for efficiency gains, and denying adaptation (Bardi, 2011), the last few decades of environmental research have provided further scientific support for the view that the never-ending pursuit of growth is incompatible with biophysical reality (Meadows *et al.*, 2004). The work of Graham Turner (2012), in particular, provides rigorous support for the 'limits to growth' analysis.

In 1973 a supporting analysis was offered by the Buddhist economist Ernst Schumacher in his provocative text *Small is Beautiful: A Study of Economics as if People Mattered*. Schumacher faulted conventional economic theory for failing to address the issue of macroeconomic 'scale', that is, for never asking the question of how much growth is 'enough' and instead just assuming that a bigger economy is always better. Challenging the orthodox view that economic policy should always seek to maximise opportunities for consumption through continuous growth, Schumacher proposed that the aim, both of individuals and societies, should be to obtain the maximum amount of wellbeing with the minimum amount of consumption. Sensible though this proposal may sound, the world was not ready for it, and Wilfred Beckerman, representing economic orthodoxy, eventually responded to Schumacher's arguments asserting that 'small is stupid' (Beckerman, 1995).

Over the next few years there were several developments of sociological significance that provided further support for growth scepticism. Theorists such as Richard Easterlin (1974), Fred Hirsch (1976), and Tibor Scitovsky (1992 [1976]), variously provided arguments and evidence to the effect that 'more growth' did not always mean 'more happiness' or 'more wellbeing'. Once the basic material needs of a society are met, some of these theorists argued, further growth in per capita income contributes little or nothing to overall wellbeing. Scitovsky explained this finding on the grounds that, beyond basic material needs, human beings simply do not find the consumption and accumulation of material things all that fulfilling, contrary to the culturally entrenched promises of advertisements (see also, Kasser, 2002). A related explanation offered by Easterlin and Hirsch was essentially that once basic material needs are met, people tend to become more concerned about relative wealth than absolute wealth and, consequently, start engaging in wasteful status competition that is necessarily a zero-sum game (see also, Veblen, 2009 [1899]). It is a zero-sum game because if one person's status is increased, someone else's status must have relatively decreased, typically leaving overall satisfaction unchanged (Easterlin, 1995). As Hirsch (1976) argued, this indicates that there are 'social limits' to growth. These sociological insights, among others, challenge the assumption that more consumption is always better, raising further doubts, at least in relation to affluent societies, about the validity of the growth model as a path of social progress (see Alexander, 2012a). In more recent years this work has evolved, with Tim Jackson's *Prosperity without Growth* (2009) deserving of special note, if only for the attention it brought to post-growth economic perspectives, rather than for any original contribution it made to the literature.

From the 1970s onward, ecological economist Herman Daly built upon and developed this diverse tradition in important ways, paying close attention to the emerging environmental predicament and its impact on questions of macroeconomic scale (Daly and Farley, 2004). Two aspects of Daly's work are of particular significance. The first is his notion of a 'steady state' economy (Daly, 1973), which can be understood as a modern expression of Mill's notion of a 'stationary state' economy. Daly criticises growth-orientated neoclassical economics for treating the natural environment as a subset of a boundless, price-dependent economy, proposing instead that the economy ought to be considered a subset of the finite environment, the biophysical limits of which an economy cannot justifiably exceed. Merging environmentalist and economic perspectives, Daly (1996) argues that sustainable development in the developed world necessarily entails a radical shift away from 'growth economies' toward a steady state economy. By this he means an economy that continues to develop in response to new technologies and changing market and cultural forces, but without growing beyond the sustainable biophysical limits of the planet. In framing his steady-state perspective in biophysical terms rather than in terms of GDP, Daly also acknowledges his intellectual debts to Frederick Soddy (see Daly, 1980) and Nicholas Georgescu-Roegen (1971), whose writings highlighted the close connection between energy and economics (an issue discussed further below). The ecological footprint analysis developed by Mathis Wackernagel and William Rees (1996) is also of immense value in this context, as it is a tool for measuring how large an economy is in relation to the carrying capacity of its environment (see Global Footprint Network, 2013), and therefore provides some guidance on questions of 'scale', which are so fundamental to post-growth or steady-state perspectives.

The second aspect of Daly's scholarship deserving of acknowledgement is the work he pioneered with John Cobb developing 'alternative indicators' to GDP (Daly and Cobb, 1989). Daly and Cobb were early critics of GDP and painstakingly exposed its many defects as a proxy for social wellbeing. GDP, they argued, is merely a measure of total economic activity that makes no distinction between activity that contributes to wellbeing and activity that does not. For example, GDP treats market expenditure on guns, anti-depressants, and cleaning up oil spills, no differently to expenditure on education, solar panels, and bicycles. They also pointed out that GDP says nothing at all about the level or nature of *non-market* activity in a society, such as community engagement or the functioning of ecosystems; nor does GDP say anything about the distribution of wealth in a society (see also, Stiglitz, Sen, and Fitoussi, 2010). That last point on inequality is especially important in light of recent evidence showing that economies that have broader distributions of wealth do better on a whole host of social indicators (Wilkinson and Pickett, 2010). Wanting to provide a much more nuanced assessment of overall progress and wellbeing, Daly and Cobb developed the Index of Sustainable Economic Welfare (ISEW). This index and others like it – such as the Genuine Progress Indicator (GPI), the Happy Planet Index (HPI), and the Bhutanese notion of Gross National Happiness (GNH) – take into consideration important social and ecological factors that GDP simply does not reflect (e.g., Lawn, 2006; Lawn and Clarke, 2008; Costanza *et al.*, 2009). For example, the ISEW and GPI begin with total private consumption expenditure and then make deductions for such things as resource depletion, pollution, income inequalities, loss of leisure, 'defensive expenditures', etc., and make additions for such things as public infrastructure, volunteering, and domestic work. The aim is to measure, as accurately as possible, the overall wellbeing of a nation, including its sustainability, not just its total market activity. The results from such indexes tend to show that despite steady growth in GDP over recent decades, the genuine progress of many developed nations has been stagnant or even in decline (Kubiszewski *et al.*, 2013). Put otherwise, the results indicate that growth has stopped contributing to wellbeing in the developed world and now may even be causing the very problems that growth is supposed to be solving, suggesting that many developed nations have entered a phase of 'uneconomic growth' (Daly, 1999). Redistribution of wealth and the protection of natural ecosystems are two areas of particular importance where these results have potentially revolutionary implications for how nations structure their economies.

Some of the most radical expressions of growth scepticism that have emerged over the last decade have emerged from the 'degrowth' movement (Baykan, 2007; Fournier, 2008; Latouche, 2009; Kallis; 2011; Alexander, 2012b). In broad terms, degrowth can be defined as 'an equitable down-scaling of production and consumption that increases human well-being and enhances ecological conditions' (Schneider *et al.*, 2010: 512.) Although it is not a unified doctrine by any means, an emerging consensus within the degrowth movement has resulted in the 'Paris Declaration' of 2008, which concisely outlines the basic vision. This document (to paraphrase) calls for a paradigm shift from the general and unlimited pursuit of economic growth to a concept of 'right-sizing' both global and national economies. At the global level, right-sizing means reducing the global ecological footprint (including carbon footprint) to a sustainable level. In countries where per capita footprint is greater than the sustainable global level, this right-sizing implies a reduction to this level through the process of voluntary economic contraction (i.e., degrowth). In countries where widespread poverty still remains, right-sizing implies increasing consumption to a level adequate for a decent life. This will need to involve increasing economic activity in some cases, but the Declaration holds that redistribution of income and wealth both within and between countries is a more essential part of the process. Once right-sizing has been achieved, the Declaration concludes, the aim should be to maintain a 'steady-state' economy with a relatively stable level of resource and energy consumption. The primary contribution made by degrowth scholarship is the explicit acknowledgement that sustainability implies not merely giving up further growth, but actually initiating a *phase of planned contraction* of the 'scale' of developed economies. That is a position entirely absent from mainstream environmental and political discourse, where the ideology of growth still reigns supreme.

In response to 'free-market environmentalists' or 'technological optimists' who claim that there is no conflict between growth and sustainability, and who claim that something called 'green growth' is the way forward, degrowth scholars point out that although techno-efficiency improvements have been widely applied, flows of material and energy are still increasing (see Weidmann *et al.*, 2013; Alexander, 2014). This increase in material and energy use despite efficiency and technology improvements is largely due to 'rebound effects', coupled with the inherent 'grow or die' structure of growth economies. Though not widely appreciated, 'rebound effects' are highly significant, for they mean that techno-efficiency improvements, rather than reducing material and energy use, often function merely to create revenue which is then spent on producing or consuming more of the same commodity (a primary rebound) or other commodities (a secondary rebound). If this is so, as the weight of evidence suggests it is (Polimeni *et al.*, 2009; Herring and Sorrell, 2009), technology and efficiency are fatally flawed solutions to the ecological problems of growth and over-consumption. This is not an argument against the use of appropriate technologies, however, but an argument that technology provides no escape from the biophysical limits to growth (Huesemann and Huesemann, 2011). In order to reduce environmental impact, growth sceptics argue that technology must be governed by an ethics of sufficiency, not an imperative to grow.

There is one final post-growth perspective deserving of acknowledgement, even if the intricacies cannot be explored. It builds upon the recognition by some ecological economists that there is a close connection between energy use and economic activity (Hall and Klitgaard, 2012). From this view – sometimes called 'biophysical economics' – the unprecedented levels of economic growth experienced since the industrial revolution have been largely due to the available abundance of cheap energy in the forms of coal, gas, and especially oil. Fossil fuels are finite resources, however, and energy analysts since Marion King Hubbert (1956) have known that at some time the production of finite fossil fuels will 'peak' and, after a plateau, eventually enter decline. The concern here is that, while production may plateau, demand is still expected to increase (Hirsch *et al.*, 2010), thereby putting an upward pressure on the price of fossil fuels, even as the 'energy return on investment' declines (Murphy and Hall, 2011). This phenomenon seems to be underway already in relation to oil, with crude oil production entering a plateau around 2005, causing the price of oil to increase from around $25 per barrel, historically, to an average price of $110 since 2011 (IEA, 2013a: 2). In a world that consumes 90 million barrels of oil every day, such sharp price rises have significant economic implications, by sucking discretionary expenditure and investment away from the rest of the economy. Indeed, some analysts argue that expensive oil is at least part of the reason the global economy, which is so dependent on oil for transport, pesticides, plastics, etc., is showing persistent signs of stagnation and instability (Heinberg, 2011). Furthermore, if oil constraints and other limits to growth are indeed bringing an end to more than two centuries of economic growth, then this is likely to cause havoc with the heavily indebted societies around the world that currently, under a capitalist framework, depend on growth to pay back debts and keep unemployment at bay. At the pessimistic end of the spectrum, some analysts argue that the global financial crisis was merely the first of a series of forthcoming crises that are going to increase in magnitude as the growth model fails to deal with, or even acknowledge, energy, resource, and debt limits (Tverberg, 2012). From such perspectives, the world may have an alternative to the growth model imposed upon it sooner rather than later, irrespective of whether the world wants or is ready for such an alternative (see, e.g., Clarke and Lawn, 2010).

The relationship between energy and economics also becomes problematic in the context of climate change mitigation. Currently, fossil fuels make up over 80% of the global energy supply (IEA, 2013b: 6). If nations around the world choose to decarbonise economies in response to climate change (see Wiseman *et al.*, 2013), this may well imply an end to growth, or even significant economic contraction, because there are serious doubts about whether renewable energy will be able to fully replace the energy-dense fossil fuels in a timely or affordable way (see, e.g., Trainer, 2013a, 2013b). This is not an argument against renewable energy, of course; the suggestion is merely that growth-orientated consumer societies could not be sustained if the world rapidly decarbonised to run solely or primarily on renewable sources of energy (Hopkins and Miller, 2013). A transition to 100% renewable energy, therefore, may well imply consuming significantly less energy, and in the highly developed regions of the world, energy descent would probably mean transitioning to some post-growth economic paradigm via a process of planned economic contraction, or degrowth. Kevin Anderson's work is particularly important here (see Anderson, 2013), for he is one of the only climate scientists who recognises (or is outspoken enough to say) that the world's shrinking carbon budget requires degrowth and reduced consumption in high consumption societies. That is not an implication many are prepared to accept, even amongst many or even most participants in the broad environmental movement. Indeed, this blindness – it might even be wilful blindness – is arguably the environmental movement's greatest shortcoming.

4. Obstacles on the Path to a Post-Growth Economy

While passing necessarily over many matters of detail, this review has nevertheless outlined a wide variety of issues that, in the eyes of many observers, fundamentally undermine the coherency of the growth paradigm. If once humankind lived on an 'empty planet', where the benefits of growth clearly outweighed the costs, today it seems we live on a 'full planet', where continued growth in the developed regions of the world, at least, is ecologically unsupport-able, socially unjust, and arguably not even socially desirable from a 'happiness' perspective (Diener *et al.*, 2010). Earth is struggling to absorb the impacts of the existing global economy, and despite decades of extraordinary technological advance, the ecological situation is getting worse, not better. It is very hard, therefore, to escape the conclusion that sustainability *proper* means that overdeveloped nations must enter a phase of significant degrowth in material and energy consumption, so that there is some 'ecological room' for the poorest nations expand their economic capacities in order to provide basic needs for all. When that has been achieved, humanity must figure out a way to maintain a relatively steady state economy that operates within the sustainable carrying capacity of the planet. This alternative, post-growth vision of progress may sound idealistic – and in today's neoliberal political climate it certainly lies on the intellectual fringe – but in the long term one only ever hits what one aims for, and post-growth economics have a coherency that the vision of growth decidedly lacks.

If it is indeed the case that the growth paradigm has no future – primarily due to the impossibility of its persistence in the face of the biophysical limits to growth – then the critique of growth should always be accompanied by a discussion of what the best alternatives are and how to get there. In closing this analysis, a few outstanding issues are outlined which, it will be argued, deserve and require more attention if the paradigm shift toward a post-growth macroeconomics is to come to fruition.

4.1. *How best to frame the alternative?*

As more people come to recognise the 'limits to growth', calls for an alternative macroeconomic model will surely become louder and more numerous. While this may be the catalyst that speeds up the paradigm shift to a post-growth economy – a paradigm shift which seems to be already underway – one must also accept that the growth paradigm remains, for the time being, the meta-narrative that governs the global development agenda. This dominance is partly due, no doubt, to the vested interests many corporations and political parties have in maintaining a growth economy, as well as the influence advertising and news media have in promoting materialistic values and consumerist cultures. This raises the important question of how advocates of a post-growth alternative should attempt to frame the transition. Should we try to redeem the notion of 'sustainable development'? Should we embrace the language of Mill's 'stationary state' or Daly's 'steady state' economy? Is the vocabulary of 'degrowth' required to express the magnitude of the changes required? Or should we be talking of a politics or economics of 'happiness' or 'sufficiency'? And how to deal with the fact that all post-growth economists presumably still want 'growth' in culture, renewable energy, bike lanes, leisure, wellbeing, etc. 'Degrowth in *what*?', one might suggest, is just as important as the question 'Growth in *what*?' Further ways of framing the debate might include 'wellbeing economics', 'one planet economics' or 'safe climate economics'. These issues about how best to frame the alternative to conventional growth economics are not simply cosmetic. After all, it is not enough for growth objectors merely to be correct in their diagnoses and prescriptions; if they are to have any influence, they also have to be listened to and to be persuasive, and that requires thinking about how best to frame the new narrative.

The problem with trying to redeem the language of 'sustainable development' is that its ambiguities have been exploited for many decades now, such that it has come to mean anything at all, depending on the interests it is meant to serve, and thus it means nothing much of any substance. *Everyone* seems to be in favour of 'sustainable development', which means it lacks content as a concept, and is too easily shaped and reshaped. Business as usual, more or less, has been the result. The other problem is that sustainable development has always been deeply embedded in the growth paradigm – if sustainable development means anything, it means 'green growth' or 'sustained growth' (e.g., UN, 2012). But if growth itself is the issue that needs rethinking, then sustainable development may not be the banner under which to march. It may carry too much baggage. Herein lies the value of 'degrowth' discourse – it could hardly be more explicit about its rejection of the growth paradigm and for the requirement, in the developed world, at least, for a *contraction* of resource and energy consumption. While neoliberal capitalism proved quite capable of co-opting the language of 'sustainable development' in order to avoid changing, it is hard to imagine how neoliberalism could co-opt degrowth without degenerating into Orwellian double-speak: degrowth means growth! Nevertheless, despite the coherency of degrowth as a radical vision for sustainability, it has obvious 'public relations' issues to deal with. It is difficult to imagine a mainstream campaign emerging under the banner of 'degrowth', so while it has conceptual value in positioning itself clearly *against growth*, it may not be the best term to use if mainstreaming that position is the goal. Too many people are likely to interpret the term as somehow being against 'progress', even though degrowth scholars would insist it *means* progress, albeit of a reconceived nature. Even notions of a stationary state or steady state economy can seem to imply stagnation, although, again, advocates are clear that it is only *biophysical impact* that does not grow, leaving it open for such an economy to progress or grow in cultural, technological, and moral terms.

Accordingly, the notion of 'progress' may itself be the term that needs to be reconceived, as we see happening already with the alternative indicators to GDP, such as the Genuine Progress Indicator. These indicators may be the clearest means of communicating the idea that 'genuine progress' today may not mean growth in GDP, and may even imply degrowth. The idea of a politics or economics of 'happiness', while at risk of coming across too rosy, may also bear fruit by emphasising the personal and social *benefits* that can flow from rethinking the growth paradigm (see also, NEF, 2012). An 'economics of sufficiency' has great value in highlighting the lifestyle implications of the alternative paradigm (discussed further below). While all these terminological issues ought to be borne in mind, it may be that different ways of framing the alternative may be required in different contexts. As the title of this chapter suggests, however, the phrase 'post-growth economics' may be a suitable middle-ground, in so far as it is explicitly against growth – and thus has some oppositional content – while at the same time implying that it is 'after' or 'beyond' growth, suggesting progress rather than social decline.

4.2. *The problems of debt, interest, and fractional reserve banking*

Other issues that deserve more attention within the literature of post-growth economics are financial and banking issues related to debt, interest-bearing loans, and fractional reserve banking. Sometimes post-growth scholars give the impression that 'growth' is a feature of the existing economic order that can be taken away, while leaving the essential structure of that order more or less in place. However, as Ted Trainer (2011) and others have insisted, the existing market economies are not economies that *have* growth; they are *growth economies*, which have a 'grow or die' imperative built into their very structure (Smith, 2010). Profit-seeking (or profit-maximisation) is an element of market economies that cannot easily be done away with, giving rise to various financial issues which suggest that a post-growth economy could never arise without undertaking fundamental changes with respect to banking and finance systems. One does not refer here to things like stricter regulation of predatory lending or more state support for credit unions, although it may include those things. Instead, one refers to deeper, structural issues about what to do with the mountainous personal and national debts in existence, as well as the fact that interest-bearing loans and fractional reserve banking imply and rely on an ever-expanding money supply. Individuals and governments took on huge loans over recent decades, predicated on the assumption that the future of growth would be similar to the past. But if we are reaching or exceeding the 'limits to growth', then it will become much harder or impossible for those debts to be repaid. And yet, under the existing system, things quickly break down when debts are not repaid, as exemplified by the global financial crisis, so post-growth economists must formulate coherent strategies for dealing with the problem of debt. Similarly, interest-bearing loans imply an expansion of the money supply, since borrowers have to repay the sum borrowed plus the interest. But if a post-growth economy means bringing an end to the expansion of the money supply, then it is not clear whether interest-bearing loans or fractional reserve banking can be a part of such an alternative. These questions suggest that it will be impossible to remove 'growth' from existing economies without fundamentally rethinking the nature of banking and finance systems. While these are very complex matters – calling on expertise beyond what the present author can provide – this short section will have served a worthwhile purpose if it highlights a research agenda that should be given more attention by post-growth economists. After all, however problematic the growth paradigm might be, an alternative is unlikely to be embraced *en masse* until more of its details are outlined, especially with respect to banking and finance systems that are compatible with such a post-growth alternative. These questions also raise broader issues about whether a post-growth alternative is consistent with the basic institutions of capitalism (i.e., private property and markets) or whether some form of eco-socialism is required to facilitate the transition. This is a debate that is currently underway (see Sarkar, 1999; Smith, 2010; Trainer, 2011; Lawn, 2011).

4.3. *Radical lifestyle implications of a post-growth economy*

Another area of neglect within the literature on post-growth economics relates to the lifestyle implications of a transition beyond growth. If the aim of a post-growth economy is to live within the carrying capacity of the planet, and to share the finite resources of Earth in some equitable fashion amongst the world's population (White, 2007; Vale and Vale, 2013), then it seems clear that nothing resembling the high-impact, energy-intensive, Western-style consumer lifestyles could be maintained. In a recent article, Steb Fisher (2013) outlined a case for why developed nations (his focus was Australia) would need to reduce resource consumption to about 6% of current levels if seven billion people are to live sustainably on the planet. That is 16 times less than current consumption levels! The arithmetic and assumptions can (and no doubt will be) debated, but even so, the magnitude of downshifting required for 'one planet living' is drastic, to say the least. The point is that living sustainably on a full planet does not merely mean recycling, composting, and buying efficient light bulbs, necessary though such practices may be. Rather, it means *fundamental lifestyle change* to an extent few people dare to envision (see Trainer, 2010; Alexander, 2013a). Without attempting presently to describe such a change in any detail, one planet living might involve a revolutionary shift toward organic urban agriculture, *a la* Havana in Cuba, with all households maximising food production and water collection, retrofitting their houses for energy efficiency, and living more densely within those houses; it might involve giving up private cars and regular air flights in favour of walking, biking, or using electrified public transport; it might involve vigilantly recycling and creatively reusing most, or all, wastes produced, and mending clothes and tools rather than buying new. More generally, it would surely imply doing without many comforts and conveniences that many 'first world' consumers take for granted today, like a new mobile phone every few years, superfluous kitchen gadgets or household ornaments, or cosmetic home renovations. Likewise, rather than turning on the heater or air-conditioner, we may need to put on a woollen jumper when its cold or close the curtains on hot days to keep out the heat. The changes required would be endless in number and radical in nature, but little attention is given to these issues by post-growth economists, perhaps due to an unconscious techno-optimism which assumes that technology will be able to decouple consumer lifestyles from their ecological impact. The problem is that this gives the impression that something resembling consumer lifestyles could be maintained in a post-growth or degrowth economy, when in fact the degree of ecological overshoot and the limits of technology suggest otherwise. If sustainability means degrowth, then sustainability implies a move toward lifestyles of radical simplicity (Trainer, 2012).

It must also be emphasised, however, that the lifestyles of radical simplicity required by one planet living need not imply hardship. On the contrary, radical simplicity implies focusing on what is *sufficient* to live well, and then dedicating one's time and energy to non-material sources of meaning and wellbeing. While it is certainly the case that this implies a cultural revolution in 'first world' attitudes to material consumption – and a reimagining of the 'good life' – an empirical and philosophical case can be made that people can live 'more' with significantly 'less' (Alexander, 2009; Alexander, 2012a; Alexander and Ussher, 2012).[4]

4.4. *Theories of change – democratic, eco-socialist, anarchist*

A final issue worth highlighting relates to the nature of any transition to a post-growth economy. What would drive such a

---

[4] While this discussion is focused on developed nations, obviously there lies a whole other body of issues to consider about the relevance of 'degrowth' to the Global South, as well as issues related to distribution of wealth both within and between nations. See generally, Trainer, (2010) Ch 5; Wilkinson and Pickett (2010); and White (2007).

transition? And how would it come about? These are important questions, but again, they are somewhat neglected in the literature on post-growth economics. That literature is particularly strong on the *critique* of growth (Meadows *et al.*, 2004; Jackson, 2009; Turner, 2012), and a growing body of work is being dedicated to *describing* what a post-growth economy might look like at a political and macroeconomic level (with a gap, as noted, related to finance and banking issues). Considerably less attention has been dedicated to understanding how the transition to a post-growth economy might unfold (Alexander, 2013). This is problematic because it is not enough simply to *diagnose* the problems and *describe* the best alternative. It is equally necessary to consider questions about how to mobilise communities and destabilise existing power structures, for the purpose of bringing a post-growth economy into existence. There are several broad categories of transition worth outlining, in the hope of bringing more attention to the issues under consideration.[5]

The first theory of transition could be called 'radical reformism', which can be understood to signify a transition that holds on to the basic notions of a market economy and a centralised democratic state, and argues that the changes needed for a post-growth economy must be brought about through radical parlia-mentary reform. This approach to transition is currently dominant in green circles (e.g., Jackson, 2009) and it assumes that a functioning, representative democracy will produce a post-growth economy when the citizenry are willing to vote for it. This theory envisions a post-growth culture shift first growing in strength and influence, and over time filtering upwards to eventually find political and macroeconomic expression, primarily through the legislature.

A second approach could be called 'eco-socialist', which differs from radical reformism insofar as it denies that a post-growth economy could be based on markets and private property – that is, based on an essentially capitalist framework – and holds that what is needed instead is the establishment of a strong, centralised socialist government with a deep green vision (see Sarkar, 1999). The argument, in short, is that markets have a 'growth imperative' built into their very nature (Smith, 2010), meaning that the idea of a *willingly post-growth capitalism* is essentially a contradiction in terms. Given that the capitalist class is unlikely to abdicate its power willingly, eco-socialists, like most socialists, argue that parlia-

---

[5] For a more detailed examination of these issues, see Samuel Alexander and Jonathan Rutherford, 'The Deep Green Alternative: Debating Strategies of Transition'. *Simplicity Institute Report* 14a (2014): 1-24.

mentary reform will be inadequate to the task of creating a post-growth economy, on the grounds that the capitalist state is said to be primarily a tool for furthering the interests of the capitalist class. Accordingly, eco-socialists tend to believe some form of revolution will be required, through which state power is gained for the purpose of socialising the economy and establishing, by way of centralised planning, a post-growth regulatory framework.

A third theory of transition could be called 'eco-anarchist' (see Trainer, 2010; Holmgren, 2002; Fotopoulous, 1997). This school of thought tends to agree with the socialist or eco-socialist critique of capitalism, but argues that the strategy of trying to take state power for the purpose of realising a post-growth economy is flawed. As anarchists, they believe that human beings should be self-governing at the local level and that political hierarchies inherent to centralised governments are inconsistent with a fully free and dignified existence. However, in the context of post-growth economics, eco-anarchists have a supplementary critique of the state. Governments, they argue, have an inherent bias towards growth, on the basis that public policies cost money, incentivising governments to seek economic growth to pay for those policies via a larger tax base. For these reasons it is argued that governments of any stripe – whether capitalist or socialist – will tend to pursue growth, the implication of which, eco-anarchists argue, is that a post-growth economy could never emerge from the 'top down' but could only emerge 'from below', at the grassroots level.

While these cursory reviews may well have raised more questions than they have answered, the purpose was simply to highlight the question of 'strategy'. If a post-growth economy is what is needed, theorists and activists have to put their minds to the question of where to direct their oppositional energies, for there is hardly oppositional energy to waste. Should people campaign for the Greens and try to radicalise them? Should they try to agitate and organise for a socialist revolution? Or should they essentially ignore governments and just set about 'pre-figuring' the post-growth alternative at the grassroots level, within the shell of the existing growth economy? Finally, will the transition be smooth and rational, or proceed through a series of crises and responses? These questions have no clear answers, but the movement for a post-growth economy will be stronger for taking them seriously.

5. Conclusion and Research Agenda

This literature review suggests that the foundations for a post-growth economy are becoming ever more robust and, indeed, that the movement for an economics 'beyond growth' is developing some real momentum (see, Stiglitz, Sen, and Fitoussi, 2010; Milne, 2012; Royal Government of Bhutan, 2012; Costanza *et al.*, 2014). At the same time, it is difficult to be hopeful that a smooth transition will take place in the narrowing time frame available. Vested interests (e.g., the fossil fuel industry, concentrated private media, transnational corporations, etc.) are everywhere insidiously working to maintain the status quo and resist movements for change. Nevertheless, if a robust scientific and moral case can be made for a post-growth economy, then it is the job of academics, educators, and activists to keep pushing for change, no matter the chances of success. As Bertrand Russell (2009: 45) once wrote, 'Gloom is a useless emotion'.

If it turns out that it is already too late to avoid some form of 'Great Disruption' (Gilding, 2011) as the growth economy collides with the biophysical limits to growth, then in practical terms the attempt to 'pre-figure' post-growth alternatives here and now presents itself as a coherent strategy to adopt, even if only at the micro-scale at first. Doing so will help build resilience in anticipation of future shocks, and increase the likelihood that less destructive modes of civilisation could one day emerge from the existing order. Before all else, this creative process of civilisational renewal will require infusing as ethics of sufficiency into our economic thinking, our economic practices, and, most of all, the economic systems that structure our lives.

This analysis will close by summarising some research and advocacy agendas which it is proposed could help advance post-growth economics by addressing outstanding issues highlighted by this literature review:

- Take seriously the question of how best to 'frame' the alternative macroeconomic paradigm. There may not be only one 'correct' way to do this, but reflecting on these terminological issues in relation to specific contexts and audiences may increase the likelihood of reaching a broader audience, which is obviously a necessary part of the transition.
- Give increased attention to what systems of banking and finance would be required to make a post-growth economy function, and how a transition to such systems could play out.
- Confront the question of whether a post-growth economy is compatible with the basic property and market structures of capitalism or whether fundamentally

different structures are required, and if so, what they may be.

- Honestly acknowledge the radical implications of the 'carbon budget'. Kevin Anderson (2013) has drawn most attention to this issue, by showing that keeping beneath two degrees implies degrowth in the wealthiest parts of the world. But a huge amount of work remains to be done mainstreaming this message and unpacking its implications.
- Emphasise the radical lifestyle implications of moving away from a growth economy. High-impact consumer lifestyles are inconsistent with sustainability; degrowth implies lifestyles of voluntary simplicity.
- Move beyond merely criticising growth (diagnosis) and describing the alternative (prescription), and dedicate more attention to questions of how best to *facilitate the transition* to the proposed alternative. This is partly a debate about which strategies are likely to provide the most leverage, but it also calls for 'envisioning' exercises where various post-growth futures are creatively sketched out to help more people break free from the imaginative constraints of the current growth trajectory.
- Address the whole host of further issues about how to overcome the various social, psychological, cultural, economic, legal, and political obstacles and barriers that currently obstruct the path to a post-growth economy and entrench the status quo.
- Recognise that transitioning to a post-growth economy in the developed regions of the world is going to have implications for the developing regions of the world. Give deeper consideration to issues of social justice and equity in this transition, paying particular attention to ways that a systemic redistribution of wealth could help facilitate the transition to a post-growth economy and minimise suffering as the new paradigm lays down its roots.
- Confront the thorny subject of population growth. While this issue must not be used as a scapegoat to deflect attention away from 'first world' over-consumption and the structures that promote this – the primary problems – it is clear that population growth tends to be a multiplier of everything, including ecological burden, and so global population must be equitably limited and eventually reduced.
- Clarify and collect arguments for 'grounded hope' in these extremely challenging times. Both despair and naïve

optimism are unhelpful responses – tempting though they both, at times, may be.

References

Adorno, T. 2001. *The culture industry*. London: Routledge.

Alcott, B. 2012. 'Population matters in ecological economics'. *Ecological Economics* 80: 109-120.

Alexander, S. (ed.). 2009. *Voluntary simplicity: The poetic alternative to consumer culture*. Whanganui: Stead & Daughters.

Alexander, S. 2011. 'Property beyond growth: Toward a politics of voluntary simplicity'. Doctoral thesis, Melbourne Law School. Available at: http://papers.ssrn.com/sol3/papers.cfm?abstract_id=1941069 (accessed 10 September 2013).

Alexander, S. 2012a. 'The optimal material threshold: Toward an economics of sufficiency'. *Real-World Economics Review* 61: 2-21.

Alexander, S. 2012b. 'Planned economic contraction: The emerging case for degrowth'. *Environmental Politics* 21 (3): 349-368.

Alexander, S. 2013a. *Entropia: Life beyond industrial civilisation*. Melbourne: Simplicity Institute Publishing.

Alexander, S. 2013b. 'Voluntary simplicity and the social reconstruction of law: Degrowth from the grassroots up'. *Environmental Values* 22(2): 287-308.

Alexander, S. 2014. 'A critique of techno-optimism: Efficiency without sufficiency is lost'. *MSSI Working Paper* (WP 1/14): 1-21.

Alexander, S. and McLeod, A. 2014. *Simple Living in History: Pioneers of the Deep Future*. Melbourne: Simplicity Institute Publishing.

Alexander, S. and Ussher, S. 2012. 'The voluntary simplicity movement: A multi-national survey analysis in theoretical context'. *Journal of Consumer Culture* 12(1): 66-86.

Anderson, K. 2013. *Avoiding dangerous climate change demands de-growth strategies from wealthier nations*. Available at: http://kevinanderson.info/blog/avoiding-dangerous-climate-change-demands-de-growth-strategies-from-wealthier-nations/ [accessed 25 November 2013].

Bardi, U. 2011. *The limits to growth revisited*. New York: Springer.

Baykan, B. 2007. 'From limits to growth to de-growth within French green politics'. *Environmental Politics* 513.

Beckerman, W. 1992. 'Economic growth and the environment:

Whose growth? Whose environment?'. *World Development* 20(4): 481-496.

Beckerman, W. 1995. *Small is stupid: Blowing the whistle on the greens*. London: Duckworth Publishing.

Beckerman, W. 2002. *A poverty of reason: Sustainable development and economic growth*. Oakland, CA: Independent Institute.

Boulding, K. 1997 [1966]. 'The economics of the coming spaceship Earth', in H. Jarrett (ed.). *Environmental quality in a growing economy*. Baltimore: John Hopkins Press.

Brown, L. 2011. *World on the edge: How to prevent environmental and economic collapse*. New York: W.W. Norton and Company.

Cobb, J. and Daly, H. 1989. *For the common good: Redirecting the economy toward community, the environment, and a sustainable future*. Boston: Beacon Press.

Collins, R. 2000. *More: The politics of economic growth in post-war America*. Oxford: Oxford University Press.

Coote, A. and Franklin, J. 2013. *Time on our side: Why we all need a shorter working week*. London: New Economics Foundation.

Costanza, R., Hart, M., Posner, S., and Talberth, J. 2009. 'Beyond GDP: The need for new measures of progress'. *The Pardee Papers*. No. 4, 2009: 1-37.

Costanza, R., Kubiszewski, I., Giovannini, E., Lovins, H., McGlade, J., Pickett, K., Ragnarsdóttir, K., Roberts, D., Vogli, and R., Wilkinson, R. 2014. 'Time to leave GDP behind'. *Nature*. 505: 283-285.

Daly, H. 1973. *Toward a steady-state economy*. San Francisco: W.H. Freeman.

Daly, H. 1980. 'The economic thought of Frederick Soddy'. *History of Political Economy*. 12(4): 469-488.

Daly, H. 1996. *Beyond growth: The economics of sustainable development*. Boston: Beacon Press.

Daly, H. 1999. 'Uneconomic growth in theory and fact', in *The First Annual Feasta Lecture* (16 April 1999). Available at: http://www.feasta.org/documents/feastareview/daly.htm [accessed 10 April 2010].

Daly, H. and Farley, J. 2004. *Ecological economics: Principles and applications*. Washington: Island Press.

Diener, E., Helliwell, J., and Kahneman, D. 2010. *International differences in well-being*. Oxford, New York: Oxford University Press.

Di Tella, R. and MacCulloch, R. 2010. 'Happiness adaptation to income beyond "Basic Needs"', in E. Diener, J. Helliwell, and D. Kahneman (eds). 2010. *International differences in well-Being*. Oxford, New York: Oxford University Press: 217-246.

Easterlin, R. 1974. 'Does economic growth improve the human lot?', in P. David and M. Reder (eds). *Nations and households in economic growth: Essays in honor of Moses Abramovitz.* New York: Academic Press.

Easterlin, R. 1995. 'Will raising the incomes of all increase the happiness of all?' *Journal of Economic Behavior & Organization* 27:35.

Ehrlich, P. 1970. *The population bomb.* New York: Ballantine.

Ehrlich, P. and Ehrlich, A. 1990. *The population explosion.* London: Frederick Muller.

Ehrlich, P. and Ehrlich A. 2013. 'Can a collapse of civilization be avoided?'. *Simplicity Institute Report* 13a: 1-19.

Ehrlich, P. and Holdren, J. 1971. 'Impact of population growth'. *Science* 171: 1212-1217.

Fisher, S. 'Our sustainability crisis didn't start and doesn't stop at climate change'. *The Conversation* (9 September 2013). Available at: http://theconversation.com/our-sustainability-crisis-didnt-start-and-doesnt-stop-at-climate-change-17471 [accessed 20 November 2013].

Fotopoulos, T. 1997. *Towards an inclusive democracy: The crisis of the growth economy and the need for a new liberatory project.* London & New York: Cassell.

Fournier, V. 2008. 'Escaping the economy: The politics of degrowth'. *International Journal of Sociology and International Research* 28: 528-545.

Friedman, M. 2002. *Capitalism and freedom.* Chicago: University of Chicago Press.

Galbraith, J. 1958. *The affluent society.* London: Hamish Hamilton.

Georgescu-Roegen, N. 1971. *The entropy law and the economic process.* Cambridge, Mass: Harvard University Press.

Gilding, P. 2011. *The great disruption: How the climate crisis will transform the global economy.* London: Bloomsbury.

Global Footprint Network, 2013, resources available at: http://www.footprintnetwork.org/en/index.php/GFN/page/annual_report/ (accessed 29 October 2013).

Gummer, J. and Goldsmith, Z. 2007. *Blueprint for a green economy: Submission to the shadow cabinet.* Available at: http://conservativehome.blogs.com/torydiary/files/blueprint_for_a_green_economy110907b.pdf (accessed 14 December 2013).

Hall, C. and Klitgaard, K. 2012. *Energy and the wealth of nations: Understanding the biophysical economy.* New York: Springer.

Hamilton, C. 2003. *Growth fetish.* Crows Nest, NSW: Allen & Unwin.

Heinberg, R. 2011. *The end of growth: Adapting to our new*

economic reality. Gabriola Island: New Society Publishers.

Herring, H. and Sorrell, S. 2009. *Energy efficiency and sustainable consumption: The rebound effect*. London: Palgrave Macmillan.

Hirsch, F. 1976. *Social limits to growth*. Cambridge, Mass: Harvard University Press.

Hirsch, R. *et al.* 2010. *The impending world energy mess*. Burlington: Apoge Prime.

Hollander, S. 1992. *Classical economics*. Toronto: University of Toronto Press.

Holmgren, D. 2002. *Permaculture: Principles and pathways beyond sustainability*. Hepburn: Holmgren Design Services.

Hopkins, R. 2008. *The transition handbook: From oil dependency to local resilience*. White River Junction, Vt: Chelsea Green Publishing.

Hopkins, R. and Miller, A. 2013. *Climate after growth: Why environmentalists must embrace post-growth economics*. Post Carbon Institute. Available at: http://www.postcarbon.org/reports/Climate-After-Growth.pdf (accessed 20 November, 2013).

Hubbert, M. 1956. 'Nuclear energy and the fossil fuels' (presented before the Spring meeting of the American Petroleum Institute, Plaza Hotel, San Antonio, Texas, March 7-9, 1956). Available at: http://www.hubbertpeak.com/hubbert/1956/1956.pdf (accessed 10 November 2013).

Huesemann, M., and Huesemann, J. 2011. *Techno-fix: Why technology won't save us or the environment*. Gabriola Island: New Society Publishers.

Intergovernmental Panel on Climate Change (IPCC), 2013. 'Climate Change 2013: The Physical Science Basis (Fifth Assessment Report)'. Available at: http://www.ipcc.ch/report/ar5/wg1/#.Uk6k-CjqMRw (accessed 4 October 2013).

IEA (International Energy Agency) 2013a. *World energy outlook 2013*. Available at: http://www.iea.org/Textbase/npsum/WEO2013SUM.pdf [accessed 25 November 2013].

IEA (International Energy Agency) 2013b. *Key world energy statistics*. IEA. Available at: http://www.iea.org/publications/freepublications/publication/KeyWorld2013_FINAL_WEB.pdf [accessed 20 November 2013].

Jackson, T. 2002. 'Quality of life, sustainability, and economic growth', in T. Fitzpatrick and M. Cahill (eds). *Environment and welfare: Towards a green social policy*. Basingstoke: Palgrave Macmillan.

Jackson, T. 2009. *Prosperity without growth: Economics for a finite planet*. London: Earthscan.

Kallis, G. 2011. 'In defence of degrowth'. *Ecological Economics* 70: 873-80.

Kasser, T. 2002. *The high price of materialism.* Cambridge, MA: MIT Press.

Kubiszewski, I., Costanza, R., Franco, C., Lawn, P., Talberth, J., Jackson, T., and Aylmer, C. 2013. 'Beyond GDP: Measuring and achieving global genuine progress'. *Ecological Economics* 93: 57-68.

Kuhn, T. 1962. *The structure of scientific revolutions.* Chicago: University of Chicago Press.

Lane, R. 2000. *The loss of happiness in market democracies.* New Haven: Yale University Press.

Latouche, S. 2009. *Farewell to growth.* Cambridge, UK: Polity Press.

Lawn, P. 2005. 'An assessment of the valuation methods used to calculate the Index of Sustainable Economic Welfare (ISEW), Genuine Progress Indicator (GPI), and Sustainable Net Benefit Index (SNBI)'. *Environment, Development, and Sustainability* 2: 185-208.

Lawn, P. 2006. *Sustainable development indicators in ecological economics.* Cheltenham: Edward Elgar Publishing.

Lawn, P. 2011. 'Is a steady state capitalism viable? A review of issues and an answer in the affirmative'. *Ann NY Acad. Sciences* February: 1219: 1-25.

Lawn, P. and Clarke, M. 2008. *Sustainable welfare in the Asia-Pacific: Studies using the genuine progress indicator.* Cheltenham: Edward Elgar Publishing.

Lawn, P. and Clarke, M. 2010. 'The end of economic growth? A contracting threshold hypothesis'. *Ecological Economics* 69: 2213.

Lomborg, B. 2001. *The Sceptical Environmentalist: Measuring the real state of the world.* Cambridge: Cambridge University Press.

Lovins, A. 1998. *Factor four: Doubling wealth – halving resource use.* London: Earthscan.

Malthus, T. 2007 [1798]. *An essay on the principle of population.* New York: Dover.

Mankiw, N. 2008. *The principles of economics* (5th edn). Mason, OH: South-Western.

Marcuse, H. 2002 [1964]. *One-dimensional man: Studies in the ideology of advanced industrial society.* London: Routledge.

Max-Neef, M. 1995. 'Economic growth and quality of life: A threshold hypothesis'. *Ecological Economics* 15(2): 115.

Meadows, D., Randers, J., and Meadows, D. 2004. *Limits to growth: The 30-year update.* White River Junction, Vt:

Chelsea Green Publishing.

Mill, J.S. 2004 [1848]. *Principles of political economy: With some of their applications to social philosophy.* New York: Prometheus Books.

Milne, C. 2012. 'An economy that serves people and nature, not the other way around.' Address made to the National Press Club of Australia, Canberra, 26 September, 2012. Available at: http://greensmps.org.au/content/news-stories/economy-serves-people-and-nature-not-other-way-around (accessed 14 December 2013).

Mishan, E. 1967. *The costs of economic growth.* London: Staples Press.

Murphy, D. and Hall, C. (2011a). 'Adjusting to the new energy realities of the second half of the age of oil'. *Ecological Modelling* 223: 67-71.

Murphy, D. and Hall, C. (2011b). 'Energy return on investment, peak oil, and the end of economic growth'. *Annals of the New York Academy of Sciences* 1219: 52-72.

New Economics Foundation (NEF) 2012. *Happy planet index.* Reports available at http://www.happyplanetindex.org/ (accessed 25 November 2013).

Plato, 2004. *The republic.* Indianapolis: Hackett.

Polimeni, J. *et al.* 2009. *The myth of resource efficiency: The Jevons paradox.* London: Earthscan.

Posner, R. 1986. *Economic analysis of law.* Boston: Little Brown.

Purdey, S. 2010. *Economic growth, the environment, and international relations: The growth paradigm.* New York: Routledge.

Rees, W. and Wackernagel, M. 1996. *Our ecological footprint: Reducing human impact on the earth.* Gabriola Island: New Society Publishers.

Rockstrom, J. *et al.* 2009. 'Planetary boundaries: Exploring the safe operating space for humanity'. *Ecology and Society* 14(2) Article 32.

Royal Government of Bhutan, 2012. 'The report of the high-level meeting on wellbeing and happiness: A new economic paradigm'. Available at: http://www.2apr.gov.bt/images/BhutanReport_WEB_F.pdf (accessed 14 December 2013).

Russell, B. 2009. *The basic writings of Bertrand Russell.* Oxon: Routledge.

Sarkar, S. 1999. *Eco-socialism or eco-capitalism: A critical analysis of humanity's fundamental choices.* London: Zed books.

Schneider, F., Kallis, G., and Martinez-Alier, J. 2010. 'Crisis or opportunity? Economic degrowth for social equity and ecological sustainability'. 18(6) *J Clean Prod.* 511-518.

Schumacher, E. 1973. *Small is beautiful: A study of economics as if people mattered.* Sydney: Vintage.

Scitovsky, T. 1992 [1976]. *The joyless economy: The psychology of human satisfaction.* Oxford: Oxford University Press.

Settle, M. 2010. 'Leadership move a "Storm in a Teacup" claims Prime Minister'. *Herald Scotland* (8 January 2010).

Simon, J. and Kahn, H. 1984. *The resourceful earth: A response to global 2000.* London: Blackwell Publishing.

Smith, R. 2010. 'Beyond growth or beyond capitalism'. *Institute for Policy Research & Development.* Available at: http://iprd.org.uk/wp-content/uploads/2011/02/Beyond-Growth-or-Beyond-Capitalism-by-Richard-Smith-2011.pdf [accessed 16 October 2013].

Stiglitz, J., Sen, A., and Fitoussi, J.P. 2010. *Mis-measuring our lives: Why GDP doesn't add up.* New York: The New Press.

Stratton, A. 2010. 'Cameron aims to make happiness the new GDP'. *The Guardian* (15 November 2010). Available at: http://www.theguardian.com/politics/2010/nov/14/david-cameron-wellbeing-inquiry?intcmp=239 (accessed 15 December 2013).

Theobald, R. 1961. *The challenge of abundance.* New York: Signet.

Trainer, T. 2010. *The transition to a sustainable and just world.* Sydney: Envirobook.

Trainer, T. 2011. 'The radical implications of a zero growth economy'. *Real-World Economics Review* 57: 71-82.

Trainer, 2012. 'Degrowth – do you realise what it means?'. *Futures* 44: 590-599.

Trainer, 2013a. 'Can Europe run on renewable energy? A negative case'. *Energy Policy* 63: 845-850.

Trainer, 2013b. 'Can the world run on renewable energy'. *Humanomics* 29(2): 88-104.

Turner, G. 2012. 'Are we on the cusp of collapse? Updated comparison of *The Limits to Growth* with historical data'*Gaia* . 21(2): 116-124.

Tverberg, G. 2012. 'Oil supply limits and the continuing financial crisis'. *Energy* 37(1): 27-34.

United Nations. 2012. *The future we want.* A/Res/66/88. Available at: http://daccess-dds-ny.un.org/doc/UNDOC/GEN/N11/476/10/PDF/N1147610.pdf?OpenElement (accessed 10 September 2013).

United Nations Development Program (UNDP), 2007/8. *Human Development Report.* Available at: http://hdr.undp.org/en/reports/global/hdr2007-2008/ [accessed 30 April 2011].

United Nations Department of Social and Economic Affairs (UNDSEA). 2012. *World population prospects: The 2012 revision*. Available at: http://esa.un.org/wpp/Documentation/pdf/WPP2012 Press Release.pdf [accessed 10 September 2013].

Vale, R. and Vale, B. 2013. *Living within a fair share ecological footprint*. Earthscan: London.

Vanenbroeck, G. (ed.). 1991. *Less is more: An anthology of ancient and modern voices raised in praise of simplicity*. Vermont: Inner Traditions.

Veblen, T. 2009[1899]. *Theory of the leisure class*. Oxford: Oxford University Press.

Victor, P. 2008. *Managing without growth: Slower by design, not disaster*. Cheltenham: Edward Elgar Publishing.

Von Weizsacker, E.U., Hargroves, C., Smith, M.H., Desha, C., and Stasinopoulous, P. 2009. *Factor five: Transforming the global economy through 80% improvements in resource productivity*. London: Routledge.

Weidmann, T., Schandl, H., Lenzen, M., Moran, D., Suh, S., West, J., and Kanemoto, K. 2013. 'The Material Footprint of Nations'. *Proceedings of the National Academy of Sciences (Early Edition)*. Published ahead of print, 3 September 2013: doi:10.1073/pnas.1220362110

White, T. 2007. 'Sharing resources: The global distribution of the ecological footprint'. *Ecological Economics* 64(2): 402-410.

Wilkinson, R. and Pickett, K. 2010. *The spirit level: Why greater equality makes socieities stronger*. London: Penguin.

Wiseman, J., Edwards, T., and Luckins, K. 2013. *Post carbon pathways: Towards a just and resilient post carbon future*. (CDP Discussion Paper, April 2013).

Woodward, D. and Simms, A. 2006. 'Growth isn't working: The uneven distribution of benefits and costs from economic growth. *New Economics Foundation*. Available at: http://www.neweconomics.org/publications/entry/growth-isnt-working [accessed 10 September 2013]

3

PLANNED ECONOMIC CONTRACTION
The emerging case for degrowth

If we do not change direction, we are likely to end up where we are going.
– Chinese Proverb

1. Introduction

In the most developed capitalist societies today, and increasingly throughout the world, public policy seems to be founded upon a vision of the social world in which sustained economic growth will eventually lead to a life of material abundance for all (Purdey, 2010). Attractive on the surface, perhaps, this vision of abundance treats Earth as a limitless resource to be exploited for human purposes and it promotes a materialistic attitude to life by assuming that human wellbeing consists in satisfying ever more consumer desires through market transactions. Whatever utility it may have had in the past, today there are compelling grounds for contesting this vision of abundance as well as the macroeconomics of growth that it both shapes and is shaped by (Turner, 2012; Barry, 2012; Jackson, 2009). Not only are the materialistic values underlying this vision evidently having a caustic effect on personal and social wellbeing (Pickett and Wilkinson, 2010; Kasser, 2002; Lane, 2000), but the process of globalising Western-style consumption habits is degrading the health and integrity of Earth's ecosystems and diminishing their capacity to support life in the future (Global Footprint Network, 2010; Millennium Ecosystem Assessment, 2005). A new vision is urgently needed, and with it an economics 'beyond growth'.

Even to consider looking 'beyond growth' would seem rather premature, of course, if the analysis were to be directed toward the poorest nations on the planet, where the need for further economic development, *of some form*, is immediate and obvious (see discussion of 'appropriate development' in Trainer, 2010: Ch. 5). But when the analysis is focused, as it will be presently, on the richest nations, it is much less clear why economic growth, measured by increases in Gross Domestic Product (GDP), should remain a central policy objective of governments. Indeed, there are four main arguments for why the richest nations should give up the pursuit of economic growth and try to manage without growth (Victor and Rosenbluth, 2007): (1) Continued economic growth worldwide is no longer a sustainable option due to environmental and resource constraints, so the richest nations should leave room for growth in the poorest nations where the benefits of growth are evident (Meadows *et al.*, 2004); (2) in the richest nations growth has become 'uneconomic', in the sense that it detracts from overall wellbeing more than it contributes, all things considered (Daly, 1999); (3) growth in the richest nations is neither necessary nor sufficient for meeting policy objectives such as full employment, elimination of poverty, and protection of the environment (Victor, 2008); and (4) growth in the richest nations is an ineffective and unsustainable means of reducing global poverty (Woodward and Simms, 2006). Taken together, these arguments provide the foundations for a radically new phase of macroeconomic policy in the richest nations, one in which economic growth should lose its privileged position as the touchstone of policy and institutional success (Alexander, 2011a; Stiglitz *et al.*, 2010). Whether this new 'post-growth' phase of economic transformation will need to be driven primarily from the 'top down' or 'from below' is a question fiercely debated in the literature (see, e.g., Sarkar, 1999; Jackson, 2009; Smith, 2010; Trainer, 2010) and will be briefly considered later in the analysis and in more detail elsewhere in this book.

The substantive analysis of this chapter begins by drawing on social and ecological research and economic theory in an attempt to underpin what Manfred Max-Neef (1995) has called the 'threshold hypothesis'. This hypothesis holds that 'for every society there seems to be a period in which economic growth (as conventionally measured) brings about an improvement in the quality of life, but only to a point – the threshold point – beyond which, if there is more economic growth, quality of life may begin to deteriorate' (Max-Neef, 1995: 117). The basic idea is that when macroeconomic systems expand beyond a certain size, the additional social and ecological costs of growth begin to outweigh the benefits, making any further growth uneconomic. The best way to determine whether growth is economic or uneconomic is to utilise the conceptual tools employed by many ecological economists, who have developed a number of indexes to measure and compare the benefits and costs of economic growth (e.g., the Index of Sustainable Economic Welfare [ISEW] and the Genuine Progress Indicator [GPI]). To anticipate the central finding here, in virtually every instance of where an index of this type has been calculated, the movement of the index appears to reinforce the threshold hypothesis (Lawn, 2005; Kubiszewski et al., 2013). Put more directly, there is an emerging body of evidence which indicates that many of the most developed regions of the world – including North America, Western Europe, Japan, and parts of Australasia – have entered or are entering a phase of uneconomic growth. This evidential basis has given preliminary credence to the radical notion of 'degrowth' (Kallis, 2011; Latouche, 2009; Fournier, 2008; Baykan, 2007), which has been broadly defined as 'an equitable downscaling of production and consumption that increases human wellbeing and enhances ecological conditions' (Schneider et al., 2010: 512).

Focusing on the highly developed regions of the world, this chapter draws on a wide range of literature to outline theoretically and support empirically the emerging case for degrowth. It argues that when an economy has grown so large that it has reached or exceeded the threshold point beyond which any further growth is 'uneconomic' (i.e., socially or ecologically counter-productive), economies should be reconstructed in order to achieve more specific welfare-enhancing objectives – such as eliminating poverty, lessening inequalities, and protecting the environment – and the efficient growth of GDP *or lack thereof* should be treated as a by-product of secondary importance. After outlining the emerging case for degrowth, this chapter considers the feasibility of a macro-economics beyond growth and begins sketching an outline of what such a macroeconomics might look like as a politico-economic programme. It is hoped that this analysis might help objectors to growth (and others) envision alternatives to the existing paradigm and better understand the extent of change required for justice and sustainability. In an age of widespread political paralysis, of course, it could be that change 'from below' is the most likely space for effective opposition and renewal (see Alexander and Rutherford, 2014), and, in fact, perhaps the revolution needed can *only* be driven from below (see Trainer, 2010). On the other hand, perhaps at this late stage in the game, only a committed 'top down' response is going to be able to achieve the deep changes necessary in the time available. Whatever the case, considering what governments *could* do to promote a post-growth or degrowth economics should serve as a useful clarification of some of the central issues.

2. The Social Critique of Growth

As outlined in the last chapter, the growth model of progress assumes as a matter of course that an increase in GDP per capita will contribute positively and quite directly to a nation's wellbeing. While neoclassical theory seems to accept that assumption without question, a growing body of interdisciplinary scholars, building upon the pioneering work of Richard Easterlin (1974), has been examining its empirical basis using survey analyses (Diener *et al.*, 2010). Summarised below, these scholars have found the correlation between income and subjective wellbeing to be much more nuanced than neoclassicists generally assume (for a more comprehensive review, see Alexander, 2012).

It will probably surprise no one to discover that on average people in the richest nations report higher levels of subjective wellbeing than people in the poorest nations (Diener *et al.*, 2009). But there is much evidence that now indicates that beyond a certain material standard of living, increases in personal and/or national income have a fast diminishing marginal utility (Diener *et al.*, 2010; Layard *et al.*, 2008; Lane, 2000). Put otherwise, there comes a point where rises in income become less important as a means of increasing wellbeing, and other features of life, such as more meaningful employment, more leisure time, and more social engagement, become increasingly important (Helliwell, Layard, and Sachs, 2012; Diener and Seligman, 2004).

Indeed, when comparing only the richest nations – which are the focus of this chapter – the correlation between GDP per capita and wellbeing is evidently negligible. Clive Hamilton, for example, has studied data on the richest 17 nations and found that 'there is no relationship at all between higher incomes and higher appreciation of life' (Hamilton, 2003: 26). Similarly, Richard Layard (2005: 32) has extensively reviewed the evidence and concluded that 'if we compare the Western industrial countries, the richer ones are no happier than the poorer'. In a more recent study, Layard and colleagues (2010) provide further support for this position and carefully respond to their critics (Stevenson and Wolfers, 2008; Deaton, 2008). This new study, among others (e.g., Di Tella and MacCalloch, 2010; Pickett and Wilkinson, 2010) essentially corroborates Ronald Inglehart's thesis (1996: 509) that 'although economic gains apparently make a major contribution to subjective wellbeing as one moves from societies at the subsistence level to those with moderate levels of economic development, further economic growth seems to have little or no impact on subjective wellbeing'. If this is so, the richest nations could now be confronting honestly what John Maynard Keynes (1963: 362) called our 'permanent problem' – that is, the problem of what to *do* with the freedom that material comfort provides. But instead of embracing that task, an apparently insatiable imperative for growth continues to structure not only the global economy, but the collective imagination. This is despite the mounting evidence which indicates that further growth is unlikely to contribute much to social wellbeing, at least in the wealthy parts of the world (Easterlin, 2013; Easterlin and Angelescu 2010; Diener *et al.*, 2010; Blanchflower and Oswald, 2004; Lane, 2000).

Explanations vary (often in mutually supportive ways) for why increases in individual or national income beyond some material threshold have a diminishing marginal utility. Five of the most prominent arguments are: (1) that once a person's basic material needs are satisfied, *relative* income has much more effect on subjective wellbeing than *absolute* wellbeing (Layard *et al.*, 2010), which means that growth eventually becomes a zero sum game; (2) that 'hedonic adaptation' occurs, meaning that as people get richer they generally become accustomed to the pleasure or satisfaction afforded by their increased income, nullifying the projected benefits of growth (Di Tella and MacCalloch, 2010); (3) that the material norms on which judgements of wellbeing are based tend to increase in the same proportion as the actual income of the society, again nullifying the projected benefits of growth (Easterlin, 1995); (4) beyond a certain threshold, distributive equity matters more than continuous growth (Pickett and Wilkinson, 2010); and (5) that people with materialistic value orientations tend to have lower personal wellbeing and psychological health than those who believe that materialistic pursuits are relatively unimportant (Kasser, 2002).

While the intricacies of these complex matters cannot be explored here, collectively this body of research casts considerable doubt on the assumption that getting richer will consistently lead to increased individual or social wellbeing. Indeed, the weight of evidence suggests that there are 'social limits to growth' (Hirsch, 1976) which many of the richest nations already seem to have surpassed. Although this matter is far from settled, a strong case can certainly be made that the richest nations – given appropriate institutional restructuring (see proposals in Sect. 6) – could have a lower GDP per capita without compromising, and perhaps even positively enhancing, social wellbeing (see Kubiszewski *et al.*, 2013). This counter-intuitive thesis is likely to seem much less counter-intuitive when considered in conjunction with the following ecological critique of growth, since in that broader context the high consumption lifestyles celebrated in rich countries today are plainly the driving force underlying the manifold ecological crises the world is currently facing. In other words, it is becoming increasingly clear that it is in everyone's interest – including the inhabitants of the richest nations – that contemporary Western-style cultures of consumption are quickly downscaled (Alexander, 2009; Alexander 2011b; Trainer, 2010), and so too the size of the most highly developed economies.

3. The Ecological Critique of Growth

Many credible scientific studies have shown that the human economy is degrading the planet's ecosystems in ways that are unsustainable (e.g., Global Footprint Network, 2010; IPCC, 2007; Millennium Ecosystem Assessment, 2005; Wackernagel, 2002). While this is hardly news (Meadows *et al.*, 2004), the full implications of ecological 'overshoot' are rarely acknowledged or understood, at least with respect to what it means for conventional growth economics. It is clear enough that human beings need to consume *differently* and produce commodities more *efficiently* (Arrow *et al.*, 2004). But few people – and no governments, in the developed world, at least – are prepared to accept that attaining an ecologically sustainable global economy requires a fundamental reassessment of the growth model. On the contrary, the mainstream position on sustainability seems to be that economies around the world simply need to adopt 'sustainable development', which in theory means continuing to pursue economic growth while employing science and technology to produce and consume more cleanly and efficiently (e.g., UNDP, 2007/8: 15).

This mainstream vision of how to achieve a sustainable world is coherent in theory, at best, but demonstrably it does not reflect empirical reality (see Alexander, 2014). Although many economies around the world are indeed getting better at producing commodities more cleanly and efficiently (a process known as 'relative decoupling'), overall ecological impact is nevertheless *still increasing*, because every year increasing numbers of commodities are being produced, exchanged, and consumed as a result of growing economies (Jackson, 2009, Ch. 5). We might have more fuel-efficient cars, for example, but the rebound effect is that we are also driving more and buying more cars. This is but one example of the 'Jevons paradox' that permeates market societies and beyond (Polimeni *et al.*, 2009) – a paradox, so-called, because a per unit reduction in the throughput of commodities does not always lead to reduced ecological impact, since those efficiency improvements are often outweighed by the increasing amounts of commodities that are consumed (Holm and Englund, 2009). The implication of this is that technology and efficiency improvements are not going to solve the ecological crisis, as their most optimistic advocates and popular consciousness seem to assume they can (Lovins, 1998) – at least, not unless the highly developed nations also transition away from growth economics. Efficiency without sufficiency is lost.

The fact that the global economy is already in significant ecological overshoot (Global Footprint Network, 2012) is even more challenging when we bear in mind that in the poorest parts of the world today great multitudes are living lives oppressed by extreme poverty (World Bank, 2009). The momentous global challenge, therefore, in terms of humanitarian justice and ecological sustainability, can be stated as follows: The human community must find a way to *raise* the material standards of living of the world's poorest people – which is almost certainly going to increase humanity's demand and impact on nature – while at the same time *reducing* humanity's overall ecological footprint (Meadows *et al.*, 2004).

What further exacerbates these ecological and humanitarian crises, however, is the fact that, according to the United Nations, global human population is expected to exceed nine billion by mid-century (UNDSEA, 2012). This will intensify greatly the already intense competition over access to Earth's limited natural resources and it will put even more pressure on Earth's fragile ecosystems. The problem of a greatly expanding human population, therefore, provides further compelling support for the proposition that any transition to a just and sustainable world will need to involve the most developed nations transitioning away from the growth model.

Very few people, however, including many environmentalists, seem to acknowledge or understand quite how directly the global situation undermines the legitimacy of continued growth in the richest nations. Ted Trainer (2010: 22), being a rare exception, expresses the magnitude of the problems of ecological overshoot, economic growth, and population growth in painfully clear terms: '[I]f we in the rich countries average 3% growth, and 9 billion rose to the living standards we would then have by 2070, total world output would be 60 times as great as it is today.' While this future seems to be the very aim of globalised 'development', it would be preposterous in the extreme to suggest that Earth's ecosystems could withstand the impacts of a 60-fold expansion of a global economy *already* in ecological overshoot, especially since there is no evidence that absolute decoupling of the global economy is occurring, or likely to occur, to the degree necessary. Degrowth in the rich nations seems much less 'radical' when considered in these terms. Indeed, degrowth in the richest nations would seem to be an absolutely necessary element in any solution to the global predicament – although one must also accept that the degrowth solution is effectively unthinkable in today's politico-economic climate.

4. The Economic Critique of Growth

In light of the preceding critiques, it would seem that the term 'economic growth' needs to be reconsidered. According to microeconomic theory, activity is considered 'economic' if the additional benefits of engaging in it are greater than the additional costs. For example, an extra unit of production by an individual firm is considered economic if the additional revenue generated is greater than the additional costs incurred. Similarly, an additional hour of labour is considered economic if the consumption-related utility from the money earned is greater than the leisure-related utility forgone (Lawn, 2008). Within this microeconomic framework it is accepted that there will come a point – an 'optimal' point – when the marginal costs of additional production or consumption equal the marginal benefits. This is sometimes called the 'when to stop rule' (Daly, 1999), a rule which implies that if growth occurs beyond the optimal point it will be 'uneconomic', in the sense that the costs begin to outweigh the benefits. Micro-economists are the first to label uneconomic growth 'irrational' (Becker, 1962).

However, as Philip Lawn (2008: 1) observes, 'at the macroeconomic level, growth in real GDP is labelled "economic" growth irrespective of whether it generates more additional benefits than costs'. It may well be that what most people mean by economic growth is growth of the economy, but Lawn (2008: 1) correctly points out that 'growth of something which happens to be called "the economy" is not the same as "economic growth"'. Properly understood, economic growth means growth that generates more benefits than costs, all things considered. It follows that growth that generates more costs than benefits must be judged 'uneconomic' growth. But conventional macroeconomics does not recognise a 'when to stop rule' and so has no place for the notion of an 'optimal' scale of the economy as a whole. It just assumes that a bigger economy is always better; that growth in GDP is always 'economic'. The preceding critiques of growth cast serious doubt on that assumption.

If markets functioned perfectly, perhaps a rise in GDP would always be 'economic' growth. But that is to make a notoriously implausible assumption. Economists have long acknowledged that there are 'market failures' (Pigou, 1920), however only in quite recent times have the extent and significance of those failures been comprehensively and systematically exposed (Daly and Farley, 2004: 157-220). Conventional growth economics based on GDP accounting fails to internalise many significant externalities that can be associated with economic activity, such as loss of social capital or environmental degradation (Stiglitz *et al.*, 2010; Cobb *et al.*, 1995). By failing to take such externalities into account, growth of the economy can seem 'economic' even when the economy has already exceeded its optimal scale, rendering any further growth 'uneconomic'.

Although still in need of refinement, the 'extended accounts' of the ISEW and GPI are increasingly robust tools for exposing macroeconomic externalities and internalising them (Lawn, 2005). In this way those extended accounts, and other similar ones, seek to measure as accurately as possible the true costs and benefits of growth and thereby help determine when growth is 'economic' and when it is not. Those extended accounts often use orthodox economic notions, such as cost/benefit analysis and externalities, to criticise neoclassical orthodoxy. Doing so opens up theoretical space for the notion of uneconomic growth at the macroeconomic level. Again, Lawn (2008: 1) puts the situation well:

> It is... critical that a distinction be drawn between 'economic' and 'uneconomic' growth; that indicators be established to determine what form of growth a nation is experiencing; that only 'economic' growth be encouraged; and that 'uneconomic' growth be addressed by making the transition to a steady-state economy (degrowth) at which time the sole emphasis of all economic activity should be on qualitative improvement not quantitative expansion.

Indicators such the ISEW and GPI already exist to inform us when a nation is experiencing uneconomic growth, and consistently the message delivered is that the developed nations are entering or have already entered such a phase (Kubiszewski *et al.*, 2013; Lawn and Clarke, 2010; Daly, 1999). The implication is that just as an individual firm should downscale when the benefits of doing so would be greater than the costs, so should the over-developed economies downscale. This could be called 'economic degrowth'.

For present purposes there is one final and important point in critique. Assuming the developed nations never *choose* to question the growth model – which one must admit is the most likely scenario – the issue of 'peak oil' and related energy supply problems (Hirsch *et al.*, 2010) suggests that the era of growth economics could be coming to an end nevertheless (Heinberg, 2011). Many parts of the world seem to be recovering (at least superficially) from the 'credit crunch', but the 'oil crunch' may well come to tell a different story. Whether the transition away from energy-intensive economies occurs voluntarily or is imposed by force of biophysical limits remains to be seen. It scarcely needs remarking that a well-planned, voluntary transition would be the desired path.

5. The Feasibility of a Macroeconomics Beyond Growth

Even if the multi-dimensional critique of growth outlined above is accepted, or comes to be accepted, there might still be (and probably are) doubts as to whether planned economic contraction, or degrowth, is a feasible macroeconomic policy. After all, the logic of capitalism is arguably dependent upon growth and accumulation, and as the recent financial crisis shows, an economic system dependent on growth that suffers *unplanned* economic contraction (i.e., recession) is not to be desired. Among other problems, recession causes rates of unemployment to rise, which leads to distressing economic insecurity and notoriously gives rise to a host of other social problems (Clark and Oswald, 1994). And aside from all that, growth is typically assumed to be the *solution* to unemployment, as well as the solution to other problems, like poverty and environmental degradation. How do these issues sit within a macroeconomics beyond growth? Is a macroeconomics beyond growth even possible?

Surprisingly, very little sustained attention has been given to these issues, although this tide seems to be turning. One of the most important contributions in recent years has been the in-depth analysis offered by the Canadian economist Peter Victor (2008). Although Victor focuses primarily on the Canadian economy, it can be fairly assumed (and he would insist) that his conclusions have relevance to other advanced capitalist societies since they are all governed by essentially the same macroeconomic growth paradigm. After reviewing the foundations of growth scepticism, Victor considers the familiar argument that growth is needed to achieve important policy objectives, such as protecting the environment and eliminating unemployment and poverty. In a thorough review of the evidence since 1980, he shows that recent decades of unprecedented economic growth have not eliminated unemployment or poverty in Canada; that distributions of wealth have become more unequal; that growth has generally exacerbated, not solved, environmental problems, and that greenhouse gases are still growing. On the basis that growth has been a disappointing tool for achieving these important policy objectives, Victor reasonably turns his attention to the question of whether those objectives could be better achieved in an advanced economy without relying on growth.

72

Victor uses an interactive systems model to explore the possibility of a macroeconomic framework that is not based on growth. This model allows him to consider changes in key macroeconomic variables, such as output, consumption, public spending, investment, employment, trade, and so on, in order to estimate future GDP in various scenarios, while also keeping an account of unemployment, greenhouse gas emissions, and poverty levels. By simulating a variety of scenarios, Victor illustrates that 'no growth' could be disastrous if implemented carelessly, bringing hardship to many; just as growing 'business as usual' would arguably be disastrous. But he illustrates that slower growth, leading to stability around 2030, can also be consistent with attractive economic, social, and environmental outcomes, including full employment, virtual elimination of poverty, more leisure, considerable reduction in greenhouse gas emissions and fiscal balance. Furthermore, by comparing various low-/no-growth scenarios, Victor also argues that various attractive options are available. For example, some scenarios with higher investment seem more compatible with a future in which renewable energy and efficient technology become widely adopted. Other scenarios, where GDP and GDP per capita are lower, may not adopt those measures so quickly, but the lower incomes might compensate in terms of reduced ecological impact.

On what basis does Victor draw these conclusions? One of the most important features of a macroeconomics beyond growth relate to changes in investment and the structure of the labour market. Restructuring tax policies and redirecting public spending (see discussion below) could be effective ways of changing investment strategies to realise the attractive hypothetical scenarios Victor envisages (including a shift in investment from private to public goods). The essential reasoning here is quite straightforward, even if its implementation would not be: new avenues open up for progressive politico-economic reform once growth loses its privileged position as the touchstone of policy and institutional success.

Nevertheless, this does not explain how the economy could function and be stable without growing and perhaps even shrinking to an extent, and it would be fair to say that Victor does not present a complete case. He has, however, helped get the conversation moving and his arguments provide a place to start. Victor argues that (among other things) a restructure of the labour market becomes essential. In a non-growing but qualitatively developing economy, technological advances would presumably still enhance the productivity of workers over time; but this could lead to increasing rates of unemployment, since less labour would be needed to produce the same (non-growing) economic output. This phenomenon, along with increases in population, are the main reasons why conventional macroeconomists insist that growth is essential; that is, it is needed to avoid unemployment spiralling out of control. In a macroeconomic framework not based on growth, however, Victor argues that a stable system could still be achieved, but through the alternate route of reducing the workweek and sharing work more equally amongst the population. Some of the policy issues that overall work reduction involves will be touched on in the next section. For now the critical point to note is that work reduction is one of the defining characteristics of a desirable macroeconomics beyond growth. This approach implies that average material standard of living would remain at a constant or mildly fluctuating level in a non-growing economy, since increases in productivity would result in more leisure rather than more income. This obviously contrasts sharply with the growth economics practised in advanced capitalist societies today, where increases in productivity are almost always used to increase overall material output rather than stabilising material living standards and reducing overall labour input (Robinson, 2009).

It is unfortunate that Victor focuses only on 'managing without growth' and does not specifically address the need for a period of degrowth, especially since the logic of his own analysis seems to require it, a point he gets tantalisingly close to acknowledging (Victor, 2008: 185; but see also, Victor, 2011). Nevertheless, in important respects degrowth is implicit to his argument, in the sense at least that he advocates a dedicated reduction in wasteful production and consumption as well as an absolute reduction in the ecological impacts of economic activity, not just relative decoupling. Taking Victor's analysis a few steps further, however, it would seem that some extra reductions in working hours, permitted by extra reductions in per capita income/consumption, could help facilitate a period of degrowth. But given the extent of degrowth needed, what banking and finance systems would be required? (For a critical discussion, see Trainer, 2011.) What happens to debt? Can a degrowth transition occur within a primarily market-based economy? What are the lifestyle implications of degrowth? Taken seriously, these and other issues suggest that degrowth is even more radical than Victor and other objectors to growth recognise (Trainer, 2012).

Perhaps the most compelling grounds for thinking that a post-growth or degrowth framework (of some form) is feasible is the mounting evidence indicating that it is fast becoming absolutely necessary (Turner, 2012). Continued growth of economies and population on a finite planet is a straightforward recipe for ecological (and therefore humanitarian) catastrophe, which suggests that whatever risks there are to experimenting with a macroeconomics beyond growth, there are infinitely greater risks to persisting blindly with conventional growth economics. To put it proverbially, if we do not change direction, we are likely to end up where we are going.

6. Degrowth as a Politico-Economic Programme: A Preliminary Statement

The maintenance and protection of ecological integrity, on the one hand, and the redistribution of wealth and work to eliminate poverty and lessen inequalities, are some of the central policy objectives which seem to be implied by the idea of a degrowth transition to a steady state economy. This final section sketches an outline of eight policy proposals that could begin meeting those objectives and, in doing so, initiate a degrowth process of planned economic contraction. Although I assume these proposals would be delivered by a centralised state with a democratic mandate, one of their primary aims would be to open up space for individuals and communities to begin creating a new, highly localised economy at the grassroots level.

The following list makes no claim to be comprehensive and limitation of space only leaves room to introduce the core ideas. A great deal more work would be needed to convince people of the merits and feasibility of these proposals, although some of that work is being undertaken in the burgeoning degrowth movement and related movements. But it is hoped that what follows at least serves as a useful introduction to a politics of degrowth and provides a basis for future research and discussion.

- **Explicit Adoption of Post-Growth Measures of Progress:** It is now widely recognised that GDP is not an adequate measure of societal progress (Stiglitz *et al.*, 2010). It is merely a sum of national economic activity which makes no distinction between market transactions that contribute positively to sustainable wellbeing and those that diminish it. Nevertheless, growth in GDP remains the overriding policy objective of even the richest nations. A politics of degrowth should begin by explicitly adopting some post-growth measure of progress, such as the Genuine Progress Indicator (GPI). The GPI and other such measures must not become objects of fetishisation, like GDP has become, but public support for such post-growth national accounting systems would open up the political space needed for political parties to introduce policy and institutional changes that would genuinely improve social wellbeing and enhance ecological conditions – such as the following proposals – even if these would lead to a phase of planned economic contraction. If taken seriously, these alternative indicators would imply a radical agenda for change.

- **Renewable Energy:** Anticipating the imminent stagnation and eventual decline of fossil fuel supplies, and recognising the grave dangers presented by anthropogenic climate change, a politics of degrowth would need to transition to renewable and more efficient energy systems. Climate change is the greatest 'market failure' in history. Internalising that externality would mean rapid decarbonisation (and therefore localisation) of the economy. Nuclear should not be relied on as an energy source, because the world would need approximately 14,500 nuclear plants to meet current energy demand (Pearce, 2008) – currently there are 435 nuclear plants. In a world where geopolitical conflict is likely to increase as resource scarcity becomes more severe (see Klare, 2012), upscaling nuclear seems extremely unwise, irrespective of other arguments for and against it. In an economy based primarily on renewables, it would be necessary to simply use significantly less energy (Anderson, 2013), since it is very unlikely that renewables could ever sustain energy-intensive consumer societies, nor would that be desirable even if it were possible (see, e.g., Trainer, 2013a; 2013b). Public transport, cycling, and walking would largely have to replace private automobiles.

- **Resource Caps and Rationing:** 'Free markets', so-called, seem wholly incapable of functioning to 'optimise' the economy/environment relationship; instead, the growth imperative essentially forces firms to maximise their own profits irrespective of ecological limits (see, e.g., Smith, 2010). In order to move toward 'one planet living' what may be needed is the imposition of resource caps and rationing. Resource caps would set an ecologically sustainable limit to key resource consumption, above which an economy cannot consume. They should be introduced progressively, to allow adjustment. Markets can then play a role allocating those capped resources, leaving room for 'efficient' exchanges that increase wellbeing but which do not imply an increase in material throughput. Resource caps would also do much to solve the problem of 'rebound effects', because efficiency gains in a 'capped' economy could not be directed toward increasing overall throughput. In order to ensure social justice is served at the same time, especially in crisis situations, basic rationing for essential goods may be required, including energy rationing (see, e.g., Gleeson, 2010). Western nations coped well enough with rationing during other times of 'emergency' (such as world wars), and responding to the overlapping emergencies we face may require us to cope again. There is unlikely to be a smooth transition beyond the growth paradigm.

- **Basic Income:** To eliminate poverty, capitalist societies typically rely on growing the economic pie, not slicing it differently. Once the pursuit of growth is given up, however, poverty must be confronted more directly. Some form of Basic Income may be required. Although there is considerable variety in forms of Basic Income, the core idea is relatively straightforward: Every permanent resident would be guaranteed a minimal though dignified standard of economic security. A Negative Income Tax could be introduced as a transitional step, which would provide tax credits to every adult who earns below a certain income. In these ways material destitution within a nation would be virtually eliminated (Alexander, 2011a). These policies would also open up more space for self-sufficiency by allowing individuals to get active in the informal, local economy. In fact, this would be one of the primary aims of such policies. A Job Guarantee is an alternative policy to consider.

- **Progressive Taxation and the Maximum Wage:** The Basic Income could be funded in part by restructuring the tax system. The social research reviewed earlier showed that beyond a certain material threshold – which the richest nations have evidently already exceeded – further increases in personal or national income have a diminishing marginal utility. This means that very high incomes are an extremely inefficient use of resources, in terms of wellbeing, as well as being morally questionable as a matter of distributive justice. Highly progressive income or consumption taxes could be introduced to respond effectively to this situation (Frank, 2008). For example, a progressive income tax could culminate in a 100% tax on incomes over a certain democratically determined level, thereby effectively creating a maximum wage (Pizzigati, 2004). A degrowth society need not enforce strict equality of resources, but if poverty is ever to be eliminated, the socially corrosive levels of inequality prevalent today (Pickett and Wilkinson, 2010) must be greatly reduced. Furthermore, for ecological reasons politics must do much more to reign in lifestyles of profligate consumption.

- **Working Hour Reductions:** As noted earlier, restructuring the labour market is essential for a degrowth economy to function properly. The first step down this path is to eliminate the structural biases that function to promote overwork, such as laws that treat the 40-hour work week as 'standard' and which exclude part-time employees from many non-pecuniary benefits enjoyed by full-time employees (Robinson, 2009). A second step would be to introduce something like Holland's *Hours Adjustment Act 2000*, which permits employees to reduce working hours to part-time simply by asking their employers. Discussing this legislation, John de Graaf (2009, p. 274) notes that, 'Unless there is a clear hardship for the firm – something shown in less than 5% of cases [in Holland] – the employer must grant the reduction.... This law, in the most concrete terms, allows workers to trade money for time, without losing their jobs or healthcare.' A third step would be to gradually decrease the 'standard' working week, beginning with something like France's 35-hour working week, proceeding to 28-hour working week, and in time perhaps moving to a 21-hour working week (NEF, 2010). Collectively, steps such as these would privilege leisure over consumption and systematically distribute labour in a slowly contracting economy. Given that this would also imply reduced income, a significant portion of this time not working in the formal economy would need to be redirected toward home production (e.g., food production, mending, fixing, building, etc.), through which a new, informal economy 'B' slowly arises within the old, contracting economy 'A'.

- **Worker Cooperatives:** A politics of degrowth would need to transition away from the profit-maximising, corporate models prevalent under growth capitalism and move to an economy comprised predominantly of worker cooperatives and small, locally-owned enterprises. Governments could facilitate the emergence of cooperatives (including not-for-profit enterprises) through such means as providing very attractive tax incentives, as well as preferring cooperatives when contracting with the private sector (i.e., whenever possible government spending would be directed to cooperatives). Development banks could also be established through which governments could provide credit to help establish new cooperatives that would provide socially necessary services (e.g., local and organic food production).

- **Inheritance and Bequest:** The revolutionary structural reforms needed to transition to a degrowth society – such as those proposed in this short list – are going to require funding. As noted above, highly progressive income and/or consumption taxes can provide some of the funding, however more would probably be needed, especially in order to fund the Basic Income and the transition to renewable energy systems. This socially and ecologically necessary funding could be secured by abolishing the laws of inheritance and bequest, such that upon death a citizen's property would revert to the state, rather than be passed down from generation to generation. This would also contribute significantly to realising the democratic ideals of equality of opportunity and a broad-based distribution of wealth. This restructuring of property rights also makes the point that a degrowth economy may need to come under significant social control rather than be left primarily to market forces, if it is to contract without collapsing (see Smith, 2010).

It is suggested that these eight proposals, if implemented, would go a significant way to initiating a degrowth process of planned economic contraction. Clearly, this is an eco-socialist agenda, while also leaving some place for regulated markets that genuinely serve the common good. I do not underestimate the challenges that would be faced if ever such an agenda were to be embraced, not least how a nation-state could move in this direction given how globalised capitalism has become.

But again, the proposals above do not claim to answer all questions; indeed, the aim is not really to answer *any* questions, only provoke discussion. A great many other politico-economic (and socio-cultural) changes would be necessary also, shaped and implemented in context-specific ways. Some further structural issues that would almost certainly need to be addressed include: banking and finance systems; Third World and First World debt, possibly requiring a debt 'jubilee'; food production and distribution; a binding global climate treaty based on scientific requirements;

transport; conservation of nature; advertising regulation; campaign financing; military expenditure; international law and trade; foreign aid; low-consumption education campaigns, and so forth. Some of the best places to continue exploring these issues are in the proceedings of the various degrowth or steady state conferences that have taken place in recent years (e.g., CASSE, 2011; Proceedings of Second International Conference on Degrowth, 2011), and in the publications of the Simplicity Institute.

7. Conclusion

When the extent of ecological overshoot is considered in conjunction with both projected population growth and the legitimate need for the poorest nations to develop their economic capacities, degrowth in the richest nations seems a much less radical proposal than it might first appear to be. Indeed, the logic of argument, though easily ignored, is very hard to escape, and the prospect of an energy-scarce world just makes the case clearer. This is not to say that the details of what degrowth would involve are clear; and it certainly is not to say that the prospects of degrowth being voluntarily embraced are good. It is only to suggest that it is extremely hard to conceive of a transition to a just and sustainable world without the most developed nations going through some degrowth phase of planned economic contraction. Only a technological miracle, in the strictest sense, could make degrowth unnecessary. And yet it seems it is that for which the world waits.

Given the magnitude and multifaceted nature of the global predicament, any response to it that merely tinkers with growth capitalism will be grossly insufficient. An adequate politico-economic response must reflect the gravity of the problems, and this chapter has argued that degrowth is the most coherent framework within which to formulate a response. Nevertheless, in closing it is worth acknowledging that however necessary it is for there to be a committed politico-economic response to the global predicament, such a response is highly unlikely to ever eventuate in the absence of a cultural revolution in attitudes toward Western-style consumer lifestyles. That is to say, the voluntary emergence of degrowth in a consumerist culture is essentially a contradiction in terms, such that if a politics of degrowth is ever to emerge it will almost certainly have to be driven from the grassroots up by a culture that embraces some notion of 'sufficiency' in consumption (Alexander, 2010, 2011c, 2013). As Serge Latouche (2014: 1) states, degrowth involves redefining happiness as 'frugal abundance in a society based on solidarity'. Something resembling the Voluntary Simplicity

Movement or Transition Towns, for example, would need to be mainstreamed, radicalised, and politicised before any political campaign for degrowth had any realistic chance of success (Alexander and Ussher, 2012; Trainer, 2010; Hopkins, 2008). This may sound depressingly unlikely, but that just makes it all the more important that advocates of degrowth do not focus merely on highlighting the importance of *structural change*, while neglecting the necessary *cultural preconditions* for such structural change. A cultural paradigm shift in favour of 'frugal abundance' may need to precede any co-relative political revolution.

Degrowth implies voluntary simplicity.

References

Alexander, S. (ed.). 2009. *Voluntary simplicity: The poetic alternative to consumer culture.* Stead & Daughters, Whanganui.

Alexander, S. 2010. 'Deconstructing the shed: Where I live and what I live for'. *Concord Saunterer: The Journal of Thoreau Studies* 18: 125-143.

Alexander, S. 2011a. 'Property beyond growth: Toward a politics of voluntary simplicity'. Doctoral thesis, Melbourne Law School. Available at: 'http://papers.ssrn.com/sol3/papers.cfm?abstract_id=1941069 (accessed 10 September 2013).

Alexander, S. 2011b. The voluntary simplicity movement: Reimagining the good life beyond consumer culture'. *International Journal of Environmental, Cultural, Economic, and Social Sustainability* 7(3): 133-150.

Alexander, S. 2011c. 'Looking backward from the year 2099: Ecozoic reflections on the future'. *Earth Jurisprudence and Environmental Justice Journal* 1(1): 25-59.

Alexander, S. 2012a. 'The optimal material threshold: Toward an economics of sufficiency'. *Real-World Economics Review* 61: 2-21.

Alexander, S. 2011b. 'Earth jurisprudence and the ecological case for degrowth', in P. Burdon (ed.). *Exploring wild law: The philosophy of earth jurisprudence.* Kent Town, SA: Wakefield Press.

Alexander, S. 2014. 'A critique of techno-optimism: Efficiency without sufficiency is lost'. *MSSI Working Paper* (WP 1/14): 1-21.

Alexander, S. and Rutherford, J. 2014. 'The deep green alternative: Debating strategies of transition'. *Simplicity Institute Report* 14a: 1-24.

Alexander, S. and Ussher, S. 2012. 'The voluntary simplicity movement: A multi-national survey analysis in theoretical context'. *Journal of Consumer Culture* 12(1): 66-88.

Anderson, K. 2013. 'Avoiding dangerous climate change demands de-growth strategies from wealthier nations'. Available at: http://kevinanderson.info/blog/avoiding-dangerous-climate-change-demands-de-growth-strategies-from-wealthier-nations/ [accessed 25 November 2013].

Arrow, Kenneth *et al.* 2004. 'Are we consuming too much?' *Journal of Economic Perspectives* 18(3): 147.

Barry, J. 2012. *The politics of actually existing unsustainability: Human flourishing in a climate changed, carbon constrained world.* Oxford: Oxford University Press.

Baykan, B. 2007. 'From limits to growth to de-growth within French green politics'. *Environmental Politics* 513.

Becker, G. 1962. 'Irrational behavior and economic theory'. *Journal of Political Economy* 70(1): 1-13.

Beckerman, W. 2002. *A poverty of reason: Sustainable development and economic growth.* Oakland: Independent Institute.

Blanchflower, D. and Oswald, A. 2004. 'Well-being over time in Britain and the USA'. *The Journal of Public Economics* 88:1359.

Canterbury, E.R. 2003 (3rd edn). *The making of economics: The foundation.* Singapore: World Scientific Publishing.

Center for the Advancement of Steady State Economy (CASSE), 2011. 'Enough is Enough'. *Proceedings of the Steady State Economy Conference.* Available at: http://steadystate.org/enough-is-enough/ [accessed 29 June 2011].

Cobb, C., Halstead, T., and Rowe, J. 1995. 'If GDP is up, why is America down?'. *The Atlantic Monthly* October, 1.

Clarke, A. and Oswald, A. 1994. 'Unhappiness and unemployment'. *Economic Journal* 104(424): 648-659.

Collins, R. 2000. *More: The politics of economic growth in post-war America.* Oxford: Oxford University Press.

Daly, H. 1999. 'Uneconomic growth in theory and fact', in *The First Annual Feasta Lecture* (16 April 1999). Available at: http://www.feasta.org/documents/feastareview/daly.htm [accessed 10 April 2010].

Daly, H. and Farley, J. 2004. *Ecological economics: Principles and applications.* Washington: Island Press.

Deaton, 2008. 'Income, health, and well-being around the world: Evidence from the Gallup World Poll'. *Journal of Economic Perspectives* 22(2): 53.

De Graaf, J. 2009. 'Political prescriptions', in S. Alexander (ed.).

Voluntary Simplicity: The Poetic Alternative to Consumer Culture. Whanganui: Stead and Daughters: 271-282.

Diener, E. and Seligman, M. 2004. 'Beyond money: Toward an economy of well-being'. *Psychological Science in the Public Interest* 5:1-31.

Diener, E., Diener, M., and Diener, C. 2009. 'Factors predicting the subjective well-being of nations', in *Culture and Well-Being: The Collected Works of Ed Diener*. London: Springer.

Diener, E., Helliwell, J., and Kahneman, D. 2010. *International differences in well-being*. Oxford; New York: Oxford University Press.

Di Tella, R. and MacCulloch, R. 2010. 'Happiness adaptation to income beyond "Basic Needs"', in E. Diener, J. Helliwell and D. Kahneman (eds). 2010. *International differences in well-being*, Oxford; New York: Oxford University Press: 217-246.

Easterlin, R. 1974. 'Does economic growth improve the human lot?', in P. David and M. Reder (eds). *Nations and households in economic growth: Essays in honor of Moses Abramovitz*. New York: Academic Press.

Easterlin, R. 1995. 'Will raising the incomes of all increase the happiness of all?'. *Journal of Economic Behaviour & Organization*, 27: 35-47.

Easterlin, R. 2013. 'Happiness and economic growth: The evidence'. Discussion Paper, No. 7187, January 2013: 1-30.

Easterlin, R. and Angelescu, L. 2010. 'Happiness and growth the world over: Time series evidence on the happiness – Income paradox', in H. Hinte and K. Zimmerman (eds). *Happiness, Growth and the Life Cycle*. Oxford: Oxford University Press.

Fournier, V. 2008. 'Escaping the economy: The politics of degrowth'. *International Journal of Sociology and International Research* 28: 528-545.

Frank, R. 2008. 'Should public policy respond to positional externalities'. *Journal of Public Economics* 92, 1777.

Friedman, M. 2002. *Capitalism and freedom*. Chicago: University of Chicago Press.

Global Footprint Network. 2013. Reports available at: http://www.footprintnetwork.org/en/index.php/GFN/ (accessed 3 September 2013).

Hamilton, C. 2003. *Growth fetish*. Crows Nest, NSW: Allen & Unwin.

Heinberg, R. 2011. *The end of growth: Adapting to our new economic reality*. Gabriola Island: New Society Publishers.

Helliwell, J., Layard, R., and Sachs, J. (eds). 2012. *World happiness report 2012*. New York: Sustainable Development Solutions Network.

Helliwell, J., Layard, R., and Sachs, J. (eds). 2013. *World happiness report 2013*. New York: Sustainable Development Solutions Network.

Hirsch, F. 1976. *Social limits to growth*. Cambridge, Mass: Harvard University Press.

Hirsch, R. *et al.* 2010. *The impending world energy mess.* Burlington: Apoge Prime.

Holm, S.-O. and Englund, G. 2009. 'Increased ecoefficiency and gross rebound effect: Evidence from USA and six European countries 1960-2002'. *Ecological Economics* 68: 879-887.

Hopkins, R. 2008. *The transition handbook: From oil dependency to local resilience*. Totnes, Devon: Green Books.

Inglehart, R. 1996. 'The diminishing marginal utility of economic growth'. *Critical Review,* 10, 509.

Intergovernmental Panel on Climate Change (IPCC), 2013. *Climate Change 2013: The Physical Science Basis (Fifth Assessment Report)*. Available at: 'http://www.ipcc.ch/report/ar5/wg1/#. Uk6k-CjqMRw (accessed 4 October 2013).

Jackson, T. 2002. Quality of life, sustainability, and economic growth', in T. Fitzpatrick and M. Cahill (eds). *Environment and welfare: Towards a Green social policy*. Basingstoke: Palgrave Macmillan: 97-116.

Jackson, T. 2009. *Prosperity without growth: Economics for a finite planet*. London: Earthscan.

Kallis, G. 2011. 'In defence of degrowth'. *Ecological Economics* 70, 873.

Kasser, T. 2002. *The high price of materialism*. Cambridge, MA: MIT Press.

Keynes, J.M. 1963. *Essays in persuasion*. New York: Norton.

Klare, M. 2012. *The race for what's left: The global scramble for the world's last resources*. New York: Picador.

Kubiszewski, I., Costanza, R., Franco, C., Lawn, P., Talberth, J., Jackson, T., and Aylmer, C. 2013. 'Beyond GDP: Measuring and achieving global genuine progress'. *Ecological Economics* 93: 57-68.

Lane, R. 2000. *The loss of happiness in market democracies*. New Haven: Yale University Press.

Latouche, S. 2009. *Farewell to growth*. Cambridge, UK: Polity Press.

Latouche, S. 2014. 'Essays on frugal abundance (1 of 4) – Degrowth: misunderstandings and controversies'. *Simplicity Institute Report* 14c: 1-22.

Layard, R. 2005. *Happiness: Lessons from a new science*. New York: Penguin Press.

Layard, R., Mayraz, G., and Nickell, S. 2008. 'The marginal utility of income'. *Journal of Public Economics* 92: 1846-1857.

Layard, R. *et al.* 2010. 'Does relative income matter? Are the critics right?', in E. Diener, J. Helliwell, and D. Kahneman (eds). *International differences in well-being.* Oxford, New York: Oxford University Press.

Lawn, P. 2005. 'An assessment of the valuation methods used to calculate the Index of Sustainable Economic Welfare (ISEW), Genuine Progress Indicator (GPI), and Sustainable Net Benefit Index (SNBI)'. *Environment, Development, and Sustainability* 2: 185-208.

Lawn, P. 2008. *Degrowth as a solution to uneconomic growth.* Available at: http://events.it-sudparis.eu/degrowthconference/themes/1First%20panels/Backgrounds/Lawn%20P%20Degrowth%20Paris%20april%202008%20abstract.pdf [accessed 10 April 2010].

Lawn, P. and Clarke, M. 2010. 'The end of economic growth? A contracting threshold hypothesis'. *Ecological Economics* 69: 2213.

Lovins, A. 1998. *Factor four: Doubling wealth – halving resource use.* London: Earthscan.

Mankiw, N. 2008. *The principles of economics (5th edn).* Mason, OH: South-Western.

Marshall, A. 1997 [1890]. *Principles of economics.* New York: Prometheus.

Max-Neef, M. 1995. 'Economic growth and quality of life: A threshold hypothesis'. *Ecological Economics* 15(2): 115.

Meadows, D., Randers, J., and Meadows, D. 2004. *Limits to growth: The 30-year update.* White River Junction, Vt., Chelsea Green Publishing.

Millennium Ecosystem Assessment, 2005. Available at: http://www.millenniumassessment.org/en/index.aspx [accessed 30 April 2011].

New Economics Foundation, 2010. *21 hours: Why a 21-hour work week can help us all flourish in the 21st century.* Available at: www.neweconomics.org [accessed 10 May 2011].

Pearce, J. 2008. 'Thermodynamic limitations to nuclear energy deployment as a greenhouse gas mitigation technology'. *International Journal of Nuclear Governance, Economy and Ecology* 2(1): 113-130.

Pickett, K. and Wilkinson, R. 2010. *The Spirit Level: Why greater equality makes societies stronger.* London: Penguin.

Pigou, A.C. 1920. *The economics of welfare.* London: Macmillan.

Pizzigati, S. 2004. *Greed and good: Understanding and overcoming the inequality that limits our lives.* New York: Apex Press.

Polimeni, J. *et al.* 2009. *The myth of resource efficiency: The Jevons paradox*. London: Earthscan.

Posner, R. 1986 (3rd edn). *Economic analysis of law*. Boston: Little Brown.

Purdey, S. 2010. *Economic growth, the environment, and international relations: The growth paradigm*. New York: Routledge.

Proceedings of Second international conference on degrowth, 2011. Available at: http://www.degrowth.org/Proceedings-new.122.o.html [accessed 29 June 2011].

Robinson, T. 2009. *Work, leisure, and the environment: The vicious circle of overwork and overconsumption*. Cheltenham: Edward Elgar Publishing.

Sarkar, S. 1999. *Eco-socialism or eco-capitalism: A critical analysis of humanity's fundamental choices*. London: Zed books.

Schneider, F., Kallis, G., and Martinez-Alier, J. 2010. 'Crisis or opportunity? Economic degrowth for social equity and ecological sustainability'. *J Clean Prod*. 18(6): 511-518.

Smith, R. 2010. 'Beyond growth or beyond capitalism'. *Real-World Economics Review* 53: 28-42.

Stevenson, B. and Wolfers, J. 2008. 'Economic growth and subjective well-being: Reassessing the Easterlin paradox'. *Brookings Papers on Economic Activity*: 1.

Stiglitz, J., Sen, A., and Fitoussi, J.P. 2010. *Mis-measuring our lives: Why GDP doesn't add up*. New York: The New Press.

Trainer, T. 2010a. *The transition to a sustainable and just world*. Envirobook, Sydney.

Trainer, T. 2011. 'The radical implications of zero growth economy'. *Real World Economics Review* 57: 71-82.

Trainer, T. 2012. 'De-growth: Do you realise what it means'. *Futures* 44: 590-599.

Trainer, T. 2013a. 'Can Europe run on renewable energy? A negative case'. *Energy Policy* 63: 845-850.

Trainer, T. 2013b. 'Can the world run on renewable energy'. *Humanomics* 29(2): 88-104.

Turner, G. 2012. 'Are we on the cusp of collapse? Updated comparison of *The Limits to Growth* with historical data'. *Gaia* 21(2): 116-124.

United Nations Development Program (UNDP), 2007/8. *Human development report*. Available at: http://hdr.undp.org/en/reports/global/hdr2007-2008/ [accessed 30 April 2011].

United Nations Department of Social and Economic Affairs (UNDSEA). 2012. *World Population Prospects: The 2012 Revision*. Available at: http://esa.un.org/wpp/ (accessed 10 September 2013).

Victor, P. 2008. *Managing without growth: Slower by design, not disaster*. Cheltenham: Edward Elgar Publishing.

Victor, P. 2011. 'Growth, degrowth, and climate change: A scenario analysis'. *Ecological Economics* 84: 206-212.

Victor, P. and Rosenbluth, G. 2007. 'Managing without growth'. *Ecological Economics* 61(2-3): 492.

Wackernagel, M. 2002. 'Tracking the ecological overshoot of the human economy'. *Proceedings of the National Academy of Sciences of the United States of America*, 99: 9266-9271.

Woodward, D. and Simms, A. 2006. *Growth isn't working: The uneven distribution of benefits and costs from economic growth*. London: New Economics Foundation.

World Bank. 2009. *World development indicators*. Available at http://data.worldbank.org/indicator [accessed at 29 June 2011].

4

DEGROWTH IMPLIES VOLUNTARY SIMPLICITY

Overcoming barriers to sustainable consumption

Our country is set up structurally to oppose voluntary simplicity.
— Michael Jacobson[6]

1. Introduction

The global economy is exceeding the sustainable carrying capacity of the planet, and it has been for some time (Global Footprint Network, 2012; Millennium Ecosystem Assessment, 2005). This 'ecological overshoot' is being driven by the escalation and expansion of Western-style consumer lifestyles, which are highly resource and energy intensive. It is now commonplace to acknowledge that humankind would need four or five planets if North American lifestyles were universalised (e.g., Scott, 2009: 2). With the global population expected to reach nine billion by mid-century, it is increasingly clear that these high consumption lifestyles are unsustainable and certainly not universalisable. The science of climate change, furthermore, implies that we must decarbonise consumer lifestyles without delay (IPCC, 2013; Hansen, 2011), and the spectre of 'peak oil' suggests that the supply of cheap petroleum upon which consumer societies and their growth-orientated economies are based, may be coming to an end (Murphy, 2014; Heinberg, 2011). All this means that 'business as usual' is

---

[6] Jacobson is referring here to the US, however this chapter is framed by the assumption that his comment applies, to varying degrees, to all developed nations (and in many ways to developing nations also).

simply not an option (Turner, 2012), and it may well be that the persistent delays in responding to these serious issues means that it is now too late to avoid some form of 'great disruption' to life as we know it (Gilding, 2011). What makes this admittedly gloomy situation even more troubling is that empirical research shows that many of those who have attained the Western-style consumerist ideal may not be finding such lifestyles all that fulfilling (Lane, 2000; Alexander, 2012a). Technological progress and economic growth, it would seem, cannot solve all our problems or answer for us the question of how we ought to live. For these reasons, among others, it has never been more urgent to rethink contemporary practices of consumption.

But the news is not all grim. The fact that many in the global consumer class are not finding high consumption lifestyles particularly fulfilling raises the tantalising possibility that people could *increase* their quality of life by voluntarily *reducing* their material and energy consumption. This is sometimes called the 'double dividend' of sustainable consumption (Jackson, 2005), for the reason that 'simpler' lifestyles of reduced consumption can benefit the planet while also being in the immediate and long-term self-interest of the individual (Brown and Kasser, 2005). Exchanging some superfluous consumption for more free time is one path to this 'double dividend'. Reducing superfluous consumption can also open up space for a 'triple' or even 'quadruple' dividend, on the grounds that low-consumption lifestyles of voluntary simplicity have the potential to generate communitarian or humanitarian benefits too (e.g., by leaving more resources for others in greater need). It has even been suggested that lifestyles of voluntary simplicity, focusing as they do on non-materialistic forms of meaning and fulfilment, might provide something of an antidote to the spiritual malaise that seemingly inflicts many people within materialistic cultures today (Alexander, 2011a; Myers, 2000). But if indeed there are multiple dividends to sustainable consumption, including self-interested ones, why does the global consumer class consume so much? Are we not free to step out of the rat race and simply consume less?

Unfortunately, things are not that simple. Our lifestyle decisions, especially our consumption decisions, are not made in a vacuum. Instead, they are made within social, economic, and political structures of constraint, and those structures make some lifestyle decisions easy or necessary and other lifestyle decisions difficult or impossible. Change the social, economic, and political structures, however, and different consumption practices would or could emerge. With a practical focus, this chapter seeks to develop some of the theoretical work that has already been done in this area

(Jackson and Papathanasopoulou, 2008; Jackson, 2003; Sanne, 2002; Ropke, 1999). More specifically, this chapter examines the extent to which people in consumer societies are 'locked in' to high consumption, energy-intensive lifestyles, and it explores ways that structural changes could facilitate a societal transition to practices of more sustainable consumption.

This subject should be of interest to all those broadly engaged in work on sustainability, for the reasons outlined in the opening paragraph. But it should be of particular interest to those who have been convinced that the richest nations, if indeed they are serious about realising a sustainable world, ought to be initiating a degrowth process of planned economic contraction, with the aim of moving toward a socially desirable, ecologically sustainable, steady state economy (Kallis, 2011, Alexander, 2012b). It barely needs stating that a degrowth or steady state economy will never emerge voluntarily within societies that are generally comprised of individuals seeking ever-higher levels of income and consumption. It follows that any transition to such an economy will depend upon people in those societies transitioning away from consumer lifestyles and embracing lifestyles of reduced and restrained consumption. This may seem like an unlikely cultural revolution, and it is, but if it is a *necessary cultural precondition* to the emergence of a degrowth or steady state economy, then it is an issue of critical importance that ought to be given due attention. In short, a macroeconomics of degrowth implies lifestyles of voluntary simplicity, in much the same way as a macroeconomics of limitless growth implies lifestyles of insatiable consumption. If it is the case, however, that contemporary consumer societies are structured in such a way to oppose lifestyles of voluntary simplicity, then it is important that those structures are exposed and challenged. Put otherwise, we must understand how our societies function to lock people into high consumption lifestyles and then set about changing those structures to better facilitate practices of sustainable consumption. Structural change will not be enough, on its own, of course; there also needs to be a shift in values (Murtaza, 2011). However, it is tragic to think that there are some people living consumer lifestyles today who genuinely want to consume more sustainably, but who find it difficult or impossible, for structural reasons, to actually live lives of voluntary simplicity and put those values fully into practice. It is more tragic still if those consumerist structures are inhibiting people from increasing their quality of life through reduced consumption. This chapter seeks to deepen the understanding of the relationship between consumer behaviour and the structures which shape that behaviour, in the hope that the existing barriers to sustainable consumption can be overcome.

2. The Production Angle vs. the Consumption Angle

Before commencing the primary analysis it is worth outlining briefly how the present approach to consumption differs, in critical respects, from conventional, market-based analyses. In market economies, solutions to environmental, economic, and social problems are typically viewed from what has been called the 'production angle' (Princen *et al.*, 2002). This perspective assumes that if the full costs of production were internalised to the productive process, an optimal number of various goods and services would be produced and consumed. According to this view, which has its roots in neoclassical economics, social utility will be maximised when markets are free and the price of commodities are correct, because then rational consumers can be left alone in the marketplace to satisfy their private preferences in an optimal way, within the confines of a given income (Samuelson, 1938). Given these assumptions, all market activity is utility maximising, because rational economic agents would only trade in a free market if it were in their own best interests – otherwise why would they trade? Since it is assumed that market activity is in the interests of both seller and purchaser, it follows that market activity – including market consumption – should be maximised. If the overconsumption of certain commodities is causing problems of some sort, however, this must be because the costs of production are not fully internalised to the productive process, leading to artificially cheap commodities and thus their overconsumption. Governments should respond to such problems (or 'negative externalities') by internalising them, and then leave markets alone to do their work. One central implication of the 'production angle' is that governments do not need to concern themselves with how people consume, because it is assumed that human beings are rational consumers who know best how to maximise their own wellbeing in the market. That is, it is assumed that consumers are 'sovereign', such that it would be inappropriate for governments to try to shape, intervene, or regulate consumption behaviour. In recent decades, this has been the dominant view both in economics and politics (Hamilton, 2003).

This neoclassical 'production angle' is not without its insights, and governments in market societies could do much to create the conditions necessary for markets to price commodities more comprehensively. But as contemporary philosophers of language tell us, every conceptual framework conceals as it reveals, and neoclassicism is certainly no exception. In fact, as the following sections show, the production angle has several significant blind spots, particularly with respect to understanding consumption. An alternative perspective – what has been called the 'consumption angle' (Princen *et al.*, 2002) – is beginning to receive more attention, and rightly so, because it exposes some of those blind spots in illuminating ways. In ways that will be explained, this alternative perspective rejects the assumption that getting prices right is the best or only response to today's myriad environmental, economic, and social challenges, and it rejects the assumption that consumer preferences are simply 'given' and beyond critical evaluation. By taking this position the consumption angle reveals how problems and solutions look very different when they are viewed from a perspective that does not marginalise consumption but places it at the centre of analysis. This chapter seeks to develop the consumption angle by examining the ways that social, economic, and political structures can 'lock' people into high consumption, energy-intensive lifestyles even when they desire a 'simpler life' of reduced or restrained consumption. This analytical approach can be contrasted with the production angle, not because it assumes that governments should be forcing alternative lifestyles on people, but because it recognises that governments are not neutral bystanders when it comes to consumption but are implicated always and necessarily in creating the structures that shape and guide consumer behaviour.

3. Structure and Simplicity: Exposing and Transcending Consumer 'Lock-In'

The remainder of this chapter explores, with a practical focus, some of the most important areas where consumer behaviour is shaped by structures of constraint, and it also outlines (in a preliminary way) how those structures could be changed to facilitate the transition to more sustainable practices of consumption. This critical examination begins by considering the largest multi-national survey analysis of the Voluntary Simplicity Movement (Alexander and Ussher, 2012), for this study (hereafter 'the survey') provides a firm empirical basis for understanding what barriers people face when trying to live 'simpler' lives of reduced or restrained consumption. The survey, which has been completed by more than 2,000 participants in the Voluntary Simplicity Movement, was comprised of 52 questions, one of which asked participants what is the *greatest* obstacle they face when trying to live 'simpler' lives of reduced or restrained consumption. Participants were provided with six categories and then asked to select the one that best signified their *greatest* obstacle. The categories provided were: (1) suitable transport; (2) suitable employment; (3) insufficient product information; (4) resisting consumer temptations; (5) suitable social activities; and (6) suitable housing. If participants felt those options did not reflect what they considered their greatest obstacle, then they were able to submit their alternative answer in a textbox labelled 'other'. Since only 12% answered 'other', it can be tentatively inferred that the six obstacles suggested by the survey quite accurately expose some of the greatest challenges people face when trying to live simply. This empirical finding provides some helpful guidance to those seeking to understand and dismantle the obstacles people face when trying to live more simply, and the following discussion uses the six obstacles outlined in the survey to structure the analysis. This empirically grounded approach seems particularly important given that some of the largest existing studies on policies for sustainable consumption (e.g., OECD, 2008) have failed to address some of the most important obstacles to sustainable consumption, such as transport, working hours, and housing.

3.1 *Lack of suitable transport options as an obstacle to sustainable consumption*

The question of transport provides one of the clearest examples of how structure can 'lock' people into high-impact, energy-intensive consumption. Riding bicycles and taking public transport are widely regarded as important characteristics of more sustainable consumption in transport. It is probable that simply reducing the distances and regularity of travel will also be a requirement (Moriarty and Honnery, 2008). This is primarily because driving and flying are extremely carbon-intensive modes of transportation, and climate change and peak oil both indicate that transport practices dominated by driving and flying are unsustainable in anything like their current forms. It is very likely, of course, that there will always be cars on the roads and planes in the air, but these forms of transport are likely to become much less common, and much more expensive, if the world transitions to a post-carbon future over coming decades. In short, lifestyles of sustainable consumption require people to make different decisions when 'consuming' transport, especially with respect to driving cars.

The fact is, however, escaping car culture is very difficult or impossible for many people in consumer societies today, as the survey results imply. There are undoubtedly cases where people have the option to ride their bikes to work or to take public transport, but for one reason or another choose to drive. However, there are also people who would like to cycle to work or take public transport, but for structural reasons beyond their immediate control they are unable to do so. For example, someone may be convinced of the ecological problems caused by petroleum-based driving, but in the absence of safe bike lanes or accessible public transport, this person may find themselves driving to work for lack of any other option. This exemplifies perfectly the background thesis being explored in this chapter, for it shows how 'structure' influences consumption behaviour by making some transport choices easy or necessary and other options difficult or impossible. If those structures were different, however – say, if governments decided to invest heavily in bike lanes and public transport – this would 'unlock' many people from their dependence on driving and allow them to engage in more sustainable modes of transport. Driving, therefore, is not just a matter of 'private preference'. By not investing sufficiently in sustainable transport infrastructure, governments are implicated in the structures that promote unsustainable consumption of transport.

Note how this analysis exposes how differently the issue of sustainable transport looks when viewed from the 'production angle' compared to when it is viewed from the 'consumption angle'. From the production angle, if the overconsumption of petroleum (e.g., from driving too much) is causing negative externalities (e.g., climate change, pollution, etc.), then to maximise social utility governments should attempt to internalise the costs of those externalities. This would make the production of petrol more expensive and those increased costs would be passed onto consumers. Through market forces that price increase would presumably lead to reductions in driving, until an 'optimal' amount of driving is achieved. From the consumption angle, however, the aim is not simply to internalise externalities (although that may be part of the solution). Rather, the consumption angle shows that the way people consume transport is partly a function of the structures within which their consumption decisions are made, so by changing those structures, different consumption patterns would or could emerge. Instead of merely aiming to price petrol correctly, therefore, the consumption angle suggests that governments should also try to promote alternatives to damaging consumption, such as investing heavily in sustainable infrastructure in order to dismantle existing barriers to sustainable transport consumption.

Of course, even if there were safe bike lanes and accessible public transport, some people would still choose to drive. But that is a different 'value-focused' or behavioural issue which cannot be addressed here. There is also the unexplored question of broader structural issues beyond those considered above which may also affect consumption of transport. For example, sprawling urban landscapes as well as globalised trade encourage more travel rather than less, so another way governments can promote structures of sustainable transport is to promote higher density living and more localised economies. There is also the socio-cultural structures that might lock people into driving private cars – for example, car pooling is an available option for suburban communities, but people tend to choose private driving not because they are physically locked into doing so, but because they live in cultures that value private transport rather than communal alternatives (such as car pooling or public transport). If there were a change in cultural attitudes toward car pooling, however, this would make it easier even for people in poorly designed suburbs to escape privatised transport.

For present purposes the point has been made sufficiently that external 'structures' affect consumption patterns in transport. If people are expected to consume transport sustainably, therefore, governments and communities must help create social and economic infrastructures that unchain people from carbon-intensive travel. It is not clear, however, that many governments have made this commitment in any serious way; nor is it clear that governments are receiving much pressure to do so from the cultural sphere.

3.2 Lack of suitable employment options as an obstacle to sustainable consumption

Neoclassical economic theory, upon which the production angle is based, posits that actors in market economies are free to maximise their happiness by selling as much or as little of their time as they want (Kimmel and Hoffman, 2002). The consumption angle being unpacked in this chapter calls that assumption into question. Currently, it turns out, there are structural biases in many advanced capitalist societies that function to promote overwork (i.e., working hours that are not 'optimal' or 'utility maximising'), such as laws that treat the 40-hour work week as 'standard' or which exclude part-time workers from many of the non-pecuniary benefits enjoyed by those who work full-time (Robinson, 2007). The effect of these structural biases is essentially to 'lock' many people into longer working hours than they want or need, which gives rise to cultures that tend to over-consume resources and under-consume leisure. This might lead to higher income and consumption per capita, but at the cost of quality of life and planetary health (Hayden, 1999).

This is at least part of the reason why people trying to reduce their consumption highlight 'suitable employment' as their greatest obstacle, as indicated by the results of the 'simple living' survey discussed earlier. Fifty-six percent of participants in that survey reported that if they could, they would reduce their current paid working hours and accept a proportionate reduction in income. This is not, however, a problem faced only by people who identify with the Voluntary Simplicity Movement. It is a problem endemic to many modern market societies and is a significant structural barrier inhibiting the transition to practices of sustainable consumption. For example, 28.7% of full-time workers in Australia work 50 hours per week or more; and of those workers, 46% claim they would prefer to work fewer hours, accepting a drop in pay (Australian Conservation Foundation, 2010: 11). This consumer 'lock-in' demands a political response.

One way to overcome this barrier would be to introduce a shorter 'standard' work week, such as the 35-hour work week that exists (to a diminishing extent) in France, or some more radical policy such as the 21-hour work week proposed by the New Economics Foundation (2010). Another option would be to ensure that part-time workers enjoy the same non-pecuniary benefits that full-time workers receive (on a pro-rata basis). These are policy reforms that deserve serious attention. Perhaps more importantly still, however, is the policy response that has taken hold in Holland in the form of the *Hours Adjustment Act 2000*. This path-breaking act allows employees to reduce their hours to part-time simply by asking their employers. As explained by leading work reductionist John de Graaf (2009: 274):

> Unless there is a clear hardship for the firm – something shown in less than 5% of cases – the employer must grant the reduction in hours. Workers keep the same hourly salary, full health-care, and pro-rata additional benefits like vacation time and pensions. This law, in the most concrete terms, allows workers to trade money for time, without losing their jobs or healthcare. As a result, more than a third of Dutch employees work part-time, the highest ration in the world.

This policy exemplifies one means of dismantling the structural 'lock-in' outlined above, for it opens the door to a society in which consumption is reduced in exchange for more free time. Some may object that industrial relations policies such as this will not maximise GDP per capita, but that is to miss the point. The point of an economy, after all, should be to promote quality of life for all, and if a smaller economy promotes quality of life by providing increased leisure but less income and consumption, then a smaller economy is the most economically rational option to choose. In a word, this is the rationality of degrowth (Latouche, 2009), and in many ways it would also seem to be implicit to a politics of voluntary simplicity (Alexander, 2011b).[7]

It should also be pointed out again that 'lock-in' need not just be a matter of law or infrastructure. Culture itself can create social structures that constrain or enable ways of living. For example, in many developed nations today a culture of overwork has developed, in which success in life is linked closely to one's working life. This can make it difficult for people to work less, if doing so makes them feel 'unsuccessful' according to dominant conceptions of 'success'. But if a culture came to celebrate different notions of success, then it would be easier for people to break free from the work-and-spend cycle, reduce working hours, and pursue alternative, lower-consumption lifestyles.

3.3 *Insufficient product information as an obstacle to sustainable consumption*

Conscientious or 'ethical' consumption can be understood as the practice of choosing to purchase (or not purchase) commodities on account of their ecological or social justice features, even if this means paying more for them (Lewis and Potter, 2010; Shaw and Newholm, 2002). While it is unlikely that conscientious consumption on its own could bring about the changes needed to create a just and sustainable society, this form of consumption may well need to play a significant role in such a transition (Micheletti, 2010). Accordingly, it can be argued that consumers have a duty to 'vote with their dollars', whenever possible, especially when it seems reasonably clear that commodities are not priced correctly (e.g., when prices do not include negative ecological externalities).

The importance of conscientious consumption lies in the fact that consuming this or that product sends a message, consciously or unconsciously, to the market (and to culture more broadly), affirming the product's origins, process of manufacture, and social and ecological consequences. This means that if people consume conscientiously, for the purpose of supporting only ecologically responsible and socially just businesses, producers will have an immediate economic incentive to produce differently, because

---

[7] Politicising voluntary simplicity might strike some as paradoxical, in the sense that anything mandated by law does not sound very 'voluntary'. But the position being developed herein does not suggest that 'simple living' should be *imposed* on people, but that simplicity, rather than consumerism, should be systematically privileged, supported, and encouraged when making decisions about how to structure a society (especially overconsuming societies).

producers want to produce what sells. In this way, capitalism has a sophisticated market mechanism already set up to deal with changes in consumer demands, and taken to its extreme, this mechanism has the potential to significantly change the nature of the global economy. If consumers mobilised *en masse*, for example, and boycotted all environmentally unsustainable products, global capitalism could be transformed quickly and significantly, for how we spend our money is how we vote on what exists in the world (Dominguez and Robin, 1999).

Nevertheless, conscientious consumption, like ordinary consumption, does not take place in a vacuum. Consuming conscientiously requires access to the information needed to make informed decisions, and the degree to which this information is provided to consumers can be understood as a structural issue that affects the way people consume or are able to consume. For example, suppose a person wants to buy locally grown and/or organic fruit, but the origin or farming procedures of the fruit is not stated anywhere on the label. In such circumstances, purchasing local and organic fruit is structurally difficult or impossible, irrespective of one's value system. Change the structure of this situation, however – say, by making it mandatory to label products in certain ways – and it becomes easier to purchase ethically on account of the information provided. It would also make it easier for people to 'boycott' products that they feel are unethical, and this is the flip side of the same coin. In other words, part of what it means to consume sustainably is to 'vote with your money', and in practice this means supporting businesses that produce ethically, and not supporting businesses that do not produce ethically.

The results from the 'simple living' survey, however, show that a significant proportion of people who are trying to consume more sustainably state that their greatest obstacle in this regard is 'insufficient product information'. It would seem, therefore, that inadequate product labelling is an important structural barrier in the way of more sustainable consumption practices, and one that ought to be addressed. Voluntary labelling, which results when companies want to distinguish their products from others for self-interested reasons, is one way for this to arise. Organic farmers might voluntarily label their produce 'organic', for example, knowing that some people only want to purchase organic food. 'Fair-trade' is another labelling practice that attempts to provide consumers with more confidence that the products they are purchasing are produced ethically. Another strategy is mandatory labelling, which involves state regulation of what is included on a product's label (e.g., a government might require farmers to declare whether eggs are free range or not, and provide minimum standards for this categorisation). Providing adequate and accurate information on product labels, whether mandatory or voluntary, gives consumers the option of purchasing ethically or not.

Obviously it is difficult to know where to draw the line here, since providing information on labels sometimes can be an expensive and controversial undertaking, and if the costs of labelling products in accordance with the mandatory standards are too high, this may stifle economic activity, whether ethical or unethical. But for present purposes the point is simply that conscientious consumption is not just about *wanting* to consume ethically; it is also about whether one is *able* to consume ethically, and this partly depends on the nature of the structures within which consumption takes place. Different structures make it easier or more difficult to consume ethically, and governments are partly responsible for deciding what those structures should be. While there is already some regulation of product labelling, the results of the simple living survey suggest that better and more extensive product labelling is one means of further unlocking people from structures that currently inhibit more sustainable practices of consumption.

3.4 *Exposure to consumer temptations as an obstacle to sustainable consumption*

Another way to provide consumers with information is through advertising, but this method is very much a double-edged sword. On the one hand, it is important to recognise that advertising has an important role to play providing people with information about products that could increase their wellbeing. Potentially, at least, advertising can even be important in promoting sustainable consumption (Oates *et al.*, 2008). For example, it is no good developing some new product (e.g., solar panels) if the public does not know the product exists. Therefore, the marketing of genuinely ecologically sustainable products is undeniably a good thing, on the grounds that consumers need sufficient information to make informed decisions.

On the other hand, advertising has several well-known dark sides (e.g., PIRC, 2011). As noted earlier, the paradigm of neoclassical economics assumes that human beings are rational consumers who spend their money in ways that best satisfy their 'private preferences'. But many sociologists and psychologists have levelled a sustained and devastating critique of this assumption (e.g., Brulle and Young, 2007; Kasser, 2002). They show that people do not always spend their money in ways that contribute to their wellbeing, and they also show that consumer desires are not simply 'given' in advance, but can actually be shaped by external forces, norms, or structures in society, including advertising. Advertising, that is, does not merely provide us with information. It also actively shapes our desires to some extent, often in insidious ways, and this should not really surprise us. After all, the underlying message of every advertisement is 'your life will be better if you purchase this product', and given the ubiquity of advertising in modern life, it is understandable why so many people come to think that more consumption is what is needed to increase happiness. This is especially so when advertisements deliberately play on our emotions and insecurities, rather than merely providing us with product information in impartial or objective ways. Many of the world's best psychologists do not work in universities or clinics anymore, but instead are hired by marketing agencies to apply their extremely sophisticated understandings of human psychology for the purpose of manipulating people into purchasing this or that product, without much or any concern being given to whether people need it. Not only does advertising implicitly or explicitly urge people to 'consume, consume, consume', it also has the potential to create artificial desires in people for products that they did not even know existed and which may not contribute to wellbeing in any discernable way. Accordingly, the neoclassical notion that people are purely 'rational' consumers who are informed by advertising but otherwise uninfluenced by it is scarcely credible. The results of the simple living survey provide some further evidence for this, in that a significant proportion of participants noted that 'resisting consumer temptations' was their greatest obstacle to reducing and restraining their consumption.

Once again, this can be understood to be a structural issue, further emphasising the notion that our consumption decisions are always shaped by context. Currently, people in consumer societies can be exposed to as many as 3,000 advertisements every day (de Graaf *et al.*, 2005: 165), in increasingly subtle and subliminal ways, and this relentless exposure undoubtedly affects the way people consume. Advertising is especially pernicious when directed at children (Schor, 2004). Change the nature and extent of people's exposure to advertising, however – which is a structural issue for which governments are partly responsible – and different consumption habits, and attitudes toward consumption, would result. A politics of sustainable consumption, therefore, implies rethinking the nature and extent of advertising.

One example of a progressive politics of advertising can be seen in the Brazilian city of São Paulo – the world's fourth largest city – which has implemented a ban on virtually all outdoor advertising, including advertising on billboards, neon signs, buses, trucks, and taxis. This 'Clean City Law', which came into effect in 2007, has eliminated approximately 15,000 billboards (Worldwatch Institute, 2007), creating a new social structure and a new urban aesthetic within which the city's inhabitants live. Other ways to reform advertising structures include banning advertising to children; regulating where, when, and how much advertising people are exposed to; and regulating the nature of advertising more strictly to promote more socially and ecologically beneficial messages. These options all raise various issues that require more sustained and critical attention, but the present point is simply that governments are partly responsible for the nature and extent to which people are exposed to advertising. Advertising policies create structures that either support a transition to practices of sustainable consumption or inhibit that transition. Given that 'resisting consumer temptations' has been highlighted as one the greatest obstacles faced when transitioning to lifestyles of reduced and restrained consumption, it would seem that increased regulation of advertising is one way to free people from some of the structural pressures that encourage high consumption lifestyles.

3.5 *Suitable social activities as an obstacle to sustainable consumption*

The complex relationship between consumption and structure is highlighted again when we consider why some people (as evidenced by the survey results) find socialising or social activity to be their greatest obstacle to sustainable consumption. As outlined below, human beings are not isolated and atomistic individuals whose desires are independent from those around them. Rather, anthropologists, sociologists, and psychologists have shown very clearly that human desires are shaped by the culture and social infrastructure within which they live. The complexities of this subject cannot be fully unpacked here, but two points should suffice to expose further how external structural issues often function to shape consumption habits in ways that are not always within the control of those consuming.

The first point concerns how the social meaning of consumption behaviour is culturally relative. Anthropologists have probably done the most to show that commodities play a role in human life that go well beyond their material functionality (Douglas, 1976; Miller, 2008). Commodities, they show, also function 'symbolically' as social artefacts through which people express and create their identities and in which people seek not just satisfaction but meaning and social acceptance too. 'Stuff is not just stuff', as Tim Jackson (2009: 63) aptly puts it, implying that what we own and what we purchase (especially in modern consumer societies) can be understood to be part of the 'extended self'. The important point here is that the meaning of consumption is not somehow *inherent* to the commodity or the service purchased, but is instead a social construct that is dependent on the culture within which the act of consumption takes place. Change the cultural background and the meaning of the consumption changes also, with various effects. For example, wearing a branded t-shirt of a particular kind might be of social significance in one society, at a particular time, but be meaningless in another time or place where the cultural background is different. To provide a second example, roller-skating might be the 'thing to do' in one time or place, and yet be unknown or laughed at in another time or place.

This raises issues about 'structure' because the cultural background within which consumption takes place is basically a structural 'given' beyond the immediate control of the individual. Different cultures bestow different meanings and significances to different practices of consumption, and that influences how people consume. But unless we uproot ourselves from our current culture, we do not get to choose the culture within which we live, and this is problematic when a given culture celebrates practices of consumption that may not be in the best interests of the individual, the society, or the planet. What is more problematic still, however, is that people can find themselves locked in to those practices of consumption if social and cultural norms do not provide many or any alternatives. Suppose, for example, a group of old school friends is coming to town and you are invited to a dinner one evening at an expensive restaurant; suppose also that you are trying to practise voluntary simplicity. In this scenario, to oversimplify somewhat, you are faced with the decision of either socialising with your friends despite the 'financial expense', or choosing to decline the offer in the attempt to avoid a high consumption lifestyle, but at the 'social expense' of missing out on the social event. In a different social context, however, a potluck dinner might have been 'the thing to do', in which case this predicament would never have arisen.

This type of cultural analysis could be applied to almost all consumption practices, and it raises very important points about how cultures can seduce people into high consumption lifestyles. If high-level consumption of some sort or another is needed, not just for material provision, but also for social acceptance, the social expression of one's identity, and the creation of meaning in life, then consuming less is not always as easy as one might hope. After all, reducing consumption poses new challenges if, as Mary Douglas put it, 'an individual's main objective in consumption is to help create the social universe and to find in it a creditable place' (Douglas, 1976: 243). It may be, therefore, that people live high consumption lifestyles not because they are greedy or hedonistic or indifferent to environmental concerns, but because they are trying to negotiate cultural norms of consumption in search of meaning and social acceptance. To some extent, at least, this is undoubtedly the case.

This is not to suggest, however, that consuming more sustainably in a consumer culture requires denying oneself a 'creditable place' in society. Far from it. There are ways to *enhance* or *create* meaning and social acceptance by consuming in ways that *oppose* cultural norms, and it is certainly the case that anti-consumerist movements have never advocated *renouncing* meaning or social acceptance. But it remains true that different cultural contexts make some consumption practices easier and others more difficult, and it seems to be the case that consumer cultures make consuming sustainably – including socialising in sustainable ways – much more difficult than it needs to be. All too often, the cultural presumption seems to be that socialising needs to involve spending various amounts of money, and yet there is no reason why this needs to be the case. In the absence of a community people who are socialising 'for free', however, can be drawn into consumerist modes of social activity simply to avoid being alone.

The second point, which must be dealt with even more briefly, concerns social infrastructure. The insight here is that how a society is designed from an urban planning perspective can also be understood to be a structural issue that affects how human beings socialise – including to what extent they socialise through market consumption. For example, if your local council sells your community park to developers who put a high-rise apartment block on it, this affects social space in ways that affect consumption practices. Where once parents would take their children to the park as a means of free social engagement, now they may be coerced to go to a commercial play centre, at some financial cost and arguably a diminished experience. Where once people would meet up in the community park after work and kick a ball around, in the absence of the park they may find themselves going to the movies (which costs money) or staying home (which reduces opportunities for social engagement). Again, this type of analysis could be taken in many directions, and again the point is that external structural issues affect the way people in a society consume, promoting some types of social activity (through market consumption) and opposing other types (such as free social engagement in public space). Space does not permit any detailed exploration here of what role governments could play in promoting post-consumerist forms of social engagement, but it is suggested that options will present themselves if it were ever decided that such a policy should be seriously pursued. Those options might include protecting public space from further privatisation or funding councils to organise diverse, community-based, social events. The fact is, however, overcoming barriers to sustainable social activity will probably depend (and should depend) on community-based action more than state action.

3.6 *Suitable housing as an obstacle to sustainable consumption*

Housing (whether one is purchasing, building, or renting) is typically life's greatest expense, so it is no surprise that many participants in the simple living survey highlighted 'suitable housing' as their greatest obstacle to consuming more sustainably. There are various issues here that deserve some attention, and yet we will see that addressing one issue can generate tensions with other issues, in ways that admit no obvious resolution.

One way to think of sustainable housing is in the context of 'eco-design', but the fact is that often these types of houses, despite having all the eco-features (recycled materials, solar panels, doubled-glazed windows, etc.), end up being so expensive that only a privileged few can afford them. Accordingly, they can easily be perceived as an exclusive 'bourgeois luxury'. Furthermore, it was noted earlier that living close to work can reduce one's dependency on cars, but if that means living in the inner city, this can also imply prohibitively expensive housing. This is especially so if people are seeking some land upon which to grow their own food, and yet if everyone were to have enough land to grow their own food, that could well contribute to urban sprawl in highly problematic ways. To make matters more complicated, if people decide to purchase expensive housing (e.g., eco-design, with some land, in the inner city) this may well lock them into a large mortgage, an unfulfilling job, and long hours, and this does not sit well with the 'balanced' life typically implied by lifestyles of voluntary simplicity. It is difficult to know how best to balance these competing factors.

From a different perspective – but one equally vexed – if people purchase or rent a house in much cheaper urban or even rural areas, this might allow them to reduce significantly their outgoings with respect to housing, and thus free them from some financial pressure, but it may bind them to their cars in ways that inner-city living would not. Or it might involve living in particularly unsafe parts of town. Furthermore, searching for housing in cheaper parts of the country (or the world) might open up access to a house and some land, but at the expense of taking people away from their family, friends, and broader support networks, which is a very high price to pay. Once more, for the reasons just outlined, it is no surprise that many people highlight 'suitable housing' as their greatest obstacle to sustainable consumption. We may have some conception of what a sustainable house looks like – e.g., a small, energy-efficient straw bale house, built from local materials, which is close to work, social support networks, and public transport, and which has access to a community garden – but the structure of modern societies simply does not make that a very easy option to 'choose'. The point here, which of course mirrors the points in earlier sections, is that there are structural obstacles to sustainable consumption that can make it very difficult or impossible to consume sustainably, even for those who are committed to doing so.

This issue of 'suitable housing' was deliberately dealt with last because in many ways it seems to be the hardest to solve. Any adequate solution may well involve restructuring private property rights for the purposes of redistribution, but this would be very controversial (or at least resisted fervently by vested interests determined to maintain the status quo). But perhaps that is the conclusion toward which the analysis in previous sections has been headed. It is perfectly clear that, to achieve a sustainable and just world, members of the global consumer class have to consume less, consume differently, and consume more efficiently. But it is not clear that such a transition is possible within the structural confines of consumer-capitalist society. It arguably follows that if those structures were changed in ways to facilitate the transition to 'simpler lives' of reduced and restrained consumption, nothing that resembled consumer capitalism would remain (Alexander, 2011c; Trainer, 2010).

3.7 *Other structural obstacles to sustainable consumption*

The six obstacles to sustainable consumption discussed above are by no means exhaustive. They were selected, as noted earlier, because the largest empirical analysis of the Voluntary Simplicity Movement indicates that those six obstacles are among the greatest obstacles people face when trying to reduce or restrain their consumption. It is hoped that this provides helpful, empirically grounded guidance to any policy makers who genuinely seek to free people from the structures that lock them into lifestyles of high resource and energy consumption. Given that any transition to a sustainable world entails the global consumer class reducing and restraining its consumption, figuring out how to overcome *existing barriers* to reduced and restrained consumption would seem to be a matter of considerable importance. It has been the underlying argument of this chapter that lifestyles of voluntary simplicity need to be systematically encouraged, privileged, and supported, rather than systemically opposed. This would seem to be particularly important to those who accept, as I do, that 'simpler' lifestyles of reduced and restrained consumption are a necessary cultural precondition, or at least a necessary contemporaneous supplement to any transition to a degrowth or steady state economy (Alexander, 2012b).

As well as the obstacles addressed above, many more undoubtedly exist which also deserve attention. There will be people, for example, who would like to purchase green energy from an energy provider but who find that none is presently on offer; or who would like to reduce their weekly waste disposal but who find that there are laws that require superfluous packaging; or who would like to keep a few chickens in their backyard for eggs but who find that council regulations prohibit it, etc. In fact, it is likely that when looking at the world from the 'consumption angle', almost all aspects of contemporary consumption can be seen to be affected by social, economic, or political structures that make some practices of consumption easy or necessary and other practices difficult or impossible. Currently, as we have seen, lifestyles of high consumption are structurally encouraged within consumer societies. Policy makers must recognise that these societies need to be fundamentally restructured for the explicit purpose of facilitating a transition to lifestyles of reduced consumption. But to the extent we cannot reasonably rely on sufficient action being taken by our governments, it would seem that the only option that remains is to take matters into our own hands and begin building alternative societies ourselves (Hopkins, 2008; Trainer, 2010; Alexander, 2013).

4. Toward a Politics of Voluntary Simplicity

Any transition to a sustainable and just society necessitates a shift in values away from the consumerist ethos that 'more consumption is always better' toward the post-consumerist ethos that 'just enough is plenty'. In high consumption societies of the developed world this generally means that people must consume not just differently and more efficiently, but less. Nevertheless, few people seem willing to accept this, including many environmentalists.

A value-shift toward voluntary simplicity, however, will not be enough on its own. Structural change is also needed to make the practice of voluntary simplicity a more viable alternative to consumer lifestyles. This chapter has outlined ways in which the structure of contemporary consumer societies makes lifestyles of voluntary simplicity much more difficult than they need to be. And if people accept that these societies need to consume less, consume differently, and consume more efficiently, then the structural obstacles inhibiting these practices must be removed as far as possible and as soon as possible.

It was beyond the scope of this chapter to explore in much detail the various options available, but it is hoped that this analysis provides some more insight into the nature of the problem, providing a conceptual framework within which to think fruitfully about these issues. Once it is accepted *that* structure affects consumption practices, and *how* those structures do so, the next question is what specific restructuring should actually be pursued to facilitate more sustainable consumption practices. Previous studies (e.g., OECD, 2008) have explored this question but failed to address some of the greatest barriers to sustainable consumption (e.g., transport, employment, housing, etc), an oversight that can be put down to the lack of an empirical basis with which to guide the analysis. The analysis in this chapter, however, was based on the simple living survey (Alexander and Ussher, 2012), and this study provides strong empirical grounds for thinking that the six areas addressed above represent some of the greatest obstacles to sustainable consumption.

In closing, it is worth noting that one of the biggest barriers to sustainable consumption – indeed, one of the biggest barriers to sustainability more generally – is the 'growth model of progress' that is so deeply entrenched in the developed world today, and increasingly elsewhere (Jackson, 2009). No pro-growth government will be much interested in the policies outlined in this chapter, because if the policies were successful they would generally facilitate less consumption, and this would mean less growth. Less growth is widely assumed to be a bad thing, since it is assumed that growth in GDP per capita is closely related to a nation's overall wellbeing. That assumption, however, has been subject to devastating critique for several decades now (Georgescu-Roegen, 1971; Schumacher; 1973; Daly, 1996; Meadows *et al.*, 2004), and the evidence for the critique is mounting and getting more sophisticated (e.g., Stiglitz *et al.*, 2010; Lawn and Clarke, 2010). And yet, the growth model seems to remain firmly entrenched, refusing to budge in the face of the evidence mounting in opposition. Not until a government seriously embraces a post-growth model of progress – either voluntarily or by force of ecological or financial necessity – will a top-down politics of voluntary simplicity be taken seriously. That presents two main pathways for activists for sustainable consumption: on the one hand, there is much work to be done promoting post-growth models of progress both to governments and to the constituencies upon whose mandate democratic governments depend; the other option is to direct one's energy into community-based action in the hope of 'doing for ourselves' what our governments seem unwilling or unable to do (Hopkins, 2008; Trainer, 2010). These paths are neither easy nor do they ensure success; but the longer our governments do nothing, the more it would seem that change, if it is ever to arrive, must be driven from the grassroots by a counter-culture based on practices of voluntary simplicity. If such a grassroots movement were ever mainstreamed, then, and only then, would we have the cultural conditions needed for a post-growth politics of voluntary simplicity to emerge.

References

Alexander, S. (ed.). 2009. *Voluntary simplicity: The poetic alternative to consumer culture.* Whanganui: Stead & Daughters.

Alexander, S. 2011a. 'God's away on business: The spiritual significance of voluntary simplicity'. *Earthsong: Ecology, Spirituality, and Education* 2(2): 7.

Alexander, S. 2011a. *Property beyond growth: Toward a politics of voluntary simplicity.* Doctoral thesis, Melbourne University. Available at: http://papers.ssrn.com/sol3/papers.cfm? abstract_id=1941069 (accessed 10 September, 2013).

Alexander, S. 2011c. 'The voluntary simplicity movement: Reimagining the good life beyond consumer culture'. *International Journal of Environmental, Cultural, Economic, and Social Sustainability* 7(3): 133.

Alexander, S. 2012a. 'The optimal material threshold: Toward an economics of sufficiency'. *Real-World Economics Review* 61: 2-21.

Alexander, S. 2012b. 'Planned economic contraction: The emerging case for degrowth'. *Environmental Politics* 21 (3): 349-368.

Alexander, S. 2013. 'Voluntary simplicity and the social reconstruction of the law: Degrowth from the grassroots up'. *Environmental Values* 22: 287-308.

Alexander, S. and Ussher, S. 2012. 'The voluntary simplicity movement: A multi-national survey analysis in theoretical context'. *Journal of Consumer Culture* 12(1): 66-86.

Australian Conservation Foundation (2010). Better than growth. Available at: http://www.acfonline.org.au/uploads/res/ACF_BetterThanGrowth.pdf [accessed 10 February 2012].

Brown, K. and Kasser, T. 2005. 'Are psychological and ecological well-being compatible? The role of values, mindfulness, and lifestyles'. *Social Indicators Research* 74: 349.

Brulle, R. and Young, L. 2007. 'Advertising, consumption levels, and the natural environment'. *Sociological Inquiry* 77: 522.

Daly, H. 1996. *Beyond growth: The economics of sustainable development.* Boston: Beacon Press.

De Graaf, J. 2009. 'Political prescriptions', in S. Alexander (ed.). 2009. *Voluntary simplicity: The poetic alternative to consumer culture.* Whanganui: Stead & Daughters: 274.

De Graaf, J., Wann, D., and Naylor, T. 2005 (2nd edn). *Affluenza: The all-consuming epidemic.* San Francisco: Berret-Koehler.

Dominguez, J. and Robin, V. 1999 (revised edn). *Your money or your life.* New York: Penguin.

Douglas, M. 1976. 'Relative poverty – relative communication', in T. Jackson (ed.). 2006. *The Earthscan Reader in Sustainable Consumption.* London: Earthscan.

Georgescu-Roegen, N. 1971. *The entropy law and the economic process.* London: Harvard University Press.

Gilding, P. 2011. *The great disruption: How the climate crisis will transform the global economy.* London: Bloomsbury.

Global Footprint Network, 2012. Reports available at http://www.footprintnetwork.org/en/index.php/gfn/page/world_footprint/ [accessed 10 February 2012].

Hamilton, C. 2003. *Growth fetish.* Crows Nest, NSW: Allen & Unwin.

Hansen, J. 2011: *Storms of my grandchildren.* London: Bloomsbury.

Hayden, A. 1999. *Sharing the work, sparing the planet: Work time, consumption, and ecology.* Toronto: Annandale Pluto Press.

Heinberg, R. 2011. *The end of growth: Adapting to our new economic reality.* Gabriola Island: New Society Publishers

Hopkins, R. 2008. *The transition handbook: From oil dependency to local resilience.* Totnes, Devon: Green Books.

Intergovernmental Panel on Climate Change (IPCC), 2013. *Climate change 2013: The physical science basis (Fifth Assessment Report).* Available at: http://www.ipcc.ch/report/ar5/wg1/#.Uk6k-CjqMRw (accessed 4 October 2013).

Jackson, T. 2009. *Prosperity with growth: Economics for a finite planet.* London: Earthscan.

Jackson, T. 2005. 'Live better by consuming less? Is there a double dividend in sustainable consumption?'. *Journal of Industrial Ecology* 9(1-2): 19.

Jackson, T. 2003. *Policies for sustainable consumption. A report to the sustainable development commission:* 1-77. Available at: http://www.sd-commission.org.uk/file_download.php?target

=/publications/downloads/030917%20Policies%20for%20sust
ainable%20consumption%20 SDC%20report .pdf [accessed
15 December 2010].

Jackson T. and Papathanasopoulou, E. 2008. 'Luxury or "lock in"?
An exploration of unsustainable consumption in the UK: 1968
to 2000'. *Ecological Economics* 68: 80.

Kallis, G. 2011. 'In defence of degrowth'. *Ecological Economics* 70:
873.

Kasser, T. 2002. *The high price of materialism.* Cambridge, MA:
MIT Press.

Kimmel J. and Hoffman, E. 2002. *The economics of work and
family.* Kalamazoo: Upjohn Institute for Employment
Research.

Lane, R. 2000. *The loss of happiness in market democracies.* New
Haven: Yale University Press.

Lawn, P. and Clarke, M. 2010.' The end of economic growth? A
contracting threshold Hypothesis'. *Ecological Economics* 69:
2213.

Latouche, S. 2009. *Farewell to growth.* Cambridge, UK: Polity
Press.

Lewis, T. and Potter, E. 2010. *Ethical consumption: A critical
introduction.* New York: Routledge.

Meadows, D., Randers, J., and Meadows, D. 2004. *Limits to
growth: The 30-year update.* White River Junction, Vt:
Chelsea Green Publishing.

Micheletti, M. 2010. *Political virtue and shopping: Individuals,
consumerism, and collective action.* Baskingstoke: Palgrave
Macmillan.

Millennium Ecosystem Assessment, 2005. Available at:
http://www.millenniumassessment.org/en/index.aspx.
[accessed 30 April 2011].

Miller, D. 2008. *The comfort of things.* Cambridge: Polity.

Moriarty, P. and Honnery, D. 2008. 'Low-mobility: The future of
transport'. *Futures* 40: 865.

Murphy, D. 2014. 'The implications of the declining energy return
on investment of oil production'. *Philosophical Transactions of
the Royal Society A*, 372, 20130126: 1-19.

Myers, D. 2000. *The American paradox: Spiritual hunger in an
age of plenty.* New Haven: Yale University Press.

Murtaza, N. 2011. 'Pursuing self-interest or self-actualization? From
capitalism to a steady-state wisdom economy'. *Ecological
Economics* 70: 577.

New Economics Foundation (NEF). 2010. *21 hours: Why a 21-hour
work week can help us all flourish in the 21st century.* Available
at www.neweconomics.org [accessed at 10 May 2011].

Oates, C. *et al.* 2008. 'Marketing sustainability: Use of information sources and degrees of voluntary simplicity'. *Journal of Marketing Communications* 14(5): 351.

OECD, 2008. *Promoting sustainable consumption: Good practices in OECD countries.* Paris: OECD Publishing.

PIRC (Public Interest Research Centre). 2011. *Think of me as evil? Opening the ethical debates in advertising.* Surrey: Public Interest Research Centre and WWF-UK.

Princen, T. 2005. *The logic of sufficiency.* Cambridge, Mass: MIT Press.

Princen, T., Maniates, M., Conca, K. (eds). 2002. *Confronting consumption.* Cambridge Mass: MIT Press.

Robinson, T. 2009. *Work, leisure, and the environment: The vicious circle of overwork and overconsumption.* Cheltenham: Edward Elgar Publishing.

Ropke, I. 1999. 'The dynamics of willingness to consume'. *Ecological Economics* 28: 399.

Samuelson, P. 1938. 'A note on the pure theory of consumer behaviour'. *Economica* 5: 61.

Sanne, C. 2002. 'Willing consumers – Or locked in? Policies for a sustainable consumption'. *Ecological Economics*, 42: 273.

Schor, J. 2004. *Born to buy: The commercialized child and the new consumer culture.* New York: Scribner.

Scott, K. 2009. *A literature review on sustainable lifestyles and recommendations for further research.* Stockholm: Stockholm Environment Institute.

Stiglitz, J., Sen, A., and Fitoussi, J.P. 2010. *Mis-measuring our lives: Why GDP doesn't add up.* New York: The New Press.

Shaw, D. and Newholm, T. 2002. 'Voluntary simplicity and the ethics of consumption'. *Psychology and Marketing* 19(2): 167.

Trainer, T. 2010. *The transition to a sustainable and just world.* Sydney: Envirobook.

Turner, G. 2012. 'Are we on the cusp of collapse? Updated comparison of *The Limits to Growth* with historical data'. *Gaia* 21(2): 116-124.

Worldwatch Institute. 2007. *Sao Paulo Bans outdoor advertising in fight against pollution.* Available at: http://www.world watch.org/node/5338 [accessed 11 February 2012].

5

REIMAGINING THE GOOD LIFE BEYOND CONSUMER CULTURE
A revolution in consciousness

Lately in the wreck of a Californian ship, one of the passengers fastened a belt about him with 200 pounds of gold in it with which he was found afterwards at the bottom. Now, as he was sinking, had he the gold? Or had the gold him?
— John Ruskin

1. Introduction

In the most developed regions of the world today, decades of unprecedented economic growth have all but solved the economic problem of how to attain the necessaries of life and, indeed, have resulted in most people living lives of relative luxury and comfort. Although a degree of poverty remains in these regions, exacerbated in some places by the global financial crisis, on the whole ordinary people are materially wealthy when considered in the context of all known history or when compared with the poorest billions on the planet today, who still struggle for a bare subsistence. As Clive Hamilton (2003: *xi*) puts it, 'Most Westerners today are prosperous beyond the dreams of their grandparents'. The houses of typical families are bigger than ever, and they are each filled with untold numbers of consumer products, such as multiple TVs, stereos, computers, mobile phones, racks of unused clothes, washing machines, fridges, dishwashers, dryers, vacuum cleaners, kitchen gadgets, etc. These products often overflow into garages or hired storage rooms to create spaces full of accumulated 'stuff' – or else they conveniently disappear into a growing stream of waste that ends up in landfill. Houses are often centrally heated and air-

113

conditioned, with spare rooms and two or more cars parked outside. Average wages are well above subsistence levels, meaning that most people have spare income to spend on comforts and luxuries such as alcohol, take-away food, going to the movies, fashionable clothes or furniture, books, taking the occasional holiday, etc. People generally have access to a variety of public services, including free primary and secondary education. On top of all this, democratic political systems are firmly, albeit imperfectly, established, the water is clean, and almost nobody goes hungry.

All this is indicative of vast material wealth, which it will not be suggested is a bad thing, in and of itself. But it is a prosperity which has proven extremely easy to take for granted, leaving many in the global middle class still feeling deprived despite their plenty (see generally, Hamilton and Denniss, 2005). It is also clear that universalising Western-style lifestyles would be ecologically catastrophic (Smith and Positano, 2010), which calls the legitimacy of those lifestyles deeply into question. Equally challenging to the consumer way of life is the growing body of social research indicating that affluence cannot be relied on as a path to happiness (Alexander, 2012). In other words, it seems that huge increases in material wealth have stopped contributing significantly to individual and social wellbeing in affluent societies, and indeed are beginning to undermine the ecological foundations of wellbeing (Kubiszewski et al., 2013). It is troubling, therefore, to see that even the richest nations are still focused primarily on maximising GDP. As Thoreau (1982: 261) would say, '[We] labor under a mistake'.

Is it possible that the majority of people living in the most affluent societies today have reached a stage in their economic development where the process of getting richer is now causing the very problems that they seem to think getting richer will solve? There are indeed grounds for thinking that this is so. Consumer culture, which every day is being globalised further, is failing to fulfil its promise of a better life. It has even begun taking away many of the things upon which wellbeing depends, such as community life, a work/life balance, spiritual and aesthetic experience, and a healthy natural environment (Lane, 2000). All this makes it hard to avoid the confronting questions: Is more consumption and production really the solution to these problems? Or is there, as Ted Trainer (2010) puts it, a 'Simpler Way'?

This chapter examines the simpler way known as 'voluntary simplicity', which can be preliminarily understood as a way of life in which people choose to restrain or reduce their material consumption, while at the same time seeking a higher quality of life. By addressing issues of definition, justification, and practice, this chapter aims to sketch an outline of this post-consumerist movement by bringing together many of its central elements. There is a desperate need for alternative practices and narratives of consumption beyond those prevalent in the most developed regions of the world today, and it will be argued that voluntary simplicity provides an alternative that is both coherent and attractive. The chapter concludes by considering some objections that can be levelled against voluntary simplicity.

1.1. *Structure and simplicity*

Before beginning the substantive analysis there is one important objection that needs to be anticipated at once, to avoid misunderstanding the nature of the present examination. Often people accuse advocates of voluntary simplicity of failing to appreciate structural issues that function to 'lock' many people into high consumption lifestyles. The criticism is that practising voluntary simplicity is difficult or impossible within the constraints of growth-based economies, such that 'lifestyle' responses to environmental and social justice issues are misguided and ineffective. It would follow that the real changes needed have less to do with our consumption practices, and more to do with our political and economic structures that make sustainable consumption so very hard. So far as it goes, that criticism is extremely powerful, which is to say, it is clear that mere 'lifestyle' responses to the overlapping crises facing the world today will not resolve those crises. Too many simplicity theorists give the impression that lifestyle change is enough, and for this they are justifiably reproached for being naïve.

Nevertheless, I contend that until there is a culture that embraces the ethos of voluntary simplicity at the personal or household level, there will never be sufficient social forces to induce the necessary structural changes that can support sustainable living. As it turns out, this is a point that is often lost on those hard-nosed critics who emphasise the importance of 'structure'. While I accept, without reservation, that justice and sustainability demand deep structural changes and that lifestyle responses alone are an inadequate strategy for societal transformation, the nuanced position I take is that it is nevertheless critical that a post-consumerist culture emerges to create the social conditions for the necessary structural change to take root. I do not discuss structural issues at length in this chapter, but the sub-text of this chapter (defended elsewhere, e.g., Alexander, 2011; Alexander, 2013) is that the structural changes required will seem most coherent when seen through the lens of voluntary simplicity. In short, before we can

115

expect the necessary structural changes – whether produced from the 'top down' or driven 'from below' – there needs to be a cultural revolution in attitudes toward Western-style consumption practices, and I maintain that voluntary simplicity is the most coherent lens through which to frame that necessary revolution. Until we reimagine the good life beyond consumer culture, it will be unclear why moving away from a consumer-based culture and a growth-based economy is a good idea. As Aristotle (1981) once wrote: 'A person who is going to make a fruitful inquiry into the question of the best political [or economic] arrangement, must first set out clearly what the most choiceworthy life is. For if that is unclear, the best political [and economic] arrangement must also be unclear.' This chapter seeks to outline why, especially at this moment in history, voluntary simplicity is a 'choiceworthy' life.

1.2. *Defining voluntary simplicity*

Voluntary simplicity is an oppositional living strategy that rejects the high-consumption, materialistic lifestyles of consumer cultures and affirms what is often just called 'the simple life' or 'downshifting'. Sometimes called 'the quiet revolution', this approach to life involves providing for material needs as simply and directly as possible, minimising expenditure on consumer goods and services, and directing progressively more time and energy toward pursuing non-materialistic sources of satisfaction and meaning. This generally means accepting a lower income and a lower level of consumption, in exchange for more time and freedom to pursue other life goals, such as community or social engagements, more time with family, artistic or intellectual projects, more fulfilling employment, political participation, sustainable living, spiritual exploration, reading, contemplation, relaxation, pleasure-seeking, love, and so on – none of which need to rely on money, or much money. Variously defended by its advocates on personal, social, humanitarian, and ecological grounds (discussed below), voluntary simplicity is predicated on the assumption that human beings can live meaningful, free, happy, and infinitely diverse lives, while consuming no more than a sustainable and equitable share of nature. That, at least, is the challenging ideal which seems to motivate and guide many of its advocates and practitioners (see generally, Alexander, 2009).

According to this philosophy of living, personal and social progress is measured not by the conspicuous display of wealth or status, but by increases in the qualitative richness of daily living, the cultivation of relationships, and the development of social, intellectual, aesthetic, and/or spiritual potentials. As Duane Elgin (1982) has famously defined it, voluntary simplicity is 'a manner of living that is outwardly simple and inwardly rich, ... a deliberate choice to live with less in the belief that more life will be returned to us in the process'. According to the most prominent historian of the Simplicity Movement, David Shi (2007), the primary attributes of the simple life include: thoughtful frugality; a suspicion of luxuries; a reverence and respect for nature; a desire for self-sufficiency; a commitment to conscientious rather than conspicuous consumption; a privileging of creativity and contemplation over possessions; an aesthetic preference for minimalism and functionality; and a sense of responsibility for the just uses of the world's resources. More concisely, Shi (2007: 131) defines voluntary simplicity as 'enlightened material restraint'.

Advocates are quick to point out, however, that voluntary simplicity does not mean living in poverty, becoming an ascetic monk, or indiscriminately renouncing all the advantages of science and technology. It does not involve regressing to a primitive state or becoming a self-righteous puritan. And it is not some escapist fad reserved for saints, hippies, or eccentric outsiders. Rather, advocates of simplicity insist that by examining afresh our relationships with money, material possessions, the planet, ourselves, and each other, 'the simple life' of voluntary simplicity is about discovering the freedom and contentment that comes with knowing how much consumption is truly 'enough'. Arguably, this is a theme that has something to say to everyone, especially those in consumer societies today who are every day bombarded with thousands of cultural and institutional messages insisting that 'more is always better'. Voluntary simplicity is a philosophy of living that advocates a counter-cultural position based on notions of sufficiency, frugality, moderation, restraint, localism, and mindfulness.

The notion of living simply, of course, is not new (see Alexander and McLeod, 2014). The virtues of moderation and enlightened material restraint have been integral to almost all ancient wisdom and spiritual traditions throughout history, with prominent advocates including Lao Tzu, Confucius, Buddha, Diogenes, the Stoics, Jesus, Mohammad, St Francis, the Quakers, John Ruskin, William Morris, the New England Transcendentalists (especially Thoreau), the European Bohemians, Tolstoy, Gandhi, Lenin, Richard Gregg, Helen and Scott Nearing, and many of the indigenous peoples around the world. But in postmodernity, where consumption seems to be glorified and luxury admired as never before, voluntary simplicity arguably acquires a special significance.

2. Misconceptions about Voluntary Simplicity

So as not to be misunderstood, it may be worthwhile spending a few moments clarifying some points made in preceding sections by distinguishing voluntary simplicity from what it is not.

2.1. *Glorification of poverty?*

Voluntary simplicity can be misinterpreted sometimes as glorifying or romanticising poverty, a myth encouraged perhaps by the fact that some of the more extreme proponents of simplicity – e.g., Diogenes, St Francis, Gandhi, etc. – did indeed live lives of staggering material renunciation. Such extremism can be alienating if it is considered to be a defining or necessary feature of the simple life, which it is not. There is also a risk that advocates of simplicity will be understood to be downplaying the plight of those in the world who genuinely live lives oppressed by material deprivation. It is of the utmost importance, then, to be perfectly clear on this point: voluntary simplicity does not mean poverty. Poverty, in its various dimensions, is debilitating and humiliating. Voluntary simplicity, on the other hand, can be understood as an empowering expression of freedom; a choice to live with fewer market commodities in the belief that a better life, and a better world, will result. It is about the importance of understanding and attaining material *sufficiency*, while at the same time creating a life rich in its non-material dimensions.

2.2. *Necessarily agrarian? Just for hippies?*

Living simply does not necessarily imply leaving the city to live in the country; nor does it mean becoming a hippie or joining a commune. Although some may find that an agrarian existence is a very good and natural way to live, it will not be attractive (or available) to everyone; nor will living in a hippie commune. Indeed, learning how to live more simply and sustainably in an increasingly urbanised world is surely one of the greatest challenges of our age, especially since legal and political institutions and social infra-structure make urban simple living, especially, much more difficult than it needs to be. For now, suffice it to note that voluntary simplicity is not synonymous with the 'back-to-the-land' movement or the counter-cultures that arose in the 1960s and 70s. It should be added, however, that those movements do share some common ideals with voluntary simplicity, such as anti-consumerism, self-sufficiency, the celebration of life, a deep respect for nature, and non-violent resistance to unjust features of society.

2.3. *Primitive, regressive, anti-technology?*

Voluntary simplicity, furthermore, does not mean indiscriminately renouncing all the advantages of science and technology. It does not mean living in a cave, giving up all the benefits of electricity, or rejecting modern medicine. But it does question the assumption that science and technology are always the most reliable paths to health, happiness, and sustainability. It is certainly better to accept rather than reject the advantages, though so dearly bought, which the invention and industry of humankind offer – provided, of course, that they are genuine advantages. But often with such 'modern improvements', as Thoreau (1982: 306) warned, there is 'an illusion about them; there is not always a positive advance'. Voluntary simplicity, then, involves taking a thoughtfully sceptical stance in relation to technology, rejecting those aspects that seem to cost more than they come to, all things considered. Clearly, this is far from being primitive or regressive. Just perhaps our modern technocratic societies will one day come to see that there is a sophistication and elegance to the clothesline, the bicycle, and the water tank that the dryer, the automobile, and the desalination plant decidedly lack. On a similar note, perhaps it will one day be widely accepted that there is a certain primitiveness to technological gimmicks, or that a blind faith in science can itself be 'anti-progress'. In the words of the great Leonardo da Vinci: 'Simplicity is the ultimate sophistication' (see Deger and Gibson, 2007: 262).

3. Justifying Voluntary Simplicity

With the definitional overview complete, it is now time to consider what reasons or incentives there might be for choosing a life of voluntary simplicity. The following discussion is divided into four (somewhat overlapping) sections – personal, communitarian, humanitarian, and ecological.

3.1. *Personal*

Money provides power in the market – power to purchase and consume desired commodities, whether goods or services. Consumption, by satisfying market preferences, is supposed to lead to wellbeing. In essence, this is the economic foundation of consumer culture. Its fundamental prescription is that people should seek wellbeing in higher incomes and more consumption. The problem, however, is that the pursuit of income and consumption can easily distract people from what is best in their lives, functioning to lock people into a 'work-and-spend' cycle that has no end and attains no lasting satisfaction (see, e.g., Robinson, 2007). Many simplicity theorists argue that if people in affluent societies are prepared to rethink their relationships with money and possessions, they just might be able to free up more time and energy for the pursuit of what truly inspires them and makes them happy, whatever that may be. As Richard Gregg (2009: 112) put it, living simply means 'an ordering and guiding of our energy and desires, a partial restraint in some directions in order to secure a greater abundance of life in other directions'. In this way voluntary simplicity can be seen to offer enhanced meaning and satisfaction in people's lives. The message, in more technical terms, is that lowering 'standard of living' (measured by income/consumption) can actually lead to increased 'quality of life' (measured by subjective wellbeing). It is important to emphasise, however, that this is not just about living a happier or more pleasurable life; it can also be about living more deeply and meaningfully in some existentialist, even spiritual, sense.

I begin with the personal incentives for living simply not because they are the most important, necessarily, but because I believe that if the Simplicity Movement is to expand, it must be shown that living simply does not tend to generate any significant sense of deprivation, but actually frees people from an insidiously addictive consumerism and an unhealthy relation with money and possessions. Rather than dedicating one's life to the pursuit of ever-higher levels of income and consumption, those who live simply are more likely to have a balanced working life or even work part-time, and they are more likely to seek fulfilling employment and accept a modest income, rather than get too hung about securing the highest income possible. With less time devoted to acquiring expensive commodities, 'voluntary simplifiers' (as they are sometimes called) tend to have more time to spend with friends and family, and more time to spend pursuing their private passions or civic duties. The point here is that disciplined and enlightened moderation with respect to one's material life does not tend to give rise to any sense of deprivation or sacrifice, but ultimately gives rise to a happiness, a contentment, and even a freedom significantly greater than that which is ordinarily known in the 'work-and-spend' cycle of consumer culture. In short, many people are drawn to voluntary simplicity because they want to escape the vapidity of the rat race and live more with less (see generally, Alexander and Ussher, 2012).

3.2. *Communitarian*

There are also social or communitarian incentives for embracing a life of voluntary simplicity. For example, when an individual embraces voluntary simplicity by working less, this may well benefit the individual (e.g., by creating more leisure and reducing stress). But those individual benefits will often have flow-on effects that benefit others too, such as creating more time and energy for family and friends, or more time and energy to enjoy one's civic or neighbourly responsibilities. As Cafaro and Gambrel (2009: 11) maintain, 'simplicity can help us develop social unions that enrich our lives. By fostering contentment with our status and possessions and reducing levels of dissatisfaction, simplicity can help minimise social tension and build up social capital.'

Social critics argue that community engagement is often pushed to the side by the demands of a high-consumption life. David Myers (2000) coined the term 'social recession' to describe essentially this phenomenon. A society might be booming economically, but dedicating too much attention to consumption and the acquisition of wealth, to the detriment of family and community life, can lead to an individualistic society of frantic, agitated, and alienated egos. Mark Burch (2000: 65) sums up this point exactly: 'The brutally "simple" fact is that if the quality of our family and community relationships has suffered, it's because we've chosen to do something else with our time.' What these and other thinkers propose is that affluent societies would be better off if they spent less time accumulating and consuming, and more time cultivating family and community relationships and increasing their civic engagements. The simple act of sharing something with neighbours rather than each having their own is a good example. Which community is richer: The one where each has their own? Or the community that has less but shares?

3.3. *Humanitarian*

Although there are indeed many personal and communitarian incentives for adopting voluntary simplicity, it would be an impoverished ethics that sought to justify itself solely in relation to personal or community self-interest. For that reason, it is important to recognise that there are also broader *humanitarian* reasons for adopting voluntary simplicity. In a world where extreme poverty exists amidst such plenty, living simply can be understood as a personal response to the highly skewed distributions of wealth in the world, a response that seeks as far as possible not to be implicated in a system of distribution perceived by many to be grossly unjust. In a similar vein, living simply is also understood to be an act of sharing, an act of human solidarity, by trying to resist high levels of consumption that cannot be shared by all.

We live in a world of limited resources. There is only so much stuff to go around, and with the global population expected to exceed nine billion around the middle of this century, competition over resources can be expected to intensify greatly. One obvious way to share with others, then, is simply to take less – to try to take only what one needs to live a dignified life, and no more. Taking less may not be easy, of course, especially in cultures that celebrate extravagance. But it is hard to imagine how the problems of poverty will ever be solved if the materially rich and materially comfortable continue seeking ever-higher levels of consumption. Furthermore, economic growth and the so-called 'trickle down effect' is not a solution upon which we should rely for humanitarian relief (Woodward and Simms, 2006). Challenging though it may be to admit, a necessary part of the solution to poverty involves those in the global consumer class showing some enlightened, compassionate restraint in relation to their material lives. As Gandhi once said, 'Live simply so that others may simply live'.

3.4. *Ecological*

As well as personal, communitarian, and humanitarian reasons for living simply, there are, of course, also *environmental* reasons. It has long been recognised that consumption and ecological impact are closely linked, and from this correlation it follows that reducing consumption can be an effective means of reducing ecological impact. Indeed, it is becoming increasingly clear that simpler living, in the sense of reduced and more efficient consumption, is not just to be desired but is necessary to save our planet from (further) grave ecological harm (Trainer, 2010). This is especially so in the most developed nations, where lifestyles of reduced consumption, supported by structural change (as noted above), will be a necessary part of any transition to a sustainable future. This has been acknowledged in several of the leading international policy documents on the environment which have emerged in recent decades. Agenda 21, for example – the main policy document to emerge from the Rio Earth Summit in 1992 – argued that 'the major cause of the continued deterioration of the global environment is the unsustainable pattern of consumption and production, particularly in the industrialised countries'. This document called for the following actions:

a) To promote patterns of consumption and production that reduce environmental stress and will meet the basic needs of humanity.

b) To develop a better understanding of the role of consumption and how to bring about more sustainable consumption patterns.

In more recent years, this message has been widely affirmed. When the World Summit convened in Johannesburg in 2002, 'changing consumption and production patterns' was identified as one of three 'overarching objectives' for sustainable development. What these and other reports imply is that fundamental lifestyle change with respect to private consumption is one of the main preconditions to ecological sustainability. But as yet, the international and political responses to sustainability issues have been grossly inadequate – which again highlights the importance of driving change from the personal, household, and community levels (Hopkins, 2008; Trainer, 2010). That could be considered the 'political' dimension of voluntary simplicity, an issue discussed elsewhere (see Alexander, 2011; Alexander, 2013).

4. Practising Voluntary Simplicity

It is all very well to theorise about the simple life – to debate definitions and evaluate justifications – but theory is empty if it is not grounded upon practice. Accordingly, the following sections seek to enrich the preceding theoretical discussions by providing a brief exposition of how the idea of voluntary simplicity is actually *lived* by participants in the movement.

4.1. *A non-universalist disclaimer*

Any discussion of the practice of simplicity ought to begin by acknowledging that there is not one way to live simply. There is no Doctrine or Code of Simplicity to follow, as such; there is no Method or Equation of Simplicity into which we can plug the facts of our lives and be told how to live. That is precisely what the idea cannot do. Voluntary simplicity, it could be said, is more about questions than answers, in the sense that practising simplicity calls for creative interpretation and personalised application. It is not for 'experts', therefore, or for anyone, to prescribe universal rules on how to live simply. We each live unique lives and we each find ourselves in different situations, with different capabilities, and different responsibilities. Accordingly, the practice of simplicity by one person, in one situation, may very well involve different things to a different person, in a different situation. Furthermore, simple living is not so much a destination as it is an ongoing creative process. But, as I have implied, I do not think that this practical indeterminacy is an objection to the idea.

With that non-universalist disclaimer noted, a few general remarks will now be made on what a simple life might look like in practice and how one might begin to live it (see also, Alexander, Trainer, and Ussher, 2012).

4.2. Money

Although practising simplicity is much more than just being frugal with money and consuming less – it is also a state of mind – in a market economy spending wisely plays a central role. In *Your Money or Your Life,* Joe Dominguez and Vicki Robin (1999) provide elaborate financial exercises for readers to undertake which seek to provoke reflection on the real value of money and the real cost of things. Such exercises may sound mundane and a bit pointless – most people believe themselves to be careful, rational spenders – but if they are carried out with precision the results may well surprise, and perhaps even shock. One might find that seemingly little purchases add up to an inordinate amount over a whole year, which may raise new and important questions about whether the money might have been better spent elsewhere, not at all, or exchanged for more time by working less. Then consider how much would be spent in each category over 10 years. The aim of this exercise is not to create tightwads, as such, but smart consumers who are conscious of the time/life/ecological cost of their purchases. After all, as Thoreau (1982: 286) would insist, 'The cost of a thing is the amount of... life which is required to be exchanged for it'. When exploring voluntary simplicity in this light, one might well find that some reductions and changes to spending habits, rather than inducing any sense of deprivation, will instead be life-affirming.

When it comes to spending money in accordance with the ethos of voluntary simplicity, it is also important to bear in mind Vicki Robin's profound democratic insight: that how we spend our money is how we vote on what exists in the world. Purchasing something sends a message, consciously or unconsciously, to the marketplace, affirming the product, its ecological impact, its process of manufacture, etc. Simple living, therefore, involves shopping as conscientiously as possible, directing one's monetary 'votes' into socially and ecologically responsible avenues and boycotting irresponsible avenues. A tension can arise here, of course, because shopping conscientiously or 'ethically' tends to be, but is not always, more expensive (a point deserving of more analysis than can be offered here). If it is true, however, that market expenditure is a vote on what exists in the world then it would seem that the global consumer-class has the potential to become a non-violent revolutionary class and change the world, partly through changing its spending habits. *Simplicity is the new spectre haunting capitalism.* Never before have so many people had the option of casting off the chains of consumer culture, stepping out of the rat race, and living (and spending) in opposition to the existing order of things. Money is power, and with this power comes responsibility.

4.3. *Housing*

As noted in the last chapter, housing is typically life's greatest single expense, so those living simply must think especially carefully about where they live and why, and how much of their lives they are prepared to spend seeking a 'nicer' place to live. Exactly what kind of shelter does one need to live well and to be free? Obviously, we must answer this question for ourselves – at least, within the constraints of our own socio-economic context – but again the words of Thoreau (1982: 290) might give us a moment's pause: 'Most people appear never to have considered what a house is, and are actually though needlessly poor all their lives because they think that they must have such a one as their neighbours have'. The 'McMansions' which are so prevalent in the suburbs of North America and increasingly elsewhere are extremely resource-intensive and very expensive. In opposition to that trend, participants in the Simplicity Movement are exploring alternative ways to accommodate themselves and their families, by embracing smaller, much more modest and energy-efficient homes. In particular, some are exploring co-housing arrangements, 'green design', and other forms of low-impact development, including eco-villages. More radical participants are building their own straw bale or mud houses, making shacks out of abandoned or second-hand materials, or converting shipping containers into homes.

4.4. *Clothing*

The historic purpose of clothing, as Thoreau pointed out, was to keep us warm and, in time, for reasons of modesty. Today its dominant purpose seems to be fashion and the conspicuous display of wealth and status. People can, of course, spend thousands and thousands of dollars on clothing, if they wish. But those who live simply tend to 'dress down', wearing functional, often second-hand clothing. Such clothing can be generally obtained at a minimal expense. Dressing down, it should be noted, does not necessarily imply giving up 'style' or puritanically denying self-expression through what one wears. But it does seem to imply rejecting high fashion (and all its stands for) in favour of some 'alternative' aesthetic. In this way, dressing down can be understood to be an outward statement of simplicity; an effort, however small, to express aesthetically one's opposition to consumer culture. Hundreds of billions of dollars are spent each year in the fashion industry. Just imagine if even half of that money were redirected toward green energy or humanitarian initiatives. We would lose so little and gain so much. Again, how we spend our money is how we vote on what exists in the world.

4.5. *Food*

Eating locally, eating organically, eating out in moderation, eating less or no meat, eating simply, lightly, and creatively, and, as far as possible, growing one's own fruit and vegetables – these are some of the key characteristics to food production and consumption in the lives of many simplifiers. Given some thought and a little discipline, some people are discovering that a nutritious, environmentally sensitive diet can be obtained at a surprisingly low cost. Although this short description points to the main characteristics of food production and consumption within the Simplicity Movement, there are, of course, a great many complexities with it, including issues of property rights and access to land, which cannot be addressed presently (see Alexander, 2011).

4.6. *Work*

Rethinking attitudes to work is central to the way many participants in the Simplicity Movement approach simple living. Charles Siegel (2008: 8) poses the critical question: 'Should we take advantage of our increasing productivity to consume more or to have more free time?' If people keep raising their material standard of living every time they come into more money – through a pay rise, for example, or through some new technology which increases productivity per hour – working hours will never decrease and may even rise. Indeed, many Westerners, especially North Americans, Britons, and Australians, are working longer hours today than they were in the 1970s, despite being considerably more productive (Robinson, 2007). Generally speaking, they have directed all their wealth and productivity gains into consuming more and have not taken any of those gains in terms of increased free time. But why, one might ask, should people always be working for more consumer products and services and not sometimes be content with less? Why should people not accept a lower material standard of living (e.g., old clothes, smaller house, no car, no luxury travel, etc.) and work half as much? Who can say what wonders such a cultural style might not bring! Thoreau's opinion on working hours seems to exemplify the perspective held by many participants in the Simplicity Movement (Thoreau, 1982: 636):

> Those slight labors which afford me a livelihood, and by which it is allowed that I am to some extent serviceable to my contemporaries, are as yet commonly a pleasure to me, and I am not often reminded that they are a necessity. So far I am successful. But I foresee that if my wants should be much increased, the labor required to supply them would become a drudgery. ... I wish to suggest that a man may be very industrious, and yet not spend his time well.

The basic idea here is that if people can embrace simple living and stop the upward creep of material desire, they can take some or all of their pay rises or productivity gains, not in terms of more consumption, but in terms of more free time. And this raises the questions: Are we forced by the 'curse of labour' to work so much? Or are we freer than we think we are? The Simplicity Movement is an example of a social movement where people are enjoying the benefits of exchanging money and consumption for more free time.

5. Criticisms of Voluntary Simplicity

The Simplicity Movement has not been free from criticism. Three of the more prominent criticisms will now be considered.

5.1. *A leisure expansion movement*

The Simplicity Movement is sometimes described, occasionally even by its advocates (Segal, 1999: 13), as a leisure expansion movement. The criticism sometimes implicit in this description is that voluntary simplicity is a self-centred, narrowly hedonistic philosophy of life available only to a privileged few. While voluntary simplicity by its very nature is indeed 'an ethic professed and practiced primarily by those free to choose their standard of living' (Shi, 2007: 7), the broad-based affluence in the developed world today means that the choice of voluntary simplicity is available *to some degree* to the vast majority of people. Put otherwise, downshifting does not just mean selling the Porsche and buying a Prius, or retiring at 40 and living off the income of investment properties. It can be practised by all those who have a degree of discretionary income. Furthermore, the simple life is not just about improving one's own life through leisure expansion. The Simplicity Movement may indeed be a leisure expansion movement *for some*, which, as I argued above, in itself is no grounds for criticism; in fact, trading income/consumption for more free time is one of the most important cultural shifts needed in the developed world today. But to characterise the Simplicity Movement *merely* as a leisure expansion movement is to betray an ignorance of the diverse motivations people actually have for adopting voluntary simplicity, which often include environmentalism and social justice (Alexander and Ussher, 2012). Bearing those ethically-based motivations in mind, the fact that simple living can also be described as a form of 'alternative hedonism' seems to provide, not grounds for criticism, but further support for the Simplicity Movement.

5.2. *Consumption as meaning and identity*

A more sophisticated critique of voluntary simplicity arises out of theories of consumption that recognise that commodities have come to play a role in our lives that go well beyond their material functionality (see Miller, 2008). These theories hold that commodities also function symbolically as social artefacts through which people express and create their identities and in which people seek not just satisfaction but meaning and social acceptance. 'Stuff is not just stuff', as Tim Jackson (2009) puts it, implying that what we own (especially in modern consumer societies) can be understood as part of the 'extended self'. This understanding of consumption raises important questions about voluntary simplicity, because if consumption is needed not just for material provision but also for social acceptance, the social expression of one's identity, and the creation of meaning in life, then what exactly are advocates of voluntary simplicity asking people to give up? What would reducing consumption actually mean if, as Mary Douglas (2006 [1976]: 243) put it, 'An individual's main objective in consumption is to help create the social universe and to find in it a creditable place'. The symbolic function of consumption does seem to present a challenge to the idea of voluntary simplicity, but the challenge is not as forceful as it may first appear. Psychologist Philip Cushman (1990) has argued that the 'extended self' created through consumption is actually an 'empty self', one that is constantly in need of being 'filled up' with consumer artefacts. Although consumption may indeed be a medium through which individuals in modern societies increasingly seek to find meaning, there is a great deal of evidence (supplemented by strong intuitions, perhaps) which suggests that seeking meaning in consumption is not fulfilling its promise of a happy and meaningful life (Alexander, 2012). Furthermore, anti-consumerist movements in their various forms have never advocated *renouncing* meaning but, on the contrary, they have always sought to *create* and *enhance* meaning through opposition to mainstream consumption habits. As Jackson contends, 'the insight that a certain amount of consumer behaviour is dedicated to an (ultimately flawed) pursuit of meaning opens up the tantalising possibility of devising some other, more successful, less ecologically damaging strategy for creating and maintaining personal and cultural meaning'. In the Simplicity Movement, it could be argued, that 'tantalising possibility' is becoming a reality.

5.3. *Escapist or apolitical*

Finally, for present purposes, the Simplicity Movement has been criticised also for being 'escapist' or 'apolitical', a criticism that, it cannot be denied, has some weight. Leading sociologist on voluntary simplicity Mary Grigsby (2004: 12) notes that participants in the Simplicity Movement 'don't generally talk about policy initiatives, instead focusing on the individual as the primary mechanism for change'. While the individual may well be the primary mechanism for change, many in the Simplicity Movement do not seem to recognise that, if change is what is truly sought, much more attention must be dedicated to political engagement. That is to say, reformative efforts must not be limited to personal transformation, but must also employ 'grassroots' or 'bottom up' forces to reshape structures and institutions (Alexander, 2013; Trainer, 2010). This is especially so given the many difficulties and forms of resistance people face when seeking to practise simplicity within political, legal, and economic structures that seem to be inherently opposed to reducing the levels and impacts of market consumption. It would be wrong to suggest that voluntary simplicity is an impossible living strategy, but the pro-growth structures of advanced capitalist societies certainly make living simply much more difficult than it needs to be, and this is inhibiting the expansion and impact of the movement. Accordingly, to the extent that the Simplicity Movement currently seeks to escape that structure rather than transform it, it properly deserves criticism. It should be noted, however, that this is not a criticism that touches on anything necessary or intrinsic to the Simplicity Movement. It just makes the point that historically the movement has been lacking in political consciousness. Fortunately, there are emerging signs of the movement's politicisation (Alexander and Ussher, 2012), although obviously much more action is needed.

In order to socially reconstruct political, legal, and economic structures, the movement will need to expand and organise at the social level, and this will require, to begin with, more individuals making personal commitments to live in opposition to the Western-style consumerist ideal and create for themselves, as far as possible, an alternative conception of the good life. Having increasing numbers of individuals confronting the dominant culture by reimagining the good life is necessary for creating fertile conditions for a politics of simplicity, but it will not be sufficient to bring about significant structural change in the absence of collective action. Politicising the movement will need to involve networking with others who are doing the same. But a large part of the problem at present is that the movement's collective action agenda is unorganised and underdeveloped. As Grigsby notes, 'the ideas of voluntary simplicity need to be developed to link their complaints and demands to clearly articulated and plausible policies that can be carried into existing political structures to bring about institutional change'. There are also simplicity theorists who embrace less conventional politics, such as Ted Trainer's eco-anarchism (2010), David Holmgren's permaculture strategy (2013), and Saral Sarkar's eco-socialism (1999). This is not the place to examine the political significance of simple living or the various strategies for bringing about structural change (see Alexander and Rutherford, 2014), but it should be clear that, to confront the overlapping crises we face today, a politics without an ethical foundation in simple living will fail to resolve those crises.

6. Conclusion

There is something painfully obvious about the need for most individuals and households in consumer cultures to consume less, differently, and more efficiently. This chapter has suggested, however, that this challenge need not sound so depressing. On the contrary, participants in the Voluntary Simplicity Movement see reimagining the consumerist ideal not as a matter of sacrifice or deprivation, but as a coherent path to genuine wealth and freedom. As Lao-Tzu once said, 'Those who know they have enough are rich'.

References

Alexander, S. (ed.). 2009. *Voluntary simplicity: The poetic alternative to consumer culture*. Whanganui: Stead and Daughters.

Alexander, S. 2011. 'Property beyond growth: Toward a politics of voluntary simplicity'. Doctoral thesis, Melbourne Law School. Available at: http://papers.ssrn.com/sol3/papers.cfm?abstract_id=1941069 (accessed 10 September, 2013).

Alexander, S. 2012a. 'The optimal material threshold: Toward an economics of sufficiency'. *Real-World Economics Review* 61: 2-21.

Alexander, S. 2013. 'Voluntary simplicity and the social reconstruction of law: Degrowth from the grassroots up'. *Environmental Values* 22: 287-308.

Alexander, S. and McLeod, A. 2014. *Simple Living in History: Pioneers of the Deep Future*. Melbourne: Simplicity Institute.

Alexander, S. and Rutherford, J. 2014. 'The deep green alternative: Debating strategies of transition'. *Simplicity Institute Report*, 14a: 1-24.

Alexander, S. and Ussher, S. 2012. 'The voluntary simplicity movement: A multi-national survey analysis in theoretical context'. *Journal of Consumer Culture* 12(1): 66-88.

Alexander, S., Trainer, T., and Ussher, S. 2012. 'The simpler way: A practical action plan for living more on less'. *Simplicity Institute Report* 12a: 1-43.

Aristotle, 1981. *The politics* (revised edn). London: Penguin Classics.

Burch, M. 2000. *Stepping lightly: Simplicity for people and planet*. Gabriola Island: New Society Publishers.

Cafaro, P. and Gambrel, J. 2009. 'The virtue of simplicity'. *Journal of Agricultural and Environmental Ethics* 23(1): 85.

Cushman, P. 1990. 'Why the self is empty'. *American Psychologist* 45(5): 599-611.

Deger, S. and Gibson, L. (eds). 2007 (2nd edn). *The book of positive quotations*. Rubicon Press: Minneapolis.

Douglas, M. 2006 [1976]. 'Relative poverty – relative communication', in T. Jackson (ed.). 2006. *The Earthscan Reader in Sustainable Consumption*. London: Earthscan.

Dominguez, J. and Robin, V. 2008 (revised edn). *Your money or your life: Transforming your relationship with money and achieving financial independence*. London: Penguin.

Elgin, D. 1998 (revised edn). *Voluntary simplicity: Toward a way of life that is outwardly simple, inwardly rich*. New York: William Morrow.

Gregg, R. 2009 [1936]. 'The value of voluntary simplicity', in S. Alexander (ed.). *Voluntary simplicity: The poetic alternative to consumer culture*. Whanganui: Stead & Daughters Ltd, 2009.

Grigsby, M. 2004. *Buying time and getting by: The voluntary simplicity movement*. Albany: State University of New York Press.

Hamilton, C. 2003. *Growth fetish*. Crows Nest, NSW: Allen & Unwin.

Hamilton, C. and Denniss, R. 2005. *Affluenza: When too much is never enough*. Crows Nest, NSW: Allen & Unwin.

Holmgren, D. 2013. 'Crash on demand: Welcome to the brown tech future'. *Simplicity Institute Report*. 13c: 1-23.

Hopkins, R. 2009. *The transition handbook: Creating local sustainable communities beyond oil dependency (Australian and New Zealand Edition)*. Lane Cove, Australia: Finch Publishing.

Jackson, T. 2009. *Prosperity without growth: Economics for a finite planet*. London: Earthscan.

Kubiszewski, I., Costanza, R., Franco, C., Lawn, P., Talberth, J., Jackson, T., and Aylmer, C. 2013. 'Beyond GDP: Measuring and achieving global genuine progress'. *Ecological Economics* 93: 57-68.

Lane, R. 2000. *The loss of happiness in market democracies*. New Haven: Yale University Press.

Miller, D. 2008. *The comfort of things*. Cambridge: Polity.

Myers, D. 2000. *The American paradox: Spiritual hunger in an age of plenty*. London: Yale University Press.

Offer, A., 2006. *The challenge of affluence: Self-control and well-being in the United States and Britain since 1950*. Oxford, New York: Oxford University Press.

Robinson, T. 2009. *Work, leisure, and the environment: The vicious circle of overwork and overconsumption.* Cheltenham: Edward Elgar Publishing.

Sarkar, S. 1999. *Eco-socialism or eco-capitalism: A critical analysis of humanity's fundamental choices.* London: Zed books.

Segal, J. 1999. *Graceful simplicity: Toward a Philosophy and Politics of the Alternative American Dream.* Berkeley: University of California Press.

Siegel, C. 2008. *The politics of simple living.* Berkeley: Preservation Institute.

Smith, J. and Positano, S. 2010. *The self-destructive affluence of the first world: The coming crises of global poverty and ecological collapse.* New York: Edwin Mellen.

Shi, D. 2007 (revised edn). *The simple life: Plain living and high thinking in American culture.* Athens: University of Georgia Press.

Thoreau, H. 1982. *The portable Thoreau.* Bode, C. (ed.). New York: Penguin.

Trainer, T. 2010. *The transition to a sustainable and just world.* Sydney: Envirobook.

Woodward, D. and Simms, A. 2006. 'Growth isn't working: The uneven distribution of benefits and costs from economic growth'. London: New Economics Foundation.

6

TED TRAINER AND THE SIMPLER WAY
A sympathetic critique

Although the changes required are immense, in most towns and suburbs the essentials could largely be achieved in months – at negligible dollar cost – if enough of us wanted to make them... But designing and building is not the problem. That's easy. The problem is developing the understandings and values whereby ordinary people will want *to design and build new systems, and will delight in doing so.*

– Ted Trainer

1. Introduction

For several decades Ted Trainer has been developing and refining an important theory of societal change, which he calls The Simpler Way (1985, 1995, 2010a). His essential premise is that over-consumption in the most developed regions of the world is the root cause of our global predicament, and upon this premise he argues that a necessary part of any transition to a sustainable and just world involves an adoption of materially far 'simpler' lifestyles by the over-consumers. That is the radical implication of our global predicament which most people, including most environmentalists, seem unwilling to acknowledge or accept, but which Trainer does not shy away from, and, indeed, which he follows through to its logical conclusion. This chapter outlines and presents a sympathetic critique of Trainer's complex position (2010a, 2010b, 2011, 2012b), a position that can be understood to merge and build upon various strains of socialist, anarchist, and environmentalist thinking (e.g., Morris, 2004; Gorz, 1994; Bookchin, 1990; Meadows, Randers, and Meadows, 2004).

Trainer's work is an important and original contribution to the debate surrounding eco-socialism. Although he assumes an essentially Marxist account of capitalism, and argues that state power is generally employed in the service of private capital expansion, it will be seen that Trainer rejects the underlying growth paradigm that traditionally shaped both capitalist and socialist economics (Hamilton, 2003). Furthermore, he rejects the conventional Marxist strategy of taking control of the state, and instead advocates a radically low-consumption, anarchist answer to the question of social and economic transformation. The new, zero-growth economy, he argues, will never be introduced from the 'top down', but must be built from the grassroots up, without reliance on state support. Nevertheless, Trainer also addresses the issue of structural change in ways that are typically neglected by grassroots eco-social movements (e.g., Hopkins, 2008). He is also uniquely rigorous in his critique of renewable energy, despite being unconditionally in favour of it, which advances sustainability discourse in critically important ways, and with challenging implications.

My analysis of these issues is designed in part to bring more attention to a theorist whose work has been greatly under-appreciated, so the discussion is more expository than critical. But I also raise questions about Trainer's position and develop it, where possible, in the hope of advancing the debate and deepening our understanding of the important issues under consideration.

2. The Global Predicament

Trainer's vision of The Simpler Way can only be understood in relation to his diagnosis of the global situation, which arises out of the 'limits to growth' analysis (Meadows, Randers, and Meadows, 2004). While the figures and statistics on resource depletion and environmental degradation are well known (e.g., MEA, 2005), Trainer maintains that their significance is not generally acknow-ledged or fully understood. The global economy, he argues, is far beyond the levels of resource and energy use that can be maintained for much longer (Global Footprint Network, 2012), let alone extended to all people. Add to this situation the fact that the global human population is expected to increase to nine billion in the next few decades, and the magnitude of our problems becomes clear. 'Our way of life', he concludes, 'is grossly unsustainable' (Trainer, 2010a, 19). To make matters worse, there is also a mounting body of evidence indicating that the richest nations are experiencing a breakdown of social cohesion and a stagnating quality of life (Wilkinson and Pickett, 2010; Lawn and Clarke, 2010; Lane, 2000), which implies that even if we could globalise and sustain consumer societies over the long term, we may not want to (Alexander 2009, 2011a).[8]

The problems, however, do not end there. In addition to the ecological and social issues just noted, Trainer joins many ecological economists (e.g., Daly, 1996) in highlighting the absurdity of the prevailing attitudes toward economic growth. The growth project continues to define the global development agenda (Purdey, 2010), despite evidence indicating that the existing global economy is already exceeding the sustainable carrying capacity of the planet (Global Footprint Network, 2012). Although the intricacies of the critique cannot be detailed here, the growth project faces additional challenges from those who argue that the peaking of oil and the bursting of credit bubbles are in the process of undermining the very possibility of continued growth (see Heinberg, 2011; chapters 7 and 8 in this book).

In line with much socialist theory, the moral that Trainer draws from this analysis is that the affluence enjoyed in rich countries is built on a global economic system that is, at its core, patently unjust. It is a system that enables the rich countries to take far more than their fair share of the world's resources, while depriving the poorest countries of the resources needed to live even a minimally decent existence. Not only that, rich nations work hard to entrench and maintain their empires using coercive aid contributions, trade power, 'structural adjustment packages', and, whenever necessary, military force (Trainer, 2010a, chapters 5 and 8). For all these reasons, among others discussed below, Trainer concludes that capitalism cannot be fixed or reformed; it has to be replaced. While Trainer is hardly alone in making that claim, the following sections show that he builds upon it in original ways.

---

[8] Trainer dedicates very little attention to the issue of overpopulation, which many will consider a significant weakness to his position. He is very aware of the problem, of course, which he builds into his diagnosis of the global situation; and he recognises the importance of stabilising and reducing population. But he could strengthen his position by discussing population issues in more detail. It is worth noting, however, that even if the world's population stopped growing today (at 7.2 billion), the planet would remain dangerously overburdened by high consumption lifestyles, so focusing primarily on consumption has some justification. There is certainly a risk that the population problem gets used to deflect attention away from what is the more fundamental problem of overconsumption, and perhaps this explains why Trainer has largely avoided the population debate so far.

3. The Limits of Technology and Renewable Energy

Before examining the alternative proposed by Trainer, his critical perspectives on technology and renewable energy will be outlined, as his claims on these subjects contradict widely held assumptions. Most people, including many environmentalists, seem to believe that Western-style lifestyles can indeed be sustained and even globalised, provided the world transitions to systems of renewable energy and produces commodities more cleanly and efficiently. This assumption is reflected especially clearly in international political discourse on environmental issues (e.g., UNDP, 2007/8), which consistently pushes the message that we can decouple economic growth from ecological impact, or even that we need *more* economic growth in order to fund environmental protection initiatives and thus save the planet (Beckerman, 2002). Trainer casts considerable doubt on the possibility of any technological 'fix' to ecological problems.

3.1 *Technology cannot sustain the growth paradigm*

Trainer's general point on technology is that the extent of ecological overshoot is already so great that technology will never be able to solve the ecological crises of our age, and certainly not in a world based on economic growth and with a growing global population. Amory Lovins (1998) is probably the best-known advocate of technological solutions to ecological problems, most famous for his 'factor four' thesis. He argues that if we exploit technology we could have four times the economic output without increasing environmental impact (or maintain current economic output and reduce environmental impact by a factor of four). But if the rich world continues to grow at 3% per year until 2070, and by that stage the poorest nations have attained similarly high living standards – which seems to be the aim of the global development agenda – the total world-economic output (and impact) could well be as much as 60 times larger than it is today (Trainer, 2010a, 21). If we assume that sustainability requires that fossil fuel use and other resource consumption must be half of what they are today – and the greenhouse problem probably requires a larger reduction than this (Hansen, *et al.*, 2008) – then what is needed is something like a factor 120 reduction in the per unit impact of GDP, not merely a factor 4 reduction (Trainer, 2007, 117). Even allowing for some uncertainty in these calculations, the claim that technological fixes can solve the ecological crises and sustain the growth paradigm is simply not credible. Trainer argues that the absolute decoupling necessary is just beyond what is remotely possible. The final nail in the coffin of techno-optimists is the fact that despite decades of extraordinary technological advance, the overall ecological impact of the global economy is still increasing (Jackson, 2009, Ch. 5), making even a factor four reduction through technological advance seem wildly optimistic.

3.2. *Renewable energy cannot sustain consumer societies*

Trainer (2007) has also levelled a narrower critique of technological solutions, which focuses on renewable energy. Resisting the common assumption that renewable energy systems can drive growth economies and support consumer societies, Trainer set himself the task of examining the crucially important and largely neglected question of what the *limits* of renewable energy sources might be.

This is not the place to review in detail Trainer's arguments and research. For the facts and figures, readers are referred to Trainer's books and essays (2007, 2010b, 2012a, and especially 2013a and 2013b). But the critical findings of his research can be easily summarised. After examining the evidence on varieties of solar, wind, hydro, biomass, and other kinds of energy sources, as well as energy storage and distribution systems, Trainer concludes the figures just do not support what almost everyone assumes; that is to say, they do not support the argument that renewable energy can sustain consumer societies. This is because the enormous (and globally growing) quantities of electricity and liquid fuels required by consumer societies today simply cannot be provided for by any mixture of renewable energy sources, each of which suffers from various limitations arising out of such factors as intermittency of supply, storage problems, resource limitations (e.g., land for biomass competing with food production), and inefficiency issues. Ultimately, however, the fundamental issue at play here is the cost. Trainer provides evidence showing that existing attempts to price the transition to systems of renewable energy are wildly understated (2012a).

This challenging conclusion, however, only defines the magnitude of the *present* problem. If we were to commit ourselves to providing nine or ten billion people with the energy resources currently demanded by those in the richest parts of the world, then the problems and costs become greater by orders of magnitude. The challenges are exacerbated further by the existence of the 'rebound effect', a phenomenon that often negates the expected energy use reductions of efficiency improvements (Holm and Englund, 2009;

Jackson, 2009, Ch. 4). At times, efficiency improvements can even be the catalyst for *increased* energy consumption – the 'Jevons' paradox discussed in Ch. 1 (see also, Polimeni, *et al.*, 2009). Going directly against the grain of mainstream thinking on these issues, Trainer is led to conclude that renewable energy and efficiency improvements will never be able to sustain growth-based consumer societies, primarily because it would be quite unaffordable to do so.

It is of the utmost importance to emphasise that this is not an argument against renewable energy as such; nor is it an argument more broadly against the use of appropriate technologies to achieve efficiency improvements. Trainer argues without reservation that the world must transition to full dependence on systems of renewable energy without delay and exploit appropriate technology wherever possible (Trainer, 2007, 117). But given the limitations and expense of renewable energy systems, any transition to a just and sustainable world requires a *vastly reduced demand for energy* compared to what is common in the developed regions of the world today, and this necessitates giving up growth-based, consumer societies and the energy-intensive lifestyles they support and promote.

4. The Radical Implications of a Zero-Growth Economy

The implications of the foregoing analysis can hardly be exaggerated. If it is accepted that the global economy is already in ecological overshoot, that the poorest nations on the planet have a right to increase their standards of living to some dignified level, that the global population may exceed nine billion within a few decades, and that technology will be unable to solve the various ecological crises, then it would seem that the richest nations must give up the pursuit of continued growth and create some zero-growth or steady state economy. In fact, the extent of the global predicament implies that the richest nations even need to go through a phase of planned economic contraction, or degrowth, before stabilising in a steady state economy of a sustainable scale (Lawn and Clarke, 2010; Kallis, 2011; Alexander, 2012a).

If people were to accept this diagnosis, or something like it, what would that actually mean for the most developed, growth-based economies? Trainer (2011) argues that even those who essentially agree with the diagnosis outlined above, and who accept that the world has indeed reached the 'limits to growth', rarely perceive the radical implications that would flow from giving up the growth economy. To be sure, ecological economists have been pointing out the contradiction between the limitless pursuit of economic growth and ecological sustainability for many decades (e.g., Daly, 1996), and in recent years the critique of growth has gained some momentum (Jackson, 2009). But Trainer maintains that the implications of a steady state economy have not been understood well at all, least of all by its advocates. Most advocates proceed as if we could and should eliminate the growth element of the present economy while leaving remaining structures more or less intact. Trainer provides three main criticisms of this position.

His first criticism is that eliminating the growth element of the present economy, while leaving the rest more or less as it is, cannot be done. This is because the present economy 'is not an economy which *has* growth; it is a *growth-economy*, a system in which the core structures and processes involve growth' (Trainer, 2011: 71). It follows, he argues, that 'if growth is eliminated then radically different ways of carrying out many fundamental processes have to be found' (*ibid.*). In particular, giving up growth would seem to necessitate changing the fundamentals of the existing finance and banking systems, as Trainer explains:

> If you do away with growth then there can be no interest payments. If more has to be paid back than was lent or invested, then the total amount of capital to invest will inevitably grow over time. The present economy literally runs on interest payments of one form or another; an economy without interest payments would have to have totally different mechanisms for carrying out many processes... Therefore *almost* the entire finance industry has to be scrapped, and replaced by arrangements whereby money is made available, lent, invested, etc. without increasing the wealth of the lender (2011: 77, emphasis in original).

Critics of growth rarely discuss or even acknowledge this issue, and yet it seems fundamental. Abolishing interest payments would touch the very core of growth-based economies, and it is not clear that a zero-growth economy could ever emerge if an interest-based system were to persist (Douthwaite and Fallon, 2011). This is certainly an issue to which progressive economists must dedicate much more attention because people are unlikely to give up the present monetary system until they have a detailed picture of a viable alternative. On a different note, eliminating poverty in a zero-growth economy could not be achieved by continued growth (i.e., by a rising tide lifting all boats), since growth itself would come to an end (Woodward and Simms, 2006). Instead, eliminating poverty in a zero-growth economy could only be achieved by a redistribution of wealth and power, both nationally and globally. Thus, a zero-growth economy must be much more egalitarian than any capitalist society, past or present. Fortunately, this broad-based redistribution of wealth is likely to produce healthier and happier societies compared to those societies in which wealth is highly polarised (Wilkinson and Pickett, 2010).

Trainer's second major point of criticism is that critics of growth typically proceed as if economic systems were the only or the primary things that have to be fixed. But Trainer argues that the major global problems facing us cannot be solved 'unless several fundamental systems and structures within consumer-capitalist society are radically remade' (2011: 71). For example, and most importantly, there would need to be a radical change in cultural attitudes toward consumption. This is because a zero-growth economy would never voluntarily arise, or be able to function, within cultures generally comprised of individuals seeking ever-higher levels of income and consumption. Accordingly, before growth economics can be overcome, some notion of economic sufficiency must be embraced at the cultural level (Alexander, 2011c, 2013a). As Trainer frankly notes, 'What is required is much greater social change than Western society has undergone in several hundred years' (2011: 17). The point is that a zero-growth economy depends on much more than changing the fundamentals of economic structures. It also implies 'an utterly different worldview and driving mechanism' (*ibid.*: 77).

For present purposes, Trainer's third and final major point of criticism – which again distinguishes his position from those of most other growth sceptics – relates to what he believes is the inextricable connection between growth and the market system. If there is to be no growth, he argues, '*there can be no role for market forces*' (2011: 78, his emphasis), a point he develops in the following terms:

> The market is about maximising; i.e., about producing, selling and investing in order to make as much money as possible from the deal, and then seeking to invest, produce and sell more, in order to again make as much money as possible. In other words, there is an inseparable relation between growth, the market system and the accumulation imperative that defines capitalism. If we must cease growth, we must scrap the market system (*ibid.*).

There are several issues with this analysis that deserve comment, although the first may be a criticism of expression merely, one that is important (for reasons of clarity) but can potentially be easily resolved. When Trainer asserts without any qualification that 'there can be no role for market forces' in a zero-growth economy, and that 'we must scrap the market system', this seems to misrepresent his own position, given that a close reading of his entire oeuvre shows that his position is much more nuanced. For example, when Trainer talks of 'scrapping' the market system, he does not mean that this must be done all in one go, as his language implies. His subtler position is that it would be a long process of phasing down the current economy and building up a new one. Furthermore, in the most complete statement of his perspective, Trainer (2010a) never calls for the abolishment of money *per se* (although he does call for its significant diminishment and reconceptualisation); nor does he deny that people in a zero-growth economy would still exchange goods and services with each other (although, again, he argues that such practices would play much less of a role than they do in consumer societies today and would be driven by different motives). But if a zero-growth economy could and should involve money and formal exchange *to some degree*, then it seems that it does not scrap the market system, as the above passages claim. After all, to purchase or formally exchange anything is to engage in 'market activity' (according to conventional usage of that phrase, at least), and there is no reason to think that such market activity is *necessarily* always driven by an ethics of profit-maximisation. Indeed, in Trainer's vision of a zero-growth economy (described below), market activity would not be driven by an ethics of profit-maximisation, but presumably by some ethics of genuine mutual benefit and concern.

It is important that Trainer refines or clarifies his expression of these points, because his blunt claim that the market must be 'scrapped' is not going to gain any support from those of us who are certain that market activity of some form, to some degree, will always have the potential to advance the human situation, even in a zero-growth economy. With some justification, Trainer criticises market activity when it is driven by an ethics of profit-maximisation, which, he argues, is morally repugnant in terms of human interaction, even leaving aside its connection with growth economics. But that seems to be a criticism of the *values* presently driving market activity, rather than a criticism of market activity as such, which could be driven by very different values. My point is that there is no need to 'scrap the market system' in order to create a zero-growth economy (Alexander, 2011c); but obviously whatever markets exist in a zero-growth economy would need to take on very different forms.

5. A Friendly Critique of Transition Initiatives and Permaculture

If the world ever manages to create a tapestry of highly localised, zero-growth economies, and by doing so arguably solve the greatest ecological and social challenges of our times, Trainer believes that it will have to be due to something like the Transition Towns movement (Hopkins, 2008). This nascent movement is primarily a community-orientated response to the dual crises of peak oil and climate change (among other things) and is based on the principles of permaculture (Holmgren, 2002). Although framed in slightly different terms, Trainer and others in the 'deep green' environmentalist camp have been arguing for something akin to Transition and permaculture for decades (Trainer, 1985; Trainer, 1995). Trainer therefore justly finds it immensely encouraging to see these movements bursting onto the global scene in recent years. But for all their promise, Trainer worries that these movements need to radically alter their visions and goals if they hope to make a significant contribution to solving the global predicament.

In his 'friendly critique' of the Transition Towns movement, Trainer (2009a, 2009b) articulates his concerns in some detail. 'Everything depends,' he begins, 'on how one sees the state of the planet, and the solution' (Trainer, 2009a: 1). He goes on to argue that if people do not understand the nature and extent of the crises we face, they will tend to misconceive the best responses to those crises, and set about working toward goals that cannot solve the problems. That is his primary concern about the Transition movement. He is worried that there is too much emphasis merely on building 'resilience' within consumer-capitalist society, and too little attention given to what Trainer believes is the more ambitious but necessary goal of replacing the fundamental structures of consumer-capitalist society. Setting up community gardens, food co-ops, recycling centres, permaculture groups, skill banks, home-craft courses, local currencies, etc. are all good things, and the Transition movement is doing all of these things, and much more. But Trainer (2009a: 1) contends that it is a 'serious mistake' to think these types of activities are enough, on their own, to create a new society. The existing economy, he argues, is quite capable of accommodating these types of activities without being threatened by them, prompting Trainer to speak of 'the insufficiency of resilience' (Trainer, 2009a: 1). What is required, he insists, is that Transition adopts a more radical vision, one which involves replacing the core institutions of consumer-capitalism, not merely reforming them or building resilience within them.

Trainer's 'friendly critique' understandably received some serious attention by participants in the Transition movement, including prominent figures Rob Hopkins (2009) and Brian Davey (2009). Although Hopkins (2009: 1) senses that he and Trainer ultimately 'agree on most things' in terms of what needs to happen, he did respond to some of Trainer's concerns in ways that deserve attention. Most importantly, Hopkins (2009: 1) drew the distinction between 'what is made explicit in Transition and what is kept implicit'. While Hopkins acknowledged that Trainer is right about the need to replace consumer capitalism, he did not accept that explicitly stating that goal should be a central part of Transition, for the simple reason that most people will be overwhelmed to the point of paralysis by so ambitious a project, or alienated by the language it employs. Hopkins is the most prominent figure in the Transition movement and his advocacy of the movement is a large part of its successes. Ever the diplomat, he masterfully walks the fine line between radical and reformer, and I believe he does this for pedagogical reasons. Whereas Trainer calls a spade a spade – and a revolution a revolution – Hopkins is more circumspect. My sense is that Hopkins and Trainer share a similar vision of the desired end-state, but in the hope of gaining a greater audience (which is obviously a necessary and important goal) Hopkins seems less prepared to state his radical vision quite so openly. This does not imply that Hopkins has a secret agenda that he is hiding from people. The point is simply that when activists for change talk about what needs to be done and how we might get there, we must put our minds to the extremely important question of how best to express ourselves, what language to use, and what means of persuasion best advances the causes at hand. After all, it is no good speaking the truth if it is expressed in such a way that most people are unwilling or unable to absorb the message. Indeed, it is probably fair to say that poor 'advocacy' is one of the greatest failures of the broader Green movement to date. At the same time, it is no good being listened to if the message is misconceived. These are some of the complex challenges faced by the Transition movement and the Green movement more generally, and Trainer and Hopkins deserve credit for grappling with them. Unsurprisingly, how best to proceed remains (and may always remain) an open question – one about which reasonable people can disagree.

Brian Davey's heartfelt response to Trainer's analysis was more fiery and less diplomatic than Hopkins', but it raises an equally important point. Like Hopkins, Davey does not so much reject Trainer's position on what needs to be done so much as he calls for greater realism in terms of the practical challenges faced by Transition. As Davey explains in terms directed at Trainer: 'it took me years with others to develop a successful community garden project. When I look at your description of all the things that you say the Transition Movement must do I want to scream with frustration' (Davey, 2009: 1). Davey hastens to add that his is not an ideological objection to Trainer's critique but a practical one: 'We are struggling already – the number of people with organisational and social entrepreneurial skills to set things up is small. There are lots willing to follow but few willing, or able, to lead' (Davey, 2009: 1). Furthermore, Davey laments that Trainer's vast agenda and critique of existing Transition practices 'serves more to discourage than anything else because it tells us all the things that we have to do and that we are already doing, in many cases run ragged with voluntary overwork – is still not enough'. We can be certain that Trainer never intended his message to discourage (Trainer, 2009b), but if that could be its effect then it provides Trainer and other sympathetic critics with some food for thought. At the same time, if it is to fulfil its potential, Transition must welcome constructive criticism and be prepared to discuss its weaknesses and failures.

It is likely that Davey's legitimate concerns could have been ameliorated had Trainer expressed himself somewhat differently from the outset. Trainer's point, which I feel is a valid one, is that existing Transition practices can be easily accommodated within consumer capitalism, and that more is required if fundamental change is ever to eventuate. But by insisting on more radical change, Trainer did not adequately acknowledge the immense practical challenges of such an undertaking (challenges of which he is very aware), and this led to Davey's exasperated reply. In my view, many people in Transition probably agree with something like Trainer's ambitious vision (outlined in more detail below), but the practical realities of realising the project are painfully present to activists at every turn, and so less ambitious projects are undertaken in order to achieve something rather than nothing. This is indeed my experience of the Transition Initiative with which I am personally involved. For these reasons I would suggest that Transition may not actually lack a sufficiently radical vision (or visions); instead, it may simply be that the limited resources and energies presently available to the Transition movement results in actions that seem and are moderate and inadequate, but which are nevertheless necessary building blocks for more ambitious undertakings in the future.

From little things big things grow. That must be the hope the Transition movement clings to as it struggles unsuccessfully (at present) to bring about the enormous changes that are necessary. Without that hope, many people would probably be immobilised by despair. We should always keep one eye on the big picture, no matter how distant or imposing it may seem, which is Trainer's point. But Hopkins and Davey remind us that any big picture will inevitably be comprised of countless, seemingly insignificant brushstrokes, each of which is a necessary part of the whole.

6. Anarchism and The Simpler Way

In this final substantive section I wish to provide some more detail on the new society that Trainer envisions (2010: Ch. 4), as well as outline the strategy he believes is essential to its realisation. No doubt, some will find Trainer's alternative society rather 'utopian' in outlook, but one of the functions of utopian writing is to provide details on alternative forms of lifestyle, in order to inspire movements to bring them into existence (de Geus, 1999; Alexander, 2013b). One could also defend Trainer on the grounds that it is infinite growth on a finite planet that seeks to defy reality, and that The Simpler Way is framed to acknowledge reality, not transcend it. In any case, Trainer's goal seems to be more about describing what he considers *necessary* for a sustainable and just society, not what he considers to be *likely*, and that goal ought to be borne in mind when assessing what follows.

6.1 *What would The Simpler Way look like?*

Perhaps the most important feature of The Simpler Way economy is that it moves away from the highly industrialised and globalised growth economies we know today, and moves toward small and highly self-sufficient local economies which use mainly local resources to meet local needs. These will be zero-growth economies that are sustained on much lower levels of resource consumption and ecological impact – perhaps 90% lower (Trainer 2010a: 2). This implies that material living standards will be far lower than what is common in consumer societies today – which is an absolutely essential part of any adequate response to the global predicament – but basic needs for all will be met and high living standards will be maintained because people will be living and working cooperatively in enjoyable and spiritually rewarding communities. These lifestyles of voluntary simplicity, therefore, do not mean hardship or deprivation (Alexander, 2012b; Alexander and Ussher, 2012). They just mean focusing on what is *sufficient* to live well, rather than constantly seeking increased consumption and greater affluence.

Although private firms will remain in the new economy, cooperative enterprises will be common too, and, where necessary, financing of appropriate new ventures will be obtainable on zero interest from a community-owned bank. The most important decisions about how the economy should meet the needs of the community will be placed under social governance. Town meetings will be held regularly and committees formed to discuss matters of social, economic, and ecological importance, and a Community

Development Cooperative (Trainer 2010a: 303) will be established to help organise and administer the community's essential goals and ventures, such as full employment and the elimination of poverty. Because overall consumption and production levels will be so greatly reduced from levels common in consumer societies today, the energy demands of this new economy will also be greatly reduced, meaning that renewable energy will easily be able to supply the energy required. The new economy, therefore, will be a post-carbon economy. Aside from renewable energy systems, however, technology would be quite basic – Trainer suggests we imagine something like 1950s technology – but this would nevertheless be more than sufficient for the purposes outlined above.

How would the community's needs be met? Organically grown food would be eaten in season and mainly produced in intensive home gardens and community gardens, as in small farms on the edge of urban settlements. For ecological and social justice reasons, meat consumption would reduce significantly. Permaculture principles and animal labour would greatly reduce the need for agricultural machinery, although Trainer (2010a: 82) anticipates that a small number of motorised vehicles and farming machines would still make sense, which would run on very limited ethanol produced from biomass, or electricity. Surplus production would be sold or exchanged in local markets for other necessary items, or left at the community centre for distribution. Common property – including much land that was once roads or parking lots – would be dug up and redeveloped productively into 'food forests' and maintained by community working bees. The concrete and bitumen could be recycled as building materials and the bitumen lumps could be stacked to create animal pens. The fashion industry would essentially come to an end, and a new aesthetic would develop based on functional, long lasting, and locally produced clothing. Houses would be small and humble but well designed or retrofitted, and they would be more densely inhabited than is common in many Western societies today. Most furniture would be homemade and overall home production of necessary goods and services would increase significantly.

Given the extent of home production and the minimal consumption of material goods, time spent in paid employment would decline dramatically, to as little as one or two days per week, but life would always remain busy and exciting because there would always be so much important work to do. Indeed, Trainer (2010a: 96) argues that in The Simpler Way the work/leisure distinction collapses. Furthermore, he anticipates that the cultural significance of things like television and computerised entertainment would decline markedly, or even disappear, and this would leave much more time for engaging in creative, productive, and more fulfilling activity. 'There would be little need for transport to get people to work,' Trainer explains, 'because most work places would be localised and accessible by bicycle or on foot... Railway and bus production would be one of the few activities to take place in large centralised heavier industrial centres' (*ibid.*: 93). Another implication of the new circumstances would be that international travel and trade would be rare, due to the greater appreciation and productivity of one's own locality, as well as the far greater fuel costs associated with travel and shipping in an age of declining petroleum supplies (Rubin, 2008).

Trainer (2010a, 2012b) also presents some interesting calculations regarding the ecological footprints and dollar costs implied by the type of communities described above. While acknowledging that his calculations are not exact, the data he presents (2012b; based primarily on his own practices and 'ecological footprint' analyses) suggest that per capita resource and energy use, and GDP per capita, could be reduced by as much as 90% compared to current levels in consumer societies. Trainer notes that it may be that such great reductions will not be necessary, but he presents a case showing that 'it would be possible and easy to cut our resource consumption and ecological impact to very small proportions of present rates if we adopted the ways discussed' (Trainer, 2010a: 111).

6.2. *Trainer's anarchist response to the question of strategy*

The final matter to be considered is the critically important question of how The Simpler Way could best be realised, because it is not enough to merely 'envision' a sustainable, just, and flourishing human society. We must figure out how best to get there, and Trainer gives this question of 'strategy' due attention (2010a: Pt. 3).

Trainer's analysis begins with what is essentially a Marxist critique of the capitalist state and proceeds to offer what amounts to a fundamentally anarchist solution. The Marxist line of thinking holds that the capitalist state is essentially an instrument of capital, which functions mainly to promote and secure the interests of the rich and powerful, at the expense of almost everyone else (Marx, 1983). The primary aim of state capitalism is capital expansion, plain and simple. Although framed in slightly differently terms, Trainer is largely sympathetic to this critical understanding of state capitalism, and with good reason. It certainly seems to be the case that governments in capitalist societies (and increasingly elsewhere) are under the undue influence of corporate interests (e.g., Tham,

2010), and treat economic growth as their primary and overriding concern (Hamilton, 2003). Accordingly, appealing to those governments to create a more egalitarian, zero-growth economy seems more or less doomed to failure.

This type of analysis of the state prompted Marx (and the orthodox Left more generally) to argue that radically changing society requires taking control of the state for socialist purposes – by way of violent revolution, if necessary. This is where Trainer parts company with Marxism and shifts to the anarchist camp. While he agrees that capitalism cannot be fixed, he argues that the state is so bound up in the values, structures, and mechanisms of growth that the imperative to grow is essentially a necessary element of *all* states, not merely capitalist states. Generally speaking, Marx and the orthodox Left never considered this to be a problem, because they too were firmly situated within the growth model. After all, they hoped to take control of the state but then distribute the proceeds of continued *growth* more equitably (cf. Foster, 2000, exploring 'eco-Marxism'). If Trainer is correct, however, and all states are inextricably committed to growth, then advocates of a zero-growth economy should not waste their time lobbying governments to advance their cause. Indeed, as a matter of strategy, he argues that advocates of a zero-growth economy must essentially ignore state capitalism to death by setting about building the alternative economy themselves, without expecting any help from the state (and probably receiving a lot of resistance from it). More radically still, Trainer even maintains that 'the Green Politics goal of parliamentary solutions, [is] mistaken and useless now' (2010a: 13), perhaps even 'counter-productive' (*ibid.*: 256), on the assumption that the state will never voluntarily dissolve the structures of growth that drive ecological degradation. We have limited time, resources, and energies, Trainer argues, so we should not waste them running for office or even campaigning for the Greens, because the state will be either unwilling or unable to help us. Advocates of zero-growth should just get active in their local communities and begin building the new society amongst the grassroots, here and now. This is the sense in which Trainer positions himself as an anarchist.

A full critical assessment of Trainer's anarchism lies well beyond the scope of this chapter, but I will offer some probing, cursory remarks. My first point concerns the fact that our lifestyle decisions, including our consumption decisions, always take place within specific socio-structural contexts. That is, they occur within social, economic, and political structures of constraint, many of which are a function of laws and policies created by the state. Those structures make some lifestyle decisions easy or necessary and others difficult or impossible. Currently, as I have argued elsewhere (Alexander, 2012c), those structures not only promote consumerist lifestyles but they also make oppositional lifestyles of voluntary simplicity very difficult, and in some respects impossible. This type of structural 'lock in', which is often subtle and insidious, can suffocate any attempt to create ways of life and social movements based on post-consumerist values, because current laws and structures make the practice of living more simply extremely challenging, even for those who already hold post-consumerist values. This is highly problematic because The Simpler Way and the zero-growth economy it promotes depend on the emergence of a post-consumerist culture. There are certainly structural limits to the ability of personal 'downshifting' to affect significant change.

In one sense, this seems to support Trainer's view that the state is intimately implicated in the growth model – so implicated, it would seem, that it can even function to 'lock' people into consumerist lifestyles (Sanne, 2002). There is much to be said in support of this argument, and it casts further doubt on the prospect of governments ever giving up the growth paradigm. Accordingly, as Trainer suggests, perhaps we should not waste our time on trying to persuade our political leaders to do so – just like we would not try to persuade zebras to change their stripes. From another angle, however, the argument casts some doubt on the viability of Trainer's anarchist strategy, because if people are indeed locked into consumerist lifestyles to some extent, then 'top down' structural change may be needed to 'unlock' people from those lifestyles. If the structures were changed, different consumption practices and 'ways of life' would, or could, emerge. Only then, it could be argued, will participants in a post-consumerist social movement be sufficiently free to create a new economy in the 'grassroots' manner Trainer envisions.

One reply to this line of questioning would be to acknowledge that the structure of growth economies can indeed lock people into consumerist lifestyles, but to insist that changing those structures does not require state action, only committed community action. While this reply has some merit, it does not change the fact that existing structures function to oppose the necessary community action. I offer no solution to these unsettled issues. My purpose is only to outline the questions that can be raised when Trainer's anarchist strategy is viewed through the lens of power.

My second point about Trainer's strategy concerns his seemingly optimistic assumptions about the prospects for peaceful human cooperation for common good, in the absence of state coercion. This is an issue all anarchists must deal with, for despite the undeniable beauty of their assumptions, many would argue that there are just too many people out there with strangely configured worldviews and behavioural histories, and that state coercion is therefore necessary to keep these people from imposing themselves on society in oppressive or violent ways. This is a challenge that has a long history in the literature on anarchism (Moreland, 1998), and I acknowledge that anarchists are not without their counter-arguments. But this is not the place to review and evaluate that thorny debate. I merely point out that the debate is ongoing and is unlikely ever to be closed.

I should add, however, that Trainer's vision would seem much less 'utopian' if a case could be made that it is actually in people's immediate self-interest to live simpler lives of reduced consumption and engage in the creative process of building a new society. This may seem like a counter-intuitive possibility in an age that glorifies consumption as never before, but an impressive body of evidence is mounting which suggests otherwise (see Alexander, 2012b). In accordance with ancient wisdom traditions, this research indicates that once our basic material needs are met, getting richer does not contribute much to our overall wellbeing, compared to things like community engagement, social relations, and creative activity. What this means is that most people leading high consumption lives could actually live better on less. This is extremely encouraging news, because if this message ever entered the collective consciousness of consumer societies, it could well spark the cultural revolution in attitudes toward consumption upon which a sustainable and just world relies. That is, if people *en masse* came to see that a simple life is a very good life, the world would change quickly and in fundamental ways.

My final point about Trainer's anarchist strategy builds upon the point just made. Let us optimistically suppose that post-consumerist values were mainstreamed over the next decade, and a critical mass of people began to see the desirability and necessity of The Simpler Way. Let us suppose further that this social movement began building the new society more or less according to Trainer's vision described above. My question is this: Would there not come a time when this social movement was so large and well organised that the state simply could not ignore its demands? And at that time, could not the state be employed to advance the goals of The Simpler Way and facilitate the transition to a sustainable and just world? These are questions that I ask myself in optimistic moods, and in those moods I confess to answering them in the affirmative. After all, if one is entitled to make optimistic assumptions about the possibility of a culture embracing The Simpler Way, it seems equally permissible to assume that our governments might one day be capable of acting in more enlightened ways too. If one is an anarchist 'on principle', this will be unsatisfactory because it involves working with the state (however enlightened it may become); but if one is currently a 'pragmatic anarchist' more as a matter of strategy than principle, then this possibility should not be closed off in advance, because strategies might need to change when the world (inevitably) changes.

7. Conclusion

This chapter has outlined the key elements of Ted Trainer's theory of The Simpler Way. Many intricacies of his analysis have necessarily received insufficient attention, and many issues remain to be explored more deeply, including: What form will The Simpler Way need to take in large urban centres, where existing infrastructure is poorly designed from a sustainability perspective and where land for localised food production is particularly hard to come by? How would a transition to The Simpler Way in the rich world affect the global South? And how would existing property rights, corporate structures, and power relations, which currently entrench the status quo, need to change in order to facilitate the emergence of The Simper Way? Notwithstanding these outstanding questions, my review will be considered a success if it prompts more people to consult, engage, and develop Trainer's primary texts, where more of the details on his challenging but inspiring vision can be found.

If it is true that the essential factor in the global predicament is overconsumption, the most obvious principle for a sustainable society is that those who are overconsuming must move to far more materially 'simple' lifestyles. This is the vision that Trainer has unpacked with considerable rigour and insight; he has also outlined a strategy for its realisation. 'The task is astronomically difficult, probably impossible,' he admits (2009: 6). At the same time, he insists that the peaceful revolution required can be joyous and easily achievable, if only people decide that it is what they want. This is the message of radical hope that exists deep within the bleak global picture Trainer so meticulously describes, and it suggests that the revolutionary task is primarily about developing the consciousness needed for a transition to The Simpler Way to take place.

References

Alexander, S. (ed.). 2009. *Voluntary simplicity: The poetic alternative to consumer culture.* Whanganui: Stead & Daughters.

Alexander, S. 2011a. 'The voluntary simplicity movement: Reimagining the good life beyond consumer culture'. *International Journal of Environmental, Cultural, Economic, and Social Sustainability* 7 (3): 133-150.

Alexander, S. 2011b. 'Peak oil, energy descent, and the fate of consumerism'. *Simplicity Institute Report* 11b: 1-21.

Alexander, S. 2011c. *Property beyond growth: Toward a politics of voluntary simplicity.* Ph. D. Thesis, Melbourne Law School, University of Melbourne. Accessed 5 May 2011. http://papers. ssrn.com/sol3/papers.cfm?abstract_id=1941069

Alexander, S. 2012a. 'Planned economic contraction: The emerging case for degrowth'. *Environmental Politics* 21 (3): 349-368.

Alexander, S. 2012b. 'The optimal material threshold: Toward an economics of sufficiency'. *Real-World Economics Review* 61: 2-21.

Alexander, S. 2012c. 'Degrowth implies voluntary simplicity: Overcoming barriers to sustainable consumption'. *Simplicity Institute Report* 12b: 1-17.

Alexander, S. 2013a. 'Voluntary simplicity and the social reconstruction of law: Degrowth from the grassroots up'. *Environmental Values* 22 (2): 287-308.

Alexander, S. 2013b. *Entropia: Life Beyond Industrial Civilisation.* Melbourne: Simplicity Institute.

Alexander, S. and Ussher, S. 2012. 'The voluntary simplicity movement: A multi-national survey analysis in theoretical context'. *Journal of Consumer Culture* 12 (1): 66-86.

Beckerman, W. 2002. *A poverty of reason: Sustainable development and economic growth.* Oakland: Independent Institute.

Bookchin, M. 1990. *Remaking society: Pathways to a green future.* Cambridge, MA: South End Press.

Daly, H. 1996. *Beyond growth: The economics of sustainable development.* Boston: Beacon Press.

Davey, B. 2009. *Brian Davey responds to Ted Trainer.* Available at: http://transitionculture.org/2009/12/03/brian-davey-responds-to-ted-trainer/ [accessed 31 March 2012].

Douthwaite, R. and Fallon G. 2011. *Fleeing Vesuvius.* Gabriola Island: New Society Publishers.

De Gues, M. 1999. *Ecological utopias: Envisioning the sustainable society.* Utrecht: International Books.

Foster, J.B. 2000. *Marx's ecology: Materialism and nature*. New York: Monthly Review Press.

Gilding, P. 2011. *The great disruption: How the climate crisis will transform the global economy*. London: Bloomsbury.

Global Footprint Network, 2012. Reports available at: http://www.footprintnetwork.org/en/index.php/GFN/ (accessed 31 March 2012).

Gorz, A. 1994. *Capitalism, socialism, ecology*. London: Verso.

Hamilton, C. 2003. *Growth fetish*. Crows Nest, NSW: Allen & Unwin.

Hansen, J. *et al.* 2008. *Target atmospheric CO2: Where should humanity aim?* Available at: http://www.columbia.edu/~jeh1/2008/TargetCO2_20080407.pdf (accessed 31 March 2012).

Heinberg, R. 2011. *The end of growth: Adapting to our new economic reality*. Gabriola Island: New Society Publishers.

Holm, S.-O. and G. Englund. 2009. 'Increased ecoefficiency and gross rebound effect: Evidence from USA and six European countries 1960-2002'. *Ecological Economics* 68: 879-887.

Holmgren, D. 2002. *Permaculture: Principles and pathways beyond sustainability*. Hepburn: Holmgren Design Services.

Hopkins, R. 2008. *The transition handbook: From oil dependency to local resilience*. Totnes, Devon: Green Books.

Hopkins, R. 2009. *Responding to Ted Trainer's friendly criticism of Transition*. Available at: http://transitionculture.org/2009/09/08/responding-to-ted-trainers-friendly-criticism-of-transition/ (accessed 31 March 2012).

Jackson, T. 2009. *Prosperity without growth: Economics for a finite planet*. London: Earthscan.

Kallis, G. 2011. 'In defence of degrowth'. *Ecological Economics* 70: 873-880.

Lane, R., 2000. *The loss of happiness in market democracies*. New Haven: Yale University Press.

Lawn, P. and Clarke, M. 2010. 'The end of economic growth? A contracting threshold hypothesis'. *Ecological Economics* 69: 2213-2223.

Lovins, A. 1998. *Factor four: Doubling wealth – halving resource use*. London: Earthscan.

Marx, K. 1983. *The portable Marx* (edited by E. Kamenka). London: Penguin.

Millennium Ecosystem Assessment, 2005. Available at http://www.millenniumassessment.org/en/index.aspx. (accessed 30 April 2011).

Meadows, D., Randers, J., and Meadows, D. 2004. *Limits to growth: The 30-year update*. White River Junction, Vt: Chelsea Green Publishing.

Moreland, D. 1998. *Demanding the impossible? Human nature and politics in nineteenth-century social anarchism*. London: Continuum International.

Morris, W. 2004. *News from nowhere and other writings*. London: Penguin Classics.

Polimeni, J. *et al*. 2009. *The myth of resource efficiency: The Jevons paradox*. London: Earthscan.

Purdey, S. 2010. *Economic growth, the environment, and international relations: The growth paradigm*. New York: Routledge.

Rubin, J. 2008. *Why your world is about to get a whole lot smaller*. London: Virgin.

Sanne, C. 2002. 'Willing consumers – or locked in? Policies for a sustainable consumption'. *Ecological Economics* 42: 273-287.

Schor, J. 2010. *Plenitude: The new economics of true wealth*. New York: Penguin Press.

Tham, J-C. 2010. *Money and politics: The democracy we can't afford*. Sydney: University of New South Wales Press.

Trainer, T. 1985. *Abandon affluence*. London: Zed Press.

Trainer, T. 1995. *The conserver society*. London: Zed Press.

Trainer, T. 2007. *Renewable energy cannot sustain a consumer society*. Dordrecht: Springer.

Trainer, T. 2009a. *The Transition Towns movement: Its huge significance and a friendly criticism*. Available at: http://www.energybulletin.net/node/51594 (accessed 31 March 2012).

Trainer, T. 2009b. *Further musings from Ted Trainer*. Available at: http://transitionculture.org/2009/09/29/further-musings-from-ted-trainer/ (accessed 31 March 2012).

Trainer, T. 2010a. *The transition to a sustainable and just world*. Sydney: Envirobook.

Trainer, T. 2010b. 'Can renewables solve the greenhouse problem: The negative case'. *Energy Policy* 38(8): 4107-4114.

Trainer, T. 2011. 'The radical implications of zero growth economy'. *Real-World Economics Review* 57: 71-82.

Trainer, T. 2012a. *Renewable energy – cannot sustain an energy intensive society*. Available at: http://socialsciences.arts.unsw.edu.au/tsw/RE.html (accessed March 31 2012).

Trainer, T. 2012b. 'How cheaply could we live and still flourish', in *The Simpler Way: A practical action plan for living more on less*. S. Alexander, S. Ussher, and T. Trainer (eds). *Simplicity Institute Report* 12a, 20-43.

Trainer, T. 2013a. 'Can Europe run on renewable energy? A negative case'. *Energy Policy* 63: 845-850.

Trainer, T. 2013b. 'Can the world run on renewable energy'. *Humanomics* 29(2): 88-104.

United Nations Development Program (UNDP), 2007/8. *Human Development Report*. Available at: http://hdr.undp.org/en/reports/global/hdr2007-2008/ (accessed 30 April 2011).

Wilkinson, R. and Pickett, K. 2010. *The spirit level: Why greater equality makes societies stronger*. London: Penguin.

Woodward, D. and Simms, A. 2006. *Growth isn't working: The uneven distribution of benefits and costs from economic growth*. London: New Economics Foundation.

7

THE NEW ECONOMICS OF OIL
Energy, economics, and the twilight of growth

Increasing the oil supply to support economic growth will require high oil prices that will undermine that economic growth.
— David Murphy and Charles Hall

1. Introduction

There has been a fair bit of talk about the so-called 'death' of peak oil. These eulogies have been motivated primarily by the upsurge of shale oil production in the US (Maugeri, 2012), as well as the announcement that the premiere peak oil website, *The Oil Drum*, is shutting up shop (The Oil Drum, 2013). Even the notoriously left-leaning eco-journalist George Monbiot (2012) has announced: 'We were wrong about peak oil.'

But Monbiot is wrong about being wrong. For reasons outlined below, peak oil is very much alive and squeezing its hands ever more tightly around the throats of oil-dependent economies. In other words, it is not the dynamics of peak oil that are struggling to survive, but the industrial economies that are trying to ignore the implications of oil addiction in an age of declining energy returns on investment. The new economics of oil also have alarming implications for climate change, as Monbiot acknowledged, suggesting that this is a subject we dismiss at our own peril.

This chapter seeks to show that oil issues remain at the centre of global challenges facing humanity, despite recent claims of oil abundance, and that the challenges are only going to intensify in coming years as competition increases over the world's most important source of fossil energy. The main issue, however, is not whether we will have enough oil, but whether we can afford to produce and burn the oil we have.

This chapter focuses on the problems of expensive oil; the next chapter focuses on the problems of cheap oil. In an age of price volatility, both issues need to be considered, as they raise very different economic, political, and environmental issues.

2. Is 'Peak Oil' Dead or Alive?

Peak oil, of course, does not mean that the world is running out of oil. There is a vast amount of oil left – approximately half of Earth's original endowment (Sorrell *et al.*, 2012; Maugeri, 2012). Over the last 150 years, however, we've picked the low-hanging fruit, so to speak, meaning that the remaining oil is harder to find and more expensive to extract (Murphy, 2014; Murphy and Hall, 2011a). With the age of cheap and easy oil at an end, oil companies are now drilling in thousands of feet of water, processing tar sands, and being forced into extremely inhospitable areas, such as the arctic, while at the same time major existing wells are in decline (Lyons and Ghalambor, 2007; Klare, 2012; Kopits, 2014). This is making it more difficult to increase the 'flow' of oil out of the ground.

When the rate of crude oil production cannot be increased, that represents peak oil. This situation is considered by many to signify a defining turning point in history, because oil demand is expected to increase as the world continues to industrialise (Hirsch *et al.*, 2010). The theory goes that as the supply of oil stagnates and the demand increases, the cost per barrel will rise, making the consumption of oil an increasingly expensive and debilitating addiction.

So is this theory alive or dead? Well, it's not a theory, it's a reality. Around 2005 the production of crude or 'conventional' oil stopped growing significantly and has been on a corrugated plateau ever since (see Miller and Sorrell, 2014: 6). Data from the Energy Information Administration show that between 2005 and 2012 there was only 0.3% average annual growth of crude oil production (see Heinberg, 2013: 6). Other mainstream institutions have acknowledged this plateau too, including the International Energy Agency (IEA, 2010: 6), which recently reiterated an acknowledgement of the crude oil peak through its chief economist, Fatih Birol (BBC, 2013). Global demand for oil, however, has continued to grow significantly (IEA, 2012), which has put upward pressure on the price of oil. Although there has been some price volatility in recent years, the IEA (2013: 6) notes that 'Brent crude oil has averaged $110 per barrel in real terms since 2011, a sustained period of high oil prices that is without parallel in oil market history'. The challenge of expensive of oil is compounded by the challenge of price volatility, in ways discussed further below.

Geopolitical instability in oil-rich regions of the world also pushes prices high (Klare, 2012), with recent developments in Libya, Syria, and Iraq being but the latest manifestation of this dynamic. Even if people reject the geological concerns over oil supply, the very real threat of ongoing geopolitical disruptions gives all oil importing nations a reason to prepare for supply disruptions (see Blackburn, 2014). This is especially so, as noted by the IEA, given that in coming years the world will come to rely increasingly on a small number of producers, mainly in the Middle East and Northern African regions where oil is shipped along 'vulnerable supply routes' (IEA, 2011: 3). It is also worth bearing in mind that the price spikes from the oil crises of 1973 and 1979, both of which induced recessions, were driven not by geology but geopolitics. It would be naïve to think that further crises could not arise, especially as competition over existing supplies continues to intensify (see Hiscock, 2012; Klare, 2012).

The upward pressure on price over the last decade has changed the economics of several sources of unconventional oil, making them more financially viable to produce when once they were not. For example, the main reason shale oil was not produced historically was because the costs of getting it out of the ground and refining it were significantly more than the market price for oil (Heinberg, 2013).

But with oil averaging above US$100 per barrel in recent years – price volatility notwithstanding – producers are more likely to be able to make money producing shale oil and other unconventional oils, even though their energy and economic return on investment (EROI) is considerably lower than conventional oil (Murphy, 2014; Murphy and Hall, 2011b). The fact that unconventional oil is much more carbon-intensive than crude oil (Hansen and Kharecha, 2008) – exacerbating an already intractable climate problem (IPCC, 2013) – does not seem to trouble oil producers or most politicians.

Driven by a decade of sustained high prices, this new production has meant that the total oil production (conventional plus unconventional oil) has been able to meet increasing global demand, even though conventional oil has shown almost no growth in recent years. Because total oil production has increased to meet demand, many commentators have declared that 'peak oil' is dead. These declarations, however, are based on a misunderstanding.

The current oil production situation does not debunk but rather confirms the peak oil argument. The peak oil position – at least, the most coherent iteration of its varieties – holds that when conventional oil reaches a plateau (and eventually declines), this will lead to an increase in price; but price increases make unconventional oils more financially viable, thus increasing their production and delaying a decline in overall production of liquid fuels. This is what we are seeing today (Brecha, 2013; Sorrell *et al.*, 2012; Miller and Sorrell, 2014).

The key factor in understanding the implications of peak oil, therefore, has less to do with total oil production, or even total reserves. Rather, it is inextricably linked to the price of oil. The peak oil school always argued that oil dependent economies would suffer when the growth of conventional oil slowed and the price of oil increased. This scenario is playing out before our very eyes. In short, the economics of peak oil are very much alive and well – just ask the struggling global economy (Tverberg, 2012).

3. Is the Shale Boom a Bubble?

Before looking more closely at the economic implications of expensive oil and declining EROI, it is worth noting that there is a serious question over whether there is even much money to be made producing shale oil, despite all the hype, or whether, by contrast, there is currently a shale 'boom' that may all-too-soon go 'bust'. Although mainstream media and institutions are reporting on the 'new age' of US oil and gas (IEA, 2012), and even going so far as to claim that the US will soon be energy independent (Citigroup, 2012), evidence suggests that such claims lack foundation.

David Hughes, for example, has conducted the most rigorous and comprehensive examination to date on shale holdings in the US – based on data for 65,000 wells – and his conclusions are strikingly at odds with popular perception. While he acknowledges that shale production provides some 'breathing room' (Hughes, 2013: *iii*), he insists that optimistic claims that the US is heading for energy independence are 'entirely unwarranted based on the fundamentals' (Hughes, 2013: *iv*; see also, Hughes, 2014). Richard Heinberg's new book reviews the evidence and is similarly critical, likening the so-called shale revolution to 'snake oil' (Heinberg, 2013).

One need not, however, rely solely on such critics as Hughes and Heinberg, respectable though their analyses may be (see also, Leggett, 2013). Strong messages have started to emerge even from within the oil and gas industry, to the effect that shale is not proving to be the energy 'saviour' that it was hoped to be even a few years ago. If it was once assumed, for example, that shale *gas* production was going to lessen the oil supply challenges (for example, by shifting transport fuels from oil to gas), voices from within the industry suggest this does not seem to be a very promising or reliable strategy (see leaked emails and documents compiled in the *New York Times*, 2014). In 2012 the CEO of Exxon Mobil, Rex Tillerson, commented on what the shale boom has done for his company, saying 'we are all losing our shirts today. We're making no money. It's all in the red' (Krauss and Lipton, 2012). In 2013, Exxon Mobil's quarterly profits were down a remarkable 57% (Gilbert, Scheck, and Fowler, 2013).

Similarly, Royal Dutch Shell has just written down its shale holdings by $2.07 billion, which helped push the company's second quarter earnings down 60% from a year earlier, as reported in the *Wall Street Journal* (Gilbert, Scheck, and Fowler, 2013). Even while the oil price was placed over $100 per barrel, *The Economist* (2013a) speculates that 'the day of the huge integrated international oil company is drawing to a close'. These are hardly intimations of a new 'golden age' in oil and gas production (IEA, 2012; Inman, 2014), despite increases in US production in recent years. After all, it is no good having vast technically recoverable resources if producing them is uneconomic. Furthermore, any fall in the price of oil – perhaps due to a further downturn in an already struggling global economy or short-term gluts – could also make some currently profitable shale holdings unprofitable, which soon enough would reduce shale production (see, e.g., Carroll and Klump, 2013; see also, Ch. 8). Even the IEA has reduced its enthusiasm for US shale, with chief economist Fatih Birol telling the *Financial Times* that shale represents 'a surge, rather than a revolution' (Makan and Hume, 2013). Indeed, a recent IEA 'Medium Term Market Report' indicates that the US 'surge' may level off as early as 2016 (see Mushalik, 2014). Given that US oil growth in recent years has disguised a production drop in the rest of the world (see Mushalik, 2013a), this imminent plateau in US production is significant.

Closer to home, the Australian Petroleum Production and Association's own *Oil & Gas Gazette* reported in June 2013 that the 'shale gale is little more than hot air', that '... the whole shale oil and gas game still looks like a net negative cash flow business', and that production has been driven '...not by any notion of ongoing profitability of the business' (Strachan, 2013: 4). While the future of the shale boom remains an open question, the fact that industry insiders are already expressing doubts about its long-term significance suggests that shale is not an energy source our economies should be relying on to meet ongoing supply.

Given that shale oil production is, in fact, currently doing the most to meet growing oil demand, any shale oil 'bust' is likely to have significant implications for an already strained oil market. Such a bust would also expose the stagnating production around the rest of the world, which is currently disguised (to the uncritical observer) by shale production gains (see data sources presented in Mushalik, 2013a). But even if there is no bust, as such, what seems beyond dispute is that the era of cheap and easy oil (averaging $20-25 historically) is over, owing primarily to the crude oil peak. Readers may recall the words of the Chevron advertisement from 2005, which noted 'the age of easy oil is over' (see Dodson and Sipe, 2008: 33).

A further reason to believe the price of oil will continue to face upward pressures over the long term is the fact that global *demand* for oil is expected to keep growing significantly. Much of this demand is coming from places like China and India, where energy intensive industrialisation is escalating at extraordinary rates, and where cheap cars are opening the door for hundreds of millions of new drivers who will need fuel. Naturally this increase in global demand is putting growing pressure on oil supply around the world.

The fact the consumption of oil in the US has gone down in the last few years is not a sign that 'peak oil' has been negated by 'peak demand' (*Economist*, 2013b), but that peak oil has increased the price of oil so much that ordinary consumption practices have become unaffordable, suggesting 'demand destruction' is a more appropriate term than 'peak demand'. Given the close link between energy and economic growth (see, e.g., Ayers and Warr, 2009) this demand destruction has economic implications.

What is less widely appreciated, however, is the fact that huge increases in consumption are occurring *within oil exporting nations* (e.g., in Russia and the nations in OPEC) (see, e.g., Rubin and Buchanan, 2007; Heinberg, 2011). This rise in consumption is making it more difficult for those nations to maintain existing exports, for obvious reasons. As consumption grows within oil exporting nations, and as production stagnates, there is a great incentive for those exporting nations to keep more oil for themselves, which means that the OECD nations, for example, should not assume that they are going to get the same proportion of global oil production as they do presently. Indeed, as a result of the crude oil peak, exports also seem to have peaked around 2006 (see data sources presented in Mushalik, 2013b). Since internal supplies of most importers are also declining (Hirsch *et al.*, 2010), this gives rise to a situation where most importers and exporters are wanting more oil, while they are also facing stagnating or decreasing production. This is the 'oil crunch' that is likely to define the 21st century, a crunch that is in fact in the process of unfolding in the form of increased competition, increased production costs, and ultimately, price volatility caused by expensive oil.

But can the world economy afford expensive oil?

4. The New Economics of Oil

The economic significance of the crude oil peak is clearest when we 'do the maths'. In what follows, I briefly unpack the economic implications of the price of oil rising from its historical average of around $25 per barrel[9] to an average of around $105 per barrel in recent years. I use the US as a test case, and then move on to the global situation. (Again, the following chapter considers the implications of the price of oil falling, which raises a very different but intimately related set of problems.)

The following type of analysis could be repeated for all nations, with particular significance for oil importing nations. Even allowing for different assumptions regarding the price of oil, the essential conclusion is difficult to deny: due to the minimal growth of crude oil production, there is now upward pressure on the price of oil as EROI declines, and this is having a debilitating effect on oil-dependent economies, especially oil importing nations, as the peak oil school predicted. Here are some figures:

The US currently consumes 18.605 million barrels of oil per day (mbpd) (EIA 2013a), with net imports of 7.412 mbpd (EIA, 2013b). If crude oil production had continued growing at historic rates and prices had remained at the historic price of $25 per barrel, this would mean that the US today would be spending $465 million on oil every day, or $170 billion per year. At $25 per barrel, the US expenditure on net oil imports would be $185 million per day, or $68 billion per year. These figures are still high, but remember, these calculations are based on cheap oil.

At the price of around $105 per barrel, however, the US is spending a total of $2 billion per day on oil, or the equivalent of $713 billion per year. With respect to oil imports alone, the US is currently spending $778 million per day, or $284 billion per year. The critical point is the *difference* between these two scenarios, because that arguably represents the economic implications of the crude oil peak. Put otherwise, if crude oil had not peaked and the price of oil remained at around $25 per barrel, the US would be spending around $1.5 billion *less* per day on oil, or $543 billion *less* per year. Most importantly, however, the US would be spending almost $600 million *less* per day on oil imports, or $216 billion *less* per year.

I highlight the import costs, in particular, because that is money that is being sucked out of the US economy – or any oil importing economy. The extent of imports means that these figures

---

[9] For historical data on the price of oil, see http://www.wtrg.com/prices.htm, accessed 10 September 2013.

are hugely significant. Surely the US economy would be doing much better today (at least, growing faster) if it did not have to send out of the country, due to the rise in oil prices in recent years, an extra $600 million every day on oil imports. What would the US look like today if it had an extra $600 million *every day* to spend on renewable energy, schools, hospitals, or public transport?

Even leaving the issue of imports to one side, however, the increase in overall oil expenditure would have, and is having, an impact of its own, because this increased oil expenditure is drawing money away from the rest of the economy. Overall, were it not for the price increase, the US would have an extra $1.5 billion per day to spend in the broader economy, or $543 billion per year. Instead, all that money is being spent on expensive oil, which is distorting the economy (Kerschner *et al.*, 2013; Murphy, 2014; Kopits, 2014). Is it any wonder oil-dependent economies are struggling to grow their economies? Could it be that expensive oil signifies the twilight of industrial growth, as we have known it?

Another way to think of all this is in terms of oil expenditure as a proportion of GDP. In 2012, the GDP of the US was approximately $15 trillion. If the US were paying historic average prices for oil, total oil expenditure would only be 1.13% of GDP. However, at the price of $105, total oil expenditure would be 4.75% of GDP. In other words, over the last decade or so, the costs of expensive oil have absorbed an extra 3.62% of GDP.

These figures are worrying, especially if oil continues to increase in price as global demand grows, exports decline, production costs increase, and overall production slows. James Hamilton (2011) has shown that 10 of the last 11 recessions in the US were preceded by high oil prices. By way of comparison with the figures above, Hamilton (2011: 5) notes, 'in 2008, the U.S. consumed 7.1 billion barrels of oil at an average price of $97.26/barrel, for an economic value of $692 billion, or 4.8% of GDP.' We all know how the US economy looked in 2008-2009, in the midst of the global financial crisis, and the analysis above suggests that oil expenditure in the US is getting dangerously close to the level at which it could induce another recession (Murphy, 2014; Murphy and Hall, 2011a-b).

Even if expensive oil does not induce recession, it seems clear that expensive oil makes growth very difficult, and this provides some grounds for thinking that we are entering the twilight of growth globally (Heinberg, 2011). The above analysis, after all, can be repeated for the world as a whole, producing figures that are equally sobering. The world currently consumes around 90 million barrels of oil per day (IEA, 2012), and if each barrel were $25, that would be a global oil expenditure of $2.25 billion per day. At $105, however, the world spends $9.45 billion per day on oil, or $3.5 trillion per year. This is a difference of $7.2 billion every day, an extra cost to the global economy which is largely a result of crude oil having peaked. It lacks credibility to pronounce the death of something that is costing the global economy $7.2 billion per day – or $2.6 trillion extra per year. If people had listened to the warnings of the peak oil school, we could have broken our addiction to oil by now and had this money to spend on other things. Unfortunately, oil expenditure continues to grow. At the same time, the peak oil school, in good health, is strangely pronounced dead.

As these figures show, peak oil as a concept and phenomenon is alive and well, and placing an ever tighter stranglehold on the global economy. The global economy struggles to withstand the economic impacts of high oil prices, primarily because so much trade is now international and therefore dependent on oil for the transportation (and production) of goods. When oil prices get so high that the economy cannot function – which seems to be what happened in 2008 when oil reached $147 per barrel – the economy struggles to grow, and this reduction in economic activity means a reduction in oil demand, leading to a fall in the price of oil (Heinberg, 2011). This fall in price is what happened after the Global Financial Crisis hit in 2008 (Rubin, 2012), and it is what happens whenever the demand for oil is reduced because of economic recession. Low oil prices, however, then aid economic recovery, but as economies recover from recession and begin to grow again, this puts more demand pressure on stagnating oil supplies, and the cycle repeats itself. This is what Murphy and Hall (2011b: 52) call the 'economic growth paradox: increasing the oil supply to support economic growth will require high oil prices that will undermine that economic growth'.

In short, as oil production slows or stagnates, oil prices may continue to increase until they reach an economic breaking point, crashing or destabilising economies, which would lead to a crash in oil prices; the low oil prices would then facilitate economic recovery, which puts more demand pressure on oil, leading prices to rise till economic breaking point, and so on and so forth. This cycle of bust-recovery-bust is what we may face in coming years and decades, and ultimately economic contraction is what we may have to prepare for. The world is unlikely to escape this unhappy cycle until it transitions beyond a growth-based economy and breaks its addiction to oil (see Alexander, 2012; Alexander, 2014).

This point about breaking our addiction to oil deserves some brief elaboration, because it raises the spectre of what Tom Murphy (2011) has called the 'energy trap'. In order to break the addiction to oil, economies dependent on oil will need to invest huge amounts of money and energy in building new social and economic infrastructures that are not so heavily dependent on oil (e.g., efficient public transport systems to incentivise people to drive less, organic food systems, renewable energy systems, etc.). But since this transition has not yet seriously begun, the necessary investment of money and energy is going to be required at a time when money and energy are scarcer than they have been in recent decades. This places us in the 'energy trap'. Politicians are going to have a short-term incentive *not* to invest extra money and energy in new infrastructure, since people will already be feeling the pinch of high oil prices. This means that there will be very little or no surplus money and energy to direct towards the necessary infrastructure projects. But while passing the buck, so to speak, will provide some short-term relief for people and politicians, it only delays the inevitable need for that new infrastructure. A delay only exacerbates the problem, however, since the necessary investment will then need to come later, at a time when energy and money are scarcer still, the price of oil is probably even higher, and the time frame for change is tighter.

When oil gets expensive, everything dependent on oil gets more expensive, like transport, mechanised labour, industrial food production, plastics, among many other things. This pricing dynamic sucks discretionary expenditure and investment away from the rest of the economy, causing debt defaults, economic stagnation, recessions, or even longer-term depressions. That seems to be what we are seeing around the world today, with the risk of worse things to come (Tverberg, 2012). This should provide us all with further motivation to rapidly decarbonise the economy, not only because oil has tended to be painfully expensive in recent years, but also because the oil we are burning is getting more carbon-intensive. I, for one, can think of many better things on which to spend $2.6 trillion dollars per year – things such as renewable energy, bike lanes, better public transport, and organic food production (Heinberg and Lerch, 2010).

The maths of peak oil suggest that we have entered a new era of energy and economics, one in which expensive oil is going to make it increasingly difficult for oil dependent economies to grow their economies. After two centuries of sustained economic growth, this surely marks a significant turning point in history, but little attention is being given to this issue at the macroeconomic and political levels. Where are the politicians acknowledging this issue and giving it due public attention?

In the absence of a robust understanding of these issues, most economists and politicians around the world are still crafting their policies based on flawed, growth-based thinking, not recognising that the new economics of energy mean that the growth model, which assumes cheap energy inputs, is now dangerously out-dated. The climatic implications of exploiting unconventional oils make the maths more worrying still (McKibben, 2012; Hansen and Kharecha, 2008). Granted, we are not running out of oil any time soon, but there will come a time when we run out of economically cheap, environmentally affordable oil, and, in fact, it seems that time is already upon us.

5. Conclusion

Peak oil turned out to be a more complex phenomenon than theorists originally anticipated. It has not been experienced as a precise 'moment' or 'event', but rather as a dynamic interplay between various forces that have provoked some adaptive adjustments (such as demand destruction or increased investments) in incremental and multidimensional ways. There may never be a 'shock moment' of peak oil's arrival; instead, peak oil may continue to play out as a gradual, unplanned transition to a new set of energy and consumption patterns that are less oil dependent, giving rise to social, economic, and ecological impacts that no one can predict with any certainty. The evolving interrelationship of geological, geopolitical, economic, cultural, and technological variables has continued to surprise analysts – both the 'cornucopians', who claim there is nothing to worry about, and the 'doomsayers', who think collapse is imminent, as well as everyone in between. No doubt there will be more twists still to come in this energy tale. But what seems clear is that the consequences of peak oil are not going away.

Whether the next twist arrives in the form of a new war or financial crisis, a new technology, a bursting shale bubble, or perhaps a radical cultural shift away from fossil fuels in response to climatic instability, intellectual integrity demands that analysts continue to revise viewpoints as further evidence continues to arrive. This issue is too important to be governed by ideology.

References

Adams, C. 2014. 'Oil price fall threatens $1 trillion of projects'. *Financial Times* (15 December 2014). Available at: http://www.ft.com/cms/s/0/b3d67518-845f-11e4-bae9-00144feabdc0.html#axzz3MbJePVES (accessed 16 December 2014).

Alexander, S. 2012a. 'The sufficiency economy: Envisioning a prosperous way down'. *Simplicity Institute Report* 12s: 1-32.

Ayres, R. and Warr, B. 2009. *The economic growth engine: How energy and work drive material prosperity*. Cheltenham, UK: Edward Elgar Publishing.

Brecha, R. 2013. 'Ten reasons to take peak oil seriously'. *Sustainability* 5(2): 664-694.

British Broadcasting Corporation (BBC). 2013. 'Hard-talk' (interview with Fatih Birol). Available at: http://www.youtube.com/watch?v=pYUj1ere2BI, (accessed 10 September 2013).

Carroll, J. and Klump, E. 2013. 'Oil's $5 trillion permian boom threatened by $70 oil'. *Bloomberg*, 25 October 2013. Available at: http://www.bloomberg.com/news/2013-10-24/oil-s-5-trillion-permian-boom-threatened-by-70-crude.html (accessed 25 October 2013).

Citigroup. 2012. 'Energy 2020: North American the New Middle East'. Available at: https://ir.citi.com/%2FSyMM9ffgfOZgu StaGpnCw5NhPkvdMbbn02HMA05ZX%2BJHjYVS07GqhxF2 wMk%2Bh4tv7DEZ5FymVM%3D (accessed 17 October 2013).

Dodson, J. and Sipe, N. 2008. *Shocking the suburbs: Oil vulnerability in Australian cities*. Sydney: University of New South Wales Press.

Economist, The 2013a. 'The global oil industry'. *The Economist*, 3 August 2013.

Economist, The 2013b. 'The future of oil: Yesterday's fuel'. *The Economist*, 3 August 2013.

Gilbert, D., Scheck, J., and Fowler, T. 2013. 'Shale boom profits bypass big oil'. *The Wall Street Journal*, 1 August 2013.

Gilbert, D. and Scheck, J. 2014. 'Big oil feels the need to get smaller'. *Wall Street Journal*, 2 November 2014. Available at: http://www.wsj.com/articles/big-oil-feels-the-need-to-get-smaller-1414973307

Hamilton, J. 2011. 'Historical oil shocks'. *National Bureau of Economic Research*. Working Paper 16790. Available at: http://www.nber.org/papers/w16790.pdf (accessed 10 September 2013).

Hamilton, J. 2012. 'Oil prices, exhaustible resources, and economic growth'. *National Bureau of Economic Research*. Working Paper 17759. Available at: http://www.nber.org/papers/w17759.pdf (accessed 10 September 2013).

Hamilton, J. 2014. 'Oil prices as indicator of global economic conditions'. *Econobrowser*, 14 December 2014. Available at: http://econbrowser.com/archives/2014/12/oil-prices-as-an-indicator-of-global-economic-conditions (accessed 15 December 2014).

Hansen, J. 2012. 'Game over for the climate'. *International Herald Tribune*, 9 May 2012.

Hansen, J. and Kharecha, P. 2008. 'The implications of "Peak Oil" for atmospheric CO2 and climate'. *Global Biochemical Cycles* 22: GB3012, 1-10.

Heinberg, R. 2011. *The end of growth: Adapting to our new economic reality.* Gabriola Island: New Society Publishers.

Heinberg, R. 2013. *Snake oil: How fracking's false promise of plenty imperils our future.* Santa Rosa, CA: Post Carbon Institute.

Heinberg, R. and Lerch, D. 2010. *The post carbon reader: Managing the 21st century's sustainability crises.* Healdsburg: Watershed Media.

Hirsch R., Bezdek, R., and Wendling, R. 2010. *The impending world energy mess.* Burlington" Apoge Prime.

Hiscock, G. 2012. *Earth wars: The battle for global resources.* Singapore: John Wiley & Sons.

Hughes, J.D. 2013. 'Drill, baby, drill: Can unconventional fuels usher in a new era of energy abundance'. *Post Carbon Institute Report.* Available at: http://www.postcarbon.org/reports/DBD-report-FINAL.pdf (accessed 10 September 2013).

Hughes, J.D. 2014. 'Drilling deeper: A reality check on government forecasts for a lasting tight oil and shale gas boom'. *Post Carbon Institute Report.* Available at: http://www.postcarbon.org/publications/drillingdeeper/ (accessed 10 December 2014).

Inman, M. 2014. 'Natural gas: The fracking fallacy'. Nature, 3 December 2014.

International Energy Agency 2004. *World energy outlook 2010.* Available at: http://www.worldenergyoutlook.org/media/weowebsite/2008-1994/weo2004.pdf (accessed 10 December 2014).

International Energy Agency 2010. *World energy outlook 2010: Executive summary.* Available at: http://www.worldenergyoutlook.org/media/weowebsite/2010/WEO2010_es_english.pdf (accessed 10 September 2013).

International Energy Agency 2011. *World energy outlook 2011: Executive summary.* Available at: http://www.worldenergyoutlook.org/media/weowebsite/2011/executive_summary.pdf (accessed 10 September 2013).

International Energy Agency 2012. *World energy outlook 2012: Executive summary.* Available at: http://www.iea.org/publications/freepublications/publication/English.pdf (accessed 10 September 2013).

International Energy Agency 2013. *World energy outlook 2013: Executive summary.* Available at: http://www.iea.org/publications/freepublications/publication/WEO2013_Executive_Summary_English.pdf (accessed 10 February 2014).

Intergovernmental Panel on Climate Change (IPCC), 2013. *Climate change 2013: The physical science basis (Fifth Assessment Report)*. Available at: http://www.ipcc.ch/report/ar5/wg1/#.Uk6k-CjqMRw (accessed 10 October 2013).

Kerschner, C., Prell, C., Feng, K., and Hubacek, K. 2013. 'Economic vulnerability to peak oil'. *Global Environmental Change*, 23: 1424-1433.

Klare, M. 2012. *The race for what's left: The global scramble for the world's last resources*. New York: Picador.

Kopits, S. 'Oil and economic growth: A supply-constrained view'. Presentation delivered at Columbia University, 11 February 2014.

Kraus, C. and Lipton, E. 2012. 'After the boom in natural gas'. *New York Times*, 20 October 2012.

Leggett, J. 2013. *The Energy of nations: Risk blindness and the road to renaissance*. London: Routledge.

Lyons, G. and Ghalambor, W.C. 2007. 'Production decline analysis'. In *Petroleum Production Engineering*. Burlington, VT: Gulf Professional Publishing: 97-105.

Maugeri, L. 2012. *Oil: The next revolution*. Available at: http://belfercenter.ksg.harvard.edu/files/Oil-%20The%20Next%20Revolution.pdf (accessed 10 September 2013).

McKibben, B. 2012. 'Global warming's terrifying new math'. *Rolling Stone*, 19 July 2012.

Meijer, R. 2014. 'Will oil kill the zombie?' *Automatic Earth*, 12 December 2014. Available at: http://www.theautomaticearth.com/will-oil-kill-the-zombies/ (accessed 10 December 2014).

Miller, R. and Sorrel, S. 2014. 'The future of oil supply'. *Philosophical Transactions of the Royal Society A* 372, 20130179: 1-27.

Monbiot, G. 2012. *False summit*. Available at: http://www.monbiot.com/2012/07/02/false-summit/ (accessed 10 September 2013).

Murphy, D. 2014. 'The implications of the declining energy return on investment of oil production'. *Philosophical Transactions of the Royal Society* 372, 20130126: 1-19.

Murphy, D. and Hall, C. 2011a. 'Adjusting to the new energy realities of the second half of the age of oil'. *Ecological Modelling* 223: 67-71.

Murphy, D. and Hall, C. 2011b. 'Energy return on investment, peak oil, and the end of economic growth'. *Annals of the New York Academy of Sciences* 1219: 52-72.

Murphy, T. 2011. 'The energy trap'. Available at: http://physics.ucsd.edu/do-the-math/2011/10/the-energy-trap/ (accessed 10 September 2013).

Mushalik, M. 2013a. 'US shale hides crude Oil peak in rest of world'. Available at: http://crudeoilpeak.info/us-shale-oil-hides-crude-oil-peak-in-rest-of-world (accessed 15 October 2013).

Mushalik, M. 2013b. 'Shrinking crude oil exports a tough game for oil importers'. Available at: http://crudeoilpeak.info/shrinking-crude-oil-exports-a-tough-game-for-oil-importers (accessed 15 October 2013).

Mushalik, M. 2014. 'IEA report implies US crude may start to peak 2016'. Available at: http://crudeoilpeak.info/iea-report-implies-us-crude-production-may-start-to-peak-2016 (accessed 10 December 2014).

Rubin, J. 2012. *The end of growth: But is that all bad?* Toronto: Random House.

Rubin, J. and Buchanan, P. 2007. *OPEC's growing call on itself*. CIBIC, Occasional Report 62.

Sorrell, S., Speirs, J., Bentley, R., Miller, R., and Thompson, E. 2012. 'Shaping the global peak: A review of the evidence on field sizes, reserve growth, decline rates and depletion rates'. *Energy* 37(1): 709-724.

Strachan, P. 2013. 'Shale gale little more than hot air'. *Oil & Gas Gazette*, June 2013.

The Oil Drum. 2013. 'Live until 31 august, oil drum successors discussion, and user profiles'. Available at: http://www.theoildrum.com/node/10081 (accessed 10 September 2013).

Tverberg, G. 2012. 'Oil supply limits and the continuing financial crisis'. *Energy* 37(1): 27-34.

8

THE PARADOX OF OIL
The cheaper it is, the more it costs

There will be oil, but at what price?
– Chris Nelder and Gregor Macdonald

1. Introduction*

It would be fair to say that the timing of the sudden drop in the price of oil from June 2014 took energy and financial analysts by surprise. After averaging around US$110 per barrel since 2011 (IEA, 2013: 6), suggesting a 'new normal', as of February 2015 the price of oil had fallen to around US$50 per barrel. But although the timing of this price drop was not forecast by analysts with any precision, there are economic, geological, and geopolitical dynamics at play in light of which the price volatility we are seeing is not actually that surprising.

In my article 'The New Economics of Oil' (Alexander, 2014) – published a few months prior to the fall in price – I explained why expensive oil has a stagnating effect on oil-dependent economies, which I argued could lead to a drop in oil demand and thus a sharp fall in price.[10] I also explained why expensive oil can incentivise

---

*The author would like to thank Josh Floyd, Matt Mushalik, and Jonathan Rutherford for very helpful comments on an earlier draft. Any errors are the responsibility of the author.

[10] To quote from p. 9: 'In short, as oil production slows or stagnates, oil prices may continue to increase until they reach an economic breaking point, crashing or destabilising economies, which would lead to a crash in oil prices; the low oil prices would then facilitate economic recovery, which puts more demand pressure on oil, leading prices to rise till economic breaking point, and so on and so forth. This cycle of bust-recovery-bust is what we may face in coming years and decades...' (Alexander, 2014).

greater investment in production while disincentivising consumption, a dynamic that can increase oil production faster than
demand and thereby generate short-term oil gluts that can also lead
to price volatility, only via a different route.[11] Both of these dynamics
go a long way to explaining the current state of oil markets. While
the exact timing of the current fall in prices may have come as a
surprise to everyone, including me, the phenomenon itself is quite
comprehensible when one recognises the intimate connection
between energy (especially oil) and economics. As we will see, the
ever-present influence of geopolitics is shaping oil markets too.

What is so frustrating about the state of much oil commentary
today is the tendency for analysts to focus on the immediate or
short-term situation, often from a purely financial/economic
perspective, neglecting the larger social, political, and environmental contexts in which oil markets unfold. When those larger
contexts are given due attention, it becomes clear that oil is a
commodity that defies reductive analysis and which cannot be
understood unless one looks through a multi-dimensional, interdisciplinary lens.

In this chapter I outline and analyse various explanations for
why the price of oil has fallen so dramatically in recent months and
present some considered but tentative hypotheses about what we
can expect from the oil markets in coming years. I also hope to
challenge the naïve conclusion – drawn all-too-hastily in the
mainstream media – that the drop in price somehow debunks the
analytical framework of the 'peak oil' school (see, e.g., Sakya, 2015).
Although it may sound counter-intuitive, cheap oil is actually a
complicated function or symptom of peak oil dynamics, and far
from solving oil problems, the drop in price is merely creating new
problems of equal or greater weight, in ways that will be explained.
Those who claim that the effects of cheap oil are 'clearly positive' are
at best being simplistic and are at worst just plain wrong (see, e.g.,
The Economist, 2014a).

The main conclusion defended below is that so-called 'cheap
oil' (at ~$50 per barrel) is just as problematic as expensive oil (at
$100+ per barrel), but for very different social, political, economic,
and environmental reasons. Just as expensive oil suffocates
industrial economies that are dependent on cheap energy inputs to

---

[11] To quote from p. 5: 'The peak oil position – at least, the most coherent
iteration of its varieties – holds that when conventional oil reaches a plateau
(and eventually declines), this will lead to an increase in price; but price
increases make unconventional oils more financially viable, thus increasing
their production and delaying a decline in overall production of liquid fuels'
(Alexander, 2014).

function, cheap oil merely propagates and further entrenches the existing order of global capitalism that is in the process of growing itself to death (Turner, 2014). The fall in prices also undermines the oil industry by scaring off capital investment in an age when the costs of establishing and drilling new fields is relentlessly on the rise (Kopits, 2014), due to declining energy returns on investment (Murphy, 2014). Cheap oil therefore is likely to retard mid-to-long-term production, setting the scene for a foreseeable mid-range supply crunch that will soon enough push prices back up (see Kent and Faucon, 2015; Mushalik, 2015a).

Accordingly, we should not be fooled by this current period of depressed prices. As the world continues to replace the easy 'conventional' oil with ever-more marginal 'unconventional' oils (e.g., deepwater, shale oil, tar sands, etc.) and alternative 'biofuels', the laws of physics will forever be putting upward pressure on production costs. So despite currently depressed prices, it remains true to say that we live in an age of expensive oil, a position that might seem contradictory if interpreted superficially but which is actually accurate when interpreted in geological context: the low-hanging fruit is gone. The only way oil will remain cheap over the long term is if our economies are doing so poorly from a conventional growth perspective that we cannot afford for oil to be any more expensive, making oil demand weak and keeping prices deflated (see Meijer, 2014a).

Looking at the current situation from a different angle, cheap oil also makes renewable energy alternatives less 'cost competitive', which will have disastrous ramifications on climate change mitigation by disincentivising the necessary transition beyond fossil fuels at a critical time. This ecological issue is typically overlooked by those oil analysts who are blinded by the apparent, short-term economic benefits of cheaper oil. Herein lies the paradox of oil: the cheaper it is (economically), the more it costs (environmentally).

For these types of reasons I will argue that there is no 'optimal' price for oil in much the same way as there is no 'optimal' price for heroin. This analogy between oil and heroin may appear like a polemical exaggeration, but I hope to show that it is, in fact, worryingly apt. When heroin is expensive, addicts cannot afford what they desperately need, or feel they need, and suffer accordingly. Expenditure on more worthwhile things is cut back in order to fund the increasingly expensive and debilitating addiction. But when heroin is cheap and readily available, the negative effects of addiction become even more pronounced through over-consumption, and the addiction only deepens as hopes of rehabilitation fade. Oil acts as industrial civilisation's own form of heroin, and whether it is cheap or expensive, addicts today are in as much trouble as ever.

2. Energy and Economics

Before focusing on the specific issue of the recent fall in prices, I will briefly describe the fundamental changes that have taken place over the last decade with respect to the relationship between oil demand, geology, and economic activity (for more detail, see Alexander, 2014). Only by understanding these changes can we begin to gain insight into the diverse forces that shape oil markets today.

Throughout most of the 20th century oil supply was able to meet increasing demand without much trouble. Leaving aside the geopolitical oil crises of 1973 and 1979, cheap oil in the range of $20-25 was readily available.[12] Naturally, industrial economies came to rely on these cheap energy inputs and structured their societies accordingly, assuming energy costs would remain marginal and that economic growth trajectories could be maintained indefinitely. Around 2005, however, conventional crude oil production stagnated (Miller and Sorrell, 2014: 6) and the theory of 'peak oil' began being taken seriously by more people and more institutions (see Munroe, 2010).

As discussed in the last chapter, peak oil refers to the point where the 'rate' of oil extraction reaches its highest point ever. This point arrives not because oil is 'running out' but because the 'low-hanging fruit' (the easy-to-produce oil) has already been discovered and produced, leaving only the more marginal oil reserves. When the easy oil is gone, producers have to run faster and faster (or drill more and more, and in less ideal places) merely to stay in the same place (see, e.g., Likvern, 2012). Producing oil, that is, has diminishing marginal returns. Eventually the producers cannot maintain supply rates, and the flow of oil stops growing or peaks and eventually begins to fall, despite the fact there is still lots of oil left.

But this is not merely a geological phenomenon. In ways outlined below, the geology and the economics (and the geopolitics) become intertwined, forming a complex interrelationship, with various factors giving shape to the rise, peak, and decline of oil supply. The primary concern of the peak oil school is that the peak arrives while demand for oil keeps on growing. According to basic economic principles, a stagnating supply coupled with increasing

---

[12] For historical data on the price of oil, see http://www.wtrg.com/prices.htm, accessed 10 January 2015.

demand would lead to a spike in oil prices, and this would place a huge financial burden on oil-dependent economies, with destabilising effects.

As conventional oil supply began to stagnate in 2005 while global demand continued to increase, the price of oil began a steady incline, moving from its historic average of $20-25 per barrel (where it sat even in the late 20th century) to over $100 by 2008. This basic dynamic played out as the peak oil school predicted (see, e.g., Heinberg, 2003; Heinberg, 2011), even if the interplay between geology, economics, technology, culture, and geopolitics proved to be more complicated and nuanced than petroleum geologists and other analysts anticipated. Today conventional crude oil remains on what is often called a 'corrugated' or 'undulating' plateau (see Jackson and Smith, 2014), a phenomenon that has been acknowledged by mainstream institutions, including the International Energy Agency (see, e.g., IEA, 2010: 6; BBC, 2013). In other words, conventional crude oil seems to have peaked. Any gains from now on, if they occur, will be negligible.

Nevertheless, as the rate of conventional crude oil production stopped growing, the consequent rise in the price of oil made various unconventional oils more economically viable, facilitating their production and incentivising the development of new or more refined technologies (including 'fracking' techniques). What this meant was that global supply of oil was able to keep up with a growing global demand, delaying a 'peak' in overall liquid fuels.

But meeting this growing demand came at a huge cost and the intimate relationship between energy and economics became clearer. No longer could oil be considered a marginal cost of negligible economic significance to the processes of production. After a century of cheap energy inputs, industrial economies (especially the oil importers) found their dependence on oil to be an increasingly debilitating financial burden (Ayres and Warr, 2009; Murphy and Hall, 2011a; Ayres, 2014; Tverberg, 2015).

It is worth being clear about the extent of this financial burden. By 2012 the global economy was consuming around 90 million barrels of oil every day (mbpd), and when trying to maintain those levels of consumption the difference between oil at $25 per barrel and oil priced over $100 per barrel becomes hugely significant. To be precise, it constitutes an extra cost to the global economy of around $7.2 billion dollars per day, or $3.6 trillion dollars per year – money that would otherwise have been spent in the broader economy. If we look specifically at the US – the world's largest oil consumer – the rise in the price of oil from $25 to over $100 meant that the US was spending an extra $600 million every day on oil imports, money that was not just being sucked into the energy sector but being sucked out of the national economy all together (see Alexander, 2014).

In light of these figures, it is not difficult to understand why 10 of the last 11 recessions in the US have been associated with high oil prices (see Hamilton, 2011) or why the implosion of the global economy in 2008 correlated so closely with the oil price spiking at $147 per barrel (Hamilton, 2012; Murphy and Hall, 2011b). When oil gets expensive, everything dependent on oil gets more expensive, like transport, mechanised labour, industrial food production, plastics, among a host of other things. This pricing dynamic siphons discretionary expenditure and investment away from the rest of the economy – or out of the national economy altogether – causing debt defaults, economic stagnation, recessions, or even longer-term depressions (Tverberg, 2012). While it would be too one-dimensional to argue that expensive oil was the *only* cause of the global financial crisis (and the ongoing economic stagnation), it would be just as blind to deny the defining role expensive oil played both in the global financial crisis and the state of the deflated global economy today (see generally, Ayres, 2014).

3. The Two Principal Factors Influencing the Fall in the Price of Oil

Against this background the two principal factors influencing the fall in the price of oil over the last six months can be inferred with a degree of confidence. The first is a demand-side factor; the second, a supply-side factor. These are not mutually exclusive and in fact they have fed off each other to exacerbate their individual effects, hence why the fall in price has been so dramatic.

The demand-side factor influencing the price drop is that the global economy is deflated (see Hamilton, 2014; Mearns, 2014), in large part owing to several years of expensive oil, averaging over $100 since 2011. As explained above, this has had a suffocating effect on expected growth trajectories. The EU and Japan economies remain very weak; China's growth is slowing; and the Russian economy is sinking quickly, all of which reduces oil demand, and expected demand (see Meijer, 2014b). When economic growth is strong, oil demand is high; when economies are weak, stagnant, or in recession, oil demand is weak.

When oil demand is weak while supply is maintained, however, basic economic principles dictate that the price of oil will fall, and this is precisely what we have seen. Another way to frame this demand-side point is to say that when oil is expensive, it becomes increasingly unaffordable, especially when wages stagnate, and this unaffordability induces 'demand destruction' which puts less pressure on oil supply chains. It could even be said that there is not so much a glut of cheap oil as there is a glut of consumers who cannot afford expensive oil (see Mushalik, 2015b). Consequently, the reduced pressure on the oil markets manifests in reduced prices. All this is perfectly comprehensible, even if the exact timing of the effects could never be predicted with any precision. Economics is not a hard science.

The second principal factor influencing the currently depressed prices can also be understood in relation to the prolonged period of expensive oil in recent years, but this time from the supply-side. Historically, the vast reserves of unconventional oil around the world (especially in the tar sands of Canada and Venezuela, and the shale oil plays in the US) have been under-exploited, because the capital expenditure needed to extract oil from them have been so great that it would have been 'uneconomic' to do so. But once conventional oil began to plateau around 2005, putting supply pressure on global oil markets, this induced the steady rise in the price of oil. As oil reached beyond $100 and seemed to stabilise it suddenly appeared as if much more of these unconventional oils could be produced for a profit. This naturally provoked something of an investment frenzy, especially in the US and Canada, resulting in the significant 'up tick' in US oil production and the steady rise in Canadian tar sands production. Several years of 'manic drilling' (*The Economist*, 2014a) have resulted in a short-term glut in oil supply, and whenever there is a glut in supply, prices inevitably fall. (Why the 'glut' is likely to be short-term is addressed further below.) A recent boost in Libyan oil production has also magnified this temporary oversupply (see Patterson, 2014).

It is worth highlighting the important interactions here between the demand-side and the supply-side dynamics. As we have seen, expensive oil places a burden on oil-dependent economies, making it difficult to maintain expected or desired growth trajectories and inducing demand destruction. But just as oil demand was weakening due to poor economic performance, the very same phenomenon of expensive oil was bringing new supply chains to the market. If these supply and demand dynamics were at play in isolation, they would have produced a drop in the price of oil. When they occur together – that is, when demand is being destroyed by expensive oil just as expensive oil is incentivising increased production – it should come as no surprise that at some point the markets would react. In the last six months or so, we have seen precisely that occur (see Berman, 2015).

4. Why Cheap Oil is a Mixed Blessing (and Ultimately a Curse)

As noted in the introduction, the sudden and drastic fall in the price of oil has been widely interpreted as 'good news' for economies. In a superficial sense, this is quite an understandable reaction. While many people seem resistant to the thesis that expensive oil inhibits economic growth, more people seem willing to accept the thesis (which is the flip side of the same coin) that cheap oil is good for economic growth. In an age of deep economic uncertainty and widespread economic instability, anything that is perceived to be good for growth is generally regarded as something worth celebrating. Unfortunately, the implications of cheap oil are far more complicated and by no means so positive.

It is certainly true that cheap oil makes conventional economic growth easier than if oil were expensive, so if returning to historic growth trajectories is considered the ultimate goal, then the celebration of the falling price of oil is justified, so far as it goes. But the following analysis unpacks the situation in more detail and fleshes out some of the intricacies in this situation in order to show why cheap oil is likely to cause as many problems as it solves.

The first thing to note is that, irrespective of the current market price of oil, the energy return on investment (EROI) of oil is in terminal decline (Murphy, 2014). We must not forget that it is 'net energy' that is the important measure of energy supply, not total barrels extracted and consumed. Due to declining EROI, it is possible that oil production can increase in gross supply while net energy from oil can be flat or in decline.[13] Indeed, this would disguise the 'peak' in useful energy supply from oil. Could we be at that point now even though total liquid fuels still seem to be creeping upward? It is hard to be sure, but it is important that we put our minds to this subtle phenomenon, because it is on its way, if not already upon us.

The increasing financial costs of production, however, are easier to quantify. Oil's declining EROI translates as increasing costs

---

[13] This could happen as high-EROI conventional oil is replaced with low-EROI unconventional oil. Suppose, for example, the world at one time produces 90 mbpd with an EROI of 30:1 (meaning that 3 mbpd were invested in ordered to produce 90 mbpd, giving a 'net energy' surplus of 87 mbpd). Suppose, a few years later, the world produces 95 mbpd, but of that oil, 60 mbpd has EROI of 20:1, and 35 mbpd has an EROI of only 5:1 (meaning that 10 mbpd were invested to produce 95 mbpd, giving a 'net energy' surplus of 85 mbpd). In this case, gross oil production would have increased, obscuring the fact that 'net energy' has actually declined.

of production, especially in new oil fields. According to a recent analysis (Kopits, 2014: 43), capital expenditure in the large oil firms has been rising at 11% per annum since 1999. When the price of oil was hovering above the $100 mark, it made economic sense to invest and produce many of these unconventional oils, because despite the increasing costs of production, it seemed a profit could still be made. But now that oil has dropped to around $50 per barrel, a large proportion of this new production no longer seems profitable.

For example, the Monetary Policy Report of the Bank of Canada (2015) recently reported as follows:

> Based on recent estimates of production costs, roughly one-third of current production could be uneconomical if prices stay around US$60, notably high-cost production in the United States, Canada, Brazil and Mexico (Chart 4). More than two-thirds of the expected increase in the world oil supply would similarly be uneconomical. A decline in private and public investment in high-cost projects could significantly reduce future growth in the oil supply, and the members of the Organization of the Petroleum Exporting Countries (OPEC) would have limited spare capacity to replace a significant decrease in the non-OPEC supply.

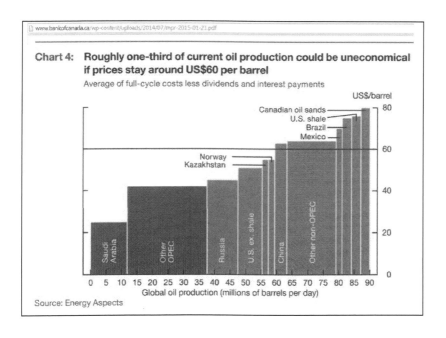

Chart 4: **Roughly one-third of current oil production could be uneconomical if prices stay around US$60 per barrel**

Average of full-cycle costs less dividends and interest payments

Source: Energy Aspects

In much the same vein, a recent report in the *Financial Times* (see Raval, 2014) concludes that the Canadian oil sands have a break-even price of $80 per barrel, US shale plays and other areas of tight oil around $76; Brazil's deep-water fields are thought to require $75 to break even and Mexican projects around $70. If these estimates are even roughly accurate, the recent price drop to around $50 per barrel means that all these technically recoverable oil resources may become vulnerable to their own high (and increasing) production costs. Needless to say, profit-seeking businesses will not produce oil that costs $70+ if they can only sell it for $50 (see Carroll and Klump, 2013).[14]

Of course, significant portions of the 'costs of production' occur in the early stages of setting up a field for drilling, which means that most of the *current projects* already have 'sunk costs'. Because of this, most of those projects are not going to stop producing in the short term. But at $50 or $60 per barrel, many if not most *new* unconventional oil projects may not be profitable, and investors and oil companies alike are already beginning to show signs of caution or withdrawal. Notably, in November 2014, there was a 40% drop in new oil and gas permits in the US, which is being attributed to the lower price of oil (Hays, 2014). Similarly, since October 2014, rigs in the US have fallen by 34% (see Mushalik, 2015d; Inman, 2015a; Inman, 2015b), according to the Baker Hughes index. The foreseeable consequences, as reported in the *Economist* (2014a), are as follows:

> A rash of bankruptcies is likely. That, in turn, would bespatter shale oil's reputation among investors. Even survivors may find the markets closed for some time, forcing them to rein in their expenditure to match the cash they generate from selling oil. Since shale-oil wells are short-lived (output can fall by 60-70% in the first year), any slowdown in investment will quickly translate into falling production.

A different article in *The Economist* (2014b) is even more explicit:

> Wood Mackenzie, a research consultancy, estimates that the 'break-even price' of American projects is clustered around $65-70, suggesting many are vulnerable (these calculations exclude

---

[14] Again, this was anticipated in Alexander (2014: 6): '…it is no good having vast technically recoverable resources if producing them is uneconomic. Furthermore, if the price of oil were to drop to some extent – perhaps due to a further downturn in an already struggling global economy – this could also make some currently profitable shale holdings unprofitable, which soon enough would reduce shale production.'

some sunk costs, such as building roads). If the oil price stays at $70, it estimates investment will be cut by 20% and production growth for America could slow to 10% a year. At $60, investment could drop by as much as half and production growth grind to a halt.

This is hugely significant, especially when it is recognised that the growth in US shale oil and Canadian tar sands in recent years has been essentially the only thing that has disguised peaking production of liquid fuels in the rest of the world (Mushalik, 2013). In fact, the current oil situation, which some are claiming debunks 'peak oil' may in fact be announcing its arrival. Conventional oil production is already on a corrugated plateau that almost certainly represents the highest 'peak' it will ever reach, but it could be that the current supply and demand dynamics mark the onset of peak 'liquid fuels'. As oil analyst Ron Patterson (2015) notes:

> Peak oil will be the point in time when more oil is produced than has ever been produced in the history of the world, or ever will be in the future of the world. It is far more likely that this period will be thought of as a time of an oil glut rather than a time of an oil shortage.

Could it be that 2015-17 will be the oil 'glut' that marks the peak in 'liquid fuels'? If cheap oil is in the process of jeopardising future production, as it seems to be doing, and/or if the 'shale boom' peters out in the next year or two (Energy Watch Group, 2013; Heinberg, 2013; Hughes, 2013; Hughes, 2014; Mushalik, 2014) this near-term peak could indeed eventuate. A new study conducted by Goldman Sachs (see Adams, 2014) concludes that the lower oil prices means that $1 trillion of oil investment funds are now at risk of being withdrawn from projects, and this would reduce production by 7.5 million barrels of oil per day over the coming decade. Since that study was undertaken prices have fallen further. Even before the price slump, in fact, the biggest oil companies were shelving expansion plans and shredding operations with profit margins too tight to justify (Gilbert and Scheck, 2014; Tverberg, 2014). Maintaining current production looks like it is going to be a Herculean task.

Nevertheless, the foreseeable consequence of a production and investment drop will be a tightening of global oil supply, thus increasing the price of oil, especially if demand increases at the same time. This upward pressure, of course, could potentially bring some of the high-cost producers back online, although investors will be more cautious and funds will be harder to come by, for fear of another price collapse. Furthermore, if the economy cannot accommodate a return to expensive oil, we may see a subsequent price slump, yet again, and a further production drop for the reasons just outlined. This is a volatility that we can expect to see in coming years and decades. It is too simplistic to suggest that lower prices mean that oil troubles are over. They are merely challenging oil-dependent economies in new ways, primarily by threatening to render huge amounts of existing production 'uneconomic'. At the World Economic Forum in 2015, the chief economist of the International Energy Agency, Fatih Birol (as quoted in Mushalik, 2015c), described the oil situation as follows:

> In 2015 we expect oil and gas upstream investments to decline $100 billion or 15%. And the big chunk of it will come from the high cost areas. And this will have implications, not perhaps immediately but for 2016-17. And if this comes together with a stronger demand this will have strong implications for the price and the markets.

Another issue that needs to be borne in mind is the economic instability that arises in oil-*exporting* nations when the price of oil drops so suddenly and deeply. Significant exporters such as Russia, Iran, Iraq, and Venezuela are highly dependent on high oil prices to balance their fiscal budgets (see Herszenhorn, 2014). In October 2014 the International Monetary Fund assessed what oil price different governments needed to balance their budgets, and drew some disturbing conclusions: Russia needs oil at $101 per barrel; Iran needs $136; Venezuela and Nigeria need $120 (see Viscusci, Patel, and Kennedy, 2014). When we recognise that oil and gas make up 50% of Russia's federal budget, it becomes clear that a drop in price from $110 (June 2014) to $50 (February 2015) more than halves that oil revenue stream. Nobody knows what Putin might do, for example, if he finds himself with his back against the wall. More generally, if cheap oil means extreme economic hardship for exporters, this could well provoke social discontent and political instability. We see the geological and economic issues quickly become infused with the geopolitics.

There are further geopolitical complexities and speculations concerning the recent fall in the price of oil. For instance, there is some speculation that Saudi Arabia desires these lower prices because cheap oil can be expected to undermine competition in global oil markets – especially the US shale plays and Canadian oil sands, both of which require higher prices to maintain existing production over the long term (see Meijer, 2014a; Solomon and Said, 2014; Critchlow, 2015). Saudi Arabia for decades has been the so-called 'swing producer' that increased or decreased production as necessary to stabilise the price of oil where it could. Recently, however, Saudi Arabia has made it clear that it has no intention of reducing its production to push the price of oil higher (Defterios, 2014). It knows that cheap oil will undermine its competition.

Furthermore, the prospect of cutting Saudi production would raise further concerns about its effect on oil prices. According to the secretary general of OPEC, Abdalla Salem el-Badri: 'If we cut production then there will be spare capacity and producers will not invest, or postpone projects. The market will rebound back higher than the $147 we saw in 2008' (as quoted in Critchlow, 2015).

Perhaps most importantly, with cheap oil Saudi Arabia is able to punish or put pressure on some of its (and the US') geopolitical enemies, including Iran and Russia – two oil exporters that are much harder hit by $50 oil than the wealthier Saudi Arabia (see, e.g., Mazzetti, Schmitt, and Kirkpatrick, 2015). As of early 2015, the Russian economy seems particularly weak and unstable, and there is some speculation that the US has colluded with Saudi Arabia to flood the markets for this very purpose (see, e.g., Elliot, 2014; Whitney, 2014; Topf, 2015), even if this hurts US shale producers. In fact, some analysts argue with plausibility that oil markets, in our neoliberal era, provide a means for the US government and the broader 'Transnational Elite' to insidiously wage economic war, especially against Russia (for more detail, see Fotopoulous, 2014). It is very difficult to know how far these geopolitical influences are shaping the oil markets – and space does not permit a more elaborate analysis – but there certainly seems to be more than plain 'supply and demand' issues at play.

It seems to me that the geology is fundamental, which then enters a dialectical relationship with the economics, leaving the very real geopolitical tensions and strategies to play out against that background. As usual, the environmental issues tend to be ignored.

5. The Environmental Costs of 'Cheap' Oil

The analysis above has focused primarily on the central role energy plays in economic processes, touching also on a couple of important geopolitical issues. The environmental impacts of oil consumption are too often left out of this picture. Not only does oil consumption facilitate the depletion of natural resources and the devastation of biodiversity as a result of ever-expanding, globalised economies, perhaps most importantly, we now know that the consumption of oil and other fossil fuels contributes directly to climate change (IPCC, 2013; Hansen and Kharecha, 2008).

Analysts tend to try to deal with these issues in isolation, exemplified most strikingly by Fatih Birol. On the one hand, his position as chief economist of the IEA demands that he does all he can to ensure that enough affordable oil is supplied to global markets in such a way that facilitates stable economic growth. In fact, that is essentially the reason the IEA was formed, in the wake of the 1973 oil crisis. On the other hand, Birol sees the world continuing its addiction to fossil fuels in such a way that is locking humanity into decades of high carbon living. The implications of this on climate change will be disastrous, as the chief economist acknowledges. He seems to be torn apart by the contradiction of trying to facilitate conventional (oil-dependent) growth economics in the grim context of climate change.

At least Fatih Birol is forthright enough to acknowledge the intractable problem posed by this situation, even if he still tries to address the problems in isolation. Environmentalists often fail to understand how destabilising it would be, from a conventional economic perspective, to swiftly and significantly reduce oil consumption. Economists, however, are often too quick to celebrate the economic benefits of cheap oil, neglecting to mention the fact that cheap oil will incentivise increased fossil fuel consumption at a time when the world's climate scientists are crying out that we must swiftly move away from fossil fuels (IPCC, 2013).

According to carbon budget analyses (e.g., Carbon Tracker 2013), between 60-80% of known fossil fuel reserves must be left in the ground if the world is to have a good chance of keeping temperature rises less than two degrees above pre-industrial levels. Climate scientists Kevin Anderson and Alice Bows (2011) have shown that in order to keep within a fair share of the carbon budget, the wealthier nations need to decarbonise their economies by 8-10% per annum over coming decades. Guess what would happen to the price of oil if oil availability were reduced by 8-10% per annum as a climate change response strategy? Even reducing availability at 3-4% per annum would produce a price spike to unprecedented highs and probably crash many economies just like in 2008. But cheap oil only makes continued consumption of oil more affordable, while at the same time making renewable energy alternatives less price competitive. In this light, cheap oil is a catastrophe for climate-response strategies. As the *Financial Times* reports: 'falling oil prices threaten to make economies more carbon-intensive and less energy efficient' (Wolf, 2014; see also, Zumbrun, 2015).

The reality is that if a peak and decline in liquid fuels is not imposed upon us for geological-economic reasons, we should nevertheless be embracing it voluntarily for reasons of climate mitigation. Of course, I do not claim that this climate-response strategy is likely. I only claim that the challenge of climate change clearly shows that the question of how to deal with a peak and decline of oil supply is more relevant today than ever before.

These points ultimately highlight the incoherence of talking of 'cheap oil'. The only reason it can be considered 'cheap' is because the environmental costs of oil consumption are 'externalised'. If the costs of climate change, biodiversity loss, pollution, and resource depletion were built into the price of oil, there is no way it would be 'cheap'. And what of the social and economic costs that will be borne by future generations? In decades to come, as climate change wreaks havoc on global food systems and increases the severity and regularity of extreme weather events, how will today's language of 'cheap oil' be received? I suspect that $50 oil will be seen for what it is – something that came at far too great a cost.

This, once more, is the paradox of oil: the cheaper it is, the more it costs.

6. Conclusion

What, then, lies ahead for oil markets? The short answer is that nobody really knows. There are too many economic, geopolitical, technological, and social variables at play for any certainty. Black swans could lie around every bend in the river. The unpredictable actions of OPEC have significant implications: will they cut production after their next meeting? It is anybody's guess. There is also the ever-present possibility of ongoing geopolitical disruptions, as evidenced especially by the instability in several oil-rich nations, such as Iraq, Iran, and Russia. If a new war broke out in any of these areas, or if Russia's economic decline intensified, markets would be thrown into further turmoil. This could push prices back up very quickly, but high prices could assist the producers of non-conventional oil that need high prices to make any money. However, the point I have been labouring is that those high prices could again squeeze the life out of oil-dependent economies and place further obstacles in the way of 'economic recovery'. Another global financial crisis would only overturn the oil markets again, as happened in 2008, leading to a pricing collapse. There is also the threat of the 'carbon bubble' bursting, if shareholders in fossil fuel companies begin to worry that their shares could become 'stranded assets' should nations or the international community decide to take climate change seriously (see Alexander, Nicholson, and Wiseman, 2014).

In light of all this, my view is that we should expect continued price volatility. That may sound like 'hedging my bets' but the fact is that the oil situation is so unstable that cycles of 'bust-recovery-bust' are the most likely future we face. It could well be that we will see a further fall in the price of oil, although claims of $20 oil (see Worstall, 2015) seem very unlikely to be realised. If oil ever fell to this price it would necessarily be short-lived, for the reasons outlined above: many unconventional producers need prices of $70+ per barrel simply to break-even. Indeed, the IEA recently reported that 'a price rebound... seems inevitable' (see Kent and Faucon, 2015). Where to? Again, no one can be sure, but the high production costs of unconventional oil suggest that a reasonable 'floor' for oil prices in the mid-to-long term (within a couple of years) may be in the $80+ range – higher if the shale boom goes bust or if war or political instability enters the scene more significantly. But remember, part of my argument is that there is no 'safe operating space' for oil prices. The 'floor' of oil prices is likely to be too high (for the economy); just as the 'ceiling' is likely to be too low (for the climate). We live in paradoxical times indeed.

What we do know is that the EROI of oil is in terminal decline, and it is this geological reality which means that there will forever be upward pressure on the price of oil, and that is forever going to put pressure on oil-dependent, growth-orientated economies. As Murphy and Hall argue: 'increasing the oil supply to support economic growth will require high oil prices that will undermine that economic growth' (Murphy and Hall, 2011a: 52). This is the world we now live in.

In the introduction to this chapter I stated that there is no 'optimal' price for oil. It should now be clearer what I meant. In an age of increasing capital expenditure on new oil fields, due to declining EROI, oil needs to be sufficiently expensive for oil supply to keep up with demand. But when oil is too expensive, economies that rely on cheap energy inputs cannot function and demand dries up, reducing the price of oil. Some analysts argue that there is a 'narrow ledge' (Nelder and Macdonald, 2011) where the price of oil is high enough to procure the necessary investments and production but not so high as to inhibit so-called 'healthy growth' of the economy. That may have been the case in recent history, but my suspicion is that this 'narrow ledge' has itself now crumbled away. There is no longer an 'optimal price' that falls within such a ledge. Oil is now *either* too cheap to procure ongoing investments and production *or* too expensive for oil-dependent economies to function well (perhaps even *both* too cheap to meet demand *and* too expensive for growth). When these issues are placed in the context of climate change and the need to transition beyond fossil fuels, it becomes clear that there is no such thing as cheap oil.

In short, industrial civilisation now finds itself between a rock and a hard place; or, to change the metaphor, we now find ourselves in 'checkmate', with nowhere to move. Our only option is to start playing a different game – a game 'beyond oil' – a choice we should have made many years, if not decades, ago. Unfortunately, building a post-petroleum civilisation (Trainer, 2010; Alexander, 2012) would require a bravery and boldness that we have hitherto lacked. Can we yet muster the courage?

The challenge, admittedly, is to find ground between naïve optimism and despair.

References

Adams, C. 2014. 'Oil price fall threatens $1tn of projects'. *Financial Times*, 15 December 2014. Accessed 10 January 2015 at: http://www.ft.com/intl/cms/s/0/b3d67518-845f-11e4-bae9-00144feabdc0.html#axzz3RxSpUHzf

Alexander, S. 2012. 'The sufficiency economy: Envisioning a prosperous way down'. *Simplicity Institute Report* 12s, 1-31.

Alexander, S. 2014. 'The new economics of oil'. *MSSI Issues Paper* No. 2, March 2014: 1-15.

Alexander, S., Nicholson, K, and Wiseman, J. 2014. 'Fossil free: The development and significance of the fossil fuel divestment movement'. *MSSI Issues Paper* No. 4, September 2014: 1-16.

Anderson, K. and Bows, A. 2011. 'Beyond "dangerous" climate change: Emission scenarios for a new world'. *Philosophical Transactions of the Royal Society* 369: 2-44.

Ayers, R. and Warr, B. 2009. *The economic growth engine: How energy and work drive material prosperity*. Cheltenham: Edward Elgar Publishing.

Bank of Canada 2015. 'Monetary Policy Report'. Accessed 17 February 2015 at: http://www.bankofcanada.ca/wp-content/uploads/2014/07/mpr-2015-01-21.pdf

Berman, A. 2015. 'No oil price rebound yet: An explanation in two charts'. *The Petroleum Truth Report*, 11 February 2015. Accessed 17 February 2015 at: http://www.resilience.org/stories/2015-02-11/no-oil-price-rebound-yet-an-explanation-in-two-charts

British Broadcasting Corporation (BBC) 2013. 'Hard-talk' (interview with Fatih Birol). Accessed 10 September 2013 at: http://www.youtube.com/watch?v=pYUj1ere2BI

Carbon Tracker 2013. 'Unburnable Carbon 2013: Wasted Capital and Stranded Assets'. *Carbon Tracker Initiative*. Accessed 10 January 2015 at: http://www.carbontracker.org/report/wasted-capital-and-stranded-assets/

Carroll, J. and Klump, E. 2013. 'Oil's $5 Trillion Permian Boom Threatened by $70 Oil'. Bloomberg, 25 October 2013. Accessed 25 October at: http://www.bloomberg.com/news/2013-10-24/oil-s-5-trillion-permian-boom-threatened-by-70-crude.html

Critchlow, A. 2015. 'Saudi Arabia Increases Oil Output to Crush US Shale Frackers'. *Telegraph*, 27 January 2015. Accessed 15 February 2015 at: http://www.telegraph.co.uk/finance/news bysector/energy/11372058/Saudi-Arabia-increases-oil-output-to-crush-US-shale-frackers.html

Defterios, J. 2014. 'Saudi Arabia: We'll Never Cut Oil Production'. *CNN Money*, 22 December 2014. Accessed 10 January 2015 at: http://money.cnn.com/2014/12/22/news/economy/saudi-arabia-oil-production/

Economist, The 2014a. 'Sheiks v shale'. *The Economist*. 6 December 2014. Accessed 25 January at: http://www.economist.com/news/leaders/21635472-economics-oil-have-changed-some-businesses-will-go-bust-market-will-be

Economist, The 2014b. 'In a bind: Will falling oil prices curb America's shale boom'. *The Economist*, 6 December 2014. Accessed 25 January 2015 at: http://www.economist.com/news/finance-and-economics/21635505-will-falling-oil-prices-curb-americas-shale-boom-bind

Elliot, L. 2014. 'Stakes are high as US plays the oil card against Iran and Russia'. *The Guardian*. 10 November 2014. Accessed 10 January 2015 at: http://www.theguardian.com/business/economics-blog/2014/nov/09/us-iran-russia-oil-prices-shale

Energy Watch Group 2013. 'Fossil and Nuclear Fuels – The Supply Outlook'. March 2013. Accessed at: http://energy watchgroup.org/wp-content/uploads/2014/02/EWG-update2013_short_18_03_2013.pdf

Fotopoulos, T. 2014. 'Oil, Economic Warfare, and Self-Reliance'. *Inclusive Democracy Weekly Column*, 27 October 2014. Accessed 15 February 2015 at: http://www.inclusivedemocracy. org/journal/vol10/vol10_no1-2_Oil_economic_warfare_and_self-reliance.html

Gilbert, D. and Sckeck, J. 2014. 'Big oil feels the need to get smaller: Exxon, Shell, Chevron pare back as rising production costs squeeze earnings'. *Wall Street Journal*, 2 November 2014. Accessed 10 January 2015 at: http://www.wsj.com/articles/big-oil-feels-the-need-to-get-smaller-1414973307

Hamilton, J. 2011. 'Historical oil shocks'. National Bureau of Economic Research, Working Paper 16790. Accessed 10 September 2013 at: http://www.nber.org/papers/w16790.pdf

Hamilton, J. 2012. 'Oil prices, exhaustible resources, and economic growth'. National Bureau of Economic Research, Working Paper 17759. Accessed 10 September 2013 at: http://www.nber.org/papers/w17759.pdf

Hamilton, J. 2014. 'Oil prices as an indicator of global economic conditions'. *Econbrowser*, 14 December 2014. Accessed 25 January 2015 at: http://econbrowser.com/archives/2014/12/oil-prices-as-an-indicator-of-global-economic-conditions

Hansen, J. and Kharecha, P. 2008. 'The Implications of "Peak Oil" for Atmospheric CO2 and Climate'. *Global Biochemical Cycles* 22: GB3012, 1-10.

Hays, K. 2014. 'Exclusive: New U.S. oil and gas well November permits tumble by nearly 40%'. *Reuters*, 2 December 2014. Accessed 10 January 2015 at: http://www.reuters.com/article/2014/12/02/us-usa-oil-permits-idUSKCN0JG2C120141202

Heinberg, R. 2003. *The Party's Over: Oil, War, and the Fate of Industrial Civilisation*. Gabriola Island: New Society Publishers.

Heinberg, R. 2011. *The End of Growth: Adapting to Our New Economic Reality*, New Society Publishers, Gabriola Island.

Heinberg, R. 2013. *Snake Oil: How Fracking's False Promise of Plenty Imperils our Future*. Santa Rosa, CA: Post Carbon Institute.

Herszenhorn, D. 2014. 'Fall in oil prices poses a problem for Russia, Iraq, and others'. *New York Times*, 15 October 2014. Accessed 10 January 2015 at: http://www.nytimes.com/2014/10/16/world/europe/fall-in-oil-prices-poses-a-problem-for-russia-iraq-and-others.html?_r=1

Hughes, J.D. 2013. 'Drill, Baby, drill: Can unconventional fuels usher in a new era of energy abundance'. Post Carbon Institute Report. Accessed 10 September 2013 at: http://www.postcarbon.org/reports/DBD-report-FINAL.pdf

Hughes, J.D. 2014. 'Drilling deeper: A reality check on US Government forecasts for a lasting tight oil and shale gas boom'. Post Carbon Institute Report. Accessed 10 January 2015 at: http://www.postcarbon.org/publications/drillingdeeper/

Inman, M. 2015a. 'The investment gap'. *Beacon*, 12 January 2015. Accessed 20 February 2015 at: https://www.beaconreader.com/mason-inman/the-investment-gap

Inman, M. 2015b. 'Early signs of the Bakken oil slow down'. *Beacon*, 26 January 2015. Accessed 20 February 2015 at: https://www.beaconreader.com/mason-inman/early-signs-of-the-bakken-oil-slow-down?ref=profile

International Energy Agency 2010. 'Global energy outlook 2010: Executive summary. Accessed 10 September 2013 at: http://www.worldenergyoutlook.org/media/weowebsite/2010/

WEO2010_es_english.pdf

International Energy Agency 2013. 'World energy outlook 2013: Executive summary'. Accessed 10 February 2014 at: http://www.iea.org/publications/freepublications/publication/ WEO2013_Executive_Summary_English.pdf

Intergovernmental Panel on Climate Change (IPCC) 2013. 'Climate change 2013: The physical science basis (Fifth Assessment Report)'. Accessed 10 October at: http://www.ipcc.ch/ report/ar5/wg1/#.Uk6k-CjqMRw

Jackson, P.M. and Smith, L.K. 2014. 'Exploring the undulating plateau: The future of global oil supply'. *Philosophical Transactions of the Royal Society* 372(2006): 20120491.

Kent, S. and Faucon, B. 2015. 'Oil-price rebound predicted: IEA adds to chorus of voices saying glut with abate'. *Wall Street Journal*, 9 February 2015. Accessed 10 February 2015 at: http://www.wsj.com/articles/demand-for-opec-crude-will- rise-this-year-says-group-1423482563

Kopits, S. 2014. 'Oil and economic growth: A supply-constrained view'. Presentation delivered to the Center on Global Energy Policy, Columbia University, 11 February 2014. Accessed 15 January 2015 at: http://energypolicy.columbia.edu/ sites/default/files/energy/Kopits%20-%20Oil%20and%20 Economic%20Growth%20%28SIPA,%202014%29%20- %20Presentation%20Version%5B1%5D.pdf

Likvern, R. 2012. 'Is shale oil production from Bakken headed for a run with "the Red Queen"'. *The Oil Drum*, 25 September 2012. Accessed 20 February 2015 at: http://www.theoildrum. com/node/9506

Mazzetti, M., Schmitt, E., and Kirkpatrick, D. 2015. 'Saudi oil is seen as lever to pry Russian support for Syria's Assad'. *New York Times*, 3 February 2015. Accessed 10 February 2015 at: http://www.nytimes.com/2015/02/04/world/middleeast/saud i-arabia-is-said-to-use-oil-to-lure-russia-away-from-syrias- assad.html?ref=todayspaper

Mearns, E. 2014. 'The 2014 oil price crash explained'. *Energy Matters*, 24 November 2014. Accessed 10 January 2015 at: http://euanmearns.com/the-2014-oil-price-crash-explained/

Meijer, R. 2014a. 'Cheap oil a boon for the economy? Think Again'. *The Automatic Earth*, 29 November 2014. Accessed 10 January 2015 at: http://www.theautomaticearth.com/2014/11/cheap- oil-a-boon-for-the-economy-think-again/

Meijer, R. 2014b. 'The price of oil exposes the true state of the economy'. *The Automatic Earth*, 27 November 2014. Accessed 10 January 2015 at: http://www.theautomaticearth. com/2014/11/the-price-of-oil-exposes-the-true-state-of-the-economy/

Miller, R. and Sorrell, S. 2014. 'The future of oil supply'. *Philosophical Transactions of the Royal Society A* 372, 20130179: 1-27.

Munroe, R. 2010. 'Energy security: An annotated military/security bibliography (2010 update)'. *Resilience*, 28 September 2010. Accessed 10 January 2015 at: http://www.resilience.org/stories/2010-09-28/energy-security-annotated-militarysecurity-bibliography-2010-update

Murphy, D. 2014. 'The implications of the declining energy return on investment of oil production'. *Philosophical Transactions of the Royal Society A* 372, 20130126: 1-19.

Murphy, D. and Hall, C. 2011a. 'Adjusting to the new energy realities of the second half of the age of oil'. *Ecological Modelling* 223: 67-71.

Murphy, D. and Hall, C. 2011b. 'Energy return on investment, peak oil, and the end of economic growth'. *Annals of the New York Academy of Sciences* 1219: 52-72.

Mushalik, M. 2013. 'US shale hides crude oil peak in rest of world'. Accessed 15 October 2013 at: http://crudeoilpeak.info/us-shale-oil-hides-crude-oil-peak-in-rest-of-world

Mushalik, M. 2014. 'IEA report implies US crude production may start to peak 2016'. *Crude Oil Peak*, 14 August 2014. Accessed 10 January 2015 at: http://crudeoilpeak.info/iea-report-implies-us-crude-production-may-start-to-peak-2016

Mushalik, M. 2015a. 'NorthConex road tunnel contract signed only days after US$150 oil price warnings in Davos'. *Crude Oil Peak*. Accessed 15 February 2015 at: http://crudeoilpeak.info/northconnex-road-tunnel-contract-signed-only-days-after-us-150-200-oil-price-warnings-in-davos

Mushalik, M. 2015b. 'Peak affordable oil'. *Crude Oil Peak*, 2 February 2015. Accessed 5 February 2015 at: http://crudeoil/peak.info/peak-affordable-oil

Mushalik, M. 2015c. 'Free oil! Next stop free oil crunch'. *Crude Oil Peak*. 15 February 2015. Accessed 20 February 2015 at: http://crudeoilpeak.info/free-oil-next-stop-free-oil-crunch

Mushalik, M. 2015d. 'US drilling count'. *Crude Oil Peak*, 13 February 2015. Accessed on 17 February 2015 at: http://crudeoilpeak.info/us-drilling-rig-count

Nelder, C. and Macdonald, G. 2011. 'There will be oil, but at what price?' *Harvard Business Review*, 4 October 2011. Accessed 10 January 2015 at: https://hbr.org/2011/10/there-will-be-oil-but-can-you

Patterson, R. 2014. 'OPEC October MOMR and other news'. *Peak Oil Barrel*, 10 October 2014. Accessed 10 January 2015 at:

http://peakoilbarrel.com/opec-october-momr-news/

Patterson, R. 2015. 'Texas RRC oil and gas production data'. *Peak Oil Barrel*, 20 January 2015. Accessed 25 January 2015 at: http://peakoilbarrel.com/texas-rrc-oil-gas-production-data/

Raval, A. 2014. 'Oil price plunge means survival of fittest: Crude oil at $70 puts at least 1.5m b/d of projects 2016 at risk'. *Financial Times*, 10 December 2014. Accessed 10 January 2015 at: http://www.ft.com/intl/cms/s/0/51cc00ba-7f85-11e4-86ee-00144feabdc0.html#axzz3RxSpUHzf

Sakya, P. 2015. 'BP PLC, Shell PLC and Petrofac PLC: Why peak oil theory was wrong'. *Yahoo Finance*. Accessed 25 January 2015 at: https://uk.finance.yahoo.com/news/bp-plc-shell-plc-petrofac-093705013.html

Solomon, J. and Said, S. 2014. 'Behind OPEC decision: A Saudi fear of US shale'. *Wall Street Journal*, 22 December 2014. Accessed 10 January 2015 at: http://online.wsj.com/public/resources/documents/pageone122214.pdf

Topf, A. 2015. 'Did the Saudis and the US collude in dropping oil prices?' *On Line Opinion*, 5 January 2015. Accessed 20 February 2015 at: http://www.onlineopinion.com.au/view.asp?article=16981&page=0

Trainer, T. 2010. *The Transition to a Sustainable and Just World*. Envirobook, Sydney.

Turner, G. 2014. 'Is Global Collapse Imminent? An Updated Comparison of *The Limits to Growth* with Historical Data'. *MSSI Research Paper* No. 4 August 2014.

Tverberg, G. 2012. 'Oil supply limits and the continuing financial crisis'. *Energy* 37(1): 27-34.

Tverberg, G. 2014. 'Beginning of the end? Oil companies cut back on spending'. *Our Finite World*, 25 February 2014. Accessed 20 February 2015 at: http://ourfiniteworld.com/2014/02/25/beginning-of-the-end-oil-companies-cut-back-on-spending/

Tverberg, G. 2015. 'A new theory of energy and the economy: Part I – Generating economic growth'. *Our Finite World*, 21 January 2015. Accessed 20 February 2015 at: http://ourfiniteworld.com/2015/01/21/a-new-theory-of-energy-and-the-economy-part-1-generating-economic-growth/

Viscusci, G., Patel, T., and Kennedy, S. (2014) 'Oil at $40 possible as market transforms Caracas to Iran'. *Bloomberg Business*, 1 December 2014. Accessed 10 January 2015 at: http://www.bloomberg.com/news/articles/2014-11-30/oil-at-40-possible-as-market-transforms-caracas-to-iran

Whitney, M. 2014. 'The oil coup'. *Counterpunch*, 16 December 2014. Accessed 10 January 2015 at: http://www.counterpunch.org

/2014/12/16/the-oil-coup/

Wolf, M. 2014. 'Two cheers for the sharp falls in oil prices'. *Financial Times*, 2 December 2014. Accessed 10 January 2015: http://www.ft.com/intl/cms/s/0/18a2df62-7949-11e4-9567-00144feabdc0.html#axzz3RxSpUHzf

Worstall, T. 2015. 'Citigroup: Oil's heading to $20 and Opec's days are over'. *Forbes*, 10 February 2015. Accessed 15 February 2015 at:http://www.forbes.com/sites/timworstall/2015/02/10/citigroup-oils-heading-to-20-and-opecs-days-are-over/

Zumbrun, J. 2015. 'Oil's plunge could help send its price back up'. *Wall Street Journal*, 22 February 2015. Accessed on 22 February 2015 at: http://www.wsj.com/articles/oils-plunge-could-help-send-its-price-back-up-1424632746

9

VOLUNTARY SIMPLIFICATION AS AN ALTERNATIVE TO COLLAPSE
Prosperous descent in the Anthropocene

A society or other institution can be destroyed by the cost of sustaining itself.
— Joseph Tainter

1. Introduction

The global, industrialised economy is in gross ecological overshoot (Global Footprint Network, 2012), and yet population is expanding and great multitudes living in poverty justly seek material advancement. Despite this ecological overshoot, nations, both rich and poor, pursue continued growth of their economies without apparent limit (Hamilton, 2003), vastly increasing energy and resource demands on an already overburdened planet. This process of industrialisation, barely 300 years old, has produced what some theorists are now calling 'the Anthropocene' – an era in which human impact on Earth has been so severe that it constitutes a new geological epoch. This is an era where biodiversity is in sharp decline and resource scarcity looms, and where carbon emissions are threatening to destabilise our climatic systems with potentially catastrophic consequences (Friedrichs, 2013; Turner, 2012).

Are we, the participants of industrial civilisation, thus destined to face the same fate as other great civilisations in history, having risen to such great heights, only to fall? Admittedly, it challenges the imagination to envision a time when our present civilisation is being studied as Rome is studied today, as an object of history – as a dead

199

civilisation. But is this the future we face? Or is there a door hidden in the wall, through which we might be able to negotiate some alternative path and escape what seems to be our impending fate? These are the ambitious themes addressed in this chapter, by offering a sympathetic critique of the work of Joseph Tainter, in which seemingly minor disagreements and refinements are shown to have major implications.

2. Overview

In 1988 Joseph Tainter published his seminal work, *The Collapse of Complex Societies*, in which he presented an original theory of social complexity that he offered as the best explanation for the collapse of civilisations throughout history. Social complexity, in Tainter's sense, refers to the way civilisations develop their methods of organisation, production, and behaviour in response to societal 'problems' that arise. For example, increasing social complexity in order to solve problems might involve developing technical abilities, establishing new institutions, diversifying social, economic, and political roles, as well as increasing production and information flows, all of which require energy and resources. Tainter's central thesis, outlined in more detail below, is that while increasing social complexity initially provides a net benefit to a society, eventually the benefits derived from complexity diminish and the relative costs begin to increase. The diminishing returns on complexity arise from the fact that, when trying to solve societal problems, 'inexpensive solutions are adopted before more complex and expensive ones' (Tainter, 2011a: 26), meaning that over time the energy and resource costs of problem-solving tend to increase and the relative benefits decrease. As the benefits of complexity continue to diminish, there comes a point when all the energy and resources available to a society are required just to maintain the society, at which point further problems that arise cannot be solved and the society then enters a phase of deterioration or even rapid collapse. That is, civilisations can be destroyed when the costs of sustaining their complexity become unaffordable. This is the essential dynamic that Tainter argues 'can explain collapse as no other theory has been able to do' (Tainter, 1995: 400). Not only is Tainter's theory of historical interest, many believe it has implications for how we understand the world today.

One of the most challenging aspects of Tainter's theory is how it reframes – one might even say revolutionises – sustainability discourse (Tainter, 2003; Tainter, 2011a; Allen, Tainter, and Hoekstra, 2003). Tainter argues that sustainability is about problem solving and that problem solving increases social complexity. But he also argues that social complexity requires energy and resources, and this implies that solving problems, including ecological problems, can actually demand *increases* in energy and resource consumption, not reductions. Indeed, Tainter (2006: 93) maintains that sustainability is 'not a passive consequence of having fewer human beings who consume more limited resources', as many argue it is; he even goes as far as to suggest that 'voluntary simplification' – which refers to the process of choosing to reduce energy and resource consumption – may no longer be an option for industrial civilisation (e.g., Tainter, 2011a), for reasons that will be explained. Instead, Tainter's conception of sustainability involves subsidising ever-increasing complexity with more energy and resources in order to solve ongoing problems.

While Tainter's theory of social complexity has much to commend it, in this chapter I wish to examine and ultimately challenge Tainter's conclusion that voluntary simplification is not a viable path to sustainability. In fact, I will argue that it is by far our best bet, even if the odds do not provide grounds for much optimism. Part of the disagreement here turns on differing notions of 'sustainability'. Whereas Tainter seems to use sustainability to mean *sustaining the existing civilisation*, I use sustainability to mean *changing the form of civilisation* through voluntary simplification, insofar as that is required for humanity to operate within the carrying capacity of the planet (Vale and Vale, 2013). Given that Tainter (1988) seems to accept, as we will see, that his own conception of sustainability will eventually lead to collapse, I feel he is wrong to be so dismissive of voluntary simplification as a strategy for potentially avoiding collapse. It is, I argue, our only alternative to collapse, and if that is so, voluntary simplification ought to be given our most rigorous attention and commitment, even if the chances of success do not seem high. I feel Tainter is flippant about our best hope, and given what is at stake, his dismissal of voluntary simplification should be given close critical attention. Furthermore, even if attempting to sustain the existing civilisation through ever-increasing complexity continues to be humanity's dominant approach to solving societal problems, I maintain the alternative path of voluntary simplification remains the most effective means of building 'resilience' (i.e., the ability of an individual or community to withstand societal or ecological shocks). This is significant because it justifies the practice and promotion of voluntary simplification, *irrespective of the likelihood of it ever being broadly accepted*. Directed toward the highly developed regions of the world, I argue that environmental sustainability requires voluntary simplification; but if that strategy is not widely embraced, I maintain we should still embrace the strategy *as far as possible*, in order to build resilience in preparation for forthcoming civilisational deterioration or collapse. The aim is not to achieve some passive socio-ecological stasis, but to move toward a way of life that achieves some form of dynamic equilibrium within ecologically sustainable limits.

While I accept that problem solving generally implies an increase in social complexity, the thesis I present below is that there comes a point when complexity itself becomes a problem, at which point voluntary simplification, not further complexity, is the most appropriate response. Not only does industrial civilisation seem to be at such a point today (Homer-Dixon, 2006; Slaughter, 2010), or well beyond it (Gilding, 2011), I hope to show, albeit in a preliminary way, that voluntary simplification presents a viable and desirable option for responding to today's converging social, economic, and ecological problems. This goes directly against Tainter's conception of sustainability, while accepting much of his background theoretical framework.

3. Tainter's Theory of Complexity and Collapse

This is not the place to review the historical details that serve to underpin Tainter's theory (1988). For present purposes, what is required is simply an outline of the structure of his position, which can be done quite briefly.

3.1. *The dynamics of social complexity*

The foundation of Tainter's position, as already noted, is that social complexity increases when human beings set out to solve the problems with which they are confronted. Since problems continually arise, there is persistent pressure for growth in complexity (Tainter, 2011b: 91). Both historically and today, such problems might include securing enough food, adjusting to demographic, climatic, or other environmental changes, dealing with aggression within or between societies, organising society, and so on. Indeed, the challenges any society might face are, for practical purposes, 'endless in number and infinite in variety' (Tainter, 2011a: 33), and responding to problems generally requires energy and resources. Social or cultural 'complexity' is the term Tainter uses to describe this development in human organisation and behaviour.

In order to understand the dynamics of social complexity, it can be helpful to begin by focusing on prehistoric times (prior to the uptake of agriculture), when human life was about as simple as can be. During these times, the main problem human beings faced was securing an adequate food supply, and this was solved relatively easily by hunting wild animals and gathering wild plants. Interestingly, anthropologists have concluded that prehistoric hunter-gatherers were the most leisured societies to have ever existed (Sahlins, 1974; Diamond, 1998), which confirms that food supply was generally secure and easily obtained. It seems that once essential biophysical needs were adequately met, hunter-gatherers stopped labouring and took rest rather than work longer hours to create a material surplus for which they did not seem to desire.

This form of life was sustained by a minimal and largely static supply of energy – essentially just food, and eventually fire. This tightly constrained energy supply placed strict bounds on the types of society that could arise, for the reason that more 'complex' social organisations and behaviours require greater supplies of energy. In other words, hunter-gatherer societies had no food (i.e., energy) surplus to feed any non-food specialists – such as soldiers, craftspeople, bureaucrats, aristocrats, and so forth – so there was very little differentiation in social roles. Accordingly, for hundreds of thousands of years, early hunter-gatherer societies did not develop any significant degree of social complexity, in Tainter's sense of the term.

Things began to change, however, around 10,000 years ago as a consequence of the agricultural revolution (Diamond, 1998: Ch 6). The greater productivity of agriculture for the first time gave human societies a significant boost in their food (i.e., energy) supply, and this set in motion the development of social complexity that continues to this day. Being so much more productive than foraging, agriculture meant that not everyone had to spend their time producing food, and this gave rise to an array of non-food specialists, including those noted above and many more. Furthermore, the sedentary nature of agricultural societies made it practical to begin producing and accumulating new material artefacts (e.g., houses, furniture, collections of tools, etc.), all of which would have been too cumbersome for nomadic peoples to justify creating, or too energy-intensive.

Eventually wind energy (boats, windmills, etc.) and hydro energy (waterwheels) further enhanced humankind's energy surplus (Smil, 2004), paving the way for further increases in social complexity. The greatest energy revolution, however, was of course initiated early in the 18th century, when humankind first began harnessing on a large scale the extraordinary potential of fossil fuels. This provided the vast energy foundations required to establish and maintain a form of life as complex as industrial civilisation. While it is believed that hunter-gatherers had no more than a dozen distinct social personalities, modern European censuses recognise as many as 20,000 unique occupational roles, and industrial societies may contain more than 1,000,000 different kinds of social personalities (Tainter, 2011a: 25). If nothing else, this is evidence of unprecedented social complexity.

At this stage it is important to note that social complexity does not always follow an energy surplus, but often precedes a surplus. In fact, Tainter argues that complexity *typically* precedes an energy surplus (Tainter, 1988; Tainter, 2000). While he accepts that historically there were a few isolated 'revolutions' in energy supply that certainly made further complexity possible, he argues that normally complexity arises when new problems present themselves, and in solving those problems societies are forced to find a way to produce more energy, if that is possible. This contrasts with the isolated situations (following an energy revolution) when societies voluntarily become more complex due to an availability of surplus energy. As Tainter puts it, 'Complexity often compels the production of energy, rather than following its abundance' (Tainter, 2006: 92). This is significant because it means that increasing complexity often is not voluntary, in that it is typically a response to the emergence of unwanted problems, rather than being a creative luxury chosen in response to the availability of surplus energy. This is a point to which we will return as the case for and against voluntary simplification is assessed.

3.2. *Diminishing marginal returns of complexity*

At the centre of Tainter's theory lies his idea that social complexity is an economic function that has diminishing marginal returns. Complexity is an economic function in the sense that it involves a balancing of costs and benefits. That is, when a society solves a problem by becoming more complex it will receive the benefits of solving the problem, but it will also incur the costs of doing so. These costs will include, most importantly, energy and resources, but also costs like time and annoyance. For example, when hunter-gatherer societies discovered agriculture and became aware that its methods could produce more food than foraging, they had to balance the benefits of transitioning to an agricultural society with the costs. The costs were that early farming techniques were more labour-intensive than foraging; the benefits were that agriculture was much more productive per acre, and this extra productivity might have provided a welcome opportunity to support non-food specialists or solved a society's food crisis (perhaps brought on by overpopulation or overhunting depleting available resources).

This same balancing exercise takes place every time a society considers responding to a problem by creating a new institution, adding new bureaucrats, developing some new technology, or establishing some new social system, etc. Societies choose complexity – that is, choose to solve the problems they face – when it seems that the benefits of doing so will outweigh the costs. Critically, there must also be the energy and resources available to actually subsidise the problem-solving activity (or at least the potential to acquire more energy and resources, if current supplies are already exhausted in simply maintaining existing complexity).

Tainter's most original insight, however, is that complexity is subject to diminishing returns, which is to say, over time the benefits of complexity diminish and the ongoing costs of maintaining or increasing complexity augment. He explains that this is because 'humans always tend to pick the lowest hanging fruit first, going on to higher branches only when those lower no longer hold fruit. In problem-solving systems, inexpensive solutions are adopted before more complex and expensive ones' (Tainter, 2011a: 26). In other words, over time increments of investment in complexity begin to yield smaller and smaller increments of return, which is another way of saying that the marginal return on complexity starts to decline.

Eventually, Tainter argues, the costs of solving a problem will actually be higher than the benefits gained. At this point further problems will not or cannot be solved, and societies become vulnerable to deterioration or even rapid collapse. Another way of expressing this is to say that there comes a point in the evolution of societies when all the energy available to that society are exhausted in simply maintaining the existing level of complexity. When further problems arise, as history tells us they inevitably will do, the lack of an energy surplus means that new problems cannot be solved and thus societies become liable to collapse.

This highlights the point explained above about how complexity is not always, and not even normally, a voluntary response to surplus energy, but instead is usually required for a society to sustain itself as new problems emerge. Societies can be destroyed, however, when the costs of sustaining their complexity become unaffordable. This is the essential dynamic that Tainter argues 'can explain collapse as no other theory has been able to do' (Tainter, 1995: 400).

4. Implications of Tainter's Theory on Sustainability Discourse

As noted, Tainter's theory of social complexity and collapse has profound implications on sustainability discourse. There are, of course, many strains of sustainability discourse, but Tainter (2011b) argues that all the dominant varieties look inadequate once the implications of his theory are grasped. His main target is 'voluntary simplification', which refers to the strategy of voluntarily consuming fewer energy and resources as a response to societal problems (including environmental problems). But he also levels his critique against sustainability arguments based on pricing commodities correctly and market exchange; rationing resources; reducing population; or producing commodities more efficiently through technological advance (Tainter, 2011b). For present purposes, the focus will be on voluntary simplification, since it is the most important and by far the most original of Tainter's critiques. Tainter (2011b: 93-4) frames and dismisses voluntary simplification in the following terms:

> *Voluntarily reduce resource consumption.* This strategy is constrained by the fact that societies increase in complexity to solve problems. Resource production must grow to fund the increased complexity. To implement voluntary conservation long term would require that a society be either uniquely lucky in not encountering problems, or that it not address the problems that confront it.

I will now examine this position and offer an alternative assessment of it.

4.1 *Tainter's critique of voluntary simplification*

Tainter maintains that the argument for sustainability based on voluntarily consuming less and reducing social complexity follows logically from what he considers a flawed assumption – the assumption that surplus resources and energy *precede* and *facilitate* innovations that increase complexity. 'Complexity, in this view, is a voluntary matter. Human societies became more complex by choice rather than necessity. By this reasoning, we should be able to choose to forgo complexity and the resource consumption that it entails' (Tainter, 2011a: 31). Tainter rejects that reasoning. In his view, complexity is generally forced upon societies as they respond to new problems, not voluntarily embraced due to an energy surplus, and this leads Tainter to reject voluntary simplification as a path to sustainability:

> Contrary to what is typically advocated as the route to sustainability, *it is usually not possible for a society to reduce its consumption of resources voluntarily over the long term.* To the contrary, as problems great and small inevitably arise, addressing these problems requires complexity and resource consumption to increase (Tainter, 2011a: 31, emphasis in original).

Elsewhere, Tainter (2006: 99) arrives at the same conclusion: 'Sustainability is an active condition of problem solving, not a passive consequence of consuming less.' More directly still, he insists that 'sustainability may require greater consumption of resources rather than less. One must be able to afford sustainability' (2006: 99). He even concludes a recent essay with the following statement: 'Developing new energy is therefore the most fundamental thing we can do to become sustainable' (Tainter, 2011a: 33). His essential argument, therefore, is that if we have enough energy to solve the problems we face, civilisation will not deteriorate or collapse. The flip side of that argument, of course, is that if we cannot secure the necessary energy, our future looks much bleaker – that is, we will be destined to repeat the history of all previous civilisations that have collapsed according to the same logic of diminishing returns on complexity (Tainter, 1988; Tainter and Patzek, 2012).

Despite Tainter's approach to sustainability being coherently and rigorously argued (if one accepts his assumptions), his position directly contradicts those who advocate reducing overall energy and resource consumption, which is the strategy this chapter is defending. For reasons already outlined, Tainter rejects that strategy as nice in theory but naïve in practice, perhaps even impossible. Given that Tainter is equally dismissive of the other approaches to sustainability (e.g., population reduction, internalising externalities, technological advancements, etc.), one can understand why he resigns himself to the fact that 'the study of social complexity does not yield optimistic results' (Tainter, 2006: 99). In fact, there is something deeply tragic in Tainter's view, because it suggests that civilisation, by its very nature, gets locked into a process of mandatory growth in complexity that eventually becomes unsupportable. Furthermore, history provides a disturbingly consistent empirical basis for this tragic view (Tainter, 1988), leading Tainter (2006: 100) to conclude that 'all solutions to the problem of complexity are temporary.' This seemingly innocuous statement is actually profoundly dark, for it implies that ultimately and inevitably social complexity will outgrow its available energy supply. Despite this situation, or rather, because of it, Tainter (2006: 100) argues that '"success" consists substantially of staying in the game', and he believes that sustainability in this sense depends on developing new energy sources to subsidise ongoing problem-solving activity.

4.2. *Problems with Tainter's conception of sustainability*

Before offering a different response to the diminishing returns of complexity, it may be worth spending a moment further considering Tainter's proposed solution, for even if we were to accept the underlying logic of his analysis, his thesis that sustainability should be pursued by increasing energy supply is highly problematic, to say the least.

First of all, production of the world's most important source of energy – conventional petroleum (i.e., crude oil plus condensate) – seems to have 'peaked' or reached an undulating plateau (see IEA, 2010a; Miller and Sorrell, 2014). This has led to increased development of non-conventional oil, but this is notoriously more expensive to produce and has far lower energy and economic returns on investment (Hall and Murphy, 2011; Murphy, 2014). What this means is that the world will eventually be facing a future with less net energy derived from oil supplies, not more; it is only a question of timing. Furthermore, being non-renewable resources, a similar pattern of stagnation and decline will eventually apply to other fossil fuel sources too (coal and gas), as well as fuels for nuclear energy. This is the so-called 'peak everything' argument (Heinberg, 2007), and it presents Tainter's approach to sustainability with what is probably an unsurmountable obstacle. That is, just as we need more energy to subsidise further complexity and respond to new societal or ecological problems, overall energy and resource supplies look poised to plateau and diminish (Klare, 2012).

Secondly, the science of climate change (IPCC, 2013) suggests very strongly that if we maintain or increase existing levels of fossil fuel consumption, we are likely to face increasingly dire consequences over the course of this century and beyond (Gilding, 2011). Again, this casts grave doubt on Tainter's energy-based solution to sustainability problems. He argues that we must secure increased energy supplies to solve new and ongoing problems, but if increasing social complexity in that way requires continuing to burn more fossil fuels, then it seems clear that the world's problems are going to get considerably worse, not better (Hansen, 2011). At the same time, if the world chooses to stop consuming fossil fuels –

which currently make up more than 80% of global energy supply (IEA, 2010b: 6) – then obviously Tainter's approach fares no better, because he argues quite rightly that we need energy to solve problems. From his perspective, then, it seems that 'we're damned if we do, and we're damned if we don't,' as the saying goes.

Given the problems of 'peak everything' and climate change, Tainter naturally highlights the importance of transitioning to cleaner, renewable sources of energy (Tainter, 2011b). Such a transition is certainly to be desired, but unfortunately it is very unlikely to provide a timely supply of energy at the level Tainter's path to sustainability would require. Leaving to one side the fact that the transition to renewables is taking place at a disturbingly slow rate while emissions continue to rise (Jackson, 2009: 72), the more fundamental problem seems to be the inherent limitations to renewable energy sources. Ted Trainer (e.g., 2013a; 2013b; 2012), for example, has spent the best part of a decade examining the evidence on varieties of solar, wind, biomass, geothermal, etc., as well as energy storage systems, such as hydrogen and batteries. He concludes that the figures do not support the widely held assumption that renewable energy can sustain the global economy in anything like its current form. This is because the enormous quantities of electricity and oil required today simply cannot be converted to any mixture of renewable energy sources, each of which suffers from various limitations arising out of such things as intermittency of supply, redundant plant, storage problems, resource limitations (e.g., rare metals, land for biomass competing with food production, etc.), and inefficiency issues. Ultimately, however, the cost is the fundamental issue at play here (due primarily to the amount of redundant plant required to accommodate base-load and intermittency). Trainer provides evidence showing that existing attempts to price the transition to systems of renewable energy are wildly understated, especially if future growth in energy production is taken into consideration. This is not a message most 'green' people want to hear.

It is of the utmost importance to emphasise that this is not an argument against renewable energy; nor is it an argument more broadly against the use of appropriate technologies to achieve efficiency improvements. It seems clear enough that the world must transition to dependence on systems of renewable energy without delay and exploit appropriate technology wherever possible (IPCC, 2013). We cannot afford not to! But given the limitations and expense of renewable energy systems, it seems highly unlikely that Tainter's approach to sustainability – the approach that argues that we need to increase energy supply to solve ongoing problems – can be subsidised by renewable energy sources. Furthermore, as outlined above, maintaining or increasing consumption of fossil fuels will be either compromised by peak oil or rendered uneconomic due to the enormous costs of adapting to a changing climate. Tainter's approach to sustainability, therefore, cannot be accepted, even if one accepts his background theoretical framework.

5. Can Civilisational Collapse be Avoided?

Tainter's conception of sustainability faces further problems in that it is not really about sustainability, as such, if sustainability is meant to refer (as it normally is) to something being sustained *over the long term*. The phrase 'over the long term' is vague, deliberately so, but it is intended to emphasise Tainter's view that civilisations could never be sustainable into the deep future (say, over tens of thousands of years). According to Tainter, the tendency of all societies to become more complex over time, coupled with the diminishing marginal returns on complexity, means that eventually all societies get locked into a process of mandatory growth in complexity that eventually becomes unsupportable. This theory of social complexity implies that all societies have an inbuilt tendency to collapse, and this is why Tainter's conception of sustainability is necessarily compromised. After all, if one were to accept his assumptions, the idea of sustainability as meaning a civilisation being sustained over the long term is actually a contradiction in terms. Civilisation is *inherently* unsustainable according to Tainter's logic, and this is why he is required to weaken his conception of sustainability to mean merely 'staying in the game' as long as possible (2006: 100). But he also insists that all solutions to complexity are only temporary, and that is why I refer to Tainter's view as 'tragic'. Not only is it tragic, it is disconcertingly plausible (Tainter, 1988; Turner, 2012).

While I accept Tainter's view that problem solving generally implies an increase in social complexity, and that social complexity has diminishing marginal returns, the thesis I outline below is that there comes a point when complexity itself becomes a problem – that is, there comes a point when the costs of further complexity exceed the benefits – at which point voluntary simplification, not further complexity, is the most appropriate response. Tainter believes this is not an available response. He asserts that such a response would 'require that a society be either uniquely lucky in not encountering problems, or that it not address the problems that confront it' (Tainter, 2011b: 93-4). I hope to show, however, that on this critical point he is in error.

Furthermore, I will argue that given the tendency of societies to become more complex than they can afford to be, long-term sustainability, in the sense of being sustained into the deep future, requires that societies embrace voluntary simplification when the costs of complexity exceed the benefits. If they do not, they collapse. Another way of expressing my argument is to say that as the benefits of social complexity diminish and become outweighed by the costs, the benefits of voluntary simplification increase. To be clear, I do not argue that voluntary simplification is *likely* to be embraced as a response to existing crises; my argument is that it is the *only* alternative to collapse, and thus it is a strategy we should do our very best to adopt, no matter our prospects of success. Indeed, given the devastating consequences of any collapse scenario, voluntary simplification becomes a moral imperative.

5.1. *Does voluntary simplification mean solving fewer problems?*

Building upon the analysis so far, voluntary simplification can be defined more precisely as *choosing a form of life in which the overall consumption of energy and resources is progressively reduced and eventually stabilised at a level that lies within the planet's sustainable carrying capacity; and because social complexity requires energy and resources, voluntarily reducing energy and resource consumption would generally imply a reduction in social complexity.* This definition of voluntary simplification raises many questions, which I will now endeavour to answer, or begin answering.

Most importantly, the definition must be situated in the context of Tainter's theory of social complexity, for in that context the notion of voluntarily reducing energy and resources seems like an incoherent strategy to achieve sustainability. This demands an immediate explanation, because if one were to accept that solving problems generally requires energy and resources – and I do accept that – it would seem to follow that voluntary simplification means *choosing to solve fewer problems.* I will now try to explain that the apparent incoherency here disappears when we take a closer look at what Tainter means when he uses the term 'problem', which is a central concept in his theory. It seems that Tainter oversimplifies here what is a complex term, and that misunderstanding or misuse locks him into the tragic worldview outlined above. I believe that clearing up this misunderstanding provides the key to escaping Tainter's tragedy.

211

5.2. *The indeterminacy of 'problems' and its implications*

In Tainter's view, societies increase their social complexity when they solve the problems with which they are presented. However, Tainter employs the term 'problem' as if it were self-defining and unambiguous. He assumes that a society just knows what is and what is not a problem, which of course is not an unreasonable assumption. On closer inspection, however, it can be seen that a 'problem' in Tainter's sense is actually a radically indeterminate notion, requiring various value judgements in order to give it content. There are at least three causes of this indeterminacy.

First of all, indeterminacy can arise over the very question of what constitutes a problem. For example, if a nation perceives a problem of national security, it may wage war on a threateningly powerful neighbouring state, rather than risk being attacked by surprise. Solving the 'problem' of security, therefore, might require (a) creating an army; and (b) if the war were successful, defending a larger territory, perhaps requiring a larger army still. This solution to the problem of security is a classic example of how increasing social complexity can require increased energy and resources. However, the 'problem' here is by no means something independent of human values or perspectives. That is, the problem is not just imposed on the society for it to deal with as best it can. There are *choices* involved about what problems to focus on. For example, rather than seeing the problem as being one of 'security', a different society might have seen a problem of 'economic growth', and rather than waging war, this alternative society might have tried to solve its problem by seeing if it could create a relationship of mutual benefit with its neighbours, perhaps through trade. Even through this simple example (which could be endlessly multiplied) it can be seen that the 'problems' that exist for any given society are often a value-laden function of their perspective or goals, not externally imposed challenges that arise independently.

A second cause of indeterminacy lies in the fact that there is rarely only one means of solving a particular problem. In the example above, the problem of security could have been solved by waging war, building a defensive wall, trying to negotiate a treaty, some mixture of these strategies, or through some other strategy entirely. Likewise, the problem of 'economic growth' could have been solved by creating new trade relationships, developing new technologies, marketing goods more effectively, or perhaps realising that growth was not actually so important (or was even harmful). Just as different perspectives might produce or dissolve certain problems, different perspectives also provide different ways of dealing with the problems that do exist (or are perceived to exist).

Significantly, this means that shifts in perspective, values, or desires can affect the level of energy or resources that are needed to deal with societal problems.

Finally, indeterminacy can also arise over the question of 'whose' problems have to be solved, for society is not a harmonious entity with a single set of goals and desires. This raises distributive questions of real importance. All societies have a limited pool of energy and resources, and the nature of any society is shaped significantly by how those limited resources are distributed and to what ends those resources and directed. Accordingly, when a society invests energy and resources to solve certain 'problems', we are entitled to ask questions about whose interests are being served by addressing those particular problems as opposed to other problems. It may be, after all, that some people in a society do not see such and such a problem as being a legitimate problem, or perhaps they see other issues that are not being addressed as more urgent problems. Tainter, it should be noted, is not wholly unaware of this issue. He writes: 'In a hierarchical institution [or society], the benefits of complexity often accrue at the top, while the costs are paid primarily by those at the bottom' (Tainter, 2006: 100). But he does not seem to appreciate that this is evidence of indeterminacy over what constitutes a problem; nor does he seem to appreciate how all these causes of indeterminacy impact on his theory. Even in a context of energy descent, for example, it could be that many civilisational problems (including environmental problems) could be solved if existing concentrations of wealth were redistributed toward solving those problems, rather than merely satisfying the indulgences of a small global elite.[15] Less positively, in circumstances of civilisation deterioration or collapse, the most likely outcome of socio-economic stress is that poverty is forced on the poorest social classes while the elite continue to reap the benefits of complexity.

My point in exposing these three indeterminacies is to show that 'problems' are not objective phenomena that exist independently of humankind and which we must simply deal with the best we can. Rather, problems are often the product of a particular worldview or value-system, in the sense that they only exist as problems because society (or a particular subset of society) desires a certain state of affairs. This is not always the case, of course, and my argument must not be interpreted otherwise. Some problems – climate change, for example – will obviously not

---

[15] Note, for example, the recent Oxfam study showing that the world's 85 richest people now own as much as the poorest half of humanity. See R. Fuentes-Nieva and N. Galasso, 'Working for the Few: Political Capture and Economic Inequality' (Oxfam Briefing Paper, 20 January 2014).

disappear merely because human beings decide to think differently about the world. But many perceived problems and perceived solutions are in fact dependent on the way human beings view the world, or dependent on whose particular perspective is adopted. What this means is that if the world came to be looked at through a different lens of understanding, a society might well find that it was faced with different problems, and perhaps different solutions would present themselves to existing problems. Again, this is significant because it means that changing perspectives or values can affect the level of energy or resources that are needed for a society to deal with its problems.

The implications of this analysis are potentially profound. Most importantly, the analysis opens up space within Tainter's theory for voluntary reductions in energy and resources. The key point is this: *the energy intensity of industrial civilisation is primarily a function of the values that produce or shape the perception of its problems.* Those values also produce and shape the perception of what constitutes a solution to perceived problems. Change those values, however, and many of the energy intensive problems industrial civilisation currently feels the need to solve may well disappear. Although in places Tainter seems to acknowledge this (Tainter, 2003: 215), he does not appear to grasp its implications for his own conception of sustainability. If energy intensive problems can be solved or rather dissolved by changing one's values or perspective, this will reduce the overall energy requirements for 'problem solving', thus opening up space for voluntary simplification. When this is understood, the apparent incoherency of voluntary simplification (i.e., the perceived implication that it would require choosing 'to solve fewer problems') disappears. Simplification might instead involve solving different problems, or perhaps solve the same problems in different, less energy-intensive ways. Tainter does not seem to appreciate this, for otherwise he would not dismiss simplification so readily. He argues that voluntarily reducing consumption would require that a society be either uniquely lucky in not encountering problems, or that it not address the problems that confront it (Tainter, 2011b: 93). But the analysis above shows that there is a third option: rethinking both what constitutes a problem and what constitutes an appropriate response. It may be that many problems that industrial civilisation currently invests in are not actually problems that need to be solved, or not solved in such energy intensive ways. For example, we could 'solve' the 'problem' of transport with more bikes and fewer cars (Floyd, 2013), suggesting that sustainability is not always about *maintaining* a certain way of life but actually *changing* it, perhaps in fundamental ways. The critical point to appreciate is that this type of analysis could be reproduced through essentially limitless examples. There is always room for a society to rethink its problems, rethink its solutions, and, importantly, *rethink how it prioritises the energy and resources it has available for problem solving*. If a society does this effectively it may find that it can solve all of its most important problems while reducing its consumption of energy and resources within sustainable levels (and redistributing its energy and resources when responding to new problems that arise). Doing so, of course, may produce a very different type of society.

5.3. *How might Tainter respond?*

One way Tainter might respond to this analysis is to argue that it seems to ignore the tendency of all societies to increase in complexity. Even if Tainter accepted, as he might well do, that there is room to reduce the energy intensity of industrial civilisation in the short term, he might nevertheless reiterate that societies are constantly faced with new problems, such that any attempts at voluntary simplification will eventually be rendered unsuccessful by the inexorable pressure to increase social complexity in response to new problems. For that reason, the costs of maintaining society will still tend to increase over the long term. Tainter might insist, therefore, that my analysis has not been able to provide any escape from the inherent tendency of civilisations to grow in social complexity until they cannot afford the costs of their own existence.

While I accept that societies will constantly be faced with new problems and that solving them will tend to increase social complexity, this is not fatal to the position I am defending. It would only be fatal if it were assumed that voluntary simplification is a passive or static form of life, as opposed to one that is dynamic and evolving. But I would argue that achieving sustainability, far from being passive or static in any way, must be a strategy that is self-reflective and constantly in flux. Again, if in places Tainter might seem to accept this point, he does not seem to appreciate what it means for his dismissal of voluntary simplification. The thought processes, behaviours, and institutions which voluntary simplification might represent cannot be static or unchanging, but must constantly respond to new circumstances and opportunities in new ways. Granted, if voluntary simplification meant reducing consumption and then returning to old ways of living, one can understand why social complexity would tend to increase over time, negating any initial benefits of voluntary simplification. But if voluntary simplification is considered an ongoing process, in which people and societies continually seek to reduce and restrain consumption, while also rethinking how best to invest the energy and resources at their disposal, then there is no reason to think that a society cannot be sustained, over the long term, on an environmentally sustainable level of energy and resource consumption, while still solving its most important problems (including new problems). Voluntary simplification, therefore, is not about achieving a stasis; it is about actively working on reaching and then maintaining some form of dynamic equilibrium within sustainable limits. This will not be easy, of course; but it is possible.

A second way Tainter might respond to my analysis is to say that there is already room for it within his own theory (Tainter, 2003). Although this would require a degree of self-contradiction, the response would seem to have some initial justification. After all, in his historical analysis, Tainter states that the Byzantine Empire (which survived the collapse of the Roman Empire in the fifth century) is an example, albeit the only one he claims, where 'a large, complex society systematically simplified, and reduced thereby its consumption of resources' (2011a: 31). At first instance, this seems to be the strategy I am defending. But after acknowledging Byzantine simplification, Tainter immediately adds that '[w]hile this case shows that societies can reduce consumption and thrive, it offers no hope that this can be commonly done' (Tainter, 2011a: 31). More importantly, however, Tainter points out that simplification by the Byzantine Empire was both forced — that is, made necessary by a gross insufficiency of resources — and temporary (Tainter, 2011a: 31). Since I am defending a strategy of simplification that is both voluntary and practiced over the long term, the Byzantine example is not evidence that voluntary simplification already fits within Tainter's theory. Rather, establishing the viability of voluntary simplification extends Tainter's theory in a way that avoids his tragic conclusions.[16]

A third way Tainter might respond to my analysis is by stating that, even if simplification were an available strategy, it will not be voluntarily embraced on the grounds that people will perceive that it is against their own interests. In fact, when considering whether voluntary simplification is possible, he states: 'I am confident that usually it is not, that humans will not ordinarily forgo affordable

---

[16] Although the term 'voluntary' suggests that simplification is purely a choice to embrace or forego, it should be noted that while simplification is currently a 'choice', soon enough it may become *necessary* due to resource or energy scarcity that may *impose* simplification upon industrial civilisation. My argument, therefore, is essentially that simplification is coming whether we want it or not, so we should 'choose' and plan for this necessity (in advance of its imposition) rather than have it imposed upon us through collapse.

consumption of things they desire on the basis of abstract projections about the future' (Tainter, 2011a: 31). Although Tainter's position here has some intuitive force, it is far from being self-evident. Tainter seems to assume (without being explicit about it) that reducing consumption is against one's self interest, but that assumption, despite being culturally entrenched, is empirically debatable, and in consumer societies it is most probably false. Indeed, there is now a vast body of social and psychological research (see Alexander, 2012a) indicating that many if not most Western-style consumers are actually mis-consuming to some extent, in the sense that they could increase their wellbeing while reducing their consumption. The intricacies of that research cannot be explored here, but if it can indeed be shown, as I believe it can, that large portions of high-consumption societies would benefit from exchanging superfluous material consumption for more time to pursue non-materialist forms of wellbeing, this would provide further support for the argument that voluntary simplification is not only possible, but desirable. If more people came to see this, one would expect simplification to be voluntarily embraced.

Nevertheless, while that might be so at the individual or community level, the question of whether *governments* will ever voluntarily initiate overall reductions in societal production and consumption is more challenging. After all, governments depend for their existence on taxes, and a larger economy means more taxable income, so a process of voluntary simplification is almost certainly not going to be initiated from the 'top down'. The overriding objective of governments around the world is to grow their economies without apparent limit (Hamilton, 2003; Purdey, 2010), and continued growth requires (among other things) a citizenry that seeks ever-higher material standards of living. This growth model of progress is arguably a reflection of an underlying belief that social progress requires more energy and resources in order to increase existing standards of living and solve ongoing problems. But if the global economy has now reached a stage where the growth model is causing the very problems it was supposed to solve, as many argue it has (Meadows *et al.*, 2004; Jackson, 2009; Trainer, 2010a; Heinberg, 2011), then voluntary simplification provides the most coherent path forward, especially for the most highly developed regions of the world (Alexander, 2012b). Although the prospects of governments embracing some 'top down' policy of voluntary simplification seem very slim, it is also clear that governments create many of the structures within which social movements operate, and those structures can function either to facilitate or inhibit a process of voluntary simplification. While an examination of ways governments could facilitate such a process lies beyond the scope of this chapter, the 'growth imperative' structurally built into modern economies suggests that if voluntary simplification is to emerge, it may well have to be driven 'from below'.

6. Escaping Tainter's Tragedy 'From Below'

While still marginal, there are several overlapping social movements that suggest that the seeds of voluntary simplification have already been sown at the grassroots level. The most long-standing of these social movements or subcultures is based on the idea of 'voluntary simplicity', which can be understood as a way of life in which people choose to reduce or restrain their material standard of living while seeking a higher quality of life (Alexander, 2009; Alexander and Ussher, 2012).[17] This counter-cultural attitude toward material wealth seems to be as old as civilisation itself (Vanenbroeck, 1991), with philosophers, prophets, and poets throughout history high-lighting that 'the good life' lies not in the accumulation of material possessions but in various non-materialistic sources of wellbeing, such as social relations, connection with nature, and peaceful, creative activity. In the 1960s and 70s, as modern environmentalism took hold, the eco-village movement emerged (Walker, 2005), which involved creating intentional communities, often on the fringe or beyond urban centres, in the hope of showing that sustainable, post-industrial forms of life were possible. Toward the end of the 1970s the term 'permaculture' was coined (Holmgren and Mollison, 1978), which is a complex notion that essentially refers to the ideal of designing social and economic systems that work with nature, rather than against it. In more recent years the Transition Towns movement has burst onto the global scene as a positive, community-based response to the dual crises of peak oil and climate change, through which people come together in an attempt to build resilient communities and local economies in the face of government inaction (Hopkins, 2008).

---

[17] The term 'voluntary simplicity' has long been used to refer to a way of life in which people choose to reduce or restrain their material consumption while seeking an increased quality of life. By way of distinction, I use the term 'voluntary simplification' in this chapter to refer specifically to a living strategy within the context of Tainter's theory of social complexity. While there is much overlap in the practical implications of these two ideas, conceptually they ought to be kept distinct. 'Voluntary simplicity', one might say, opposes 'consumerism' or 'materialism', whereas 'voluntary simplification' opposes increasing 'social complexity' in Tainter's sense.

Space does not presently permit a detailed examination of these movements. The purpose of mentioning them is merely to suggest that they exemplify, in various ways and to various degrees of influence, the process of voluntary simplification 'from below'. The reduced-consumption lifestyles of voluntary simplicity can be understood to be freeing up energy and resources to solve more important problems, or to solve problems *by* reducing wasteful consumption; eco-villages can be understood to be attempting (with various degrees of success) to build communities that can be sustained over the long term within the carrying capacity of the local environment; permaculture can be understood to be a design system that seeks to achieve sustainability by working with nature's limits and minimising waste of energy and resources; transition towns in many ways can be understood to be a mixture of all three previous movements, with the added virtue of emphasising the importance of building a post-carbon world within the existing society through committed grassroots, community-based activity. These are all gross oversimplifications of rich and diverse social movements, but if we were to take the best insights from each of them and begin shaping our societies on that basis (see Odum and Odum, 2001; Trainer, 2010a), that might just be enough to realise the concept of voluntary simplification defended in this chapter and thereby escape Tainter's tragedy – the tragedy of a civilisation increasing in complexity until it collapses. As I argued above, the energy intensity of industrial civilisation is primarily a function of the values that produce or shape the perception of its problems and solutions. But the social movements just outlined embody values that contrast with the pro-growth, materialistic values upon which industrial civilisation is built, and this means that if those alternative values were ever mainstreamed they would tend to produce a different perception of what problems needed to be solved and in what ways. This shift in values would open up space for voluntary simplification. It would require a much longer work to provide details on what the process of voluntary simplification would look like in practice, and how or whether it could ever come about, but in closing this chapter one brief example will be offered to help clarify the essential strategy.

6.1. *What would voluntary simplification look like in practice?*

Let us focus on food, given that it is an essential need for all societies. Currently, in the developed world at least, food production relies on extraordinarily complex social and economic systems. A single product in one's cupboard could well have had several dozen people in some way work on its production and distribution. Each of the substances within the product (e.g., salt, sugar, spices, vegetables, fruit, minerals, oils, etc.) could have been sourced from different parts of the world, come together at different times in the process of manufacture, having been shipped, driven and/or flown by people other than the producers. Furthermore, the glass jar or packaging could have been produced in one place, the paper for the label produced in another place, the inks for the label produced yet somewhere else, and the logo designed and printed somewhere else again. Once the product is finally complete, it would be shipped, driven and/or flown to a retailer who then stocks the shelves with hundreds or thousands of items all made in similarly complex ways. One study (Salleh, 2007) in Australia concluded that the items in a single basket of food from a supermarket typically travel 70,000 kilometres to the table (aggregating the distance each item travels).

Moreover, this complex process relies in less obvious ways on the entire system – i.e., a system of energy production that powers the manufacturers and supermarkets, factories that make nuts and bolts required to make the trucks that transport the food, universities that educate the engineers who make the factories and trucks – and so on, ad infinitum. Not only is this system of food production and distribution exceedingly energy intensive (mainly due to the fossil fuels needed for fertilisers, pesticides, irrigation, electricity, plastics, and transport), but in many ways it is also very insecure, because each step in the process is critical, meaning that if one step gets interfered with the whole process can break down. Such insecurity was exemplified by the trucker's strike in the UK in 2000. The nation realised very quickly how dependent it was on the globalised food system, because when the truckers were not trucking, food was not getting to the supermarkets. Before long supermarket officials were calling members of parliament advising them that without the lines of transport open to restock the shelves, supermarkets had about three days of food. In the words of one commentator, the nation was only 'nine meals from anarchy' (Simms, 2008). Industrial food production, we see, is extremely energy intensive and hugely complex, but partly for those reasons it is not very resilient in the face of systemic disturbances.

Compare industrial food production with the far simpler methods in hunter-gatherer societies. Everyone is involved in sourcing food, all food is locally sourced, and no fossil fuels are required. People, that is, were self-sufficient. The argument of this chapter is certainly not that we return to the extreme simplicity of hunter-gatherer societies (and even if those methods were desired, they would not be productive enough to feed anywhere near seven billion people). Rather, the argument here is that less complex and less energy intensive ways of providing food for ourselves can be achieved without compromising quality of life and perhaps contributing positively to quality of life. It is very doubtful whether strict self-sufficiency is the most desirable form of food production, and often it would not be possible. But complex societies could become far more self-reliant, and benefit from this, if only they made a commitment to source much of their own food locally, grow it organically, exchange surpluses at local markets, and eat it in season. This is one concrete example of voluntary simplification.

Governments could certainly help in this process, but presuming they will not do much, there is still much room for individuals, households, and communities to take considerable steps. Cuba in the 1990s provides an instructive example here (Percy *et al.*, 2010; Friedrichs, 2010; Friedrichs, 2013). When their oil supply was drastically cut after the fall of the Soviet Union, their industrialised food production and distribution essentially came to an end, replaced almost overnight with local and organic systems. Certainly the state played a significant role here, and this shows that governments can facilitate simplification in positive ways. But individuals and communities were the primary agents of change here. They just did what needed to be done. Voluntary simplification of food production might involve embracing something resembling the Cuban response throughout the industrialised world, both in rural and urban centres, *but prior to it becoming a necessity*. Voluntary simplification, after all, will be a very different experience than involuntary simplification, even if the actions are largely the same. This process of re-establishing local and organic food production would make the system less complex (e.g., more people would be farmers and gardeners, exchanging fossil energy for human labour), which in turn would lessen the energy demands of industrial societies. We see this process already underway, albeit in small subcultures, in the eco-village, permaculture, transition towns, and voluntary simplicity movements outlined above. What is needed is for those movements to become the centre of culture rather than exist on the fringes.

The same type of analysis could be applied to all aspects of industrial civilisation, including: the way energy is produced and used; the way we transport ourselves; the way we organise ourselves and our economies; the way we attend to our health or educational needs; the way we clothe ourselves; the way we entertain ourselves; and so on (see Trainer, 2010a). Rather than solving the problem of water security by creating expensive and energy intensive desalination plants, for example, people could simply use less water; rather than addressing obesity with expensive diet pills or liposuction, people could choose to eat better and do more exercise; rather than buying a clothes dryer, people could dry their clothes on a string outside; etc., etc; Voluntary simplification, as we have seen, involves rethinking problems, rethinking solutions, and rethinking how we prioritise the limited energy and resources we have available for problem solving. This is where the practical implications of this analysis become clearest. The task is to evaluate, personally and socially, how and where energy and resources are used and for what purposes; to isolate those areas where those resources are being wasted or misdirected; to redirect or redistribute those resources toward solving the most pressing social and ecological problems; and, where possible, reducing the overall energy-intensity of our ways of living even if this involves reductions in social complexity. If a household, community, or society does this effectively it may find that it can solve all of its most important problems, including new ones, while reducing its consumption of energy and resources (or at least not getting locked into ever-increasing consumption and complexity). But this process is not about achieving some passive ecological, social, or economic stasis; it is about constantly working on reaching and then maintaining some form of dynamic equilibrium within ecologically sustainable limits. Given that presently the global economy is far exceeding the sustainable carrying capacity of the planet (Global Footprint Network, 2012), it follows that voluntary simplification implies creating very different social and economic systems.

As I have argued elsewhere (Alexander, 2013; Alexander, 2014), an ecologically sustainable society would probably end up looking something like Ted Trainer's (2010a) vision of The Simpler Way, which is a vision of highly self-sufficient, low-carbon economies that use mostly local resources to meet local needs. These would be zero-growth economies (Trainer, 2011) that were sustained on much lower levels of resource consumption and ecological impact. This implies that material living standards would be far lower than what are common in consumer societies today, but basic needs for all could be met and high quality of life could be maintained. Embracing lifestyles of voluntary simplicity, therefore, does not necessarily mean hardship or deprivation (Alexander, 2012a; Alexander and Ussher, 2012). It just means focusing on what is *sufficient* to live well, rather than constantly seeking increased consumption and greater affluence. If, however, industrial civilisation continues to pursue that latter path of growth without limits in an attempt to universalise affluence, it will meet the fate of all previous civilisations, with all the suffering that implies (Turner, 2012). To avoid this what is required, first and foremost, is voluntary simplification, but this depends first and foremost upon a revolution in consciousness.

7. Conclusion

Industrial civilisation is at a point in history when it is faced with the pressing issue of whether it can afford the problem of its own existence. Like a growing number of others, I do not believe that it can afford this, at least, not for much longer. The ongoing financial crisis is a barely disguised metaphor for this question of affordability, and it presents all of us living in industrial civilisation with the question of how best to respond to this problem – the problem of whether civilisation can afford the costs of its own complexity.

We are hardly the first to be faced with this problem; indeed, all previous civilisations have faced it. But perhaps we can be first, thanks to Joseph Tainter, to understand the dynamics at play. Perhaps we can even respond in such a way as to avoid the collapse scenario that has marked the end of all other civilisations. Prior civilisations attempted to sustain themselves and avoid collapse by continuing to increase complexity in response to new problems, but always this strategy has resulted in collapse, because eventually the energy and resources needed to subsidise increased complexity becomes unavailable. Nevertheless, this seems to be the very response industrial civilisation is taking presently, and indeed it is the one which Tainter himself recommends as the best course of action. As he puts it, 'modern societies will continue to need high-quality energy, and securing this should be the first priority of every nation with a research capability' (Tainter, 2011b: 94). This advice from Tainter is very problematic, given that energy-intensive problem solving led to collapse on all other occasions in history, of which he is very aware. The advice appears more problematic still if one accepts that the world is facing a future of 'energy descent'. But Tainter's advice follows the logic of his own assumptions. While I accept that complexity generally has diminishing marginal returns, in this chapter I have tried to show, albeit in a preliminary way, that voluntary simplification is actually a viable and desirable response to this challenging dynamic. In doing so, I have turned Tainter's solution on its head: where he sees the solution to civilisation's problems in further complexity, I maintain the best, and probably the only, solution lies in voluntary simplification.

However, given that voluntary simplification seems unlikely to be widely embraced as a response to the problem of complexity, one hesitates before claiming that voluntary simplification will produce an environmentally sustainable way of life. While achieving sustainability by way of voluntary simplification is still an option available to us, the odds of it being selected do not look promising at all. Nevertheless, for those who substantially agree with the analysis outlined above, voluntary simplification still remains the best strategy to adopt and promote even if industrial civilisation continues to marginalise it. This is because if voluntary simplification is not embraced on a sufficiently wide scale to avoid social, economic, or ecological collapse, it nevertheless remains the most effective way for individuals and communities to build resilience. It would free up more energy and resources to deal with systemic disruptions. In the current milieu, therefore, perhaps the ability to withstand forthcoming shocks is the best we can hope for.

References

Alexander, S. (ed.). 2009. *Voluntary simplicity: The poetic alternative to consumer culture.* Whanganui: Stead & Daughters.

Alexander, S. 2012a. 'The optimal material threshold: Toward an economics of sufficiency'. *Real-World Economics Review* 61: 2-21.

Alexander, S., 2012b. 'Planned economic contraction: The emerging case for degrowth'. *Environmental Politics* 21(3): 349-68.

Alexander, S. 2013. *Entropia: Life beyond industrial civilisation.* Melbourne: Simplicity Institute Publishing.

Alexander, S. 2014. 'Ted Trainer and the Simpler Way: A sympathetic critique'. *Capitalism Nature Socialism* 25(2): 95-111.

Alexander, S. and Ussher, S. 2012. 'The voluntary simplicity movement: A multi-national survey analysis in theoretical context'. *Journal of Consumer Culture* 12(1): 66-88.

Allen, T., Tainter, J., and Hoekstra, T. 2003. *Supply-side sustainability.* New York: Columbia University Press.

Diamond, J. 1998. *Guns, germs, and steel.* London: Vintage.

Floyd, J. 'Energy, complexity, and interior development in civilisational renewal'. *On the Horizon* 21(3): 218-229.

Friedrichs, J. 2010. 'Global energy crunch: How different parts of the world would react to a peak oil scenario'. *Energy Policy* 38: 4562.

Friedrichs, J. 2013. *The future is not what it used to be: Climate change and energy scarcity.* Cambridge, MA: MIT Press.

Gilding, P., 2011. *The great disruption: How the climate crisis will transform the global economy*. London: Bloomsbury.

Global Footprint Network, 2012. Reports available at: http://www.footprintnetwork.org/en/index.php/gfn/page/world_footprint/ (accessed 10 February 2012).

Hall, C. and Murphy, D. 2011. 'Energy return on investment, peak oil, and the end of economic growth'. *Annals of the New York Academy of Sciences* 1219: 52.

Hamilton, C. 2003. *Growth fetish*. Crows Nest, NSW: Allen & Unwin.

Hansen, J. 2011. *Storms of my grandchildren*. London: Bloomsbury.

Heinberg, R. 2007. *Peak everything: Waking up to the century of declines*. Gabriola Island: New Society Publishers.

Heinberg, R. 2011. *The end of growth: Adapting to our new economic reality*. Gabriola Island: New Society Publishers.

Holmgren, D. 2002. *Permaculture: Principles and pathways beyond sustainability*. Hepburn: Holmgren Design Services.

Holmgren, D. and Mollison, B. 1978. *Permaculture One*. Melbourne: Transworld Publishers.

Homer-Dixon, T. 2006. *The upside of down: Catastrophe, creativity, and the renewal of civilisation*. Washington: Island Press.

Hopkins, R. 2008. *The transition handbook: From oil dependency to local resilience*. Totnes, Devon: Green Books.

International Energy Agency. 2010a. *World energy outlook 2010: Executive Summary*. IEA Report. Available at: http://www.iea.org/Textbase/npsum/weo2010sum.pdf (accessed 22 December 2011).

International Energy Agency (IEA). 2010b. *Key world energy statistics*. Available at: http://www.iea.org/textbase/nppdf/free/2010/key_stats_2010.pdf [accessed 20 June 2012].

Intergovernmental Panel on Climate Change (IPCC), 2013. Climate Change 2013: The Physical Science Basis (Fifth Assessment Report). Available at: http://www.ipcc.ch/report/ar5/wg1/#.Uk6k-CjqMRw (accessed 4 October 2013).

Jackson, T. 2009. *Prosperity without growth: Economics for a finite planet*. London: Earthscan.

Klare, M. 2012. *The race for what's left: The global scramble for the world's last resources*. New York: Picador.

Meadows, D., Randers, J., and Meadows, D. 2004. *Limits to growth: The 30-year update*. White River Junction, Vt.: Chelsea Green Publishing.

Miller, R. and Sorrell, S. 2014. 'The future of oil supply'. *Philosophical Transactions of the Royal Society A* 372,

20130179: 1-27.

Murphy, D. 2014. 'The implications of the declining energy return on investment of oil production'. *Philosophical Transactions of the Royal Society A* 372, 20130126: 1-19.

Odum, E. and Odum, H. 2001. *A prosperous way down: Principles and policies*. Colorado: University Press of Colorado.

Percy, E. *et al.* 'Planning for peak oil: Learning from Cuba's "Special Period"' *Urban Design and Planning* (2010) 163(4): 169.

Purdey, S. 2010. *Economic growth, the environment, and international relations: The growth paradigm*. New York: Routledge.

Salleh, A. 2007. 'Food miles can mislead'. ABC Science. Available at: http://www.abc.net.au/science/articles/2007/11/28/2103395.htm (accessed 10 January 2012).

Simms, A. 2008. 'Nine meals from anarchy: Oil dependence, climate change, and the transition to resilience'. Available at http://www.scribd.com/doc/51097356/Nine-Meals-From-Anarchy (accessed 22 December 2011).

Slaughter, R. 2010. *The biggest wake up call in history*. Indooroopilly, Australia: Foresight International.

Tainter, J. 1988. *The collapse of complex societies*. Cambridge: Cambridge University Press.

Tainter, J. 1995. 'Sustainability of complex societies'. *Futures* 27(4): 397.

Tainter, J. 2000. 'Problem solving: Complexity, history, sustainability'. *Population Environments* 22(1): 3.

Tainter, J. 2003. 'A framework for sustainability'. *World Futures* 59: 213-223.

Tainter, J. 2006. 'Social complexity and sustainability'. *Ecological Complexity* 3: 91.

Tainter, J. 2011a. 'Resources and cultural complexity: Implications for sustainability'. *Critical Reviews in Plant Sciences* 30: 24.

Tainter, J. 2011b. 'Energy, complexity, and sustainability: A historical perspective'. *Environmental Innovation and Societal Transitions* 1: 89.

Tainter, J. and Patzek, T. 2012. *Drilling down: The Gulf oil debacle and our energy dilemma*. New York: Copernicus.

Trainer, T. 2010a. *The transition to a sustainable and just world*. Sydney: Envirobook.

Trainer, T. 2011. 'The radical implications of zero growth Economy'. *Real World Economics Review* 57: 71.

Trainer, T. 2012. 'Can Australia run on renewable energy? The negative case'. *Energy Policy* 50: 306-14.

Trainer, T. 2013a, 'Can Europe run on renewable energy? A negative case'. *Energy Policy* 63: 845-850.

Trainer, T. 2013b. 'Can the world run on renewable energy'. *Humanomics* 29(2): 88-104.

Turner, G. 2012. 'Are we on the cusp of collapse? Updated comparison of *The Limits to Growth* with historical data'. *Gaia* 21(2): 116-124.

Vale, R. and Vale, B. 2013. *Living within a fair share ecological footprint*. London: Earthscan.

Vanenbroeck, G. (ed.). 1991. *Less is more: Ancient and modern voices raised in praise of simplicity*. Vermont: Inner Traditions.

Walker, L. 2005. *Eco-Village at Ithaca: Pioneering a sustainable culture*. Gabriola Island: New Society Publishers.

10

RADICAL SIMPLICITY AND THE MIDDLE CLASS

Exploring the lifestyle implications
of a 'Great Disruption'

The human race has had long experience and a fine tradition in surviving adversity. But now we face the task for which we have little experience, the task of surviving prosperity.

– Alan Gregg

1. Introduction

How would the ordinary middle-class consumer – I should say middle-class citizen – deal with a lifestyle of radical simplicity? By radical simplicity I do not mean poverty, which is involuntary and full of suffering and anxiety, and thus universally undesirable. Rather, I essentially mean a very low but biophysically sufficient material standard of living, a form of life that will be described in more detail below. In this chapter I want to suggest that radical simplicity would not be as bad as it might first seem, provided we were ready for it and wisely negotiated its arrival, both as individuals and as communities. Indeed, I am tempted to suggest that radical simplicity is exactly what consumer cultures need to shake themselves awake from their comfortable slumber; that radical simplicity would be in our own, immediate, self-interests. In this chapter, however, I will only defend the more modest thesis that radical simplicity simply *would not be that bad*. Establishing that thesis should be challenging enough.

Of course, if a radically lower material standard of living were to be imposed upon us suddenly by force of circumstances and

229

without anticipation and some preparation, I acknowledge that most people would find such a dramatic change terrifying and painful – an existential disaster. Such a response would be quite natural and understandable, for we would have our identities and worldviews shaken beyond recognition. But I will argue that if such dramatic change were to be stoically anticipated and prepared for, it would not be that bad. If this argument is correct, it would seem that the middle class could benefit greatly from anticipating and preparing for radical simplicity, even if it never arrives, which, in our lifetimes or even our children's lifetimes, it may not. Then again, *it may* – for any number of ecological, economic, political, and social reasons – and this possibility, whatever its likelihood, is ultimately my reason for addressing the subject of radical simplicity. It is my assumption that consumer lifestyles have a time limit and that this time limit is fast running out. If the global financial system does not collapse under the weight of its own debt, perhaps induced by rising oil prices or the bursting of financial bubbles, then at some point our trembling ecosystems will collapse, taking industrial civilisation down with them. Either way, consumerism and the growth paradigm that supports it have no future, a diagnosis that I will not attempt to defend here but rather take as given (see previous chapters). When consumerism's time is up, we will all be living more simply, to varying degrees, whether we want to or not.

No one can be sure exactly when time will be up, or how the closing bell will sound, but whether time runs out next year, next decade, or next century, the inevitable demise of consumerism is a subject that deserves our consideration today, because time will *eventually* run out, and probably sooner than most would like to think. It would be best that this event is prepared for, preferably by adjusting the way we live at once, but if that is too much to expect, then at least by adjusting the way we think. It should go without saying, of course, that it would be far better to embrace simplicity by design than have it embrace us through disaster.

1.1. *Of the middle class, addressing the middle class*

It will already be clear that I am writing this chapter from the perspective of an 'insider' – a member of the so-called 'middle class' – a point that I admit with some unease. Despite dedicating most of my energies toward advocating post-consumerist lifestyles of 'voluntary simplicity', and having taken significant measures to practise this lifestyle (so far as one can within the constraints of a consumer society), I am very aware that I remain a member of the middle class, enjoying many of the essential comforts this lifestyle brings. For example, I have a computer, obviously, and solar-generated electricity to run it; there is a fridge next door, with some food in it, and there is a productive vegetable garden outside, so I am not hungry; and I have sufficient clothes and a roof over my head, so I am warm. Not only that, I have the leisure, health, education, and security to study the world's problems, so without saying anything more about my standard of living, I have said enough already to place myself decidedly in the middle class. While I may barely scrape out a living as a part-time academic, in the global context, I know that I am fabulously wealthy.

I assume because the reader is also in front of a computer or wealthy enough to buy this book, with all the security and privilege that this generally implies, that I am also writing *for* the middle class, broadly defined. There may be some readers who genuinely fall outside this admittedly vague socio-economic category, but only a few, and possibly none. We are, I shall assume, in the soup together; or, as Thoreau (1982: 314) once put it: 'I should not thus unblushingly publish my guilt if I did not know that most of my readers were equally guilty with myself, and that their deeds would look no better in print'. I feel that the subject of this chapter demands these preliminary admissions, since few of us could really claim to have experienced the radical simplicity that this chapter will attempt to describe and understand. Nevertheless, life, being what it is, occasionally requires that we try to understand things that we have never experienced. I believe this is one of those times.

2. The Lifestyle Implications of a 'Great Disruption'

In order to frame the present analysis I want to pose a 'collapse scenario', with the aim of understanding what might become of middle-class consumer lifestyles in the event of what Paul Gilding (2011) calls a 'Great Disruption'. Let me begin by providing some context.

Gilding argues, as many have argued, that '[t]he earth is full' (Gilding, 2011: 1). This presents a massive problem for humanity, especially when we recognise that continued growth remains the dominant economic paradigm globally. Although the global economy already far exceeds the sustainable carrying capacity of the planet (Global Footprint Network, 2012; Meadows *et al.*, 2004), every nation on the planet still seeks continued economic growth. The pursuit of growth, in some form, may be justifiable for the poorest nations on the planet, whose basic needs are not adequately met, but on an already 'full earth', increased resource and energy consumption in the richest nations simply cannot be justified. What is required, particularly in the richest nations, is an economics of sufficiency (Alexander, 2012a). This would involve the rich nations embracing a phase of planned economic contraction, or 'degrowth', in order to create ecological room for humanity's poorest to prosper as well as leave room for the diversity of life on the planet to flourish (Alexander, 2011a-c; 2012b). This radically unconventional economic strategy is all the more necessary given that there are expected to be nine billion people on the planet within a few decades, all of whom will desire, with every justification, a dignified standard of living. This population expansion, however, will place further demands on an already overburdened biosphere.

Needless to say, the prospects of voluntary degrowth in the rich world are slim to non-existent, and that is why we can expect global capitalism to grow itself into a fatal crisis (Turner, 2012). In this sense growth capitalism resembles a snake that is eating its own tail, one seemingly unaware that it is consuming its own life-support system. Climate change and oil supply issues are arguably the clearest signs that this crisis of malconsumption is already in the process of unfolding, a situation exacerbated by the ongoing global financial crisis, which everyday is threatening to intensify. All this means that drastic changes almost certainly lie ahead of us. Things will change, Gilding (2011: 1) notes, 'Not because we will choose to change out of philosophical or political preference, but because if we don't transform our society and economy, we risk social and economic collapse and descent into chaos'. To put it proverbially, if we do not change direction, we are likely to end up where we are going.

Under the force of its own historical momentum, however, and blinded by its growth fetish, capitalism marches on as if everything were fine. But everything is not fine, to put it mildly, and it is only a matter of time before the so-called beneficiaries of growth capitalism realise that there cannot be a healthy economy without a healthy planet. My own view is that any transition to a just and sustainable economy is unlikely to be smooth, and that if such an economy were ever to emerge, it will probably be sparked not by some revolution in consciousness, but by some crisis or series of crises that essentially force upon humanity a radically alternative, post-consumerist way of living. I believe the revolution in consciousness required to prosper under an economics of sufficiency will arrive en masse, if at all, only *after* a crisis. This, at least, is one path that lies before us, and perhaps it is the best we can hope for.

Since mountains of evidence in support of radical change have not persuaded the rich world to rethink its economic trajectory, it would seem now that the only path left is for us to be persuaded, so to speak, by a 'Great Disruption' of some form. That is the scenario that will frame the following discussion. This will probably strike some people as rather too dramatic, but I feel it may prove to be a useful analysis even for those optimists who believe that there will be a smooth transition to a sustainable economy.

I do not wish to speculate about what form the Great Disruption might take (e.g., economic, ecological, militaristic, a mixture of these, etc.) or its likelihood. But for those who accept, as I do, that a Great Disruption of some form is certainly *possible*, and potentially imminent, its lifestyle implications should be of considerable interest and concern. And if it turns out that we never see a Great Disruption in our lifetimes, the following analysis might nevertheless bear fruit by bringing into sharper focus our relationship to the material world. My hypothesis is that this sharper focus might give rise to the insight that consumer affluence is much less important than most people in the middle class think it is.

3. Envisioning and Evaluating Radical Simplicity

Suppose, then, that at some stage in the foreseeable future some form of Great Disruption brings vast portions of the global economy to a grinding halt. How might such a destabilising event or series of events affect the lifestyles of the consuming middle class? Assuming it would impose some form of radical simplicity upon large parts of the developed world – which, as noted, is presently the focus – what would this look like and how bad would it be? Those are the main questions I will now consider.[18] Readers are encouraged to adjust the analysis to fit their own circumstances, so far as that might be necessary. I will structure the following discussion by considering, in turn, various aspects of a typical middle-class life and envisioning and evaluating the changes that could be brought about by a Great Disruption.

3.1 *Water*

It makes sense to begin with water, this being one of life's most basic necessities. Accessing seemingly limitless clean water by simply turning on the tap is one of those things that are most easily

---

[18] The impacts of a 'Great Disruption' on the developing world, or on a rural setting, would raise very different sets of issues. I must leave those analyses for another occasion.

taken for granted in the developed world. This is especially so given that in many places tap water is grossly under-priced, and sometimes not priced at all.[19] If, due to some Great Disruption, the water mains ever stopped functioning, almost all urban centres would at once be thrown into utter chaos, and in the absence of some well-coordinated civil emergency program, many people would die within the week. The consequences would be so grim, in fact, that we must assume that the *first thing* a society in the midst of collapse would do is ensure the functioning of its mains water supply. Governments should be aware of their responsibilities here and be sufficiently prepared to coordinate any necessary repairs or maintenance to the water mains, even in a context of social turmoil. If the government fails, local communities would have to act for themselves and do whatever needed to be done – or else perish.

Let us assume, however, that even in the event of a Great Disruption, the water mains would remain functional, or at most be down for a day or two at a time, which should be manageable for those with a moderate storage of bottled water or a water tank with some water purification tablets. It is easy enough to be prepared in this regard, so it makes sense to be so. It may be that some time after the Great Disruption, depending on its severity, governments would no longer have the capacity to run centralised water services, but by that stage we can imagine that some alternative, localised system of water capture and purification would have been developed. Human beings are a resourceful bunch, a point that too many collapse theorists ignore (but which techno-optimists exaggerate to the point of delusion). It should also be remembered that existing infrastructure, such as roofs and roads, are remarkably good at collecting water, and it would not be hard for vast amounts of water to be captured through these means, provided there was sufficient rainfall. Whether those means could actually supply sufficient amounts of water for a dense urban or suburban settlement, however, is an open question about which I will not presently speculate.

Rather than worrying about the water mains failing, I believe a more useful approach is to consider what would happen if water supplies remained relatively secure but became much scarcer and consequently much more expensive. Suppose, for example, that after some economic crash or sustained climatic aberration, new

---

[19] Between 2008-9, water in Australia was on average $1.93 per 1,000 litres, and for industry water averaged $0.12 per 1,000 litres. See Australian Bureau of Statistics:
http://www.abs.gov.au/ausstats/abs@.nsf/Lookup/by%20Subject/1301.0~2012
~Main%20Features~Water~279 (accessed 7 March 2014).

financial or regulatory constraints meant that most people were only able to draw from the water mains around 50 litres of water per day, per person. To put this figure in some context, average household water consumption in the US is around 370 litres; in Australia it is around 230 litres per day; and in Britain it is about 150 litres. At the other end of the spectrum, institutions like the United Nations and the World Health Organisation hold that 20 litres per person, per day is close to the minimum needed for bare, sanitary subsistence, and that figure is sometimes used as a baseline in refugee camps.

On the basis of these figures it probably follows that having only 50 litres per day would come as a great shock to most people in the developed world, especially those people accustomed to levels of consumption many times higher. Be that as it may, I wish to suggest that life with 50 litres of clean water per day would not actually be that bad, if it were approached thoughtfully and with the right attitude. Indeed, after a period of personal and cultural adjustment, I believe it would quickly become a very tolerable and mostly painless 'new normal'. Naturally, one's attitude and frame of mind when dealing with such a significant reduction in water consumption would be the key factor. If people compared the 'new normal' to how things used to be, they would probably feel terribly impoverished and suffer accordingly; but if people remembered that several billion people in the world today lack secure access to minimally sufficient amounts of clean water, then having 50 litres of clean water per day should suddenly seem like an extraordinary privilege for which people should be immensely grateful; to complain would be a gross perversity. The critical point to note is that the same circumstances of radical simplicity would be experienced in totally different ways, depending on the mind-set that was brought to the experience. Fortunately, that mind-set is within our control, even if the circumstances may not always be.

With a daily supply of only 50 litres, water for drinking would obviously get first priority, and remaining supplies would need to be distributed among things like cooking, washing, cleaning, and sanitation. It might well be that less water could be used in cooking if people were more mindful; clothes might be washed less regularly, which would probably bring some balance to a culture that is arguably excessively concerned with cleanliness; lawns would not be watered and vegetable gardens would be watered from water tanks or greywater systems; and so on and so forth. Innumerable water-saving strategies could well prove that high water consumption is really a product of wastefulness, such that great reductions would not take away from us anything that is actually necessary for a good life. Even if we had to give up showering and bathing in the accustomed fashion, I believe that we would nevertheless be fine. It may be a requirement of a dignified life to be able to wash oneself regularly – achievable with a bucket of water and some soap – but one could live with dignity without showering or bathing in the accustomed fashion.

This idea of cleaning ourselves with a bucket of water exemplifies, with some clarity and specificity, the challenging thesis I am proposing in this chapter. Radical simplicity with respect to water consumption would be a cultural shock, no doubt, but if it were thoughtfully considered, it should not turn out to be that bad, provided we had minimally sufficient supplies. That is, we could all live full, dignified, and meaningful lives even if we had to bathe with a bucket – and if we thought we could not we would be guilty of either pomposity or a failure of imagination.

3.2 Sanitation

Just like if the water mains stopped functioning, urban centres would be thrown into disorder very quickly if our systems dealing with sewerage broke down for any length of time. If suddenly we could not flush the toilet, there would be a significant risk that urban centres would quickly become plagued by waste-borne diseases, so proper sanitation systems can also be considered one of life's basic necessities. But what exactly is a 'proper' sanitation system? Is it a requirement, for example, that one defecates into drinking-quality water, as is customary in the developed world? Surely this practice is amongst our greatest shames and indulgences. In the State of Victoria, Australia, where I live, the government is investing billions of dollars in a desalination plant, apparently *so that* Victorians can continue to defecate in drinking-quality water. One might have thought that it would have been more sensible to begin flushing our toilets with greywater, which would save millions of litres of water *every day*, and cost almost *nothing* (e.g., collect shower water in a bucket), but apparently most people in the developed world would find that an intolerable inconvenience. As if we did not have more important things to be spending our money on! While our river systems degrade, we still seem to think that our bourgeois excrement deserves drinking-quality water, an issue upon which posterity is unlikely to judge us kindly. If we only had 50 litres of drinking water per day, however, I suspect that we would not defecate into any of it, and I am sure our excrement would be just fine. Furthermore, we would discover that the world would not come to end.

While I do not think that our existing sewerage systems are on the brink of breakdown, it may be that in hard (or enlightened) economic times people would move away from dependence on the centralised sanitation infrastructure for self-interested reasons; that is, people would do so not because they would be required to develop non-centralised systems, such as composting toilets, but because they would become aware of the many benefits of doing so. Not only do composting toilets require almost no water and avoid the energy-intensive processing required by centralised systems, they also retain for household use the nutrients from human excrement all of which are currently wasted under existing methods. The human digestive system is far from perfect, meaning that urine and faeces contain many nutrients – nutrients that are valuable for enriching soils, such as nitrogen, phosphorus, potassium, carbon, and calcium. When human excrement is composted properly (by mixing it with additional carbon material, such as paper or sawdust) it does not smell, and over time natural biological processes destroy harmful pathogens, making the end product a safe and nutrient-rich form of manure – or, as it is sometimes called, 'humanure' (Jenkins, 2005). In a collapse scenario we would all be growing more of our own food (discussed below), and this will require improving and maintaining soil quality as cheaply and effectively as possible. In such times, and without discretionary income with which to purchase compost and fertilisers, the composting toilet will become an obvious choice. Far from being a regressive step, this would be a positive advance, and one that we would get used to very quickly.

In polite society today one must not talk about human waste. In the midst of a Great Disruption, however, figuring out how to build a composting toilet may well become dinnertime conversation. My apologies if this discussion has offended the bourgeois sensibility.

3.3 *Food*

Of all our basic needs, food might become the most immediately pressing necessity in the context of a Great Disruption. This is because we currently rely on an incredibly complex line of food production and distribution, which means that the system lacks resilience – that is, lacks the ability to withstand shocks. It lacks resilience because when any one link in the production and distribution chain breaks down, the entire system can stop working. One example of this (as outlined in Ch. 9) can be seen from the impacts of the truckers strike during the year 2000 in the UK. The nation realised very quickly how dependent it was on the industrial food system, because when the truckers were not moving and delivering produce, food was not getting to the supermarkets. Before long supermarket officials were calling members of parliament advising them that without the lines of transport open to restock the shelves, supermarkets had about three days of food. In the words of one commentator, the nation was only 'nine meals from anarchy' (Simms, 2008). The reader is asked to consider how he or she would do if required to provide food for oneself and one's family in the absence of a functioning industrial food system.

It is unlikely, I should think, that the industrial food system would break down immediately or entirely, so for present purposes, being strictly self-sufficient is a goal that is far too extreme to warrant much analysis, and is probably impossible. Even in a dire collapse scenario, we can expect our households to 'import' various foods in various forms, if not from around the world, then certainly from rural contexts. This, in fact, would be an absolute necessity in urban contexts, because growing space simply does not permit anywhere near strict self-sufficiency. A recent study of Toronto, Canada, for example, concluded that the city could *possibly* produce 10% of its own fruit and vegetables, if available public growing space within the city's boundaries were converted to agriculture (MacRae *et al.*, 2010). This implies that even if urban agriculture were enthusiastically embraced on public land, the city would still need to import (or grow on private urban land) 90% of its fruit and vegetables, to say nothing of its meat, minerals, and other goods. While some cities may be able to do considerably better (e.g., Havana), the Toronto study clearly shows that urbanites around the world are extremely dependent on functioning food production and distribution systems. What if there was a long-term shock to those systems? Or what if high oil prices made industrially produced food much more expensive?

These questions are intended to provoke some self-reflection about how we urbanites feed ourselves. At the very least, in a Great Disruption all households and communities would maximise their own food production – in much the same way 'relief gardens' arose during the Great Depression and 'victory gardens' arose during World War II. Necessity is a great motivator. Increasing urban food production would involve digging up lawns and turning them into productive vegetable gardens, and planting fruit trees (which, one should note, take years to provide substantial supplies) in all available spaces. Nature strips would be cultivated; parks would be turned into small farms; suitable roofs would become productive, and generally all food-producing potential would be quickly realised. As noted in the previous chapter, this is essentially what happened in Cuba when the Soviet Union broke down and suddenly stopped providing the Cubans with significant portions of the oil needed to maintain their industrialised food systems. Almost overnight Cuba became a bastion of organic (non-petroleum based) food production, including in its urban contexts, and it can be hoped that this response would be immediately replicated whenever and wherever the industrial food system experienced a Great Disruption (see Friedrichs, 2013). When there is risk of hunger, the bourgeois aesthetic that appreciates a flourishing 'English lawn' suddenly seems trivial or even distasteful (literally).

Assuming, however, that considerable portions of urban food consumption would always need to be imported – a challenge that would be lessened to some extent, no doubt, by a great re-ruralisation or 'urban flight' – the issue becomes what kind of diets should be expected in the event of a Great Disruption to the industrial food system. First of all, we should get used to supply shocks to various goods; the luxury of popping down to the supermarket to pick up some [insert desired food product here] might become a thing of the past. Imagine, for example, doing without rice or oranges or coffee for months or years on end. A dreadful thought, perhaps, but we would survive perfectly well without these and other such (non-local) luxuries. Secondly, higher oil prices or economic contraction might make many currently affordable food products unaffordable, with similar affects on ordinary food consumption habits. We simply may not be able to afford many of the products some people take for granted today, even if they were available. Moreover, in tight economic times, take-out food and restaurants might largely disappear.

Again, these eventualities, if they were not anticipated, would probably be experienced as a terrible cultural shock, and many would think we had returned to the dark ages. But the purpose of this chapter is to suggest that such supply or price shocks, provided sufficiently nutritious diets were still available, would not be that bad. We might not eat at restaurants anymore, but simple potluck dinners among friends and neighbours would probably become commonplace again. Furthermore, while having 10,000 products waiting for us in supermarkets might be a desirable convenience, life would be quite tolerable (although very different) if there were only 100 food products available, even if they were two or three or four times as expensive as they are today. In such circumstances, our diets would certainly change, and we would probably eat less and waste less; certainly we would eat less meat. But generally we would be fine, and perhaps even better off. That is the general message this chapter seeks to present for consideration. If we were mentally prepared for it, radical simplicity in the terms outlined above would not be that bad.

But what if the lights suddenly went out?

3.4 *Electricity*

An uninterrupted electricity supply, provided at very affordable prices, sits alongside clean tap water, flush toilets, and supermarkets, as one of the defining characteristics of the affluent lifestyle under consideration in this chapter. Electricity is so central to our conception of the good life that we can barely imagine life without it for any length of time. During those very rare occasions when there is a blackout and the electricity supply is cut off, admittedly we manage well enough, although usually it is only for a few minutes or at most a few hours. Perhaps in the midst of a particularly severe natural disaster – which most of us have not experienced – the electricity is off for a few days or a week. But part of the reason we manage so well is that we assume (with some justification) that it is a temporary glitch in the system and that by the time we have thought about finding the torch the lights are back on. When we imagine life without electricity, we think of tribal Africa. But what if, in the developed world, a Great Disruption were to impact on our accustomed electricity supply in unpredictable ways? Would it be the catastrophe we might first think it would be?

It would probably push the present analysis beyond the realm of credibility to speculate about a *sudden and permanent* breakdown of the electricity supply in the developed world. That is highly unlikely. But if the global economy were to continue deteriorating for one reason or another, the developed nations which rely on continued growth would probably find themselves facing very difficult decisions about how to spend their much more limited funds. It may well be that maintaining the power grid would not receive the financial support it required, and this might lead to disruptions in the electricity supply to degrees people have not known for many generations. In an age when so much business activity is facilitated by computers, regular and prolonged cuts to the electricity supply would certainly create many difficulties, at least at first; and many households would be angered if regular blackouts interrupted the cooking of dinner or the watching of their favourite television shows. But in the greater scheme of things – and when we remember that most people on the planet have no electricity at all – would constant interruptions to our supply really be so bad? Are we so delicate?

I wish to suggest that we are not, although again this depends on the frame of mind one brings to experience. If we persist with the assumption that uninterrupted electricity is our God-given right, then a Great Disruption would feel like the sky was falling in. But if we consider such a disruption possible (however unlikely) and prepare for it, at least mentally, then things would not be as tragic as we might first suppose. Imagine, for example, that long interruptions of a few days or more became relatively commonplace; and imagine further that electricity became so expensive that the use of every appliance became a considered luxury. Even in these admittedly challenging circumstances, I propose that a strong and resilient attitude would mean that people could easily absorb the shocks, without much trouble.

In practical terms, expensive electricity would immediately make us more conscious of our casual consumption habits. Lights would religiously be turned off as we left the room, and the use of appliances, including the television, would be carefully thought through in economic terms. Instead of putting on the heater, we would put on a woollen sweater. This cultural shift, certainly, would bring no real hardship at all, and certain subcultures within the developed world have already developed these habits out of choice. More radical cultural change, however, is the subject of this chapter – but perhaps more radical changes could also be absorbed without much hardship. Suppose, for example, that households – *your* household – could only draw (or afford) one third as much electricity from the grid, with prolonged blackouts regularly but unpredictably interfering with planning. Yes, we might go to bed earlier during blackouts and rise with the sun, and yes, various business transactions would be delayed at considerable inconvenience. But soon enough drastic reductions in the amount and regularity of electricity would become a 'new normal', which even delicate souls would quickly get used to. Most businesses would adapt (and get by just as they did before electricity was taken for granted), as would affluent societies more generally. Life would go on, albeit very differently.

3.5 *Clothing*

The issue of clothing is an interesting one to consider in the context of a 'collapse scenario', because it brings to the surface the fact that consumption is a context-dependent, social practice. By this I mean that people consume things (especially clothing) not only for what they *do*, but also for what they *mean* or *symbolise* within any particular social context. Clearly, the primary function of clothing is to keep us warm, and its secondary function, at least in our state of society, is to cover nakedness. However, those functions are almost forgotten in an age, such as our own, where clothing's purpose has evolved to become primarily about expressing one's identity or social status. Even the so-called 'alternative' crowds, which explicitly reject 'high fashion', nevertheless are engaged in social positioning through their embrace of an alternative clothing aesthetic. In the context of a Great Disruption, however, the fashion industry would be amongst the first things to die, and I would like to suggest that this would be no great loss at all.

Consider, for example, if we *never again* had the opportunity or discretionary income to buy new clothing. This could well be experienced as a severe identity crisis for those who have come to define themselves through fashionable clothing. But the reality is that if one were mentally prepared for the possibility, no real harm could come from wearing last season's colours or a sewing patch over the knee (Thoreau, 1982). Indeed, I would suppose that most people could survive a decade or even more quite happily without adding to their existing wardrobes, for it is arguably the case that almost everyone in the developed world has superfluous clothing. In a Great Disruption, wearing fashionable clothing would be amongst the least of our concerns, although a new aesthetic would probably develop in which people would try to make the best of what little they had – call it 'post-fashion-collapse chic'. Human beings are a creative bunch, and 'style' would not disappear so much as evolve in a collapse scenario. Nevertheless, human beings will still typically satisfy their most pressing needs first, and in the midst of a deep economic crisis, for example, looking trendy will be of negligible concern. We would salvage clothing diligently and get very good at sewing and mending, and in terms of keeping us warm and covering nakedness, our clothing requirements would be sufficiently met without much trouble.

As Thoreau (1982: 278) once wrote: 'A man who has at length found something to do will not need a new suit to do it in', adding that 'if my jacket and trousers, my hat and shoes, are fit to worship God in, they will do; will they not?' It is an interesting question to consider, if not in relation to the worship of God, necessarily, then at least in relation to living passionately in circumstances of radical simplicity. Old clothes will do, will they not?

3.6 *Transport*

Global conventional oil production has flattened since 2005 (Miller and Sorrell, 2014), and this has been the primary cause of why oil prices over the last decade have increased several times over (see chapters 7 and 8). As new fields struggle to offset the rapid decline in existing fields; as production costs climb radically; and as the developing world continues to increase its demand on the stagnating supplies of oil, price increases can be expected over the long term. As has been argued elsewhere (Heinberg, 2011; Rubin,

2012; Alexander, 2014), globalised, industrial economies are dependent on cheap oil, and when expenditure on oil rises beyond a certain threshold – which some argue is about 5.5% of GDP (Murphy and Hall, 2011a-b) – then oil-dependent economies struggle, often to the point of recession or even depression. This may well be what we are seeing in the world today, and worse things may lie ahead (Tverberg, 2012). Indeed, expensive oil might be one of the primary drivers of the Great Disruption that is being speculated about in this chapter.

What would be the transport implications of a Great Disruption brought about through expensive oil? First of all, plane travel would become a rare luxury enjoyed only by the privileged few. While many will insist that this would be a great loss, I shall beg to differ. I have no doubt that travelling the world and seeing diverse cultures is a mind-expanding experience, but to think that one cannot have equally mind-expanding experiences in one's own locality betrays a failure of imagination. How presumptuous of people to travel to the other side of the world, one might argue, when we have not even seen – *really* seen – our own backyards; our own locality. Just perhaps, unimagined wonders await those who dare to take a closer look. It may well be that there are cheap, low-carbon, and equally fulfilling travel options that are closer to home than we might first think, if only we were to look at the world in a different way.

A second and arguably more important implication of expensive oil would be the impacts it would have on driving. Not only would petrol be more expensive, but a Great Disruption would mean most people would have considerably less discretionary income, and these issues together would mean that people would simply have to drive much less, or not at all. Public transport, where available, would be used much more regularly, probably pushed to the limits of its capacity and beyond. Cycling or walking would immediately become the default mode of transport (bringing with it various health and environmental benefits), and who knows, perhaps even the horse might return to our streets. When driving was necessary and viable, car-pooling would become the norm. There would be no more driving to the corner store to pick up a pint of milk.

A more complex issue related to transport – one that cannot be explored in any detail here – concerns the relocalisation of economy that expensive oil would induce (Rubin, 2009). Currently many people are 'locked in' to car travel by virtue of the fact that they live far away from where they work; and most businesses rely to various extents on global trade. But production is likely to move far closer to home – perhaps return to the home – as oil prices continue to rise and should economies continue to contract (Holmgren, 2012). This is likely to bring with it various hardships and insecurities, but for present purposes the point is that it would also 'unlock' people (and businesses) from long-distance travel. When our communities are forced to relearn the arts of self-reliance, car culture will disappear even more quickly than it arose. On the upside, all that time commuting could then be put to more useful or fulfilling pursuits re-engaging our local communities and revitalising our local economies.

3.7 *Technology*

Another defining feature of affluent societies is the advanced technologies that we have at our disposal, which generally are available at very affordable prices. In Australia, for example, the income procured from working less than two hours at the minimum wage can purchase a DVD player; and functioning televisions are often left out on the street simply because they are not of the new flat-screen variety. In a global and historical context, do we realise how rich we are?

In the homes of ordinary middle-class families there is an array of technologies that would have baffled people only a few generations ago. Furthermore, today it is not unusual even for children to have (and to expect) the most advanced technologies, such as iPods, Xboxes, and mobile phones. Computers, microwave ovens, dishwashers, stereos, kitchen gadgets, vacuum cleaners, washing machines, clothes dryers, air-conditioning units – all these things and so much more can be found in the typical homes of what I am calling the middle class. These technologies are so readily available that it might be hard to imagine life without them. But let us try.

Doing without computers is perhaps the hardest to imagine, because modern life is so extremely dependant on them. Let us remember, however, that people survived quite well in the 1950s without computers, so there is no reason to think that life without them would mean returning to the Stone Age. Indeed, so much time is currently spent in front of computers today that their disappearance (or huge limitation of accessibility) could well be a positive advance, forcing people to engage in more face-to-face communication and probably to spend more time outside.

The technologies in computers are so sophisticated that they arguably depend for their production on a functioning industrial economy, so it could be that a Great Disruption makes computers either unavailable or shockingly expensive. The same might apply to many other technologies currently taken for granted. With a little

Stoic resilience, however, I feel we could generally adjust to their absence without much difficulty. I suspect the washing machine might remain an extremely valuable labour-saving device, and our fridges would be one of the last things to go; but life would go on even if these things became rare luxuries; and life would certainly go on if we had to do without mobile phones, microwave ovens, vacuum cleaners, dishwashers, etc. In exchange for stereos (wonderful though they are) we would probably enjoy the greater pleasure of live music. It would be a far 'simpler' existence, no doubt, but we would survive well enough if we managed the transition wisely. Once again, being mentally prepared is the first step toward healthy adaptation – a step worth taking, I contend, even if such radical simplicity never arrives in our lifetimes.

Perhaps the most worrying aspect of a life with less technological capability concerns renewable energy systems. Like computers, solar panels and huge wind turbines probably depend for their production on a functioning and globalised industrial economy, so in the event of a Great Disruption we should not assume that the production of renewable energy systems would continue unaffected, however much we would benefit from them. Nuclear energy probably depends to an even greater extent on a functioning industrial economy, so in the event of a 'crash' nuclear energy may not be an option (supposing it was considered desirable).

For want of space I will not open up these cans of worms any further, other than to note that responding to climate change depends on greatly reducing the amount of energy we use and producing what little energy we do use from renewable sources (Trainer, 2013a-b). In the absence of hi-tech renewable energy systems, our alternatives would probably be either living like the Amish or continuing to burn fossil fuels – and we all know which of those alternatives is more likely to be chosen. By now the reader could also guess which of those alternatives I would advocate, but a better path still would be managing to take the best things from an Amish-style existence (adding a strong dose of alternative hedonism, perhaps) while at the same time taking advantage of hi-tech renewable energy systems and other 'appropriate' technologies that are available and affordable.

3.8 Television and Social Media

How a culture spends its leisure says a lot about the nature of the society. Currently, most Westerners spend more time watching television than doing anything else, other than sleeping and working; often several more hours each day are spent on Facebook. One does not have to be a 'high brow' elitist to question whether this is really the best use of our freedom. Technologies like television and Facebook are not good in themselves. Like fire, each of them is either good or bad depending on how much of it there is and how it is used. Should a Great Disruption take these things away from us, I contend that in this respect at least our cultures should be decidedly enriched. Suddenly we would find ourselves having to fill our time in other, less passive ways, but far from being bored, we would discover that there was much important and meaningful work to be done building a new civilisation.

A more complex issue, related to the discussion of computers above, concerns the Internet. As transport gets more difficult and costly, it may be that electronic communication becomes more important than ever, especially with respect to distributing knowledge. Without exploring this issue further, let us hope that we are able to exploit the best of our technologies, while avoiding their seductive pitfalls. As ever, the notion of 'appropriate technology' and 'appropriate use' thereof are critically important.

3.9 *Discretionary Income*

A more general point about the lifestyle implications of a Great Disruption pertains to discretionary income. In developed nations today, average wages are well above subsistence levels, meaning that most people have discretionary income to spend on non-essential goods and services, like alcohol, movie tickets, take-away food, books, magazines, fashionable clothing, the occasional holiday, etc. The huge economic consequences of a Great Disruption, however, would mean that the discretionary income we take for granted today might well disappear completely, or be reduced to extremely minimal levels. No longer would people be able to afford to pay others for 'services' like cleaning, cooking, accounting, repairs, etc. Such work and much more would return to the household. The ordinary person would become a 'jack-of-all-trades', or at least be able to barter various skills for others in an informal economy. Since the existing division of labour in market economies has left most of us with very narrow skill sets, having to do things ourselves would require a great 're-skilling', a culture-shift already underway in the Transition movement (Hopkins, 2008). It seems to be the case that human beings get considerable enjoyment from being self-reliant, for learning life skills and applying them can be a very satisfying process. This means that the inability to pay for services may often come with a significant silver lining.

The same economic forces that would reduce discretionary income for 'services' would also mean that we would have little or no spare income with which to buy non-essential 'goods'. Currently if we find ourselves desperately in need of something, it will probably be available at a reasonably affordable price in a store nearby. In a collapse scenario this luxury will disappear, with supply chains being disrupted and prices (relative to discretionary income) going through the roof. This situation would signify the dawn of the 'salvage economy' and the 'sharing economy', both of which may already be upon us. Should we need something and be unable to purchase it, our options would be: (1) reconsider whether we *really* need it, and perhaps do without it; (2) salvage it; or (3) borrow it from someone in our community (and perhaps lend them something in return). For example, rather than everyone on the street having pruning tools (or some other good), perhaps only one or two people will have them, or perhaps a community tool shed will be set up so that everyone has access to tools even if there were very few tools in the community. This would greatly increase the 'efficiency' of our consumption, because currently many if not most of our purchased goods sit wastefully idle for most of their life. Sharing more of our stuff would not be difficult.

Similarly, it should go without saying that, in a collapse scenario, all luxury spending would essentially disappear completely, also without any real hardship. Someone might regret not being able to afford a new kitchen, to replace the worn carpet, or to holiday in Thailand, but it would be their own fault if they considered this a good reason to despair. Surely the good life consists in something other than merely the consumption of luxury goods? To again draw upon the words of Thoreau (1982: 269): 'Most of the luxuries, and many of the so-called comforts of life, are not only not indispensible, but positive hindrances to the elevation of mankind', and on that basis Thoreau (1982: 290) urged people not be like the man who complained of 'hard times because he could not afford to buy him[self] a crown'.

3.10 *Public Services*

In closing the analysis, a few words should be offered about the decline in public services that would no doubt follow from a Great Disruption. I have been assuming that a Great Disruption would have huge economic implications, and it follows that this would affect the ability of governments to provide many public services, at least to the extent we might be accustomed to today. With a much smaller spending capacity (due to a contracting economy), governments would have to radically rethink their budgets, and this could well have significant implications for ordinary people. Many social provisions – such as unemployment benefits, health benefits or subsidies, investment in public infrastructure or the arts, etc. – might well disappear or be greatly reduced, just when they are needed most. Other public services or provisions would also receive much less financial support, such as fire services, police forces, local councils, environmental protection programmes, etc. This would obviously change the nature of society greatly, and I will not suggest that the changes would necessarily be absorbed without suffering. But it can be argued that dependence on a strong state has been one reason the strength of many communities have been weakened in recent decades; after all, one might feel less obliged to care for one's poor or elderly neighbours if that is considered something that the state should be doing. While I do not want to take that argument too far, in the absence of a strong welfare state communities would have to care for their own again, and this challenge could well revitalise the spirit of neighbourliness and solidarity that has been lost in many consumer cultures today (Lane, 2000). New community organisations and systems would have to be established to deal with crime, consumer waste, infrastructure repairs, or to feed the hungry. We would end up with very different, highly localised and self-governing communities, but all the hardship this transition would bring with it might ultimately be worth it. It just might give us a more direct, authentic, and participatory democracy, and that is probably a necessary step along the path toward creating a sustainable democracy.

Of course, it would be infinitely better if we created a sustainable democracy *in advance* of a Great Disruption.

4. Conclusion

In this chapter I have tried to describe in some detail what a life of radical simplicity might look like and to suggest that radical simplicity would not be that bad, provided the transition was anticipated and wisely negotiated. Indeed, the subtext of this chapter has been that such a transition would actually be in our own, immediate self-interests, although above I merely tried to provoke consideration over the slightly less ambitious thesis – that radical simplicity simply would not be that bad.

By way of review, the elements of radical simplicity which I have outlined above include: having only 50 litres of clean water per day; using a composting toilet; growing food in every available space and dealing with less variety and more expensive food; consuming about one third the amount of electricity currently used and dealing with regular blackouts; never buying new clothes; using only public transport or bicycles to get around and never flying; doing without many technologies, such as mobile phones, vacuum cleaners, microwave ovens, stereos, dishwashers, clothes dryers, and possibly also washing machines, computers, and fridges; watching no television and having no time for Facebook; having little or no discretionary income to spend on non-essential goods or services; and, finally, dealing with the absence of many public services that are currently taken for granted. Undoubtedly, if ordinary Western-style 'consumers' suddenly found themselves living a lifestyle of radical simplicity, they would feel greatly impoverished and suffer accordingly. But if people were to accept that the meaning of life does not consist in the consumption of material things, then radical simplicity should be no obstacle to living a happy and fulfilling life. Given that consumption is a social practice, however, it may be extremely difficult to voluntarily embrace radical simplicity in advance of its external imposition, but we now have more than enough reasons to be moving in the direction of voluntary simplicity and trying to drag culture along with us (Alexander, 2009; Alexander and Ussher, 2012).

I can anticipate at least two objections to this analysis, the first coming from the optimists and the second from the pessimists. From the optimistic perspective, people might object that my analysis is predicated on far too gloomy an outlook; that the chances of radical simplicity being imposed upon the developed world by some Great Disruption are so slim that we need not bother ourselves with thought-experiments like mine. This objection assumes that we will always have enough food, water, electricity, technologies, discretionary income, and public services to maintin the existing standard of living. To these optimists I would respond by noting that our planet is struggling to withstand the impacts of one billion 'consumers', and so the idea that this way of life could be globalised to nine or ten billion people over coming decades (which seems to be the goal of 'development') is dangerously unrealistic, even absurd. At some stage our ecosystems will declare their 'limits to growth', and indeed they are already in the process of doing so (Meadows *et al.*, 2004; Turner, 2012). The next few decades are not going to look like the last few decades (Friedrichs, 2013), and if the developed world does not voluntarily move toward a less consumption-orientated way of life, then it would seem reasonable enough to expect that such a way of life will be involuntarily imposed upon us. It is only a question of timing. Moreover, even if radical simplicity never arrives in our lifetimes (or ever), I hope that the analysis above might nevertheless have brought into sharper focus our relationship to the material world. When we take a second look at our lives (Burch, 2012), we could well discover that affluence is much less important than we might have first thought it was, and that the best things in life really are free.

From the pessimistic perspective, an objection to my analysis could be that a Great Disruption is indeed in store for us, but that the impacts are going to be far more tragic than those I have described. In other words, it might be objected that I have romanticised radical simplicity, and that radical simplicity actually means suffering, plain and simple. This objection, however, is based on a misunderstanding of my project. I understand very well that a Great Disruption could play out in various ways, including the possibility that famine, disease, and violence would lead to widespread poverty and death. In such circumstances, of course, there would be no 'upside of down', and certainly a much darker analysis could have been written. But from the outset I distinguished radical simplicity from poverty and have made no attempt to paint true poverty in rosy colours. Nobody wants to be cold, hungry, and sick. Radical simplicity, however, as I have described it, means a *secure but biophysically minimal material standard of living*, and my purpose has been to defend the thesis that life would not be so bad if we found ourselves without many of the comforts of middle-class life, provided our basic needs were still met.

In the end, the view of the world outlined above arises out of a particular conception of what it means to be human. It poses the question, 'What is it that makes life worth living?' and answers that question by saying, 'Something *other* than the limitless consumption of material things.' Consumption just does not satisfy our universal craving for meaning, and the sooner the world realises this the better it will be for everyone and the planet. If we do not choose to learn this, eventually we will be taught it.

References

Alexander, S. (ed.). 2009. *Voluntary simplicity: The poetic alternative to consumer culture*. Whanganui: Stead and Daughters.

Alexander, S. 2011. 'Property beyond growth: Toward a politics of voluntary simplicity'. Doctoral thesis, Melbourne Law School. Available at: http://papers.ssrn.com/sol3/papers.cfm?abstract_id=1941069 (accessed 10 September 2013).

Alexander, S. 2011b. 'The voluntary simplicity movement:

Reimagining the good life beyond consumer culture'. *International Journal of Environmental, Cultural, Economic, and Social Sustainability* 7(3): 133-150.

Alexander, S. 2011c. 'Peak oil, energy descent, and the fate of consumerism'. *Simplicity Institute Report* 11b.

Alexander, S. 2012a. 'The optimal material threshold? Toward an economics of sufficiency'. *Real-World Economics Review* 61: 2-21.

Alexander, S. 2012b. 'Planned economic contraction: The emerging case for degrowth'. *Environmental Politics* 21(3): 349-368.

Alexander, S. 2014. 'The new economics of oil'. *Melbourne Sustainable Society Institute* Issues Paper No.2, March 2014.

Alexander, S. and Ussher, S. 2012. 'The voluntary simplicity movement: A multi-national survey analysis in theoretical context'. *Journal of Consumer Culture* 12(1): 66-88.

Burch, M. 2012. 'Mindfulness: The doorway to simple living'. *Simplicity Institute Report* 12n.

Friedrichs, J. 2013. *The future is not what it used to be: Climate change and energy scarcity.* Cambridge, MA: MIT Press.

Gilding, P. 2011. *The great disruption: How the climate crisis will transform the global economy.* London: Bloomsbury.

Heinberg, R. 2011. *The end of growth: Adapting to our new economic reality.* Gabriola Island: New Society Publishers.

Holmgren, D. 2012. 'Retrofitting the suburbs for the energy descent future'. *Simplicity Institute Report* 12i: 1-8.

Hopkins, R. 2009. *The transition handbook: Creating local sustainable communities beyond oil dependency (Australian and New Zealand Edition).* Lane Cove, Australia: Finch Publishing.

Jenkins, J. 3rd (ed.). 2005. *The humanure handbook: A guide to composting human manure.* White River Junction, VT: Chelsea Green Publishing.

Lane, R. 2000. *The loss of happiness in market democracies.* New Haven: Yale University Press.

MacRae, R. *et al.* 2010. 'Could Toronto provide 105 of its fresh vegetable requirements from within its own boundaries? Matching consumption requirements with growing space'. *Journal of Agriculture, Food Systems, and Community Development* 1(2).

Meadows, D., Randers, J., and Meadows, D. 2004. *Limits to growth: The 30-year update.* White River Junction, Vt: Chelsea Green Publishing.

Miller, R. and Sorrell, S. 2014. 'The future of oil supply'. *Philosophical Transactions of the Royal Society A* 372, 20130179: 1-27.

Murphy, D. and Hall, C. (2011a). 'Adjusting to the new energy realities of the second half of the age of oil'. *Ecological Modelling* 223: 67-71.

Murphy, D. and Hall, C. (2011b). 'Energy return on investment, peak oil, and the end of economic growth'. *Annals of the New York Academy of Sciences* 1219: 52-72.

Odum, E. and Odum, H. 2001. *A prosperous way down: Principles and policies*. Colorado: University Press of Colorado.

Rubin, J. 2009. *Why your world is about to get a whole lot smaller*. London: Virgin.

Rubin, J. 2012. *The end of growth: But is that all bad?* Toronto: Random House.

Simms, A. 2008. 'Nine meals from anarchy: Oil dependence, climate change, and the transition to resilience'. Available at: http://www.scribd.com/doc/51097356/Nine-Meals-From-Anarchy (accessed 22 December 2011).

Thoreau, H. 1982. *The portable Thoreau*. C. Bode (ed.). New York: Penguin.

Trainer, 2013a. 'Can Europe run on renewable energy? A negative case'. *Energy Policy* 63: 845-850.

Trainer, 2013b. 'Can the world run on renewable energy'. *Humanomics* 29(2): 88-104.

Turner, G. 2012. 'Are we on the cusp of collapse? Updated comparison of *The Limits to Growth* with historical data'. *Gaia* 21(2): 116-124.

Tverberg, G. 2012. 'Oil supply limits and the continuing financial crisis'. *Energy* 37(1): 27-34.

11

VOLUNTARY SIMPLICITY AS AN AESTHETICS OF EXISTENCE

The art of ethics in a consumer age

Men have become the tool of their tools. The best works of art are the expression of man's struggle to free himself from this condition.
– Henry David Thoreau

1. Introduction

Throughout the Western philosophic tradition, ethics and morality have generally referred to the task of living in accordance with a body of objectively verifiable moral rules, of adhering to a moral code that is knowable through rational inquiry and which, by virtue of its rational basis, applies to all people in all places. Philosophers have always disagreed, of course, about which of the possible moral codes is the objectively true one. But there has been a widespread consensus that discovering such a code is the aim of moral thought and that living in accordance with such a code is the aim of moral behaviour. We can see this assumption underlying the work of almost all the great moral philosophers – from Plato, through St Aquinas, to Kant and Bentham, and beyond – and well into the 20th century this assumption remained an almost unquestioned verity (see Rorty, 1999: Ch. 4).

The logic beneath this assumption is quite understandable. If we are to live our lives according to the dictates of a moral code, even when it is not in our immediate self-interest to do so, then we should want the code to which we have subscribed to be somehow deserving of our obedience. Nobody would want to live according to moral rules if those rules were just the arbitrary assertions of some megalomaniac who simply wanted all humanity to abide by his or her personal standards of conduct. On the contrary, if anyone were to subscribe to a moral code, it would presumably always be on the condition that the code was an embodiment of some independent and verifiable moral truth, in the sense that the code reflected an objective and rational moral reality, not merely the idiosyncratic whim of some authoritarian personality.

This conception of morality as obedience to an objectively verifiable moral code makes perfect sense when one subscribes to what is often called 'the correspondence theory of truth' (see Rorty, 1991). Put simply, this theory of truth holds that the purpose of philosophical inquiry is to determine (or determine the *method* for determining) which linguistic propositions reflect metaphysical or moral reality, and which do not. Within this framework of understanding, the goal of moral philosophy is to base normative, value-laden conclusions upon secure, metaphysical foundations, foundations that are external to the human mind, eternal, objective, universal, and unchanging, and which, for these reasons, transcend all personal or contextual perspectives. According to this view of moral philosophy, which we could call Moral Realism, it is either right or wrong to act in this way or that, from which it would follow that the task of moral philosophers is to determine which acts are moral and which are not. Indeed, it could be said that using 'reason' to distinguish moral from immoral behaviour has been the defining goal of moral philosophers throughout history. This goal seems coherent enough, and in many ways it also seems quite commonsensical.

Needless to say, however, no consensus has been reached about which of the various moral codes proposed is, in fact, the objectively correct one. That is, Christians, Kantians, Utilitarians, Marxists, and so on, are still debating each other over the truth of their respective moralities. Some might suggest that this lack of moral consensus must mean that there is no moral truth, as such; that morality has no rational foundation; or, perhaps, that human beings are fundamentally irrational and thus incapable of knowing moral truth when they see it. But this does not follow, necessarily. In particular, a lack of moral consensus is not necessarily fatal to Moral Realism or the correspondence theory of truth. After all, one might still believe that, in the future, human beings will finally uncover the moral reality that lies beneath the illusion of appearances and thus gain moral enlightenment – assisted, one might suppose, by some philosopher who devises a means of proving, by way of rational demonstration, that a particular moral code is the one and only one that is *really* real; the one and only one that deserves our obedience. When this day arrives, the narrative might go, then, at last, people can finally stop debating which morality is the correct morality and instead dedicate their time and energy to actually trying to live morally.

It may be that such a day will indeed arrive. Some critical philosophers, however, such as Friedrich Nietzsche, Michel Foucault, and Richard Rorty, among many others, have argued that the very search for universal moral truth, like the search for the Holy Grail, is a dubious one – if, by universal moral truth, one means a set of objectively verifiable moral rules, grounded in metaphysical reality, that apply to all people, in all places, at all times. These 'post-metaphysical' theorists have called into question, not simply the moral codes that moral philosophers have proposed hitherto, but, more fundamentally, the very goal of seeking objective, universalisable moral codes. This scepticism arose, in various ways, out of a loss of faith in the correspondence theory of truth, which, in turn, led to a loss of faith in all forms of Moral Realism. The essential reasoning here is that since truth must be expressed in language, and since language is a human creation, so must truth, ultimately, be a human creation (Rorty, 1989). In other words, it is argued that there is no knowable metaphysical reality which language should be seeking to reflect. From this perspective, human perception and understanding is always and necessarily mediated by language – 'there is nothing outside of the text', to borrow Jacque Derrida's phrase (Derrida, 1998: 158) – and this means that knowledge, including moral knowledge, will always be a function of some conventional or 'socially constructed' linguistic framework, some paradigm of understanding. It arguably follows, therefore, that truth, knowledge, and meaning all lack the metaphysical foundations that philosophers throughout history had hoped to uncover for them. The metaphor of 'philosophy as the mirror of nature' thus loses its operational validity (Rorty, 1979). Furthermore, since language is inherently unstable and always subject to various interpretive ambiguities, there will never be one and only one moral code that is true for all people, in all places, and for all times. For even if we knew which moral code was the one and only one to obey – the Ten Commandments, for example, or Kant's 'categorical imperative', or Bentham's 'greatest happiness principle' – its context-dependent application would require interpretation, and interpretation is always a function of one or other 'interpretive community' (Fish, 1989). People may, of course, have the *experience* of moral certainty; but the 'truth' of such moral certainty will never be rationally demonstrable to all people.

What, then, becomes of moral and ethical discourse and practice if the search for a universal moral code is given up? The substantive part of this chapter begins exploring this question by turning primarily to the later works of Michel Foucault – the texts of his so-called 'ethical' turn (see especially, Foucault, 2000a). It is in these texts where Foucault develops his notion of ethics as 'an aesthetics of existence', which he presents as an alternative mode of ethical practice that can be taken up, by default, one might say, in the absence of a knowable and universalisable morality. Foucault's strategy, we will see, is to problematise the notion of 'selfhood' by arguing that the 'self', far from being as independent and autonomous as philosophers have typically supposed, is in fact inextricably shaped by external linguistic and contextual forces, such that *who we are* as individuals is not the determinate product of free decisions made by some autonomous agent, but instead the product of social and linguistic forces that are largely beyond our control. Foucault does not deny or exclude the possibility of human freedom, however, as some might infer from his early work. Foucault does insist that our identities are socially constructed entities and that we lack a transcendental or purely rational 'self', but he nevertheless carves out and secures a certain, albeit limited, degree of space within which our socially constructed identities can *act upon themselves* for the purpose of 'self-fashioning'. We may not get to choose the raw material of which our identities are constituted, but it nevertheless lies within our power to shape that raw material in various ways, just as the sculptor may make various things from a given lump of clay. According to Foucault, this relationship of the self to the self is the terrain of ethics, and when engaging the age-old ethical question, 'How am I to live?,' Foucault suggests that we avoid the traditional search for a moral code and instead ask ourselves the further question, 'What type of person should I become?'. Using aesthetic metaphors to describe and develop this process of self-creation, Foucault summarises his ethical position with the pronouncement, 'Make life a work of art' – an intriguing, provocative, but ambiguous statement that will be explored in more detail below.

The aim of this chapter, however, is not to present a thorough analysis of Foucault's notion of an aesthetics of existence. Several such analyses have appeared in recent times (after years of unfortunate scholarly neglect), and much of this emerging commentary is very probing and insightful (see especially, McGushin, 2007; O'Leary, 2002). But this is not the time to focus on furthering that critical discussion or even providing a comprehensive literature review of it. Instead, after providing a brief exposition of Foucault's ethics, this chapter will undertake to actually *apply* the idea of an aesthetics of existence to a particular subject of ethical concern, namely, to our role as 'consumers' in the context of ecological overshoot and overconsumption, primarily in the developed world. This is an area that raises ethical questions concerning how we ought to live for two main reasons: firstly, due to the impact Western-style consumers are having on the natural environment; and secondly, due to the continued existence of poverty amidst plenty. There is, however, another perspective to consider also. A large body of sociological and psychological literature now exists indicating that Western-style consumption practices are often failing to provide meaning and fulfilment, even to those who have 'succeeded' in attaining a high material standard of living (for a review, see Alexander, 2012). These three consumption-related issues – ecological degradation, poverty amidst plenty, and consumer malaise – provide ample grounds for thinking that consumption is a proper subject for ethical engagement, in the Foucauldian sense of ethics as 'the self engaging the self'. If it is the case that our individual identities have been shaped, insidiously perhaps, by a social system that celebrates and encourages consumption without apparent limit – and it would not be unfair to describe consumer societies in these terms (Denniss and Hamilton, 2005) – then it would seem that ethical practice today calls for a rethinking of our assumptions and attitudes concerning consumption, which might involve a deliberate reshaping of the self by the self.

This chapter will explore the possibility of such an ethics of consumption in the following ways. First, by explaining how neoclassical economics, which is arguably the most influential paradigm of thought in the world today, conceptualises consumption as something that benefits both 'self' and 'other' and, therefore, as something that should be maximised. To the extent that modern consumers have internalised this conception of consumption, an ethics of consumption might involve engaging the self for the purpose of changing the self and creating something new. The second way an ethics of consumption will be explored will be through an examination of the theory and practice of 'voluntary simplicity', a term that refers to an oppositional living strategy or 'way of life' with which people, somewhat paradoxically, seek an *increased quality of life through a reduction and restraint of one's level of consumption* (see generally, Alexander, 2009). The paradox, so-called, consists in the attempt to live 'more with less'. Since voluntarily living simply means heading in the opposite direction to where most people in consumer societies (and increasingly elsewhere) seem to want to go, one would expect living simply to require a fundamentally creative engagement with life and culture, especially in contemporary consumer societies that seem to be predicated on the assumption that 'more consumption is always better'. This need for a fundamentally *creative* engagement with life is what prompted the present attempt to elucidate the idea of 'voluntary simplicity as aesthetics of existence', and it is this attempt to infuse Foucauldian ethics with an emerging post-consumerist philosophy of life that constitutes the original contribution of this chapter. It is hoped that this practical application of Foucault's ethics might also prompt others to consider how ethical engagement might produce new ways of being that are freer, more fulfilling, and yet less resource-intensive and damaging than the modes of being which are dominant in consumer societies today. Could it be, for example, that the 'Death of Man', to use Foucault's phrase, was actually the first (and a necessary) phase in the demise of what one might call 'homo consumicus'? And what forms of life, what modes of being, would or could materialise with the voluntary emergence of 'homo *post*-consumicus'? These are the large questions that motivated this study and in the following pages a preliminary attempt is made to grapple with them. The aim, however, is not to legitimate 'what is already known' (Foucault, 1985: 9), since that would not be a very Foucauldian endeavour; rather, the aim is to explore whether or to what extent it is possible to 'free thought from what it silently thinks' (*ibid.*), in the hope that this might open up space to 'think differently' (*ibid.*), to think otherwise.

2. Foucault and the Art of Ethics

'Morality will gradually *perish* now', asserted Friedrich Nietzsche in 1887, with characteristic bluntness (Nietzsche, 1969: Essay III, 27). '[T]his is the great spectacle in a hundred acts reserved for the next two centuries in Europe – the most terrible, most questionable, and perhaps also the most hopeful of all spectacles' (*ibid.*). The form of morality to which Nietzsche was referring, and to which he himself was instrumental in undermining, was the form, outlined above, of morality as obedience to set of rules that are grounded in some knowable metaphysical reality. While previous philosophers had argued that human beings shared a common nature by virtue of being endowed with 'reason', Nietzsche claimed to have ended that particular myth and with it the myth of a morality knowable through an appeal to reason. Nietzsche predicted that as more people came to understand this – as more people experienced this crisis of morality to which he referred – morality itself would gradually 'perish'.

According to Foucault (1990: 49), Nietzsche's prediction has already come to pass: '[T]he idea of morality as obedience to a code of rules is now disappearing, has already disappeared. And to this absence of morality corresponds, must correspond, the search for an "aesthetics of existence".' The purpose of this first substantive section is to explore in a little more detail what this curious notion of an 'aesthetics of existence' might mean, and whether it is able, as Foucault suggested it was, to fill the void left by an absent morality. The analysis in this section, however, will be more expository and descriptive than critical, since the aim of this chapter is to build upon Foucault's ethics, not attempt to offer them a comprehensive statement or defence (see, McGushin, 2007; O'Leary, 2002). After outlining his ethics, the analysis will then attempt to develop a Foucauldian ethics of consumption.

2.1. The search for an 'aesthetics of existence'

Foucault was extremely sceptical of the claim, made throughout the Western philosophic tradition, that beneath the various manifestations of human subjectivity which have arisen throughout history there lies an ahistorical or transcendental subject that all human beings share: 'I do indeed believe', he once stated, 'that there is no sovereign, founding subject, a universal form of the subject to be found everywhere' (Foucault, 1990: 50-1). The notion of a 'universal form' of the subject is epitomised in the work of Immanuel Kant, who argued that human beings are endowed in common with rational faculties and that by correctly employing those faculties we can determine, on rational grounds, the universal moral rules that ought to govern human life. In complex ways that cannot be explored in any depth here, Foucault rejected this universal notion of 'the subject' and all that flowed from it. Just as Nietzsche had referred to the 'Death of God' to signify the loss of faith in a transcendental basis for morality, Foucault referred to the 'Death of Man' to signify the loss of faith in a basis for morality that was somehow grounded in a universal 'human nature'.

If there is no universal form of *the subject* but rather only historically specific forms of *subjectivity*, what are the implications of this on how we understand the human situation? It is in response to this type of question or self-questioning that Foucault began developing his notion of ethics as 'an aesthetics of existence'. 'From the idea that the self is not given to us,' Foucault famously pronounced, 'I think that there is only one consequence, we have to create ourselves as a work of art' (Foucault, 2000b: 262).

This aesthetic metaphor strikes many people as strange – perhaps even confronting, silly, or perverse – for we are not generally accustomed to talking about life as a work of art. We might want to say, for example, that life is one thing, art is another, and that these distinct categories should not be conflated. But the distinction between art and life was precisely what Foucault was trying to question; to get us all to question. In fact, it can be argued that Foucault was not actually using art as a 'metaphor' here at all. That is, he was not proposing that we are related to our own lives *like* the way the artist is related to his or her raw materials; instead, he was proposing that we are related to our lives *as* artists, whose raw material is life itself. As he once lamented in an interview (Foucault, 2000b: 261):

> [I]n our society art has become something which is related to objects, and not to individuals, or to life. That art is something which is specialized or which is done by experts who are artists. But couldn't everyone's life become a work of art? Why should the lamp or the house be an art object, but not our life?

Foucault's reasoning here is unusually straightforward: if the nature of 'the self' is not given to us in advance – that is, if there is no 'true self' to which we should be trying to interpret correctly and live in accordance with – then it follows, by default, that we must *create* ourselves. We are not, however, given a blank canvas to work with, so to speak; which is to say, we do not get to create ourselves from scratch, since our identities are by in large a product of social and linguistic forces beyond our control or choosing. Nobody, for example, gets to choose the categories which structure their perception of the world; rather, we are all educated into – or subjected to – a form of life, and through that process we find ourselves embedded within elaborate structures of power/ knowledge that both enable and constrict our thoughts and actions (Foucault, 1977). This education and those power/knowledge structures shape who we are as individuals and they define the nature of our subjectivity. Nevertheless, Foucault argued, we can also act upon ourselves, act upon our socially constructed subjectivities, through processes that he variously called 'self-fashioning', 'care of the self', 'techniques of the self', or 'arts of the self'. Foucault (1990: 37) defined the Greek 'arts of existence' as: 'those intentional and voluntary actions by which men not only set themselves rules of conduct, but also seek to transform themselves, to change themselves in their singular being, and to make their life into an *oeuvre* that carries certain aesthetic values and meets certain stylistic criteria'. Through these processes, in which the self engages the self, human beings have the potential to transform their subjectivities in much the same way a sculptor transforms a given lump of clay. The subject, Foucault (2000c: 290) insisted, 'is not a substance... [i]t is a form', and what form that subject takes is up to us as individual agents, at least in part. This is the creative challenge – one might say, aesthetic challenge – with which we are all burdened. We must, as Foucault (2000b: 262) proposed, 'create ourselves as a work of art'.

This proposition, however, remains ambiguous. If Foucault meant that we should all try to make ourselves as beautiful as possible, then we might fairly dismiss his argument as either ridiculous or irresponsible, or both; as an argument not worthy of any serious consideration, except perhaps to refute it briefly by showing that there is much more to life than beauty. That is not Foucault's argument, however (see especially, Foucault, 2000b: 262). Creativity, not beauty, is primary aesthetic value that defines Foucault's 'aesthetics of existence', and most of the criticism levelled at his position becomes obviously misguided when this is recognised. In other words, Foucault was no mere 'dandy' in the tradition of Charles Baudelaire or Oscar Wilde; nor was he advocating an 'aestheticisation of politics' that would simply open the door to fascism. Both of those interpretations represent superficial readings of Foucault, and they have been dealt with adequately elsewhere (e.g., O'Leary, 2002). Once more, by suggesting that we are all artists of life, Foucault was not suggesting that we should make our lives *beautiful*; instead, he was highlighting the fact that existence places upon us the burden of *creativity*. And creativity, one can argue, is a legitimate aesthetic criterion, and one that provided Foucault with a justification for employing the term 'art' as he did. After all, we are all familiar, no doubt, with works of art that are not beautiful, as such, but which are nevertheless deserving of being considered 'art' on the basis that they are worthy expressions of creativity. And this, it is argued, gets to the heart of Foucault's 'aesthetics of existence': he is not calling upon us to be beautiful 'dandies'; he is calling upon us to avoid being mere products of our socialisation and to instead be worthy expressions of creativity.

This explains, in essence, why Foucault's 'aesthetics of existence' is *aesthetic*. Life, he is suggesting, like art (or as art), is a fundamentally creative undertaking; a project that requires shaping, moulding, sculpting, and creating, in accordance with some (evolving) vision. But even if this aesthetic dimension of existence is accepted, on what basis, one might ask, could Foucault legitimately call his notion of an 'aesthetics of existence' an *ethics*? That is, so far as ethics concerns the question of 'how one ought to live', surely there is more to living ethically than merely being creative?

Undoubtedly there is, and Foucault never denied this. Nietzsche occasionally seemed to conflate ethics and creativity, such as when he argued that what mattered when giving 'style' to one's life was not whether it was good or bad but simply whether it represented 'a single taste' (Nietzsche, 1969: 2). But if that is a fair representation of Nietzsche's position – and to be fair to Nietzsche, it is not (see Nehamas, 1985) – a simplistic conflation of ethics and creativity certainly does not represent Foucault's position. In developing his aesthetics of existence, Foucault drew heavily upon the ancient Greeks, who regularly employed notions of moulding and sculpting when philosophising about the 'art of living', and Foucault's position must be understood in relation to that ancient approach. Indeed, with a nod to the Greeks, Foucault claimed that 'the problem of an ethics as a *form* to be given to one's conduct and to one's life has again been raised' (Foucault, 1990b: 263). And has been raised again, we might infer, due to the emergence of the postmodern condition in which human nature – the supposedly 'universal form' of the self – has been fragmented and is once again in need of being 'shaped' by self-engagement rather than merely 'discovered' by reason.

The ethical dimension of Foucault's aesthetics of existence deserves some further attention, however, because it remains unclear whether this approach can legitimately be called an 'ethics'. The first point here is to reiterate the important distinction Foucault draws between morality (which, from Foucault's perspective, concerns living in accordance with an objective and universal moral code) and ethics (which concerns the self's relationship with the self). Since the purpose, or at least one function, of Foucault's post-structuralist critique of metaphysics was to cast doubt on the very possibility of objective and universal forms of knowledge, including moral knowledge, it follows that his ethics would never aspire to be a new morality. Indeed, Foucault (1990c: 253-4) declared that it would be 'catastrophic' if everyone submitted to a universal moral code, and an inquiry into why he thought this would be so should shed light on the nature of his ethics as an aesthetics of existence.

Foucault thought that submission to a universal moral code would be 'catastrophic' because any code's purported or perceived universality would really be nothing more than a naturalised prejudice, and the danger here is that the particular moral perspective that has been placed under a veil of universality might blind people to relationships of domination that ought to be questioned and, if possible, opposed and transcended. Think, for example, of the colonial Americans who for centuries assumed that black slaves were not moral agents deserving of moral respect but merely animals that should be put to work. From their perspective, it was not immoral to have slaves, since slaves were not objects of moral concern. This, of course, raises the question: Might we, today, have our own moral prejudices to which we are similarly blind? The point here is that since knowledge, including moral knowledge, is always a function of a particular, socially constructed conceptual framework – one that necessarily lacks metaphysical foundations and which is therefore liable to shift or even collapse – then 'ethical' activity requires questioning the moral assumptions of dominant paradigms for the purpose of exposing their contingency; exposing the possibility of things being 'otherwise'. The goal of this ethical activity is not to replace an existing moral code with the *real* moral code, but instead to bring to consciousness the suffering, pain, domination, or oppression that existing moralities repress or deflect attention away from. Notice that this 'bringing to consciousness' is a change in the self brought about by engaging the self, and this is what ethics means for Foucault. Edward McGushin (2007: 115), in his seminal work on Foucault's ethics, notes that Foucault, far from valorising narcissism, was suggesting that 'when one takes care of oneself, an essential dimension of the self that requires attention is the relationship one maintains with others'. We can see similarities here between Foucault's aesthetics of existence and Derrida's ethics of deconstruction. As Derrida once explained: 'Deconstruction is not an enclosure in nothingness, but an openness to the other' (see Kearney, 1984: 124). This attempt to be 'open to the other' – open not just to other people but also other perspectives – is also an essential aspect to Foucauldian ethics.

This is a process, it should be noted, that has no end, because the underlying point is that *every* perspective has blind spots, so ethical activity aims to constantly renew the self for the purposes of bringing those blind spots to our attention, knowing, all the while, that a complete and undistorted perspective – the 'view from nowhere' – is always and necessarily inaccessible to us. It is on this basis that Richard Rorty (1989) highlights the ethical importance of reading widely – of reading novels in particular – because by reading as many different types of 'narratives' as possible, we are less likely to become entrenched in any one, particular narrative.

An aesthetics of existence also includes what Foucault (2000c) called 'the practice of freedom'. By this Foucault meant that transforming the self by the self is not an undertaking that is intended simply to benefit *others* but to benefit *oneself* too, by exposing the ways in which we are freer than we think we are. Think, for example, of anorexics whose lives are destroyed by a warped understanding of 'beauty'; or the status seekers whose lives are wasted by defining 'success' in relation to the number of rich and famous people they can impress. By engaging the self by the self and questioning our own assumptions – assumptions, say, about the meaning of 'beauty', 'success', 'wealth', or whatever – then we may be able to free ourselves from assumptions that are locking us into lives of self-imposed unfreedom. While we may not suffer anorexia or chronic status anxiety, Foucault suggested that we will all have our own prejudices, and thus 'the practice of freedom' means constantly aiming to 'free thought from what it silently thinks' (Foucault, 1985: 9). Again, this is not a process that has a destination. It is an ongoing, evolving process of creative self-renewal – a process of ethico-aesthetic engagement that Foucault called an 'aesthetics of existence'.

3. Problematising Consumption – Engaging the Self

Having outlined the notion of ethics as an aesthetics of existence, it is now time to apply this approach to an area of ethical concern in the hope of deepening the understanding of the practical implications of Foucault's ethical perspective. Although previous studies have incisively unpacked many of the theoretical intricacies of Foucault's ethics, and criticised, refined, and developed aspects which were only touched on above, there has nevertheless been an unfortunate failure, with rare exceptions, to actually apply Foucault's ethical insights to what one might call 'life'. Not only is this unfortunate but it arguably contradicts the defining impulse of Foucault's ethical project, which was to provide tools for engaging creatively with the question of 'how one ought to live'. Foucault, it is clear enough, was not interested in playing abstract theoretical games for the sake of it. 'I am an experimenter', he once explained, 'in the sense that I write in order to change myself and in order not to think the same thing as before' (Foucault, 2000d: 240). The very purpose of his work was to transform himself and thus his life, a process which he noted was 'rather close to the aesthetic experience' (Foucault, 1990d: 14). Why else, he asked, should a painter paint 'if he is not transformed by his own painting?' (*ibid.*). We see, then, that Foucault's ethical position is fundamentally practical in its orientation and trajectory, and something essential is missing from any discussion of his ethics if their practical implications are not explored. Indeed, Foucault's engagement with ancient Greek philosophy can be understood as a criticism of the distinction that has arisen within much modern academic philosophy between philosophy, on the one hand, and life, on the other. Just like the Greek philosophers, Foucault recognised no such distinction, and the Greek conceptualisation of philosophy as 'the art of living' ought to inform our engagement with Foucault's ethics at every turn. Otherwise, we may miss the point of it all.

3.1. *Consumption as a subject of ethical concern*

The practical implications of Foucault's ethics will now be explored by problematising the role consumption plays in our lives. After providing some theoretical context to this undertaking and explaining how the dominant paradigm of neoclassical economics may influence our thinking and behaviour as consumers, the analysis will consider whether the idea of 'voluntary simplicity as an aesthetics of existence' might provide a useful way to understand and engage ourselves ethically about how and why we consume (and live) as we do (however that might be).

As noted in the introduction, consumption presents itself as an area of ethical concern in at least three ways: first, because Western-style consumption is putting an immense and unsustainable burden on the planet's ecosystems, so much so that contemporary cultures of consumption are diminishing the capacity of the planet to support life as we know it; second, because the high consumption, resource-intensive lifestyles enjoyed by most people in the richest regions of the world coexist in a world where great multitudes live lives oppressed by material deprivation; and thirdly, because there is a large and growing body of sociological and psychological literature indicating that once our basic material needs for food, shelter, clothing, etc. are met, the limitless pursuit of more money and possessions neither produces any lasting happiness nor satisfies the human need for meaning (Alexander, 2012). Far from representing the peak of civilisation, cultures of mass consumption are showing distinct signs of widespread social, even spiritual, malaise (see, e.g., Myer, 2000). Any one of these issues, it could be argued, would be sufficient for consumption to become a proper subject for ethical engagement, in the Foucauldian sense of ethics as 'the self engaging the self'. When the three issues are considered together, the case for ethical engagement is compelling.

At once, however, we are confronted with a strange incongruity, even a contradiction, of sorts; one that seems to tear the present analysis apart. In an age when the facts of ecological degradation, extreme poverty, and consumer malaise lie quite plainly before our eyes, one might have thought that high consumption lifestyles were already a subject of widespread ethical engagement. That is, one might have expected consumption practices to be a domain of constant and dedicated ethical attention, given that overconsumption seems to be driving several of the world's most pressing problems (including the problem of consumer malaise). And yet, it can hardly be denied that any ethical engagement that takes place within consumer cultures does not, as a rule, seek to reduce or moderate consumption but rather encourage, glorify, and increase consumption – and increase it without apparent limit (Denniss and Hamilton, 2005). And here is the contradiction: consumption is at once an extremely obvious realm for ethical engagement, for the three reasons stated above, and, at the same time, engaging the self by the self for the purpose of deliberately reducing or moderating consumption seems to be more or less unthinkable within modern consumer societies. Indeed, there seems to be an almost unquestioned assumption throughout consumer societies that consumption practices are somehow 'beyond ethics', in the sense that how much we consume does not really need to inform the answer we give to the question of 'how one ought to live'. On the contrary, it is presumed that everyone is justified seeking as high a material standard of living as possible, a pursuit that is limited, it would seem, only by the laws of a so-called 'free market' economy.

This provides us with a suitable starting point, albeit a rather inauspicious one, for exploring an ethics of consumption. Why is it that an ethics of consumption is almost unthinkable in consumer cultures? In addressing this complex question it may be useful to begin by considering some of the central insights of what could be variously labelled 'post-structuralism', 'social constructionism', or 'postmodernism' – a heterogeneous body of philosophical thought of which Foucault was one of the most notable exponents (although he rejected all such labels). For present purposes, the most relevant aspect of this literature is how it variously exposes human understanding and perception to be a function of whichever linguistic framework happens to mediate our experience. The world does not categorise itself, Foucault and others argued; human beings must do that; and how we happen to categorise the world (and what meaning we attach to those categories) changes how we experience the world and ourselves, what we see, and thus how we act. But we do not get to *choose* the 'language game' we play, as such; instead, we are educated into a form of life from birth, first upon somebody's knee, and then through lessons ratified by wider society. This can make it seem as if the way we have learned to categorise the world is the one and only way to categorise the world, when, in fact, it is merely one of infinite possibilities, one of infinite means of 'socially constructing' reality. The categories and paradigms we use to think about the world generally do not seem like 'social constructions', however, or artefacts that human beings have created and thus might one day recreate. Rather, our categories or paradigms, after years of entrenchment, social affirmation, and reification, often just seem to be 'natural', 'inevitable', or 'just the way the world is' – simply a reflection of the intrinsic nature of reality that exists independently of the human mind and which, therefore, it makes no sense to doubt (see Fish, 1989).

As noted earlier, one problem with the apparent 'naturalisation' of socially constructed categories and paradigms is that this can blind us from relationships of domination (including self-domination) by directing our thought and attention elsewhere. Even if we do perceive relationships of domination, 'naturalisation' can stop us from resisting or opposing such domination on the (mistaken) grounds that it is 'inevitable' or 'just the way the world is' and, as such, cannot be avoided. This phenomenon of naturalisation (or reification) provides the battleground for critical philosophy, and critical philosophy could be broadly defined as the intellectual undertaking that aims to uncover and dismantle the systems of meaning which serve to establish and sustain relationships of domination and violence in the world. If we do not see that domination or violence even when we are looking at it, then we are guilty of what might be called 'interpretive violence'. It is for the 'archaeologist', in Foucault's sense, to excavate the foundations of human thought and expose our categories of understanding for what they are – human impositions that have shifted historically and are liable to shift again. It is for the 'genealogist', again in Foucault's sense, to study the history of those categories to determine how and why they arose, how and why they have evolved, which interests they serve, or claim to serve, and how they fit into current structures of truth and power. And finally, it is for the 'ethicist', once more in Foucault's sense, to consider to what extent our categories of understanding contribute to relationships of domination, and how an individual, through self-fashioning, might be able to escape current modes of thought and open up space for new modes of thinking and being that are less oppressive (either of oneself or others, or both).

How does all this relate to our subject of consumption? Building upon the theoretical perspective just summarised, it will now be maintained that the reason an ethics of consumption is almost unthinkable in consumer societies – despite consumption, at the same time, seeming to be an extremely obvious subject for ethical engagement – must be because the form of life into which we, modern consumers, have been educated must somehow marginalise consumption as a subject of ethical concern. This marginalisation is itself a subject of ethical concern, and so it is of some importance that we gain an understanding of why and how it occurs. This marginalisation can be best explained within, and attributed to, the exceedingly influential paradigm of neoclassical economics, and the mechanics of this marginalisation will now be explained.

3.2. Neoclassical economics and the marginalisation of consumption

Neoclassical economic theory is based on a particular conception of human beings, a conception that assumes we are all essentially 'rational, self-interested, utility maximisers'. Put simply, rationality in this sense means that human beings have goals and that they make sound decisions about how best to pursue those goals; self-interestedness, in this sense, means that human beings aim to further their own goals rather than the goals of society in general; and utility maximisation means that the goal which human beings have is to maximise their own utility (or happiness). The implications of this conceptualisation of humanity are enormous. It is argued by neoclassicists that if we place these types of human beings in a world without private property, a 'tragedy of the commons' (Hardin, 1968) would result, since people would be able to internalise the benefits of productive activity but externalise at least some of the costs, leading to 'the ruin of all' (if it were a situation of 'free access' to resources) or some non-optimal outcome (if it were a situation of 'state controlled' access to and power over resources). However, within a functioning private property system, the theory goes, both the *benefits* and the *costs* of productive activity are internalised, and it is said that this is the best means of maximising overall utility. People get back what they put in.

Furthermore, free markets must be part of this equation. Since resources are scarce relative to the demands human beings make upon them, it is important that resources find their way into the hands of those who will 'exploit' them best. The most efficient way to allocate resources, neoclassicists argue, is to allow human beings to voluntarily exchange, on mutually beneficial terms, their private property rights in free markets. Since market transactions are assumed to increase the wealth of both seller and buyer – otherwise why would the parties have traded? – neoclassicists argue that free markets are in everyone's interests and that market activity should be maximised. Obviously, a great many details have been glossed over here, but in outline this represents the dominant ideological foundations of free market capitalism.

The implications of this ideology on how we understand consumption are profound and far-reaching, although not always appreciated. It is hoped that by highlighting those implications it will become better understood how it is that consumption has been marginalised as a subject of ethical concern. Three points should suffice to explain the mechanics of this marginalisation. First, consumption within the neoclassical model is an expression of freedom, or, to employ neoclassical terminology, an expression of 'private preference'. Since consumers are assumed to be 'rational, self-interested utility maximisers', it follows that any act of consumption must be a rational act that maximises an individual's happiness. After all, with money we are able to purchase those things we desire and need most, and the neoclassical theory of consumer preferences holds that consumers always purchase that bundle of goods which maximises their happiness, given their limited income. More money means more opportunity to consume, and more consumption means having access to more of those things which contribute to happiness. So, not only is consumption considered an expression of freedom, it is also an expression of freedom that maximises an individual's happiness. At least from the individual perspective, then, more consumption would seem to be unquestionably good. So far as this line of reasoning is accepted or internalised, it is quite understandable why consumption is not considered a subject of ethical concern.

Secondly, however, from the neoclassical perspective the benefits of consumption do not flow solely to the individual who consumes. Since both parties to a market transaction are assumed to benefit from all market transactions – again, otherwise why would they trade? – consumption is conceptualised, not simply as an expression of individual freedom that maximises *individual* happiness, but also as an expression of freedom that *benefits others too*. This, in essence, is the common understanding of the 'invisible hand' argument, which holds that the pursuit of self-interest in the marketplace is the best means of promoting the common good. This perspective, in fact, provides a rather ingenious defence of greed: the more market activity one undertakes (whether transacting from the consumption or production angle), the more one benefits others, since, once again, market activity is assumed to benefit both parties in the trade. This ratifies the thesis that consumption is unquestionably good, from which it seems to follow that more consumption must always be better. Again, consumption is marginalised as a subject of ethical concern. Indeed, this 'invisible hand' argument implies that practices of consumption would only become a subject of ethical concern – or become 'immoral' – if we did *not* consume as much as possible.

For present purposes, the third and final point about how neoclassicism marginalises consumption concerns the way in which any problems caused by market activity are always approached from the 'production angle', never (or very rarely) from the 'consumption angle' (see Princen, 2005). The reasoning is as follows. Despite the first two ways in which neoclassicists conceptualise consumption as unquestionably good, no one, not even neoclassicists, can deny that market activity is causing, and has always caused, some real problems. Think, for example, of the many ecological crises we are facing today, such as climate change, the mass extinction of species, pollution, deforestation, the depletion of the ocean's fisheries, soil erosion, etc. One might have hoped that these crises would have prompted neoclassicists to finally rethink their uncritical attitudes toward consumption, to finally acknowledge that, perhaps, consumption is not unquestionably good. But this has proven to be a false hope, and perhaps this should have come as no surprise. Neoclassicism, after all, is a grand, totalising meta-narrative, which claims to have an answer to all criticisms, such that all and any of the problems caused by market activity have a purported solution *within* the free market system and without needing to rethink or revise any of the neoclassical assumptions (including the assumptions about consumption). If there is a problem caused by market activity, neoclassicists argue, this simply indicates that there has been what is called a 'market failure', which typically means that the costs of production have somehow been externalised, leading to artificially cheap commodities which, in turn, leads to the over-consumption of such commodities. But the neoclassical solution to such overconsumption does not require questioning consumption in any way. Consumption, as we have seen, is sacrosanct! Rather, the solution to such market failures is simply to attempt to internalise all externalities *from the production angle* – that is, to try to find ways to make sure that the costs of production reflect the 'true' costs (i.e., the costs *all things considered*). Once this has been achieved – if it can be achieved – any consumption that takes place is once again assumed to be at an 'optimal' level, which is to say, at a level that maximises overall utility. In this way, neoclassicism manages to retain perfect faith in the *virtue* of consumption. We might conclude, therefore, consciously or unconsciously, that since consumption is a virtue, it need not be a subject of ethical concern. Acts of consumption are beyond ethics, or, as neoclassicists put it, such acts are simply 'given'.

The point of all this has been to suggest that the paradigm of neoclassical economics is primarily responsible for why consumption has been marginalised as a subject of ethical concern within market societies and beyond. Given the essentially hegemonic role neoclassical economics plays in the world today – manifesting in the globalised political sphere as 'neoliberalism' or 'Empire' – perhaps it should come as no surprise to discover that all of us may have internalised its precepts to some degree. That is, even those who have never studied or even heard of neoclassical economics – indeed, even those who dedicate considerable amounts of time to criticising the ideology! – may still have imbibed some of its reasoning simply by virtue of living in a world that is so fundamentally shaped by it. We are, after all, social constructs, and, as explained earlier, our perception of the world and of ourselves is a function of the paradigm of understanding that we bring to experience and that we use to make sense of the world. We do not get to choose which paradigm we think with, however, since the act of choosing would be an act of thinking, and in order to think in the first place a paradigm of understanding already has to be in place. As Martin Heidegger once asserted, somewhat cryptically, 'language speaks man' (see Rorty, 1989: 50), by which he meant, we can suppose, that our notions of 'self' are not independent of language but a function of it. Donald Davidson made a similar point, but more clearly, when he wrote that 'there is no chance that someone can take up a vantage point for comparing conceptual schemes by temporarily shedding his own' (Davidson, 2011: 287). We must begin, that is, from where we are, with whom we are, rebuilding the boat of understanding one plank at a time, without ever being able to begin again from scratch.

If neoclassical economics has been internalised to some extent, consciously or unconsciously – in particular, if one has internalised the neoclassical understanding of consumption as unquestionably good – this means that the first step in any ethics of consumption might involve engaging the self by the self for the purpose of *centring* consumption; that is, for the purpose of deliberately bringing consumption into focus as a subject of ethical concern. Every conceptual framework conceals as it reveals, and whatever enlightenment one might gain from neoclassical economics, it must be acknowledged that its impressive edifice also casts shadows. Consumption, for reasons just explained, lies in the dark. An ethics of consumption must begin, therefore, by casting light in its direction, and this can only be achieved by deliberately giving the subject increased attention. Obviously, if one does not look for, or cannot see, a subject of ethical concern, it will not be a subject of ethical concern. However, even when the possibility of dedicating increased attention to consumption has been raised, which is perhaps the most difficult step, there is a second step, and that is to actually *maintain* the attention. The third step is to determine how, exactly, and in what ways, one could engage the self by the self with respect to consumption (an endeavour that is taken up in the next two sections).

Notice, here, that the terrain of ethical activity lies *within* the self, at least at first, rather than being external to it. Someone who is cognisant of the three consumption-related problems outlined above – ecological degradation, poverty amidst plenty, and consumer malaise – might initially think that living in opposition to those problems must require, say, attending rallies, campaigning for political reform, engaging in civil disobedience, volunteering, engaging with and trying to mobilise the community, etc. These are surely all important things, but if our minds are not in order, then it may be that we end up directing our time and energies to pointless or even counter-productive activity, no matter how good our intentions might be. One thinks here of the young Alcibiades, who wanted to leap into a political career, but who was ultimately persuaded by Socrates that, before he tried to take care of and assume control over others, he should first make sure he had taken care of and was in control of himself (Johnson, 2003). Otherwise, even the best intentions might go astray. Socrates was to reproach Alcibiades for being so presumptuous: 'you are not only ignorant of the greatest things, but while not knowing them you think that you do' (*ibid.*: 26). Importantly, however, Socrates was not assuming the role of advisor on the basis that he knew *more* than Alcibiades; rather, in typical fashion, Socrates assumed his role on the basis that he better understood the *limits* of knowledge; better understood that if he knew anything, it was that he knew not. In other words, Socrates knew better than any other that human understanding always has blind spots. The analysis above was intended to suggest that consumption might be one such blind spot.

Ethics was historically about living in accordance with one's 'true self', and since the true self was typically assumed to be a 'rational self', living the ethical or moral life was about living in accordance with a universally applicable moral code, knowable through reason, and which, on that basis, was deserving of obedience. When viewed from a Foucauldian perspective, however, it would seem that living the ethical life is not so much about 'becoming who one is', since, as Foucault insisted, 'the self is nothing more than the correlate of technology built into our history' (see O'Leary, 2002: 35). It could well be, as suggested above, that 'who we are' today is partly a function of various strains of neoclassicism that have been 'built into our history' and which have come to shape our identities (in ways that may not be obvious or even positive). Perhaps we have become seemingly fixed to these forms of neoclassical subjectivity, subjectivities that may produce negative effects, but which we cannot always notice because our subjectivities have been fixed in an extremely effective and thoroughly 'naturalised' way: our subjectivities, that is, may have become a 'second nature' from which it will require a massive labour to free ourselves. 'Maybe,' Foucault suggests, 'the task nowadays is not to discover what we are, but to refuse what we are.... We have to promote new forms of subjectivity through the refusal of this kind of individuality which has been imposed on us for several centuries' (Foucault, 1982: 785). This is, in essence, the point the preceding analysis made in the context of consumption practices.

4. Toward a Foucauldian Ethics of Consumption

The thesis being presented in this chapter has two central dimensions, which at this stage may be worth restating in summary form. The first dimension is that the subjectivities that have been imposed upon us by and within consumer society have marginalised consumption as a subject of ethical concern, and it was argued above that this marginalisation is best explained by and attributed to the hegemonic role neoclassical economics has played, and still plays, within consumer societies. Since human beings are socially constructed entities, it should come as no surprise that the social and institutional celebration of consumption within consumer societies has been internalised to some extent, shaping our identities and our worldviews, often in subtle ways. If it is the case, however, that cultures and structures of overconsumption are driving several of the world's most pressing problems, then it may be that ethical activity today requires that we engage the self by the self for the purpose of *refusing who are* – so far as we are uncritical consumers – and creating new, post-consumerist forms of subjectivity. Exposing the possibility self-creating such post-consumerist forms of subjectivity constitutes the second dimension of this chapter, and this second dimension will now be elaborated on by infusing the idea of voluntary simplicity with Foucault's notion of ethics as an 'aesthetics of existence'. The final section of the chapter will outline several 'techniques of the self' that could be employed by those who wish to actually *practise* the idea of voluntary simplicity as an aesthetics of existence.

4.1. *Voluntary simplicity as an 'aesthetics of existence'*

Voluntary simplicity, as described throughout this book, refers to an oppositional living strategy with which people seek an increased quality of life through a reduction and restraint of one's level of consumption (Alexander and Ussher, 2012). This way of life generally involves providing for material needs as simply and self-sufficiently as possible, minimising expenditure on consumer goods and services, and directing progressively more time and energy toward non-materialistic sources of satisfaction and meaning. As Duane Elgin (1998) has defined it, voluntary simplicity is 'a manner of living that is outwardly simple and inwardly rich, ... a deliberate choice to live with less in the belief that more life will be returned to us in the process'.

However, as we have also seen in this book, there is a misnomer at the heart of 'the simple life' – which is to say, it is not very 'simple', in the sense of being 'easy' to live or practise. Indeed, living a simpler life of reduced consumption in the midst of a consumer society is a great challenge – everything conspires against you. This is not to suggest that living simply is impossible in a consumer society, but it cannot be denied that living simply, so far as it is possible, demands a fundamentally *creative* engagement with life. It does not happen by default! By and large this is because the world is increasingly structured to encourage ever-higher levels of con-sumption, not voluntary simplicity. Therefore, those who wish to live in opposition to this trend will need, above all else, to use their imaginations – and to use them transgressively. They will need to actively reshape their lives, in their own way, and defy, avoid, reinterpret, subvert, and transcend socially entrenched norms of consumption. Furthermore, any effort to live simply in a consumer culture should not be conceived of as something that has a *destination*, as such; instead, it should be conceived of as an *ongoing creative process.*

This understanding of voluntary simplicity as an ongoing creative process is what prompted the current attempt to infuse this oppositional living strategy with Foucault's conceptualisation of ethics as an aesthetics of existence. For present purposes, 'poetry' could be used as the aesthetic trope through which this infusion could take form. Those who wish to practice voluntary simplicity, it could be said, are tasked to become 'life poets' – oppositional imagineers who must reimagine almost every aspect of the high consumption life that consumer society expects, encourages, and takes for granted. If we are prepared to broaden our conception of poetry to include more than just written or spoken verse, and define it (as did the romantic poet Percy Bysshe Shelley) as 'the expression of the imagination' (1890: 2), then to say, 'be the poet of your life', as Nietzsche (2001: 170) implored, begins to make more sense. Blurring the distinction between art and life, it suggests that we should take hold of life, as the poet takes hold of language, and shape it into something new, something worthy, something *beyond consumerism* – to imagine the best, post-consumerist life we can and then set about creating such a life. For are we not each related to our own lives in a way comparable to how the artist is related to his or her own materials? Are we not each charged with the task of creating as an aesthetic project the meaning of our own lives? The Greek and Roman Stoics were keen advocates of this form of self-cultivation, and the Stoics were in fact the inspiration for Foucault's 'aesthetics of existence'. This approach to existence, as we have seen, is to conceive of life as 'raw material' which individuals are responsible for sculpting. From this perspective, we are condemned to be artists of life, with the world condemned to be our canvas. And this chapter proposes that creating a post-consumerist life of voluntary simplicity from within a consumer society might require nothing less than the passionate exercise of our creative imagination.

Of course, Foucault insisted that we do not get to *choose* the raw material we work with, in the sense that the form one's life takes is inevitably shaped, at least in part, by the world around us – including, as I have argued, by the ideology of neoclassical economics. We exist, that is, both as creatures and creators. But insofar as we retain some space for freedom within which we can make our own decisions, then we are responsible for creating our own lives in much the same way as the sculptor is responsible for the statue; the painter for the canvas; the poet, the poem. As Jean-Paul Sartre was to propose (after qualifying his early notion of 'radical freedom' sufficiently to account for structural influences): *we can always make something new out of what we have been made into* (see Flynn, 2006: 67).

The infusion of voluntary simplicity with Foucault's aesthetics of existence presents itself most coherently, perhaps, when we consider the 'life as art' thesis in the context of Pablo Picasso's definition of art. According to Picasso, art should be understood as 'the elimination of the unnecessary' (quoted in Haenn and Wilk, 2006: 461). If it is the case that modern consumers are consuming excessively – whether in terms of nature, social justice, and/or personal wellbeing – then the creative process that voluntary simplifiers are tasked to undertake is the process of eliminating unnecessary consumption from one's life, and, in this way, make life more 'artistic' in Picasso's sense. Just as painters challenge themselves never to make unnecessary strokes of the brush; just as the poets challenge themselves never to include an unnecessary word or phrase; so must the voluntary simplifier aspire to craft a life that does not entail wasteful consumption. That is, voluntary simplicity as an art of living requires the individual to creatively eliminate unnecessary consumption from one's life. This goal will not be achieved overnight. But in a world of dangerous overconsumption – a world in which ecosystems are being degraded, great multitudes remain oppressed by poverty, and in which the suburban 'American Dream' is looking increasingly like a failed experiment – eliminating unnecessary consumption can be fairly understood as the defining goal of the 'life poet'; the defining goal of 'voluntary simplicity as an aesthetics of existence'. As Thoreau (1982: 292) once wrote: 'Men have become the tool of their tools. The greatest works of art are an expression of man's struggle to free himself from this condition.'

The reference to Thoreau here is not casual, and deserves some elaboration. Not only is Thoreau arguably the most powerful exponent of voluntary simplicity, a case can also be made that he anticipated, though in a less developed form, Foucault's notion of an 'aesthetics of existence'. Foucault's philosophical perspectivism (which underpins his ethics) could be inferred from Thoreau's (1982: 559) claim that: 'The universe is wider than our views of it' or from his suggestion that nature could support more than 'one order of understandings'. Jane Bennett (2002), in fact, has developed a post-structuralist interpretation of Thoreau with considerable insight. But Thoreau also seems to have been very sympathetic to the ideas of 'self-fashioning' and the 'art of living', as the following passage makes clear:

> I know of no more encouraging fact than the unquestionable ability of man to elevate his life by a conscious endeavour. It is something to be able to paint a particular picture, or to carve a statue, and so make a few objects beautiful, but it is far more glorious to carve and paint the very atmosphere and medium through which we look.... To affect the quality of the day, that is the highest of the arts (Thoreau, 1982: 343).

Similarly, in the conclusion to *Walden*, Thoreau (*ibid.*: 562) urged us all to 'live the life [we have] imagined'.

To some readers all this may sound grandiose, but the point being made is a serious one. 'Love your life', Thoreau (*ibid.*: 566) stated with disarming simplicity, and make no excuses. 'Every man is tasked to make his life, even in its details, worthy of the contemplation of his most elevated and critical hour' (*ibid.*: 343). Thoreau thought that there are as many ways to live 'as there can be drawn radii from one center' (*ibid.*: 266), and he desired that there 'be as many different persons in the world as possible' (*ibid.*: 325). But he also saw 'how easily and insensibly we fall into a particular route, and make a beaten track for ourselves' (*ibid.*: 562), how easily we fall into the 'deep ruts of tradition and conformity' (*ibid.*). This troubled Thoreau deeply, for he thought that if we do not live *deliberately* – that is, if we only get out of bed because of 'the mechanical nudgings of some servitor' (*ibid.*: 342) – then we are just sleepwalking through life, injuring eternity by killing time. 'Little is to be expected of that day, if it can be called a day, to which we are not awakened by our Genius' (*ibid.*: 342). Thoreau, to be sure, is speaking not so much to geniuses here, as to the genius (or poet) in us all. Take yourself and your life seriously, he is saying. Do not let yourself be swept along. Claim your freedom and exercise your capacity to create your own fate. Compose yourself! WAKE UP! 'Moral reform', Thoreau insisted, 'is the effort to throw off sleep... To be awake is to be alive' (*ibid.*: 343). With a slight change in the language, this could easily be interpreted as a Foucauldian perspective: ethical practice, one might say, is the effort to throw off 'the self' imposed upon us by society. To compose oneself is to be free.

With the basic idea of voluntary simplicity as an aesthetics of existence stated in outline, it is now time to consider, with respect to the question of consumption, ways that one might actually set about 'throwing off the self' and creating someone new.

5. Desubjectivisation: 'Techniques of the Self' and the Art of Voluntary Simplicity

In this final section, several 'techniques of the self' will be outlined which may provide a useful starting point for actually practising the ethics of voluntary simplicity as an aesthetics of existence. That is, the following 10 techniques may assist those who seek to overcome the aspects of their identities and behaviours that may have been shaped by the consumerist forces of contemporary society. The aim of these techniques is to transcend, through self-cultivation, the subjectivities that have been imposed upon us by consumer society and to create something new. It is important to note, however, that voluntary simplicity as an aesthetics of existence does not have anything to say about what form that 'new self' will ultimately take; rather, the purpose is to help break the consumerist mould of the 'existing self' so that new, post-consumerist forms of subjectivity can emerge.

5.1 *Read about consumerism and voluntary simplicity*

The importance of reading about consumerism, to begin with, lies in the fact that many of the mechanisms of consumer society are not obvious and, for that reason, can escape our notice. But if those mechanisms are not recognised or understood, they obviously cannot be resisted. Consequently, we can find ourselves shaped by those mechanisms in insidious ways. For example, the complex concept 'hedonic adaptation' (e.g., Di Tella and MacCulloch, 2010) holds that once human beings have their basic material needs satisfied, further increases in material wealth can have *short-term* influences on happiness (the so-called 'consumer buzz', of which we may be all aware), but little or no *long-term* influence on happiness (a phenomenon which may be much less obvious). That is, once human beings attain a modest material standard of living, evidence suggests that we end up 'adapting' to further increases in material wealth, which means that we typically find ourselves no better off than when we were less wealthy. If this is so, and there is considerable evidential support for this phenomenon, then this should affect the way we shape our lives, especially with respect to our pursuit of consumption. We might decide, for example, that if the pursuit of increased material wealth is unlikely to provide long-term satisfaction then that pursuit should not be the focus of our lives. But if we do not know about the process of 'hedonic adaptation', then we cannot plan our lives with the aim of avoiding consumption that is wasteful from the perspective of happiness.

A second example of the subtle workings of consumerism – from the many to choose from – is known as the 'Diderot Effect' (named after the philosopher Denniss Diderot (1769), who was the first to write about the phenomenon). The 'Diderot Effect' refers to how one consumer purchase can induce the desire for other purchases, which can induce further desires, and so on. The purchase of some new shoes looks out of place without a new outfit to match; a new car looks out of place parked in front of a shabby old house; painting the lounge can make the kitchen look even older; and replacing the sofas tempts one to replace the chairs too. This striving for uniformity in our standards of consumption – 'the Diderot Effect' – can function to lock us onto a consumerist treadmill that has no end and attains no lasting satisfaction. But if we are aware of this phenomenon, we can take steps to resist it, by foregoing the initial upgrading, for example, and thereby step off the consumerist treadmill. We can then do something else with our lives – something more ambitious, perhaps, than making sure our carpet matches our walls.

The point of these two examples is to show how consumerism can often lock us into practices of consumption that are wasteful of our time and energy (to say nothing of the waste of resources they entail). By dedicating some of our attention to the mindful study of consumerism, however, we may deepen our insight into the world, and our lives, and this may well assist us in escaping consumerism and in the planning and creation of new, post-consumerist forms of life. In other words, by deepening our understanding of consumption and its effects, we may find ourselves better able to live lives of what David Shi (2007: 131) called, 'enlightened material restraint'.

As well as reading about consumerism, it is suggested that there is also great value in reading widely about voluntary simplicity. For those of us who have been educated into a consumerist form of life, within a consumerist society, it can be very difficult indeed to imagine that alternative forms of life exist. In fact, so entrenched can we become in the consumerist form of life that we can resemble the fish that does not know it is in water. That is, we may not even recognise consumerism as consumerism – as one form of life among others – but assume instead that it is 'just the way the world is'. By reading about alternatives like voluntary simplicity, however, we can unsettle this assumption and expand our imaginations, and hopefully come to see that we have a choice in the way we live. We can change our lives, and perhaps begin changing the world, by changing our minds. Not only that, reading about voluntary simplicity can be self-fulfilling in that it can affirm and support the transition to a post-consumerist life. This is but an inflection of the old adage that what we give our attention to, we become. The choice, it would seem, is ours.

5.2 *Keep precise financial accounts and reflect on them*

Although practising voluntary simplicity is much more than just being frugal with money and spending less – it is also a state of mind – spending wisely does play an important role. In *Your Money or Your Life* – a prominent text in the literature on voluntary simplicity – Joe Dominguez and Vicki Robin (2008) provide elaborate financial exercises for readers to undertake which seek to provoke reflection on the real value of money and the true cost of things. Such exercises may sound mundane and a bit pointless – most people believe themselves to be careful, rational spenders (perhaps because that is what neoclassical economists tell us we are). But if the exercises are carried out with precision the results may well surprise, even shock. One might find that seemingly little purchases add up to an inordinate amount over a whole year, or over ten years, which may raise new and important questions about whether the money might have been better spent elsewhere, not at all, or exchanged for more time by working less. The aim of such exercises is not to create tightwads, as such, but smart consumers who are conscious of the full cost of their purchases, *all things considered*. After all, as Thoreau (1982: 286) insisted, 'the cost of a thing is the amount of what I will call life which is required to be exchanged for it'. When exploring voluntary simplicity in this light, one might well find that some reductions and changes to spending habits, rather than inducing any sense of deprivation, will instead be life affirming. Furthermore, it is often said that how we spend our money is how we vote on what exists in the world. Clearly, then, our relationship to money is an area that deserves close attention, for if we do not have a precise understanding of how we are spending our money, we can find ourselves misspending our money and thus our lives. Through the 'technique' of keeping precise accounts of our income and expenditure, however, we can bring this issue to the forefront of our attention and allow ourselves to better negotiate a fulfilling and meaningful life.

5.3 Cultivate non-materialistic sources of satisfaction and meaning

Voluntary simplicity, it could be said, is about progressively directing increasing amounts of one's attention away from the materialistic side of life toward the non-materialistic side. But cultivating a deep appreciation of non-materialistic goods often requires a certain degree of training (see generally, Burch, 2013). This training can be conceived of as an investment, of sorts, in the sense that effort expended in the early stages of development is justified on the basis that it will have positive, long-term impacts on one's life (and perhaps positive, short-term impacts also). Learning to play a musical instrument, for example – say, the cello – may require some investment in this sense before one can appreciate the joy of performance or be introduced to the profound beauty that can emanate from a cello in the hands of a competent cellist. But once that degree of competency has been attained, the non-materialistic satisfaction that can flow from playing a musical instrument is essentially limitless, and perhaps, one might even say, infinite. Another example might be reading. The more one reads, the better one gets at reading (in the sense of reading more deeply). But once a certain degree of competency has been attained, books have the potential to provide us with an inexhaustible source of non-materialistic wealth, all the better for the fact that a book itself – which is, of course, a material object – can be shared or 'consumed' without limiting its non-materialistic re-consumption by oneself or another, again and again.

At this stage some may wish to level a charge of elitism against this 'technique of the self', but such a charge would be misguided.

After all, the point of this technique is simply to consciously direct one's attention to non-materialistic goods, rather than materialistic goods, and this, in itself, makes no value judgement about which forms of non-materialistic goods should be pursued. For example, whether one learns an instrument to play music by Bach or Dolly Parton is not at issue; nor is the point to privilege Herman Hesse over Mills and Boon. The point of this technique, once more, is to deliberately cultivate satisfaction and meaning in life through non-materialistic pursuits, rather than materialistic ones. But in which non-materialistic directions one should head is not something that can be informed by a consideration of voluntary simplicity as an aesthetics of existence.

5.4 Work on overcoming status anxiety

It is sometimes said that modern consumers spend their lives working jobs they do not like, to buy things they do not need, so that they can impress people they do not like. Whether this is an exaggeration or not is less important than the issue it raises about what motivates our consumption – in particular, the issue of whether or to what extent we consume for the purpose of seeking or maintaining social status. There is in fact considerable evidence to suggest that status seeking and social positioning is highly relevant to consumption practices, especially in consumer societies (see, e.g., Hirsch, 1976). But there are at least two problems with this approach to life and to consumption: firstly, social positioning through consumption is a zero-sum game, in the sense that when one person's social status is increased, someone else's must have relatively decreased, meaning that overall social satisfaction is unlikely to change; secondly, a strong argument can be made that, ultimately, it is much more important that we have the *respect of ourselves* rather than the *respect of others*, especially since the former is within our control, and the latter is much less so. Accordingly, if we choose to care about what others think of us – and it is a choice, although it may sometimes be a difficult choice – we are giving up some of our freedom to define our lives on our own terms. It can be argued, therefore, that practising voluntary simplicity as an aesthetics of existence implies cultivating an indifference to social status, which would involve constantly thinking about what is truly valuable in life and recognising, perhaps, that it is more important to shape one's life for the purposes of gaining self-respect than for the purpose of seeking the respect of others. After all, if one merely seeks the respect of others, one might come to the end of life and have succeeded in attaining that respect, but have little respect for oneself. A case can be made that such a life would not be a successful life.

5.5 *Regularly undertake the 'deathbed experiment'*

The 'deathbed experiment', so-called, is a technique of the self (popular among the Stoics) that can assist in the evaluation of what is most important in life, including how important money, possessions, and status are to a well-lived life. The thought experiment can be expressed in the following terms: *Imagine you are on your deathbed and someone asks you about which attitudes defined your life. What would you want to be able to say?* The Stoics argued that this type of thought experiment is important for at least two reasons: first, because the technique of trying to look back on life from the vantage point of our deathbed can help us prioritise our time and attention *today* as effectively as possible; and second, it can help us accept without complaint those things we cannot change and prompt us to set about changing those things we can.

Taken seriously – and it ought to be taken seriously or not at all – the deathbed experiment can provoke us to reflect on life's 'big picture' and what role our attitudes have in shaping it. In particular, the experiment potentially has great relevance to the idea of voluntary simplicity as an aesthetics of existence, because it has implications on how we value money, possessions, and status. That is, it raises the question of what attitudes we will have toward these things on our deathbed. The purpose of considering this issue prior to lying on one's deathbed is so that our conclusions shape our thoughts and actions today; so that we have no regrets in the future; so that we can, in Nietzsche's terms, look forward to an 'eternal recurrence' of our lives.

One might suppose, for example, that a person on their actual deathbed rarely says, 'I wish I had spent more of my life working to pay for more consumer goods'. More likely, perhaps, at least in consumer societies, is that a person might come to the end of their life and have some regrets about dedicating *too much* of their time and energy toward materialistic pursuits, at the expense of various non-materialistic goods, such as time with friends and family, or time to engage in creative activity or community engagement. In short, the deathbed experiment is a tool or technique that can be used (repeatedly) to avoid the regrets of overconsumption. To paraphrase Thoreau (1982: 343), we should aim to live what is life, so that we do not, when we come to die, discover that we had not really lived.

5.6 *Acknowledge freedom by imagining alternative life paths*

Freedom, as the existentialists often insisted, can be terrifying. Freedom can be so terrifying, in fact, that we can sometimes pretend that we are bound by circumstances to live the life we are currently living when, in fact, we are really just avoiding having to deal with the reality of our own freedom. Existentialists call this living in 'bad faith'. For those brave enough to face their own freedom, however, the technique of imagining alternative, hypothetical lives can be a useful means not only of highlighting one's freedom, but also of actually expanding it. This technique involves imagining various alternative futures for your life, futures that depend merely on an act of will to initiate. Imagine, for example, radically changing careers, or deciding to dedicate your life to this or that burning passion – imagine it seriously. Imagine also, perhaps, living a radically simpler life. What would life be like? What could life be like? How could we get there?

It may be, of course, that the life one is currently living is the best life, the freest life, the most fulfilling life – in which case the alternative lives imagined need not be pursued. But by imagining alternative lives, we can become more aware of the nature and extent of our own freedom. Perhaps, as Foucault suggested, we may discover that we are freer than we think we are.

5.7 *Practise negative visualisation*

Negative visualisation refers to imagining bad things happening in your life for the purpose of preparing yourself emotionally when, as inevitably happens, something bad does actually happen. Of course, negative visualisation may also help us avoid those bad things happening in the first place, which provides further justification for this technique. Human life is such, however, that bad things sometimes occur that are entirely out of our control, so if we are mentally prepared for such occurrences, they will never seem as bad as when they strike us out of the blue.

With respect to voluntary simplicity, it can be helpful to imagine losing our entire life savings, or losing our home in a fire, or coming home one day and discovering we have been robbed of our most prized possessions. By imagining such events and considering the various ways we could respond to them, we are more likely to respond effectively should they ever occur. We would be more likely, for example, to say to ourselves, 'these are the circumstances of my life: how best can I live my life from now on, given these circumstances?'

Negative visualisation is a central 'technique' of Stoicism (see Irvine, 2009: Ch 4). The Stoics argued that it is not events that hurt us; rather, we are hurt by the *interpretations* we give to those events. This is important because, while we are not always in control of the events in our life, we are in control of the interpretations we give those events. For example, continuing the above hypothetical, suppose we arrive home one day and discover we have been robbed of our most prized possessions. This event can be 'dealt with', from an interpretive perspective, in various ways. One response is to become angry, sad, or spiteful, but they are not pleasant or desirable emotions, so responding with anger, sadness, or spite generally makes a bad situation worse. Another way to respond, however, would be to show gratitude that our prized possessions enriched our life for as long as they did; another response again would be to recognise that there are many people around the world who have almost nothing, and this can make it seem rather perverse to lament the loss of our prized, but superfluous, possessions. The point is that the same 'event' can impact on one's life in various ways depending on the 'attitude' with which we choose to deal with it. Again, the event is out of our control, but the attitude is not. To draw once more upon Nietzsche – a Stoic in his own way – one should live in the spirit of *amor fati* and 'love thy fate' (for a discussion see Han-Pile, 2011).

This technique of negative visualisation might be particularly important as the world confronts and deals with the impending 'limits to growth' (see Turner, 2012). Consumer lifestyles today are exceedingly resource dependent, and if it is the case that the planet simply cannot sustain their burdens, then consumer lifestyles as we know them today simply will not be a part of human civilisation for all that much longer. Since this means that consumer societies are likely to be maintaining a lower per capita material standard of living in the future than they are currently, it is best to 'visualise' this forthcoming transition for the purpose of preparing oneself, emotionally and otherwise, for its arrival. Economic contraction will be much harder to deal with by those who assumed that their consumer lifestyles were their God-given right, which could never be taken from them. Conversely, economic contraction will be much easier to deal with if one has anticipated it as an inevitability – perhaps, in some circumstances, a welcome inevitability. Indeed, those people who embrace voluntary simplicity may not need to look very hard to see that the limits to growth may well have an 'upside of down'. This is likely to depend, however, on one's attitude. Fortunately, the attitude we adopt in this regard is up to us. Why not, then, be an 'upsider'?

5.8 *Anticipate and avoid consumer temptations and seductions*

Everybody in consumer societies has probably had the experience of walking through a mall, or watching a television advertisement, only to discover that such experiences can give birth to new, artificially imposed, consumer desires. We may not have even known that some product existed, but after being exposed to it through sophisticated marketing techniques, we find ourselves wanting it – needing it. Not only that, just knowing about the new product can make the things we currently own seem a bit old and dated, even though, prior to discovering the new product, our current possessions were a source of satisfaction. Those same possessions can become a source of dissatisfaction.

Within consumer societies people can be exposed to as many as 3,000 adverts each day (de Graaf *et al.*, 2005: 160), and the message implicit to *every* ad is the message that our lives are not good enough as they are, but that our lives can be improved if only we buy this or that product. It seems we are easily persuaded. But we need not be passive pawns in this perverse game. If we come to accept that marketing and advertisements can seduce us ever-deeper into consumerist practices, then one 'technique' for escaping those practices is simply to anticipate and avoid as many consumer temptations and seductions as possible. For example: do not go to the mall; do not read unsolicited junk mail or glossy magazines filled with ads; watch as little television as possible, etc. By regulating as far as possible what our minds are exposed to, we can change the nature of our minds and thus our lives. If we give too much of our attention to consumer products, however, we, ourselves, might become the product.

5.9 *Keep a journal*

As noted above, one of the greatest legacies of Stoicism is the idea that, while we may not always be in control of the events that happen in our lives, we are ultimately in control of the ways in which we *respond* to those events. But although we may be in ultimate control of our responses, we do not always respond how we would have liked, and sometimes our responses can become habitual rather than considered or deliberate, at which time our freedom, our power, to respond as we wish seemingly diminishes. Keeping a journal is a good way of having a conversation with oneself about the happenings of the day. By reflecting on one's actions and taking a few moments to reflect upon one's responses to events, one becomes better able to negotiate life in the future and respond in the most fruitful ways. If one does not reflect in this way, the same mistakes can occur over and over again, and self-development essentially comes to a halt. Having a regular conversation with oneself through the keeping of a journal is likely to help us in all areas of life, but in consumer societies, it may be a particularly useful practice with respect to consumption. By critically reflecting on a regular basis upon our consumer purchases, consumer motivations, consumer insecurities, consumer expectations, consumer desires, etc. we are likely to become more conscious of the forces external to ourselves that conspire to turn us into mindless dupes who dutifully turn the cogs of the consumerist machine.

5.10 *Ask yourself, 'How much is enough?'*

This question is perhaps the central question of voluntary simplicity, and it is suggested that any attempt to practise voluntary simplicity must involve meditating upon it with exceptional dedication. Therein lies the truth of voluntary simplicity, *but not as an answer to the question, but the question itself.* Why, after all, must truth always be conceived of as an *answer*? That is, why must we deny the possibility that there could be truth awaiting us in a *question*? As it happens, however, 'How much is enough?' is an extremely unpopular question within growth-orientated, consumer societies. But it is a question that is arguably of revolutionary import, for it has the potential not only to deconstruct 'Empire', both ideologically and institutionally, it also has the potential to provide the fertile soil for growing a post-consumerist form of life.

This question, however, leads to an unexpected twist in the exploration of voluntary simplicity. We discover that it is impossible to answer the question 'How much is enough?' until we have first answered a prior and perhaps even more important question, 'Enough for *what?'* This 'prior' question challenges us to specify the point of our economic activity, for if we cannot identify its purpose we cannot know if our economic efforts have succeeded. Without some 'chief end' in mind to guide and justify our labour, we would merely be running in the ruts or acting for no conscious purpose, like the Brahmin who chained himself for life to the foot of the tree, but could not explain why he did it. The warning here, in effect, is that if we do not have a clear sense of what we are doing with our lives, or why we are heading in one direction rather than another, we will not be able to tell if our attitudes toward material things are keeping us on the right path or leading us astray.

Voluntary simplicity as an aesthetics of existence, however, can offer no guidance on the question, 'Enough for *what*?' – which is to say, we each must create as an aesthetic project the meaning of our own lives. The ethics of consumption explored in this chapter merely insists that we must face this question when shaping our attitudes toward money and material things. If we do not face that question, we cannot possibly understand the meaning or purpose of 'economy'. Once we have developed some answer to that question, however, then we are in a much better position to answer the question, 'How much is enough?' Many participants in the Voluntary Simplicity Movement (Alexander and Ussher, 2012) are discovering that much less is needed than was previously thought, and perhaps, one might hope, others will come to realise that they, too, are freer than they think they are. By needing less, people may come to realise that they would not need to work so much to provide for themselves, and it is hoped that the 10 'techniques of the self' presented above, if practised seriously, might assist in that realisation. Liberated from the limitless pursuit of more consumption and the endless labour that it demands, post-consumers are then free to set about doing something else with their lives.

6. Conclusion

It may be that Foucault scholars will take issue with aspects of the analysis above, perhaps the very nature of the analysis, and dismiss it on the grounds that Foucault would not have wanted or intended his work to be applied in this way; that his ideas have been misused or simply misunderstood. Admittedly, the ethics of consumption initiated herein will indeed need a more elaborate defence than space permits. Accordingly, consider the present sketch of 'voluntary simplicity as an aesthetics of existence' as a work in progress. But even if the present analysis in places goes further than Foucault would have ever allowed – in terms of its explicit normative content, for example – perhaps this stretching of his ethics is nevertheless 'Foucauldian', in the same way that Foucault's use of Nietzsche was at times anti-Nietzschean, but for that very reason, Nietzschean (see Foucault, 1990c: 251). After all, Foucault described his own books as 'a kind of tool-box others can rummage through to find a tool they can use however they wish in their own area.... I don't write for an audience, I write for users, not readers' (Foucault, 1994: 1). Foucault explicitly accepted, then, that it was an open question as to how the tools he provided were to be used and to what purpose they would be put. Similarly, when discussing his relationship with Nietzsche, Foucault (1977: 53-4) explained that for him 'the only valid tribute to thought such as Nietzsche's is precisely to use it, to deform it, to make it groan and protest'. The same goes for Foucault's thought, it could be said, perhaps even more so. If it is the case, then, that this chapter has taken Foucault's ethics beyond their original intent, let this simply be considered a tribute, a sincere and grateful tribute, to one of the 20th century's most brilliant and provocative ethical imaginations.

In closing, let it be noted, once more, that this chapter was designed with a practical intent; designed for the purpose of exploring an approach to consumption – the approach of 'voluntary simplicity as an aesthetics of existence' – that might actually be useful as a means of engaging the timeless question of 'how one ought to live'. It is hoped that some readers find it to be so, although in Foucauldian spirit, one must acknowledge that it need not provide answers to all readers or a complete answer to anyone. Perhaps it was always more about raising questions than providing answers, anyway. Although the question of 'how one ought to live' is timeless, answering that question inevitably takes place relative to one's own time and circumstances, relative to one's own place in history. Let this acknowledgement of our deep and inescapable historicity provide this chapter and this book with its closing theme. We are both creatures and creators of our time. As creatures, we have been shaped, in many ways, to varying degrees, into consumers. As creators, our future is always and already opening up before our very eyes.

Let us be like the poets and make things new.

References

Alexander, S. (ed.). 2009. *Voluntary simplicity: The poetic alternative to consumer culture*. Whanganui: Stead & Daughters.

Alexander, S. 2012a. 'The optimal material threshold: Toward an economics of sufficiency'. *Real-World Economics Review* 2-21.

Alexander, S. and Ussher, S. 2012. 'The voluntary simplicity movement: A multi-national survey analysis in theoretical context'. *Journal of Consumer Culture* 12(1): 66-88.

Bennett, J. 2002. *Thoreau's nature: Ethics, politics, and the wild*. Lanham: Rowman & Littlefield.

Burch, M. 2013. *The hidden door: Mindful sufficiency as an alternative to extinction*. Melbourne: Simplicity Institute Publishing.

Davidson, D. 2011. 'On the very idea of a conceptual scheme', in R.

Talisse and S. Aitkin (eds). *The Pragmatism Reader: From Peirce through the present*. Princeton: Princeton University Press.

Denniss, R. and Hamilton, C. 2005. *Affluenza: When too much is never enough*. Crows Nest, NSW: Allen & Unwin.

Derrida, J. 1998. *Of grammatology*. Baltimore: John Hopkins University Press.

De Graaf, J., Naylor, T., and Wann, D. 2005 (2nd edn). *Affluenza: The all-consuming epidemic*. San Francisco: Berrett-Koehler.

Diderot, D. 1769. 'Regrets on parting with my old dressing gown'. Available at: http://www.marxists.org/reference/archive/diderot/1769/regrets.htm (accessed 12 June 2014)

Di Tella, R. and MacCulloch, R. 2010. 'Happiness adaptation to income beyond "basic needs"', in E. Diener, J. Helliwell, and D. Kahneman (eds). *International Differences in Well-Being*. Oxford, New York: Oxford University Press.

Dominguez, J. and Robin, V. 2008 (revised edn). *Your money or your life: Transforming your relationship with money and achieving financial independence*. London: Penguin.

Elgin, D. 1998 (revised edn). *Voluntary simplicity: Toward a way of life that is outwardly simple, inwardly rich*. New York: William Morrow.

Fish, S. 1989. *Doing what comes naturally: Change, rhetoric, and the practice of theory in literary and legal studies*. Durham: Duke University Press.

Flynn, T. 2006. *Existentialism: A very short introduction*. Oxford: Oxford University Press.

Foucault, M. 1977. *Power/Knowledge: Selected interviews & other writings 1972-1977*, edited by Colin Gordon. New York: Pantheon.

Foucault, M. 1982. 'The subject and power', in H. Dreyfus and P. Rabinow (eds). *Michel Foucault: Beyond structuralism and hermeneutics*. Chicago: University of Chicago Press.

Foucault, M. 1985. *The uses of pleasure: The history of sexuality Vol 2*. New York: Random House.

Foucault, M. 1990a. 'An aesthetics of existence', in L. Kritzman (ed.). *Michel Foucault: Politics, philosophy, culture: Interviews and other writings 1977-1984*. New York: Routledge.

Foucault, M. 1990b. 'Concern for the truth', in L. Kritzman (ed.). *Michel Foucault: Politics, philosophy, culture: Interviews and other writings 1977-1984*. New York: Routledge.

Foucault, M. 1990c. 'Return of morality', in L. Kritzman (ed.). *Michel Foucault: Politics, philosophy, culture: Interviews and other writings 1977-1984*. New York: Routledge.

Foucault, M. 1990d. 'The minimalist self', in L. Kritzman (ed.). *Michel Foucault: Politics, philosophy, culture: Interviews and other writings 1977-1984.* New York: Routledge.

Foucault, M. 1994. 'Prisons et asiles dans le mécanisme du pouvoir', in *Dits et Ecrits Vol. 11.* (1994) [1974], as quoted at http://www.michel-foucault.com/quote/2004q.html (accessed 10 June 2014).

Foucault, M. 2000a. *Ethics: Essential works Vol. I,* edited by Paul Rabinow. London: Penguin.

Foucault, M. 2000b. 'On the genealogy of ethics', in Michel Foucault, *Ethics: Essential works Vol. I.* London: Penguin.

Foucault, M. 2000c. 'The ethics of the concern of the self as a practice of freedom', in Michel Foucault, *Ethics: Essential works Vol. I.* London: Penguin.

Foucault, M. 2000d. *Power: The essential works of Foucault, 1954-1984 Vol. III,* edited by J. Faubion. New York: New Press.

Han-Pile, B. 2011. 'Nietzsche and amor fati'. *European Journal of Philosophy* 19(2): 224-262.

Hardin, G. 1968. 'Tragedy of the Commons'. *Science* 162: 1243.

Haenn, N. and Wilk, R. (eds). 2005. *The environment in anthropology: A reader in ecology, culture, and sustainable living.* New York: New York University.

Hirsch, F. 1976. *Social limits to growth.* Cambridge, Mass: Harvard University Press.

Irvine, W. 2009. *A guide to the good life: The ancient art of Stoic joy.* Oxford: Oxford University Press.

Johnson, D. (ed.). 2003. *Alcibiades and Socrates.* Newburyport: Focus Publishing.

Kearney, R. 1984. *Dialogues with contemporary continental thinkers.* Manchester: Manchester University Press.

McGushin, E. 2007: *Foucault's Askesis: An introduction to the philosophical life.* Evanston: Northwestern University Press.

Myer, D. 2000. *The American paradox: Spiritual hunger in an age of plenty.* New Haven: Yale University Press.

Nehamas, A. *Nietzsche: Life as literature.* Cambridge: Harvard University Press.

Nietzsche, F. 1969. *On the genealogy of morals.* New York: Vintage Books.

Nietzsche, F. 2001. *The gay science,* edited by Bernard Williams. Cambridge: Cambridge University Press.

O'Leary, T. *Foucault and the art of ethics.* New York: Continuum.

Princen, T. 2005. *The logic of sufficiency.* Cambridge (MA): MIT Press.

Rorty, R. 1979. *Philosophy and the mirror of nature.* Princeton: Princeton University Press.

Rorty, R. 1989. *Contingency, irony, and solidarity.* New York: Cambridge University Press.

Rorty, R. 1991. *Objectivity, relativism, and truth: Philosophical papers.* New York: Cambridge University Press.

Rorty, R. 1999. *Philosophy and social hope.* New York: Penguin.

Shelley, P.B. 1890. *A defense of poetry.* Boston: Ginn and Co.

Shi, D. 2007 (revised edn). *The simple life: Plain living and high thinking in American culture.* Athens: University of Georgia Press.

Thoreau, H. 1982. *The portable Thoreau,* edited by Carl Bode. New York. Penguin.

Turner, G. 2012. 'Are we on the cusp of collapse? Updated comparison of *The Limits to Growth* with historical data'. *Gaia* 21(2): 116-124.

12

THE HOUR IS DARKEST JUST
BEFORE DAWN
Crisis as opportunity

All great changes are preceded by chaos
– Deepak Chopra

This short chapter is a transcript of a presentation delivered in October 2013 as part of the 'Festival of Ideas', at the University of Melbourne, Australia. Participants were asked to envision how Australia made the transition to a low-carbon society, back-casting on the transition from the year 2033.

As I look back from the year 2033, I would like to be able to tell you that the transition to our low-carbon society was smooth and rational. I would like to be able to tell you that, as a democracy, we shaped our nation with sensible, evidence-based decisions, and built a just and sustainable world through intelligent planning and bold leadership. I would like to be able to tell you that people did not suffer, and that our ecosystems are not permanently damaged. I would like to be able to tell you that the leatherback turtle and the orange-bellied parrot are not extinct.

But who really thought that the transition beyond consumer capitalism was going to be smooth, rational, and painless? Who really thought that Empire would lie down like a lamb at the mere request of the environmental movement? No – it was always going to be a muddy transition, punctuated with crises, and moulded with conflict, grit, and tears.

When looking back over the last few decades, one has to acknowledge that the global economy resembled not an obedient servant but a snake aggressively eating its own tail – a snake seemingly unaware that it was consuming its own life-support system. When the global economy finally choked on its own growth fetish, what was surprising was not how quickly it transformed into something else, but rather why so few people had foreseen its inevitable demise.

The lessons of history so often seem infantile when seen through the lens of hindsight.

The era of resource abundance and cheap energy was over, and this was to change everything. It was the 'new normal' that forced us to become something else, something 'other', whether we wanted to or not. The road, to be sure, was rough.

This was especially so in a highly interconnected, globalised world, burdened by excessive debt and addicted to expensive oil. One way or another, for better or for worse, the future was not much going to resemble the past. While the apocalypse never arrived, it is clear that humanity made a whole host of very, very, very poor decisions, and even the good ones came depressingly late. This was an era of great instability, uncertainty, and hardship, which, in a sense, we thoroughly deserved.

What I am trying to convey here is that humanity did not voluntarily embrace a new way of life, so much as a new way of life forcefully embraced us, with the global financial crisis of 2008 merely signifying the beginning of a long emergency that has only recently abated.

When the crises eventually hit – and I mean hit hard – it was then, and only then, that our nation was provoked into action. It was only then, in the chambers of consumer culture, that we were shaken awake from our long, dogmatic slumber.

The hour was darkest just before dawn.

◆ ◆ ◆

Every crisis, they say, is an opportunity – from which the optimist infers that the more crises there are, the more opportunities there are. Australia, I am happy to say, made the most of its crises.

When the comfortable years of consumer affluence were taken from us almost overnight, this challenged our economy – indeed, our very civilisation – to refashion itself and find or create a new identity, a new narrative of progress.

However unsettling it may have been, this identity crisis came with a surprisingly large silver lining – a silver lining that was to ignite all the positive changes that were to come later. Most importantly, it forced us to confront the question of how much we actually needed to live well and to be free. Is more always better? Or is just enough plenty? Through this period of enforced reflection we discovered several quite extraordinary things about the nature of the good life.

We discovered, for example, that our culture could thrive at a far lower material standard of living than we had thought; we also discovered that we were much hardier and more resilient than we had thought; that we were much more creative and resourceful than we had thought; and that our community spirit, which had seemingly faded in the years of consumer culture, was actually still in tact, desperately waiting beneath the surface of culture for a time when we could reengage each other, and be neighbours again.

The economic depression we lived through meant that most people had very little discretionary income, so we found ourselves sharing more (because we had to), growing more of our own food (because we had to), biking more and leaving our cars in the driveway (because we had to), travelling less, mending our clothes, reusing our waste (because we had to) – all of which reduced our ecological footprint. But somehow, at the same time, we were living more. That is to say, consumer culture was forcefully taken from us, so we had to create a new culture of consumption. We embraced a simpler way of living – and, much to our own surprise, we found it to be good. If it was not always comfortable, it was, at least, fulfilling. This is the paradox of simplicity, the wisdom of which had been lost in the consumer age: less can be more.

It was the philosopher Jean-Paul Sartre who said that the French were never as free as when the German's occupied their country during the Second World War. His point was that their lives, in the midst of crisis, were suddenly infused with meaning and purpose, in contrast with the humdrum unfreedom they had been living as comfortable middle-class consumers, with their overemphasis on status and materialistic concerns. The same could be said of Australia, and indeed the West, more generally, during the last few decades of economic contraction. In the midst of crisis, torn from our televisions and shopping malls, we were freer perhaps than we had ever been before, despite the hardships and constraints we faced. In the process of creating a new way of life, our lives were unexpectedly infused with new meaning, and that was the invisible force that drove the entire transition. As Friedrich Nietzsche once said: 'Those who have a *why* to live, can bear almost any *how*.'

It had become clear, however, that we could no longer solve the problems we faced with the same kinds of thinking that caused them. It was time to think differently, to act differently, to live differently. And if our national and state politicians were not going to act decisively in the face of crisis, then we would have to act decisively ourselves, at the community level. Australian culture underwent a silent revolution, of sorts – a renaissance of participatory democracy – which over time, in the face of much resistance, filtered upwards through the various levels of political governance, decentralising power in the process and relocalising economy.

And so, the Great Transition, as we now call it, began amongst the grassroots of local communities. After all, there was hardly going to be a progressive politics until there was a progressive culture. Agitated but inspired social movements emerged throughout the nation, in various guises and forms, representing a growing sense of dissatisfaction and disillusionment with the old ways of doing things. People had had enough of the same old story, so they began writing a new story, not with words, but with deeds.

The low-carbon society that we have today is a product of these cultural forces eventually finding political and macroeconomic expression. By reordering our priorities, and reconceptualising what progress meant for our nation, we found that investment in renewables was not financially prohibitive, even in hard economic times, but merely a matter of political commitment. But do not misunderstand me. Of course we had to make some sacrifices elsewhere. Certainly, we could not afford to sustain a growth-orientated, consumer society on renewable energy. Far from it! Huge lifestyle changes were required to support our transition to a low-carbon, steady state society. So let me be clear: we no longer live lives of consumer affluence. We are a nation of radical recyclers, menders, makers, salvagers, gardeners, and retrofitters. But do not pity us! We might live simply and creatively, but we live well. We have reimagined the good life and this is reflected in our macroeconomics of sufficiency.

Perhaps the most important feature of our new economy, therefore, is that we do not use anywhere near as much energy as we did in earlier decades. Due to the fact that our levels of production and consumption have been radically downscaled, we can now afford to produce most of our limited electricity needs with solar, wind, and hydro. By walking, cycling, using public transport, producing food organically, and relocalising much of our economy, we have also been able to reduce our consumption of oil to a small fraction of what it once was. Last year, after a political firestorm, we closed all our coal power plants.

In closing, there are four points worth emphasising about our transition to a low-carbon society: (1) that it was provoked by crisis, or rather, a series of crises; (2) that the crises brought an end to economic growth as we had known it; (3) that making the best of a post-growth economy depended upon a new culture of consumption, in which people embraced far simpler ways of living; and

(4) that we were required to consume much less energy in order to be able to afford to run our economy primarily on renewables and create a low-carbon society. Renewable energy, I repeat, could never sustain a growth-orientated, consumer society.

We are not at the post-carbon, sufficiency economy yet, but we're well on our way, and after two dark decades, the future is again looking bright.

Courage to us all.

Appendix

COLLECTED ESSAYS VOLUME II
SUFFICIENCY ECONOMY: ENOUGH, FOR EVERYONE, FOREVER

Samuel Alexander

To be published by the Simplicity Institute in 2015.

PROVISIONAL CONTENTS PAGE

1. Sketching a Paradigm of Sufficiency
A simpler way for an energy descent future

2. Degrowth and the Carbon Budget
Powerdown strategies for climate stability

3. The Optimal Material Threshold
Toward an economics of sufficiency

4. The Voluntary Simplicity Movement
A multi-national survey analysis in theoretical context

5. Sufficiency Economy
Envisioning a prosperous descent

6. Low-Tech Living as a Demand-Side Strategy
Simplicity is the ultimate sophistication

7. Disruptive Social Innovation for a Low-Carbon World
Evaluating prospects for a Great Transition

8. Voluntary Simplicity and the Social Reconstruction of Law
Degrowth from the grassroots up

9. Wild Law from Below
Examining the anarchist challenge to earth jurisprudence

10. The Deep Green Alternative
Debating strategies of transition

11. The Transition Movement
Questions of diversity, power, and affluence

12. Looking Backward from the Year 2099
Ecozoic reflections on the future

ABOUT THE AUTHOR

Dr Samuel Alexander is a lecturer at the University of Melbourne, Australia, teaching a course called 'Consumerism and the Growth Economy: Interdisciplinary Perspectives' in the Masters of Environment. He is also co-director of the Simplicity Institute and research fellow at the Melbourne Sustainable Society Institute, publishing widely on issues related to voluntary simplicity, degrowth and post-growth economics, energy descent, and transition strategies. He is author of *Entropia: Life Beyond Industrial Civilisation* (2013), editor of *Voluntary Simplicity: The Poetic Alternative to Consumer Culture* (2009), and co-editor of *Simple Living in History: Pioneers of the Deep Future* (2014). He blogs at www.simplicitycollective.com and posts most of his writings at www.thesufficiencyeconomy.com.

OTHER BOOKS FROM THE SIMPLICITY INSTITUTE

Simple Living in History: Pioneers of the Deep Future (2014), edited by Samuel Alexander and Amanda McLeod

Entropia: Life beyond Industrial Civilisation (2013), Samuel Alexander

The Hidden Door: Mindful Sufficiency as an Alternative to Extinction (2013), Mark A. Burch

FOR MORE INFORMATION, SEE THE SIMPLICITY INSTITUTE

www.simplicityinstitute.org

22487100R00183

Made in the USA
San Bernardino, CA
08 July 2015